THE STATE OF SCOTLAND'S

ENVIRONMENT AND NATURAL HERITAGE

THE NATURAL HERITAGE OF SCOTLAND

Each year since it was founded in 1992, Scottish Natural Heritage has organised or jointly organised a conference that has focused attention on a particular aspect of Scotland's natural heritage. The papers read at the conferences, after a process of refereeing and editing, have been brought together as a book. The ten titles already published in this series are listed below (No. 6 was not based on a conference).

This is the eleventh book in the series.

THE STATE OF SCOTLAND'S ENVIRONMENT AND NATURAL HERITAGE

*Edited by Michael B. Usher, Edward C. Mackey
and James C. Curran*

EDINBURGH: THE STATIONERY OFFICE

First published in 2002 by The Stationery Office Limited
71 Lothian Road, Edinburgh, EH3 9AZ

Applications for reproduction should be made to Scottish Natural Heritage,
12 Hope Terrace, Edinburgh EH9 2AS

British Library Cataloguing in Publication Data
A catalogue record for this book is available from the British Library

ISBN 0 11 497306 7

Cover illustrations: Leverburgh and Northton, Isle of Harris, Western Isles, May 1994
(© P.A. MacDonald/SNH) (inset) set against the Land Cover Map
2000 (courtesy of the Centre for Ecology and Hydrology).

PREFACE

Over the last decade there has been a growing interest in the state of Scotland's environment and natural heritage.

In 1992, Scottish Natural Heritage (SNH) was 'born' from the amalgamation of the Nature Conservancy Council for Scotland and the Countryside Commission for Scotland. The word 'sustainable' was included in SNH's founding legislation; it is said that this was the first time that the word had been used in British legislation. One of the early questions that was asked of SNH related to the state of the natural heritage in Scotland. For this reason information was brought together by many experts in many habitat types and species groups, and edited into a major report *The Natural Heritage of Scotland: an Overview* (Mackey, 1995). Whilst containing a huge amount of information on the current state of the natural heritage, that report was not designed to analyse how the state was changing. Trends are important; are things getting better or worse, and why are these changes occurring? Thus, further data were collected, and a new report entitled *Natural Heritage Trends: Scotland 2002* (Mackey *et al.*, 2001) was published.

The Scottish Environment Protection Agency (SEPA) was established in 1996 through the amalgamation of the seven River Purification Authorities in Scotland with Her Majesty's Industrial Pollution Inspectorate and through the addition of other responsibilities, notably those for air emissions and waste management previously held by the local authorities. SEPA incorporated elements of 64 predecessor bodies. Like SNH, SEPA also has the term 'sustainable development' in its founding legislation. There was considerable interest in the state of Scotland's environment at the time of the creation of this new Government Agency, and very rapidly appropriate data were collected and published as a *State of the Environment Report* (SEPA, 1996). The summaries in this initial report have been expanded and developed into more comprehensive explorations of various sectors of the Scottish environment. Water was the first sector to receive this comprehensive treatment (SEPA, 1999a), and it has been followed by reports on the quality of Scotland's air (SEPA, 1999b) and soil (SEPA, 2001).

Given the interest in both SNH and SEPA in reporting on the state of Scotland's environment and natural heritage, it was logical that the two Government Agencies should hold a joint conference to explore the present state, the trends, the future prospects, and the scope for increasingly sustainable solutions to environmental problems. This book provides an account of the conference which comprised three distinct types of presentation.

First, major reviews of Scotland's land, air, fresh water and sea were presented. Each of these was considered from different and complementary viewpoints – a speaker from SEPA looking at environmental trends, a speaker from SNH looking at natural heritage trends, and a speaker from outwith these two agencies exploring what might happen in the future.

Second, each of the other papers presented verbally at the conference addressed a more focused concern, be it climate change, biodiversity, polluting compounds, sustainability, or Scotland's place in both the European Union and the Nordic area. After presentation at the conference, and after discussion, these papers have also been written up for publication as chapters in this book.

Third, a feature of the conference was the large number of people, the majority from outwith SEPA and SNH, who wanted to show poster papers or to mount demonstrations. We were, unfortunately, unable to incorporate the whole of the wealth of this material and information in this book, but a few of the poster papers that were particularly relevant to the theme of the book have been prepared as book chapters.

We are also aware of many parallel studies that record the state and trends in particular groups of species; an excellent example is the huge volunteer effort to understand what is happening to Britain's butterflies (Asher *et al.*, 2001). However, we hope that in these 22 chapters we have encapsulated much of the core information, analysis, discussion and prediction that was presented during the conference's two days. The emphasis was not retrospective, but forward looking, seeking ways of enhancing the qualities of Scotland's environment and natural heritage in the future.

The problems of future predictions and solutions were brought home to the 300 or so delegates in a very real way. The dates of the conference were 11 and 12 September 2001, and the tragic events of the terrorist outrages in the United States were unfolding in a most horrific way as delegates grappled with understanding the state of Scotland's land. The Conference Dinner, that concluded the first day's deliberations, started with a silence in memory of the thousands killed only a few hours earlier. The television pictures and radio broadcasts revealed the enormity of the events that had taken place and emphasised the urgent need for improved national and international dialogue and the development of commonly shared values. It is a challenge and an opportunity for the global move towards sustainability to play its part in reconciling some of our serious social and cultural differences.

The meeting was held in the Conference Centre at Heriot Watt University. The facilities were excellent, and we wish to thank the staff at the University for all that they did to make the conference run smoothly. From our own organisations, we should like to thank the people who really got 'the show on the road' – Helen Forster, Sylvia Conway and Jo Newman (SNH), and Rosemary Mackintosh and Jean Skellern (SEPA). Technical advice during the planning stage was provided by Anton Edwards and Ross Doughty (SEPA) and Julian Holbrook (SNH), and we are grateful to them for the huge amount of work that they did. In editing this book, we should particularly like to thank the large number of referees who have read individual chapters and commented on them. We are convinced that the chapter authors have benefited from the refereeing process, and that the quality of this book has thereby been improved. Also, we owe a particular 'thank you' to Jo Newman who has undertaken so many of the tasks of editing manuscripts, typing letters, getting everything into electronic format, and persuading people whose deadlines have passed to get on with their task. For proof-reading we should like to thank Helen Forster and Jo Newman. Jane McNair of The Stationery Office guided the whole process to publication.

However, we do not view this publication just as a record of the event that took place in September 2001. The UNCED conference in Rio de Janeiro in 1992 was a milestone in achieving awareness of the environment. Perhaps Agenda 21 and the Convention on Biological Diversity were two of the Rio outcomes that most intimately affect the work of SNH and SEPA, and the policies of the Scottish Executive Environment and Rural Affairs Department. It was always envisaged that there would be a 'Rio +10' conference, which we now hear is scheduled to be held in Johannesburg in September 2002. As editors, we are aware of the value of this book, highlighting Scotland within the United Kingdom, as a contribution to the Johannesburg meeting. We hope that the frank accounts of the state of Scotland's environment and natural heritage, as well as the analyses of trends, are helpful in informing that conference. Scotland demonstrates some very hopeful trends and predictions for the future, but equally there are some aspects of the current state of the environment and natural heritage about which we cannot be so positive. However, the book does leave the reader with a feeling that Scotland is taking steps towards a more sustainable future. It is our hope that what started in Rio de Janeiro in 1992, and what will continue in Johannesburg in 2002, will guide all nations towards a shared commitment to the more sustainable use of the planet's resources.

References

Asher, J., Warren, M., Fox, R., Harding, P., Jeffcoate, G. and Jeffcoate, S. (2001). *The Millennium Atlas of Butterflies in Britain and Ireland.* Oxford University Press, Oxford.

Mackey, E.C. (ed.) (1995). *The Natural Heritage of Scotland: an Overview.* Scottish Natural Heritage, Perth.

Mackey, E.C., Shaw, P., Holbrook, J., Shewry, M.C., Saunders, G., Hall, J. and Ellis, N.E. (2001). *Natural Heritage Trends: Scotland 2001.* Scottish Natural Heritage, Perth.

SEPA (1996). *State of the Environment Report 1996.* Scottish Environment Protection Agency, Stirling.

SEPA (1999a). *Improving Scotland's Water Environment.* Scottish Environment Protection Agency, Stirling.

SEPA (1999b). *State of the Environment: Air Quality Report.* Scottish Environment Protection Agency, Stirling.

SEPA (2001). *State of the Environment: Soil Quality Report.* Scottish Environment Protection Agency, Stirling.

James C. Curran, Environmental Futures Manager, SEPA

Edward C. Mackey, Head of Environmental Audit, SNH

Michael B. Usher, former Chief Scientist, SNH; currently Leverhulme Emeritus Fellow, University of Stirling

February 2002

CONTENTS

LIST OF PLATES
(between pages 170 and 171)

LIST OF CONTRIBUTORS

R.W. Battarbee, Environmental Change Research Centre, Department of Geography, University College London, 26 Bedford Way, London, WC1H 0AP. E-mail: rbattarb@geog.ucl.ac.uk

J. Baxter, Scottish Natural Heritage, 2 Anderson Place, Edinburgh, EH6 5NP. E-mail: john.baxter@snh.gov.uk

H. Bennion, Environmental Change Research Centre, Department of Geography, University College London, 26 Bedford Way, London, WC1H 0AP. E-mail: hbennion@geog.ucl.ac.uk

R.V. Birnie, The Macaulay Institute, Craigiebuckler, Aberdeen, AB15 8QH. E-mail: R.Birnie@macaulay.ac.uk

P.J. Boon, Scottish Natural Heritage, 2 Anderson Place, Edinburgh, EH6 5NP. E-mail: phil.boon@snh.gov.uk

C.D. Campbell, The Macaulay Institute, Craigiebuckler, Aberdeen, AB15 8QH. E-mail: c.campbell@macaulay.ac.uk

N.G. Cameron, Environmental Change Research Centre, Department of Geography, University College London, 26 Bedford Way, London, WC1H 0AP. E-mail: ncameron@geog.ucl.ac.uk.

R. Crofts, Scottish Natural Heritage, 12 Hope Terrace, Edinburgh, EH9 2AS. Present address: 6 Old Church Lane, Duddingston Village, Edinburgh, EH15 3PX. E-mail: crofts.manson@dodin.idps.co.uk

J.C. Curran, Scottish Environment Protection Agency, Erskine Court, The Castle Business Park, Stirling, FK9 4TR. E-mail: james.curran@sepa.org.uk

J. Currie, Environment Directorate General, European Commission, 200 Rue de la Loi, B-1049, Brussels, Belgium. Present address: c/o Group Secretary's Department, Royal Bank of Scotland PLC, 42 St Andrew Square, Edinburgh, EH2 2YE.

C. Curtis, Environmental Change Research Centre, University College London, 26 Bedford Way, London, WC1H 0AP. E-mail: ccurtis@geog.ucl.ac.uk

L.C. Dale, Centre for Ecology and Hydrology, Monks Wood, Abbots Ripton, Huntingdon, Cambridgeshire, PE28 2LS. E-mail: lcd@ceh.ac.uk

J.E. Dobson, Scottish Environment Protection Agency, Clearwater House, Heriot Watt Research Park, Avenue North, Riccarton, Edinburgh, EH14 4AP. E-mail: judy.dobson@sepa.org.uk

M. Donaghy, Fisheries Research Services, Freshwater Fisheries Laboratory, Faskally, Pitlochry, Perthshire, PH16 5LB. E-mail: m.donaghy@marlab.ac.uk

C.R. Doughty, Scottish Environment Protection Agency, 5 Redwood Crescent, Peel Park, East Kilbride, G74 5PP. E-mail: ross.doughty@sepa.org.uk

U. Dragosits, Centre for Ecology and Hydrology, Bush Estate, Penicuik, Midlothian, EH26 0QB. E-mail: ud@ceh.ac.uk

K. Dunion, Friends of the Earth Scotland, 72 Newhaven Road, Edinburgh, EH6 5QG. E-mail: kdunion@foe-scotland.org.uk

A. Edwards, Scottish Environment Protection Agency, Clearwater House, Heriot Watt Research Park, Avenue North, Riccarton, Edinburgh, EH14 4AP. E-mail: anton.edwards@sepa.org.uk

N. Ellis, Scottish Natural Heritage, 2 Anderson Place, Edinburgh, EH6 5NP. E-mail: noranne.ellis@snh.gov.uk

R.J. Flower, Environmental Change Research Centre, University College London, 26 Bedford Way, London, WC1H 0AP. E-mail: rflower@geog.ucl.ac.uk

D. Fowler, Centre for Ecology and Hydrology, Bush Estate, Penicuik, Midlothian, EH26 0QB. E-mail: dfo@ceh.ac.uk

R. Fuller, Section for Earth Observation, Centre for Ecology and Hydrology, Monks Wood, Huntingdon, Cambridgeshire, PE28 2LS. E-mail: rf@ceh.ac.uk

J. Hall, Scottish Natural Heritage, 2 Anderson Place, Edinburgh, EH6 5NP. E-mail: jeanette.hall@snh.gov.uk

E.-L. Hallanaro, Päärynäpolku 1, 02710 Espoo, Finland. E-mail: eeva-liisa@nic.fi

M.P. Henton, Scottish Environment Protection Agency, Erskine Court, The Castle Business Park, Stirling, FK9 4TR. E-mail: tricia.henton@sepa.org.uk

J. Holbrook, Scottish Natural Heritage, 2 Anderson Place, Edinburgh, EH6 5NP. E-mail: julian.holbrook@snh.gov.uk

M. Hughes, Environmental Change Research Centre, University College London, 26 Bedford Way, London, WC1H 0AP. E-mail: m.hughes@geog.ucl.ac.uk

P. Hutchinson, North Atlantic Salmon Conservation Organization, 11 Rutland Square, Edinburgh, EH1 2AS. E-mail: hq@nasco.int

L. Johnston, The Macaulay Institute, Craigiebuckler, Aberdeen, AB15 8QH. E-mail: l.johnston@macaulay.ac.uk

V.J. Jones, Environmental Change Research Centre, University College London, 26 Bedford Way, London, WC1H 0AP. E-mail: vjones@geog.ucl.ac.uk

M. Kernan, Environmental Change Research Centre, University College London, 26 Bedford Way, London, WC1H 0AP. E-mail: mkernan@geog.ucl.ac.uk

A. Kerr, Greenergy Carbon Partners Ltd, Tower Mains Studios, 18 Liberton Brae, Edinburgh, EH16 6AE. E-mail: andy.kerr@greenergy.co.uk

S.J. Langan, The Macaulay Institute, Craigiebuckler, Aberdeen, AB15 8QH. E-mail: s.langan@macaulay.ac.uk

O.L. Lassière, British Waterways, Canal House, 1 Applecross Street, Glasgow, G4 9SP. E-mail: olivia.lassiere@britishwaterways.co.uk

J.A. MacDonald, Scottish Environment Protection Agency, 17 Whitefriars Crescent, Perth, PH2 0PA. E-mail: janette.macdonald@sepa.org.uk

W.G. MacGregor, Scottish Environment Protection Agency, Erskine Court, The Castle Business Park, Stirling, FK9 4TR. Present address: Innogy Hydro, Stanley Mills, Stanley, Perthshire. E-mail: bill.macgregor@innogy.com

E.C. Mackey, Scottish Natural Heritage, 2 Anderson Place, Edinburgh, EH6 5NP. E-mail: ed.mackey@snh.gov.uk

P.S. Maitland, Fish Conservation Centre, Gladshot, Haddington, East Lothian, EH41 4NR. E-mail: SavingFish@Maitland60.freeserve.co.uk

H.M. Malcolm, Centre for Ecology and Hydrology, Monks Wood, Abbots Ripton, Huntingdon, Cambridgeshire, PE28 2LS. E-mail: hmm@ceh.ac.uk

A.G. McDonald, Centre for Ecology and Hydrology, Bush Estate, Penicuik, Midlothian, EH26 0QB. E-mail: agmd@ceh.ac.uk

G.G. McFadyen, Scottish Environment Protection Agency, Erskine Court, The Castle Business Park, Stirling, FK9 4TR. E-mail: gordon.mcfadyen@sepa.org.uk

G. McGowan, Centre for Ecology and Hydrology, Hill of Brathens, Banchory, Kincardineshire, AB31 4BW. E-mail: gmcg@ceh.ac.uk

D.T. Monteith, Environmental Change Research Centre, University College London, 26 Bedford Way, London, WC1H 0AP. E-mail: dmonteit@geog.ucl.ac.uk

E. Nemitz, Centre for Ecology and Hydrology, Bush Estate, Penicuik, Midlothian, EH26 0QB. E-mail: en@ceh.ac.uk

I. Newton, Centre for Ecology and Hydrology, Monks Wood, Abbots Ripton, Huntingdon, Cambridgeshire, PE28 2LS. E-mail: ine@ceh.ac.uk

T. O'Riordan, Centre for Social and Economic Research on the Global Environment, University of East Anglia, Norwich, NR4 7TJ. E-mail: m.a.dixon@uea.ac.uk

D. Osborn, Centre for Ecology and Hydrology, Monks Wood, Abbots Ripton, Huntingdon, Cambridgeshire, PE28 2LS. E-mail: dano@ceh.ac.uk

S.C.F. Palmer, Centre for Ecology and Hydrology, Hill of Brathens, Banchory, Kincardineshire, AB31 4BW. E-mail: scfp@ceh.ac.uk

E. Paterson, The Macaulay Institute, Craigiebuckler, Aberdeen, AB15 8QH. E-mail: ed.paterson@macaulay.ac.uk

S.T. Patrick, Environmental Change Research Centre, University College London, 26 Bedford Way, London, WC1H 0AP. E-mail: spatrick@geog.ucl.ac.uk

K. Pugh, Scottish Environment Protection Agency, Greyhope House, Greyhope Road, Torry, Aberdeen, AB11 9RD. E-mail: ken.pugh@sepa.org.uk

N.L. Rose, Environmental Change Research Centre, University College London, 26 Bedford Way, London, WC1H 0AP. E-mail: nrose@geog.ucl.ac.uk

G. Saunders, Scottish Natural Heritage, 2 Anderson Place, Edinburgh, EH6 5NP. E-mail: graham.saunders@snh.gov.uk

B. Sargent, Scottish Environment Protection Agency, Erskine Court, The Castle Business Park, Stirling, FK9 4TR. E-mail: bob.sargent@sepa.org.uk

C.D. Sayer, Environmental Change Research Centre, University College London, 26 Bedford Way, London, WC1H 0AP. E-mail: c.sayer@ucl.ac.uk

P. Shaw, Scottish Natural Heritage, 2 Anderson Place, Edinburgh, EH6 5NP. E-mail: phil.shaw@snh.gov.uk

M.C. Shewry, Scottish Natural Heritage, 2 Anderson Place, Edinburgh, EH6 5NP. E-mail: michael.shewry@snh.gov.uk

R. Shore, Centre for Ecology and Hydrology, Monks Wood, Abbots Ripton, Huntingdon, Cambridgeshire, PE28 2LS. E-mail: rfs@ceh.ac.uk

G. Simpson, Environmental Change Research Centre, University College London, 26 Bedford Way, London, WC1H 0AP. E-mail: gavin.simpson@ucl.ac.uk

G. Smith, Section for Earth Observation, Centre for Ecology and Hydrology, Monks Wood, Huntingdon, Cambridgeshire, PE28 2LS. E-mail: gesm@ceh.ac.uk

G. Söderman, Finnish Environment Institute, P.O.Box 140, 00251 Helsinki, Finland. E-mail: guy.soderman@ymparisto.fi

T.H. Sparks, Centre for Ecology and Hydrology, Monks Wood, Abbots Ripton, Huntingdon, Cambridgeshire, PE28 2LS. E-mail: ths@ceh.ac.uk

M.A. Sutton, Centre for Ecology and Hydrology, Bush Estate, Penicuik, Midlothian, EH26 0QB. E-mail: ms@ceh.ac.uk

M.B. Usher, Scottish Natural Heritage, 2 Anderson Place, Edinburgh, EH6 5NP. Present address: Department of Environmental Science, University of Stirling, Stirling, FK9 4LA. E-mail: m.b.usher@stir.ac.uk

C. Wienburg, Centre for Ecology and Hydrology, Monks Wood, Abbots Ripton, Huntingdon, Cambridgeshire, PE28 2LS. E-mail: clwy@ceh.ac.uk

H. Yang, Environmental Change Research Centre, University College London, 26 Bedford Way, London, WC1H 0AP. E-mail: hyang@geog.ucl.ac.uk

A. Youngson, Fisheries Research Services, Freshwater Fisheries Laboratory, Faskally, Pitlochry, Perthshire, PH16 5LB. E-mail: a.youngson@marlab.ac.uk

FOREWORD

The 1992 Earth Summit in Rio de Janeiro set out a global agenda for developing sustainable development and safeguarding world biodiversity. We have come a long way since then. Agenda 21, Local Agenda 21 and Biodiversity Action Plans have been pursued vigorously. They are now beginning to show real results. Sustainable development has become a familiar concept, applicable to all walks of life. It is enshrined in the founding legislation of both SNH and SEPA. It is a theme that is at the heart of the work of the Scottish Parliament, and a keystone of policy for the Scottish Executive and the UK Government. The 2002 World Summit in Johannesburg will provide an opportunity to review progress since Rio and give new impetus to our work.

This book, recording the proceedings of SNH's and SEPA's joint conference in September 2001, allows examination of the links between changes in our wildlife, landscape and surrounding seas, and the quality of Scotland's air, land and water. It explores our understanding of the relationship between environmental pressures and observed changes. Contributors predict the nature, rate and direction of change, and anticipate where the main pressures will come from in future.

The land and surrounding seas of Scotland are hugely varied. We must not take for granted the features of the environment on which we depend – clean air and clean water, soil fertility, natural regulation of water flow, saltmarshes and machair, and many more. If we over-exploit our natural resources, or overstretch their capacity to regenerate, our own health and well-being will suffer. For a sustainable future we must understand ecosystem processes and the carrying capacity of the environment. Sustainable management of the environment requires integrated solutions to be adopted by all sections of society and all sectors of the economy.

Many of the environmental issues that we encounter in Scotland are common to other parts of Europe. Effective action therefore often calls for co-ordination among Member States. The preparation of a sustainable development strategy for the European Union will act as a catalyst for change, focusing on a number of the most pressing problems facing us today. In the natural heritage context these problems include climate change, threats to public health, pressures on natural resources and biodiversity, excessive generation of waste, congestion, pollution and social exclusion.

Through environmental protection and enhancement we aim to improve the quality of life for Scotland's people as an integral part of the regeneration of urban and rural communities. This will make cities more attractive, extend opportunities for people to enjoy the countryside around towns, encourage community participation and involvement, and foster understanding and appreciation of landscape and environment.

As a benchmark for the new millennium, I applaud SNH and SEPA for hosting the conference and documenting it in this book. The book emphasises that Scotland's environment, natural heritage, society and economic activity need to be viewed as a whole. The quality of our environment is vital to our quality of life, to Scottish identity and to the foundation of a modern economy. This book makes a valuable contribution to our understanding of the present state of Scotland's natural heritage and provides useful pointers for future action.

Allan Wilson MSP
Deputy Minister for Environment and Rural Development
February 2002

PART ONE

SCOTLAND IN CONTEXT

PART ONE

SCOTLAND IN CONTEXT

Scotland's distinctive biogeography, its climate, topography, geology and soils, and history of land use, are reflected in a richly varied land cover and a diversity of habitats and species. On many counts, the state of Scotland's environment and natural heritage might be thought of as extremely good. Nevertheless, a growing number of households exerts continuing development pressure on building land, on natural resources, and on goods and services. Environmental impacts arising from, for example, settlement and transport, or from farming and forestry, the legacy of industrialisation, or the over-exploitation of marine fish stocks and associated trawling damage to the sea floor, underlie the need for conservation action and sustainable resource management. The focus of this book is on Scotland and its surrounding seas. Yet many environmental pressures and their consequences are not easily contained by political boundaries.

Mackey (Chapter 1) notes that Scotland encounters and contributes to a range of environmental pressures at a European scale. It is appropriate at the outset, therefore, to consider the broader context. Indeed, in the Foreword to this book the Deputy Minister for the Environment and Rural Development, Allan Wilson MSP, looks towards the Johannesburg World Summit on Sustainable Development in September 2002. He emphasises the importance of the Scottish conference on the world stage, recalling that the United Nations Conference on Environment and Development, the 1992 Earth Summit in Rio de Janeiro, set out a global agenda for sustainable development.

Efforts that have been undertaken in Scotland on biodiversity action planning, or on tackling the causes and consequences of climate change, are practical expressions of the Local Agenda 21 message: 'think global, act local'. Reflecting a common purpose and the need for co-ordinated action, Currie (Chapter 2) notes that at least 80 per cent of environmental legislation that applies to Scotland nowadays originates in Europe. In this, he argues that Scotland has a greater role to play.

Audits of the Nordic environment (Bernes, 1993) and of the European environment (Stanners and Bourdeau, 1995) have informed environmental policy and set standards for monitoring and reporting. Air pollution provides some of the earliest and best examples of consistency in data recording and reporting. Many other aspects of the environment and natural heritage are more difficult to compare. At a European scale, Scotland is characterised by two biogeographical provinces: the 'Scottish Highlands' to the north of the Highland Boundary Fault, and the 'Atlantic' province which extends to the rest of the British Isles and western margins of continental Europe (Stanners and Bourdeau, 1995). From a Nordic perspective, Hallanaro and Söderman (Chapter 3) point to a shared glacial past and similarities among habitats and species of the uplands, coasts and seas. Differences are equally evident, arising in part from the post-glacial ecological insularity of the British Isles, as well as differences in cultural histories and contemporary climate.

Fuller and Smith (Chapter 4) explain how the global technology of satellite imagery has been applied to create a new land cover map for Scotland, providing methodological consistency at a UK scale and offering prospects for pan-European comparisons.

At a planetary scale, Scotland may appear at first sight to be relatively insignificant – for example in terms of its geographical extent, its population size and its species complement. Nevertheless, systematic studies at a country scale are vital to understanding local distinctiveness, and are the mechanism by which we can gain a wider understanding of the state of the environment and natural heritage – within the UK, within Europe and globally. On the one hand, the conference has demonstrated a richness of information at a country scale. On the other hand, country comparisons that provide clear messages about the extent to which sustainable development is being secured, and Scotland's contribution, as yet remain largely beyond our grasp.

References

Bernes, C. (1993). *The Nordic Environment: Present State, Trends and Threats.* Nordic Council of Ministers, Copenhagen.

Stanners, D. and Bourdeau, P. (eds.) (1995). *Europe's Environment: the Dobris Assessment.* European Environment Agency, Copenhagen.

1 Scotland in a European Context: Environmental and Natural Heritage Trends

E.C. Mackey

Summary

1.   A duty of care for the natural heritage in Scotland includes the full extent of land, fresh waters and the sea, the ecological functions and communities of life they support, together with the livelihood and quality of life of people.

2.   Reported environmental concerns for Europe are examined, leading to observations on apparent similarities and dissimilarities with Scotland.

3.   Farming systems and the characteristics of farmland change vary across Europe. Nevertheless, common patterns of a diminishing agricultural labour force, amalgamation, conversion of land to non-agricultural uses, simplification and intensification are all evident in Scotland.

4.   Commercial afforestation in Scotland appeared to parallel reported trends in other parts of Europe until the 1990s, since when the emphasis in Scotland has been on the re-establishment of native woodlands and the creation of woodland networks which fit the landscape better and which provide wildlife and recreation benefits.

5.   Targets have been set for the continued improvement of air and water quality in Scotland, in keeping with environmental improvements throughout much of Europe. Comparisons of urban growth, greenspace and ecosystem functions need to be supported by more systematic data gathering and reporting.

6.   The quality of Scotland's fresh waters is generally good by European standards but major investment continues to be required in waste water and sewage treatment for the protection of coastal waters, the restoration of polluted or degraded rivers and lochs, and the improvement of drinking water quality.

7.   The seas to the west and north of Scotland are among the most pristine in Europe. Land-based pollution into the North Sea is being brought under stricter control. The ecological status of commercially exploited wild fish stocks in the seas around Scotland is a matter of current conservation concern.

8.   As part of the UK, Scotland has much to contribute towards European environmental assessments and should be fully involved in the development of European indicators. In turn, Scotland would benefit from being able to see more clearly how the state of its environment and natural heritage compare in a European context.

1.1 Scottish distinctiveness in a European context

The land area of Scotland is about 78,000 km², being around 240 km at its widest and 1,350 m at its highest. The coastal length is 16,500 km at a mapping scale of 1:25,000. Territorial waters defined by the 12 nautical mile limit approach 89,000 km², somewhat larger than the land area.

The extent and stature of the British uplands may appear relatively insignificant in European terms, but their distinctive landscape character and range of ecosystems are not duplicated elsewhere in the world (Ratcliffe and Thompson, 1988). Much of the Scottish uplands are characterised by expansive tracts of blanket bog, which is more extensive in Scotland and Ireland than elsewhere in Europe. Some patterned bog types appear to be confined to Britain and Ireland. In the lowlands, despite the encroachment of agriculture, forestry and mining, Scotland still retains one of the richest surviving European concentrations of raised bog.

Extensive acid grasslands, which predominate towards the wetter west, and heather moorland on more freely drained soils to the east have been sustained by grazing and burning since the natural forest was cleared from Neolithic times onwards. As a feature of north-west European landscapes, heather moorland is extensive nowadays only in the British Isles, and particularly so in Scotland (Thompson *et al.*, 1995).

The northern and montane vascular flora of Britain is drawn from at least seven phytogeographical elements. Whilst component species are, for the most part, widely distributed in continental Europe, the mixture of alpine, arctic-alpine and arctic species is unique. On the higher mountain tops, above the natural treeline, scrub remnants give way to montane plant communities which, although small in extent compared with the main continental occurrences, exhibit considerable diversity and include several types which are either highly local or apparently absent elsewhere (Ratcliffe and Thompson, 1988).

The Caledonian pine/birch-dominated forests, which have a smaller range of species than continental boreal forests, nevertheless contain several species of plants and animals which are rare or absent elsewhere. The oceanic climate and varied topography of the western Highlands and Islands give rise to an unparalleled richness of the Atlantic bryophyte flora (Ratcliffe and Thompson, 1988). More than half of the liverworts and mosses, and over a third of the lichens, of Europe occur in Scotland. Being sensitive to air and water pollutants, many lower plants have their European stronghold along the Atlantic coast.

The botanically rich machair lands of the Hebridean islands support internationally important populations of nesting waders. Goose Management Schemes, introduced in four areas of Scotland, help to integrate productive farming on more intensively managed crops and grass with the conservation of internationally important populations of wild geese (SNH, 2002a). An abundance of invertebrates within intertidal sand and mud flats sustain large numbers of over-wintering wildfowl and waders. A long coast with, for the most part, relatively low levels of human pressure, has given rise to the preservation of much of Scotland's marine natural heritage. Of international importance are Scotland's breeding populations of seabirds and grey seals.

Situated on an island at a northern latitude, Scotland's biodiversity is distinctive. Total species richness has been estimated to be some 90,000 native species, with slightly more than 50,000 in terrestrial and freshwater environments and at least 39,000 in the surrounding seas. Around half of the overall total is accounted for by single-celled organisms, 23 per cent by plants and fungi, and 28 per cent by animals (Usher, 1997). This compares with an estimated 230,000 terrestrial species in Europe as a whole (Delbaere, 1998). As terrestrial species richness increases markedly to the south and east, Scotland is similar to Nordic countries at similar latitudes.

A remarkable feature of Scotland's species complement, which is mostly shared with other parts of the UK and Europe, is its diverse mix of Atlantic, arctic, arctic-alpine and boreal elements (SNH, 2001a). Many are on the extreme edge of their global range. Probably a greater mixture of boreal, low-, mid- and high-arctic, temperate and continental bird species breed in the British uplands than in any comparably sized part of Europe. Although most of the individual species are not scarce elsewhere in Europe, the assemblages of boreal-arctic peatland birds, and birds of the montane plateaux and corries, have no counterparts elsewhere (Ratcliffe and Thompson, 1988). Thirty-one species (ten lichens, six mosses, ten vascular plants, four insects and one vertebrate, the Scottish crossbill (*Loxia scotica*)) may be endemic to Scotland, although such numbers are subject to continual revision in the light of new knowledge.

Around 12 per cent of Scotland is designated to be of special scientific interest in terms of its floral, faunal or earth heritage characteristics, and around the same extent is designated to be of exceptional landscape value (SNH, 2001b). Many components of the natural heritage are of international importance, for example in relation to Scotland's contribution to the Natura ecological network (Box 1.1).

Box 1.1. Scotland's position in the 'Natura Barometer'.

The two main components of nature conservation policy within the EU are Council Directive 79/409/EEC on the protection of wild birds (the 'Birds Directive') and Council Directive 92/43/EEC on the conservation of natural habitats and of wild fauna and flora (the 'Habitats Directive'). Together, they establish an ecological network for protecting and conserving wildlife and habitats across the EU, known as 'Natura 2000' (*Natura 2000 Newsletter, Issue 1, May 1996*). Protected areas within the network include

- Special Protection Areas (SPAs), to conserve the 182 bird species and sub-species listed in Annex I of the Birds Directive and migratory birds, and
- Special Areas of Conservation (SAC), to conserve the 253 habitat types, 200 animal species and 434 plant species listed in Annexes I and II of the Habitats Directive.

The 2001 'Natura Barometer' (*Natura 2000 Newsletter, Issue 14, April 2001*) indicated that country assessments across the EU are as yet incomplete. The number of SPAs which have been 'classified' ranges from 13 in Luxembourg to 617 in Germany (the UK ranks sixth out of 15 Member States with 230). As a proportion of national territory, France is the lowest with 1.5 per cent and Netherlands is the highest with 24 per cent (the UK ranks eleventh with 4.6 per cent). The number of SACs which have been proposed ranges from 38 in Luxembourg to 2,507 in Italy (the UK ranks seventh out of 15 Member States with 499). As a proportion of national territory, Belgium is the lowest with 3.6 per cent and Denmark is the highest with 24 per cent (the UK ranks twelfth with 8.4 per cent).

Within the UK, Scotland accounts for slightly under half of the SPA area classified and the SAC area proposed. A European comparison of Scotland within the 'Natura Barometer' is summarised in Table 1.1 and Figure 1.1. The classified SPA area in Scotland (above and below high water mark) accounts for around 6 per cent of the national territory, somewhat below the simple mean of 9 per cent across the 15 Member States. Scotland contributes 2 per cent of the European classified area. The proposed SAC area in Scotland (above and below high water mark) would account for around 11 per cent of the national territory, again somewhat below the simple mean of 14 per cent for the 15 Member States. Scotland again contributes around 2 per cent of the European proposed area.

Table 1.1. Scotland within the 'Natura Barometer'.

Designation	Natura Barometer	Europe	UK	Scotland
Birds Directive: SPAs				
	Sites classified	2,941	230	123
	Scotland as a percentage	4	53	
	Classified area (km²)	212,473	11,165	4,911
	Scotland as a percentage	2	44	
	Percentage of UK/Scotland territory	-	5	6
Habitats Directive: SACs				
	Sites proposed	12,612	499	213
	Scotland as a percentage	2	43	
	Proposed area (km²)	418,042	21,658	8,915
	Scotland as a percentage	2	41	
	Percentage of UK/Scotland territory	-	8	11

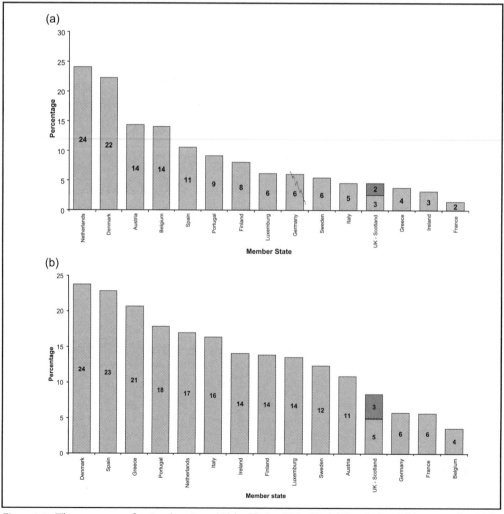

Figure 1.1. The percentage of national territory (a) classified as SPAs (Birds Directive) and (b) proposed as SACs (Habitats Directive) as at 1 March 2001.

Despite enhanced protection, wildlife sites cannot be conserved effectively in isolation and wildlife cannot be sustained exclusively on designated sites. Similarly, scenic interest and recreational enjoyment are not confined to special areas. It has become widely accepted that a set of protected areas is not enough. Instead, ecological networks which incorporate core areas, corridors, restoration areas and buffer zones, together with co-ordinated action, are essential for conserving ecosystems, habitats, species, landscapes and other natural features of European importance (Delbaere, 1998). A duty of care for the natural heritage in Scotland therefore includes the full extent of land, fresh waters and the sea, the ecological functions and communities of life they support, together with the livelihood and quality of life of people (SNH, 2002b).

1.2 How does Scotland compare?

Prominent European environmental concerns were assessed in the mid-1990s (Stanners and Bourdeau, 1995). These are examined here within the major natural heritage settings, but systematic comparisons with Scotland are hampered by a lack of definitive pan-European trend data. For example, the natural heritage is not yet represented among European indicators of sustainable development (Bosch and Stanners, 2001) and a Biodiversity Expert Group has only been convened as recently as February 2002 to consider requirements for reporting on European biodiversity. A Scottish study has been initiated to identify comparative European and other international trends (UNEP WCMC, 2002) but it is at an early stage and it has not proved easy to identify comparable data beyond the well established environmental indices of air and water quality. Consequently, the discussion that follows is necessarily a preliminary and partial view.

Land use and development have been the main drivers of change in Scotland, as in Europe. Typically, farming, forestry or urban development account for around 80 per cent of the land area in European countries (EEA, 1999). In Scotland the proportion might be as much as 94 per cent (McGowan *et al.*, 2001), with large tracts of open hill land utilised for extensive grazing, sport and recreation. In 1988, perhaps 60 per cent of Scotland's land cover (land and freshwater habitats) could be regarded as semi-natural, having been reduced by 17 per cent over four decades since the late 1950s (SNH, 2001c). However, a decade on, the 1998 estimate, albeit from a very different survey, was similar to that of 1988 (McGowan *et al.*, 2001).

The scope of discussion which follows is restricted to prominent environmental issues which have been identified within the European Union and which may be compared with trends which are evident within Scotland's natural heritage settings of farmland, forest and woodland, urban land, fresh waters and the sea. A number of cross-cutting issues, which cannot be dealt with in sufficient detail here, are nevertheless discussed by other authors in this volume. These include, for example, non-native species (Holbrook and Hall, Chapter 6), climate change (Kerr and Ellis, Chapter 16), biodiversity (Usher, Chapter 18) and hazardous substances (Pugh, Chapter 19).

1.3 Major land and water uses

1.3.1 Farmland

The rural economy has become increasingly diversified throughout Europe, with improved transport and telecommunications links. A growth of non-agricultural sectors in rural areas and tourism have emerged as alternatives to farming employment. Between 1975 and 1995, the number of agricultural holdings in the European Union (EU12) fell by 3 million, some 31 per cent (EEA, 2001).

Many European landscapes and habitats, which have come to be highly valued in social, cultural and environmental terms, have evolved through low intensity farming activities (Beaufoy *et al.*, 1994). Examples for Scotland are crofting and extensive sheep rearing. Concern has been raised about the running-down and disappearance of low-intensity farming systems throughout Europe, a dwindling rural labour force and out-migration (EEA, 1999). Agricultural intensification has taken place in areas of competitive advantage. Extensification, amalgamation, abandonment and conversion to alternative uses such as commercial forestry, have occurred where farming incomes have been poorest and where it has been most difficult to find successors within an ageing farming population.

Farming systems and the nature of change vary from country to country in Europe. Nevertheless, common factors which have been found to be associated with land marginalisation, i.e. where farming ceases to be economically viable, include the physical environment, geographical location, the size and structure of agricultural holdings, social and demographic factors, economic conditions, and, not least, the policy context (for example, around half of the annual European Union budget is expended on agriculture). Within a typology of five broad types, Scotland is an 'extensive farming region' which is said to be particularly susceptible to land marginalisation (Baldock *et al.*, 1996).

By 2000, agriculture accounted for over 40 per cent of the total land area within the European Union (EU). In comparison, agricultural holdings extended across 71 per cent of Scotland, of which 62 per cent was un-enclosed rough grazing (e.g. SEERAD, 2001).

Decline in workforce: In the late-1990s, agriculture accounted for slightly more than 5 per cent of employment within the EU. Having declined since the mid-1940s, the number of full-time employees in Scottish agriculture represented around 3 per cent of Scottish employment and 8 per cent of the rural workforce (SERAD, 1998). The number of farmers and employees in agriculture remained around 70,000 between 1991 and 2000 but the proportion of full-time workers declined. The number of full-time farm occupiers and spouses fell by 10 per cent whilst their part-time equivalents increased by 13 per cent. Part-time employment also increased, from 47 per cent to 54 per cent, as did the contracting of agricultural operations (FPD Savilles, 2001).

Amalgamation: With a considerable proportion of land being accounted for by around 1,500 large estates, the 1997 average farm size in Scotland was 122 ha compared with 62 ha in the UK and 16 ha in the EU. In 1999, 6 per cent of Scottish holdings were larger than 300 ha and accounted for two-thirds of the total agricultural area. Conversely, over half of the agricultural holdings in Scotland were smaller than 20 ha and accounted for no more than 3 per cent of the area. Between 1987 and 1999, the number of holdings of between 20 and 100 ha decreased by nearly 6 per cent whilst holdings greater than 100 ha increased by between 1 and 2 per cent. The overall agricultural area decreased by 3.1 per cent through conversion to non-farming uses (FPD Savilles, 2001).

Change of use: An estimated 19 per cent expansion of fen, marsh and swamp between 1990 and 1998 would appear consistent with reduced or abandoned grassland drainage in wetter areas. Heather moorland, encompassing wet and dry heaths as habitats of European Community interest on Annex I of the Habitats Directive, declined by 5 per cent, mainly due to woodland canopy closure and conversion to grassland. Broadleaved and mixed woodland expanded by 9 per cent, mainly on grassland but also on heath and bog habitats, arable land and road verges (McGowan *et al.*, 2001).

Simplification: Mixed farming in Scotland has declined in recent decades, with the west becoming more dominantly pastoral and the east more dominantly arable. Hedgerow length was reduced by more than half between 1947 and 1988 (Mackey *et al.*, 1998). The mixed farm area decreased by 23 per cent between 1987 and 1999 (FPD Savilles, 2001). The number of crofters, managers of small-scale mixed farms in the north-west of Scotland, fell by 23 per cent between 1960 and 1985, accompanied by reduced tillage and the replacement of traditional cattle grazing by sheep (RSPB and SCU,1992).

Intensification: In the more intensively farmed areas, concern was expressed in the 1970s that the steady elimination of non-productive land and increased efficiency of production posed threats to nature conservation in Britain (Ratcliffe, 1977). For example, the frequency of occurrence of the arable weed flora declined in Scotland between 1930-1960 and 1987-1988 (Rich and Woodruff, 1996). A 29 per cent reduction in hay stocks and an 86 per cent increase in silage stocks reflect intensified grassland management between 1987 and 1999 (FPD Savilles, 2001).

Declines in farmland birds in Scotland from the early 1970s to the late 1990s have been linked to agricultural intensification (SNH, 2001d), also identified as the prime cause of declines in farmland bird species across Europe (Delbaere, 1998). Conversely, wintering wildfowl and waders have benefited from intensively managed grasslands in the west of Scotland (SNH, 2001e). Since 1992, between 5 and 15 per cent of arable farmland has been set-aside from production on large arable farms. The weight of pesticide use, excluding desiccant on potatoes, declined by 15 per cent between 1982 and 1998, with increased frequency of spraying at lower concentrations (e.g. Snowden and Thomas, 1999). Fertiliser use remained little changed between 1983 and 1998 (e.g. Burnhill *et al.*, 1999). Nevertheless, agricultural run-off has been implicated in increased nitrate levels in some rivers between 1980 and 2000, with a 17 per cent average increase in the east and a 28 per cent average increase in the north (Landrock *et al.,* 2001). Similar trends are found in other parts of Europe (EEA, 2001), where control of nitrate run-off from agriculture has rarely been achieved and where unsatisfactory implementation of the Nitrates Directive has resulted in infraction proceedings (T. Lack in www.nmw.ac.uk/change2001).

Agricultural patterns: Farming systems and the characteristics of farmland change vary across Europe. Nevertheless, common patterns of a diminishing agricultural labour force, amalgamation, conversion of land to non-agricultural uses, simplification and intensification are all evident in Scotland. Birnie *et al.* (Chapter 5) take a closer look at the geographical characteristics of such changes within Scotland. It has been argued that conservation must become a more explicit objective of rural policy, aimed at preserving management practices which are beneficial to the natural heritage, without stifling development, and also promoting a way of life which is socially and economically attractive (Beaufoy *et al.*, 1994; Baldock *et al.*, 1996). Environmentally-friendly farming practices, such as through the Rural Stewardship Scheme (Scottish Executive, 2000), have been shown to enable wildlife such as the corncrake (*Crex crex*) in Scotland to recover or re-establish (Green and Riley, 1999).

1.3.2 *Forest and woodland*

In 1995, the average forest and woodland cover in European countries was 33 per cent (Stanners and Bourdeau, 1995). Ireland with 6 per cent and Finland with 66 per cent were at extreme ends of the scale. The extent of forest and timber production had increased by 1998, predominantly associated with replacement of old and semi-natural woodlands by more uniform forests of exotic species. The two most important causes of degradation to natural forests were reported to be air pollution (central, eastern and to a lesser extent northern Europe) and fire (southern Europe), neither being normally associated with Scottish forests.

Accounting for 17 per cent of the Scottish land area in 2000, woodland cover is relatively, but not exceptionally, low by European standards. Having been reduced to less than 5 per cent in the early 1900s, the expansion of forest and woodland has been due in large measure to commercial afforestation between the 1940s and 1980s (Mackey *et al.*, 1998).

From the 1990s onwards, however, woodland change in Scotland departs from the general European trend. Opportunities have been taken to restructure felled plantations and, through a greater emphasis on broadleaved planting and local progeny, to restore habitat diversity, ecological connectivity and the visual character of woodland within the landscape. The area of native woodland in Scotland increased by one-third between 1984 and 1999 (SNH, 2001f), and the area of farm woodland doubled between 1991 and 2000 (e.g. SEERAD, 2001), creating and restoring habitat diversity in lowland and upland environments. Five out of 14 widespread woodland birds increased in abundance between 1994 and 1999 (SNH, 2001d).

Commercial afforestation in Scotland appeared to parallel reported trends in other parts of Europe until the 1990s, since when the emphasis in Scotland has been on the re-establishment of native woodlands and the creation of woodland networks which fit the landscape better and which provide wildlife and recreation benefits.

1.3.3 *Urban land*

In 1995 it was concluded that sustainability in Europe required urban activities to be brought more into balance with the capacity of ecosystems to provide life support services important to human health (Stanners and Bourdeau, 1995). By 1999, improvements had been made in air and water quality, but urban greenspace, which ranged from 2 per cent to 70 per cent of European cities, remained at risk from development (EEA,1999).

Major air polluting industries in Scotland have been subject to control since 1863, but the most substantial improvements in air quality, especially in urban areas, have been secured since the Clean Air Act 1956 (Fowler *et al.*, Chapter 7). In general, air quality resulting from industrial and domestic pollution has tended to improve or at least remain constant over time, whilst traffic pollution has become worse. Road traffic has become mainly responsible for elevated levels of air pollution in urban areas, as well as ozone and other forms of pollution in rural areas. In general, urban air quality in Scotland is likely to be within defined thresholds. Nevertheless, problems arising from industry or heavy traffic may require locally targeted attention (SEPA, 1999a).

In the early 1900s, most rivers in Scotland were grossly polluted downstream of significant conurbations or major industries (SEPA, 1999b). Regulatory authorities were set up in 1951 but it was not until 1965 that legislation was provided to restore Scotland's rivers to a healthy condition. Major improvements to the quality of Scotland's waters have been detected from the mid-1970s onwards. Between 1980 and 1995, the monitored length of polluted river (in fair, poor and seriously polluted categories) decreased by 41 per cent. Sewage effluent, diffuse agricultural pollution, acidification and urban drainage were the main causes of river pollution in 1996, the first year in which the recording for a broader range of environmental measurements was undertaken. Between 1990 and 1995, polluted waters in estuaries were reduced by 47 per cent and in coastal waters by 55 per cent. Sewage and industrial effluent were the main causes of pollution in estuarine and coastal waters in 1996.

Community woodlands and local nature reserves have increased in number over the past decade in Scotland. The Central Scotland Woodland Initiative, based on a partnership including EU funding, is providing environmental and landscape improvements, and new recreational opportunities within Scotland's Central Belt between Glasgow and Edinburgh (www.csct.co.uk). This is a part of Scotland where development pressure is high and where the countryside has been degraded by mining and heavy engineering industries. The target of 34,000 ha of woodland by 2015 will create an attractive multi-purpose environment of woodland and farmland, towns and villages, shelterbelts and hedgerows. This transformation of the landscape will support economic regeneration and enhance the quality of life for all who live and work in the area. By 2002, the towns and cities of the Central Belt will also be connected by a restored canal network to provide a corridor of greenspace that is notable for its diversity and richness, and opportunities for recreation and relaxation (Lassière, Chapter 11).

A difficulty in making comparisons of urban greenspace is that little information is available on, for example, extent and composition, wildlife, recreation, connectivity and accessibility. In terms of overall extent, greenspace ranges from around 10 to 40 per cent of the major Scottish towns and cities (Mackey *et al.*, 2001), being neither exceptionally low nor exceptionally high by European standards.

Since the 1990s, emphasis has been placed on the utilisation of vacant and derelict land for re-development or restoration. Although the number of households rose by 18 per cent between 1981 and 1999 (Landrock *et al.*, 2001), the Countryside Survey detected no clear evidence of urban expansion between 1990 and 1998 (Haines-Young *et al.*, 2000). Between the mid-1960s and the mid-1990s, tranquillity was reduced throughout 45 per cent of a rural-urban case study area in the north-east of Scotland (Ash Consulting Group, 1998; Birnie *et al.*, Chapter 5). A projected 12 per cent expansion in housing demand from 1989 to 2012 (Landrock *et al.*, 2001) indicates continued development pressure on land in the future.

Targets have been set for the continued improvement of air (SEPA, 1999a) and water quality (SEPA, 1999b) in Scotland, in keeping with environmental improvements throughout much of Europe. Comparisons of urban growth, greenspace and ecosystem functions need to be supported by more systematic data gathering and reporting.

1.3.4 Fresh waters

By 1995, water supply problems, related both to demand and fitness for drinking, were prevalent in many parts of Europe (Stanners and Bourdeau, 1995). In Nordic and some western European countries, improvements in sewage and waste water treatment had reduced point-source pollution and heavy metal contamination, bringing about improvements to river water oxygenation and water quality. Nevertheless, diffuse pollution from intensive farming, together with spills of slurry and silage, threatened the quality of European inland waters and small streams.

Eutrophication, due to phosphorus and nitrogen in waste water and agricultural run-off, was widespread in European rivers, lakes, reservoirs, and coastal and marine waters. Nitrate thresholds for drinking water were frequently exceeded in groundwaters, and concentrations of synthetic chemicals, such as pesticides, exceed prescribed standards in many areas of intensive agriculture. In some countries, groundwater quality was also threatened by heavy metals, hydrocarbons and chlorinated hydrocarbons. With improved waste water treatment and reduced emissions from industry between 1980 and 1995, phosphorus discharges into rivers fell by 40 to 60 per cent in several European countries. Phosphorus concentrations in surface waters fell significantly, but remained ten times higher than for water of good quality at a quarter of river monitoring sites. By 1999, most countries classified 80 to 95 per cent of their river water as good or fair quality, but some classified as much as 25 per cent as poor or bad quality (EEA, 1999). The concentration of nitrate in EU rivers remained essentially unaltered from 1980 to 1999.

By 1999, nine-tenths of the 50,000 km of rivers which are classified in Scotland were of excellent or good quality (see Doughty *et al.*, Chapter 9). The quality of habitats in or near water is also an important measure of the overall quality of the aquatic environment. In 1997, 28 per cent of sites surveyed for river habitat were classified as either obviously modified (15 per cent), extensively modified (12 per cent) or heavily modified (1 per cent), reflecting the impacts of agriculture and urban development. In 1999, some 4,000 km of classified river length, and 30 of 150 classified lochs, were polluted (SEPA, 1999b). Phosphorus-rich discharges have, for example, degraded the ecological status of Loch Leven, a Ramsar Site and Special Protection Area. There, the local economic impact of a toxic algal bloom in 1992 was estimated to have approached £1 million. Whilst pollution from point sources has been progressively reduced since the 1970s, pollution from diffuse sources is now also being tackled through a catchment management plan (Loch Leven Catchment Management Project, 1999).

The European otter (*Lutra lutra*), a species of European Community interest listed in Annex II of the Habitats Directive, declined over much of its European range in the latter half of the twentieth century, particularly in the industrialised west (Mitchell-Jones *et al.*, 1999). Improved water quality in the formerly industrialised rivers of Scotland has allowed it to re-occupy much of its former range in the Central Belt (Green and Green, 1980, 1987, 1997). Nevertheless, by 2000, some 50 per cent of native freshwater fish species were thought to have declined throughout Scotland, while non-native species had generally expanded. The status of the Atlantic salmon (*Salmo salar*) is a matter of current conservation concern (Baxter and Hutchinson, Chapter 15). Pollution of the only two lochs in which it was found led to the extinction of the vendace (*Coregonus albula*) in Scotland, prior to its re-introduction into two other lochs. By 1996, the number of sites where great crested newts (*Triturus cristatus*) had been recorded since 1876 had declined by 55 per cent. About half of the world's functional populations of freshwater pearl mussel (*Margaritifera margaritifera*) are found in Scotland, but by the late 1990s 65 per cent had no juveniles and only 7 per cent were classified as near-natural. Nine breeding bird species dependant on fresh waters expanded in range between 1970 and 1990, while five species contracted (Mackey *et al.*, 2001).

The quality of Scotland's fresh waters is generally good by European standards but major investment continues to be required in waste water and sewage treatment for the protection of coastal waters, the restoration of polluted or degraded rivers and lochs, and the improvement of drinking water quality. The Water Framework Directive provides a common basis for integrated action throughout the European Union.

1.3.5 The sea

At the interface between land and sea, and between fresh and salt water, a considerable amount of European activity is concentrated around the coastal zone. In 1995, the pressures on the coast included urbanisation and transport, agriculture, tourism and recreation, fisheries and aquaculture, industry and energy production (Stanners and Bourdeau, 1995). A range of associated problems included local alterations to the natural balance of erosion and sedimentation, habitat loss and degradation, pollution from land-based sources and shipping, and environmental and amenity degradation through littering. By 1998 the North Sea was considered to be threatened by over-fishing (Saunders *et al.*, Chapter 12), high nutrient concentrations and pollution (EEA, 1998).

Much of the population and infrastructure of Scotland is located on or close to the coast, predominantly within the eastern Lowlands and the Firth of Clyde. By the late 1990s it was estimated that around 10 per cent of Scotland's coastline had been affected by intensive urban or industrial use (Ritchie, 1999). Land-claim has historically resulted in losses of intertidal mudflats, for example 50 per cent of the intertidal area within the inner Forth Estuary has been reclaimed over the past two centuries. High nitrate levels can impact on marine and coastal waters, such as in the River Ythan's estuary in the north-east of Scotland where algal mats have caused changes to invertebrate communities (SEPA, 1999b). In 2000 the Ythan catchment was designated a Nitrate Vulnerable Zone, requiring reductions in water pollution from agricultural sources. Bathing water quality achieved only 85 per cent compliance among Scottish identified bathing waters in 2000 (SEPA, 2000).

Land-based pollution from waste water and sewage is being brought under stricter control, and the input of nutrients and contaminants to the North Sea has been reduced since the dumping of sewage sludge stopped in 1998. Some of the most polluted parts of the Forth and Clyde Estuaries have improved, resulting in recolonisation by invertebrates and fish (Saunders *et al.*, Chapter 12).

Reliant upon clean, sheltered waters, Scottish mariculture has expanded from the late 1970s onwards. By 1999, some 351 salmon farm sites and 237 shellfish sites had been established around western and northern coasts. By 2001, most commercially exploited wild fish species in the seas around Scotland, including some deep-water species, were in decline and outside of safe biological limits (Saunders *et al.*, Chapter 12).

Whilst marine survey coverage has increased greatly in recent decades, the extent, abundance, status and ecology of most marine habitats and species remain poorly known. The distribution, nature and sensitivity of Scotland's marine habitats and species are still not fully documented but the importance of the marine natural heritage is now reflected in 34 proposed or candidate marine Special Areas of Conservation (SAC) covering around 3,600 km² of coast and sea.

The seas to the west and north of Scotland are among the most pristine in Europe. Land-based pollution into the North Sea is being brought under stricter control. However, the ecological status of commercially exploited wild fish stocks in the seas around Scotland is a matter of current conservation concern.

1.4 Discussion

Situated on an island at a northern latitude within Europe, Scotland is distinctive in many ways. The European importance of notable aspects of Scotland's natural heritage is expressed by the Natura network (Box 1.1). Environmental pressures and their consequences vary from country to country within Europe, but common elements are evident within Scotland. A more systematic documentation of pan-European trends, air pollution being a well developed example, would be of benefit to analysing and reporting on the state of Europe's environment.

As part of the UK, Scotland has much to contribute towards European environmental assessments. It should be involved in the development of European indicators, such as those for biodiversity. These could draw more fully on Scottish trend data and illustrative case studies, as in the recent study of biodiversity in the Nordic nations (Hallanaro and Söderman, Chapter 3; Hallanaro and Pylvänäinen, 2002). In turn, Scotland would benefit from being able to see more clearly how the state of its environment and natural heritage compare in a European context.

Acknowledgements

The views expressed here are personal, and do not necessarily reflect those of Scottish Natural Heritage. Nevertheless, the author would like to thank colleagues in the Environmental Audit Unit of Scottish Natural Heritage for the use of background material in the preparation of this chapter: Phil Shaw, Julian Holbrook, Mike Shewry, Jeanette Hall and Graham Saunders.

References

Ash Consulting Group (1998). A96 Aberdeen–Inverness tranquil areas study. Unpublished report.

Baldock, D., Beaufoy, G., Brouwer, F. and Godeschalk, F. (1996). *Farming at the Margins: Abandonment or Redeployment of Agricultural Land in Europe.* Institute for European and Environmental Policy and Agricultural Economics Research Institute, London.

Beaufoy, G., Baldock, D. and Clark, J. (1994). *The Nature of Farming: Low Intensity Farming Systems in Nine European Countries.* Institute for European Environmental Policy, London.

Bosch, P. and Stanners, D. (2001). The European Environment Agency focusing on EU policy in its approach to sustainable development indicators. Paper presented at the Conference of European Environmental Advisory Councils, Ghent.

Burnhill, P.M., Chalmers, A.G., Owen, L. and Corbett, A. (1999). *The British Survey of Fertiliser Practice: Fertiliser Use on Farm Crops for Crop Year 1998.* The BSFP Authority, Peterborough.

Delbaere, B.C.W. (ed.) (1998). *Facts and Figures on Europe's Biodiversity: State and Trends 1998-1999.* European Centre for Nature Conservation, Tilburg.

European Environment Agency (1998). *Europe's Assessment: the Second Assessment.* Elsevier Science, Oxford.

European Environment Agency (1999). *Environment in the European Union at the Turn of the Century: Environmental Assessment Report No 2.* European Environment Agency, Copenhagen.

European Environment Agency (2001). *Environmental Signals 2001. Environmental Assessment Report No. 8.* Office for Official Publications of the European Communities, Luxembourg.

FPD Savilles (2001). Trends in agricultural land use. Unpublished report.

Green, J. and Green, R. (1980). *Otter Survey of Scotland 1977-79.* The Vincent Wildlife Trust, London.

Green, J. and Green, R. (1987). *Otter Survey of Scotland 1984-85.* The Vincent Wildlife Trust, London.

Green, R. and Green, J. (1997). *Otter Survey of Scotland 1991-94.* The Vincent Wildlife Trust, London.

Green, R. and Riley, H. (1999). *Corncrakes.* Scottish Natural Heritage, Perth.

Haines-Young, R.H., Barr, C.J., Black, H.I.J., Briggs, D.J., Bunce, R.G.H., Clarke, R.T., Cooper, A., Dawson, F.H., Firbank, L.G., Fuller, R.M., Furse, M.T., Gillespie, M.K., Hill, R., Hornung, M., Howard, D.C., McCann, T., Morecroft, M.D., Petit, S., Sier, A.R.J., Smart, S.M., Smith, G.M., Stott, A.P., Stuart, R.C. and Watkins, J.W. (2000). *Accounting for Nature: Assessing Habitats in the UK Countryside.* Department of the Environment, Transport and the Regions, London.

Hallanaro, E.-L. and Pylvänäinen, M. (eds) (2002). *Nature in Northern Europe: Biodiversity in a Changing Environment.* Nordic Council, Copenhagen.

Landrock, J., Hawkins, J., Simcox, H., Smolka, Z. and Kelly, F. (eds.) (2001). *Key Scottish Environment Statistics.* Scottish Executive, Edinburgh.

Loch Leven Catchment Management Project (1999). *The Loch Leven Catchment Management Plan.* Perth and Kinross Council, Perth.

Mackey, E.C., Shewry, M.C. and Tudor, G.J. (1998). *Land Cover Change: Scotland from the 1940s to the 1980s.* The Stationery Office, Edinburgh.

Mackey, E.C., Shaw, P., Holbrook, J., Shewry, M.C., Saunders, G., Hall, J. and Ellis, N.E. (2001). *Natural Heritage Trends: Scotland 2001.* Scottish Natural Heritage, Perth.

McGowan, G.M., Palmer, S.C.F., French, D.D., Barr, C.J., Howard, D.C. and Smart, S.M. (2001). Trends in broad habitats: Scotland 1990-1998. Unpublished report.

Mitchell-Jones, A.J., Amori, G., Bogdanowicz, W., Krystufek, B., Reijnders, P.J.H., Spitzenberger, F., Stubbe, M., Thisses, J.B.M., Vohralik, V. and Zima, J. (1999). *The Atlas of European Mammals.* Poyser, London.

Ratcliffe, D.A. (1977). *A Nature Conservation Review.* Cambridge University Press, Cambridge.

Ratcliffe, D.A. and Thompson, D.B.A. (1988). The British uplands: their ecological character and international significance. In *Ecological Change in the Uplands*, ed. by M.B. Usher and D.B.A. Thompson. Blackwell Scientific Publications, Edinburgh. pp. 9-36.

Rich, T.C.G. and Woodruff, E.R. (1996). Changes in the vascular plant floras of England and Scotland between 1930-1960 and 1987-1988: the BSBI monitoring scheme. *Biological Conservation*, **75**, 217-229.

Ritchie, W. (1999). The environmental impact of changing uses on the North Sea littoral of Scotland. In *Denmark and Scotland: the Cultural and Environmental Resources of Small Nations*, ed. by G. Fellows-Jensen. The Royal Danish Academy of Sciences and Letters, Copenhagen. pp. 103-122.

Royal Society for the Protection of Birds and Scottish Crofters Union (1992). *Crofting and the Environment: a New Approach.* Royal Society for the Protection of Birds, Edinburgh.

Scottish Environment Protection Agency (1999a). *State of the Environment: Air Quality Report.* SEPA, Stirling.

Scottish Environment Protection Agency (1999b). *Improving Scotland's Water Environment: SEPA State of the Environment Report.* SEPA, Stirling.

Scottish Environment Protection Agency (2000). *Scottish Bathing Waters 2000.* SEPA, Stirling.

Scottish Executive (2000). *The Rural Stewardship Scheme.* The Stationery Office, Edinburgh.

Scottish Executive Environment and Rural Affairs Department (2001). *Economic Report on Scottish Agriculture: 2001 Edition.* Scottish Executive, Edinburgh.

Scottish Executive Rural Affairs Department (1998). *Agriculture in Scotland.* SERAD, Edinburgh.

Scottish Natural Heritage (2001a). Natural heritage trends: species diversity. Introduction. Information & Advisory Note No. 129.

Scottish Natural Heritage (2001b). *Annual Report 2000 - 2001: Facts and Figures.* Scottish Natural Heritage, Perth.

Scottish Natural Heritage (2001c). Natural heritage trends: land cover 1947-1988. Semi-natural habitats. Information & Advisory Note No. 124.

Scottish Natural Heritage (2001d). Natural heritage trends: species diversity. Breeding bird species. Information & Advisory Note No. 133.

Scottish Natural Heritage (2001e). Natural heritage trends: species diversity. Wintering bird species. Information & Advisory Note No. 134.

Scottish Natural Heritage (2001f). Natural heritage trends: forest and woodland. Native woodland. Information & Advisory Note No. 139.

Scottish Natural Heritage (2002a). *Goose Management Schemes: Natural Care.* Scottish Natural Heritage, Perth.

Scottish Natural Heritage (2002b). *Natural Heritage Futures: An Overview.* Scottish Natural Heritage, Perth.

Snowden, J.P. and Thomas, L.A. (1999). *Pesticide Usage in Scotland, Arable Crops 1998.* SERAD, Edinburgh.

Stanners, D. and Bourdeau, P. (eds.) (1995). *Europe's Environment: The Dobris Assessment.* European Environment Agency, Copenhagen.

Thompson, D.B.A., MacDonald, A.J., Marsden, J.H. and Galbraith, C.A. (1995). Upland heather moorland in Great Britain: a review of international importance, vegetation change and some issues for natural conservation. *Biological Conservation*, **71**, 163-178.

United Nations Environment Programme World Conservation Monitoring Centre (2002). The natural heritage of Scotland: International comparison of trends. Unpublished report.

Usher, M.B. (1997). Scotland's biodiversity: an overview. In *Biodiversity in Scotland: Status, Trends and Initiatives*, ed. by. L.V. Fleming, A.C. Newton, J.A. Vickery and M.B. Usher. The Stationery Office, Edinburgh. pp. 5–20.

2 Scotland's Environment: A European Opportunity

Jim Currie

Summary

1. It is estimated that over 80 per cent of environmental regulation which affects Scotland is legislated through the European Union.

2. There are major policy changes ahead as the European Union expands from its current 15 Member States. Scotland has an important role in developing these new policies.

3. It is essential that Scotland's influence comes early in the development of draft policy by the European Commission. For this to happen, contacts at all levels by both institutions and individuals need to be developed and fostered.

4. The relationship between Scotland and Brussels must be two-way. There is now a need for this relationship to be moved 'up a gear'.

2.1 Introduction

The environment and natural heritage of Scotland must be considered within a European context (Mackey, Chapter 1). Many of the problems are associated with global issues of atmospheric emissions, international trading of raw materials, and both agricultural competition and subsidy. Neither pollution nor market forces respect national boundaries. As a reflection of this, it is now estimated that over 80 per cent of environmental regulation which affects Scotland is legislated through the European Union. Amongst the questions currently on the agenda in Brussels are

- water quality standards,
- controls on air pollution,
- soil quality,
- genetically modified organisms,
- measures to tackle climate change, and
- the conservation of biodiversity.

To this list needs to be added the review of the Common Agricultural Policy and the negotiations surrounding the Common Fisheries Policy. It is obvious that policy making at the European Union level has a considerable impact on Scotland's land, air, freshwater and marine environments.

2.2 Europe and its environment

European Union leadership helped to deliver, in July 2001, a major agreement on the so-called Kyoto Protocol to mitigate global climate change, despite opposition from President

George W. Bush of the United States of America. Every country except the US has signed up to this agreement. However, in order to deliver on the European Union's commitments, it is important to review a number of policies, especially energy policy and transport policy. There has to be a substantial cut across the European Union in emissions of the so-called 'greenhouse gases'. Scotland must contribute to the European Union's target.

A review of the Common Fisheries Policy has already been launched by the European Commission. It is predicted that in early 2003 the Common Agricultural Policy will also be re-examined. Much of the change in these two major policies of the European Union will be driven by environmental considerations. Fish stocks are dwindling and their conservation, to support a sustainable fishing industry, is important. In the aftermath of the two major disease outbreaks of livestock – bovine spongiform encephalopathy (BSE) and foot and mouth disease (FMD) – agricultural systems need to be reconsidered. It is increasingly evident that "environment is not the problem, but a big part of the solution".

Scotland must have a role in the development of the European Union's environment policy. The European Commission is currently developing a ten year strategy for environmental policy. This is, and will be, discussed in the European Parliament and among Member States in the Council of Ministers. The developing strategy will deal with a very broad range of issues, from safer chemicals (Pugh, Chapter 19) and clean air (Fowler *et al.*, Chapter 7) to protecting biodiversity (Usher, Chapter 18) and environmental health. These are issues of major concern to the people of Scotland and to the Scottish economy. For example, the quality of Scotland's biodiversity is critically linked to promoting the service industries, on which Scotland increasingly depends.

2.3 Europe and sustainable development

The European Commission is also considering its sustainable development strategy in an attempt to bring the debate to the highest political level. The elements of sustainable development, for example the link between environment and human health, are more meaningful to the citizens of Europe than most politicians realise (O'Riordan, Chapter 21). It is apparent that the drive for progress is coming largely from northern European countries, with the south being much less engaged, but it is still true that there is evident failure to translate the concept and principles of sustainability into practical and demonstrable actions for government and business.

The proposed 6th Environment Action Programme 2001-2010 (CEC, 2001a) and the Sustainable Development Strategy (CEC, 2001b) are founded upon a systematic analysis of trends and prospects. Four topics have been identified where new effort and impetus are needed to secure the long-term welfare of people in Europe and around the world (Table 2.1).

2.4 Europe's links with Scotland

It is unlikely that the current administrative structures in Europe will change, whereby negotiation is conducted through the United Kingdom's representative (UK REP), with Scotland represented as part of the UK.

However, the negotiation processes happen 'downstream', after the long process of preparing and publishing the draft proposals has been completed by the European Commission. The critical question is how to influence the thinking that goes into

Table 2.1. Four topics that have been identified for new effort for the European Union's 6th Environment Action Programme (2001-2010) and for the Sustainable Development Strategy.

Topic	Commentary
Tackling climate change	With 5 per cent of the world's population, the European Union generates 15 per cent of global greenhouse gases. The objective is to stabilise concentrations of greenhouse gases at a level that will not cause unnatural variations in the Earth's climate. Compared with the 1990 baseline, it will be necessary to reduce greenhouse gas emissions by 8 per cent agreed at Kyoto by 2008-12, to reduce emissions by 20 to 40 per cent by 2020, and to achieve a long-term reduction of 70 per cent.
Protecting nature and wildlife	In the European Union, 38 per cent of bird species and 45 per cent of butterflies are threatened. In north and western Europe, 60 per cent of wetlands have been lost. Two-thirds of trees are suffering from pollution. Soil erosion is a major problem in the south. Care of the seas is required to tackle over-fishing, damage to the seabed and pollution. Objectives are to protect or restore the structure and functioning of natural systems, to halt the loss of biodiversity, and to protect soils against erosion and pollution.
Action for the environment and health	Continued improvements to air and water quality (surface, ground and coastal) will be required to achieve an environment where contaminants do not pose risks to human health. This will include reducing risks from pesticide and chemical use, and taking account of noise pollution in planning decisions.
Natural resources and waste	For the conservation of natural resources, targets include a need to reduce the quantity of waste going to land fill by 20 per cent on 2000 levels by 2010 and 50 per cent by 2050.

preparing these draft proposals. To do this requires taking initiatives 'upstream'; this can be done directly by Scotland without offending against the agreed and established UK co-ordination arrangements.

Take as an example the current thinking on agricultural reform. Scottish Ministers are now completing their own assessment of the future of agriculture. This has, to some extent at least, been made a greater priority due to BSE and then FMD. Concurrently, the European Commission is undertaking preparatory work on the future of Europe's agriculture. This is the long spoken-of 'reform of the Common Agricultural Policy'. It does not relate to a European Union of 15 Member States but to an enlarged EU of 25 or more countries. This work in Brussels is likely to generate radical new proposals by 2003. Now is the ideal time for Scotland's views to be known in Brussels. It may be too late after the preparatory work has been completed in the European Commission.

It is easy to be sceptical and ask if Brussels will listen. Experience indicates that the European Commission will listen. The European Commission is an exceptionally open and accessible bureaucracy, in a way that national Government Ministries are not, in order that account can be taken of the cultural and political diversity of the different countries in the European Union. Similarly, both the European Parliament and the Scottish Parliament are places where the parliamentarians and the public can meet and exchange ideas, so that the

Scottish experience should provide instructive mechanisms and processes to take advantage of opportunities to exert influence and direction.

Moreover, practices in Brussels have changed with more emphasis being put on discussing options before proposals are firmed up. The European Commission has borrowed from the UK the concepts of Green Papers and White Papers. Many of the preliminary ideas for new European Union policy for the environment and related areas are being published in these formats. Among the most salient examples are the current Green and White Papers on transport, energy, chemicals and the reform of the initial Common Fisheries Policy. These papers are, by definition, designed for consultation. Scotland must use this opportunity to the maximum. Scotland has an excellent representational office in Brussels – Scotland House – which can provide the entrée for Scotland's thinking on these issues. The key, though, is to input this thinking early in the process of policy development so as to maximise Scotland's influence at the preparatory stages.

2.5 Scotland and Europe: a mutualistic relationship

Most critically, Brussels also needs Scotland. In the majority of cases, successful environmental policies depend on local and regional delivery. For example, in order to tackle global warming (Kerr and Ellis, Chapter 16), it becomes crucially important to develop local traffic and transport initiatives, regional policies on reduction in energy use, and local industrial companies acting to cut CO_2 emissions. The Brussels-Scotland relationship has to be a two-way relationship.

This relationship needs to be strengthened and developed. This can be achieved at many levels, both institutionally and personally. I have, for example, given evidence to the Scottish Parliament. The European Union's Commissioner has visited Scotland, and heard about Scotland's plans to promote its environment and natural heritage. But Scotland also needs to be outward looking. Its Ministers, Parliament, local authorities and government agencies, businessmen, academics and voluntary bodies must move Scotland's relationships with Europe to a new level of engagement. I believe that this kind of proactive approach will meet with a positive response in Brussels and will better serve Scotland's environmental interests.

References

Commission of the European Communities (2001a). *Environment 2010: Our Future, Our Choice. The Sixth European Union Environmental Action Programme 2001-10.* Office for the Official Publications of the European Communities, Luxembourg.

Commission of the European Communities (2001b). *A Sustainable Europe for a Better World: a European Union Strategy for Sustainable Development.* CEC, Brussels.

3 NATURE IN SCOTLAND AND THE NORDIC COUNTRIES: SIMILARITIES AND DIFFERENCES

Eeva-Liisa Hallanaro and Guy Söderman

Summary

1.   Scotland shares many habitat types with the Nordic Countries (Iceland, Norway, Sweden, Finland and Denmark), including marine environments, sea cliffs and other coastal habitats, heaths and moors, mires, alpine terrain, and coniferous forests.

2.   The long-term exploitation of the land has deprived Scotland of some of its original habitats, particularly native coniferous forests, but has also created large areas of semi-natural habitats, such as moors. In Fennoscandia native woodland still prevails, but few heathlands are left.

3.   The flora and fauna of Scotland and the Nordic Countries have many common elements, although the insularity of Britain has hampered the spread of some terrestrial species to Scotland, and contributed to the disappearance of isolated populations of other species during the post-glacial period.

4.   Some typical boreal mammals like the elk and the beaver are absent from Scotland, as are all of the large predators. The numbers of red deer in Scotland are unrivalled in the Nordic Countries, but the related overgrazing problems are not unlike those involving reindeer.

5.   Scotland shares many environmental problems and conservation concerns with the Nordic Countries. Many threatened species are red-listed in both regions.

6.   The frameworks for nature conservation and the designation of nature reserves differ somewhat between Scotland and the Nordic Countries. The proportion of the land under protection varies between the countries.

3.1 Similar settings

During the most recent glaciation, the continental ice sheet completely covered both Scotland and the Nordic Countries, with the exception of the west coast of Jutland. The erosive effects of the ice are still clearly visible in Scotland today, in the mountains and along the intricate coastline, where landscapes bear a striking resemblance to those of the Norwegian coast.   Scotland's soils are mostly nutrient-poor and acidic, and as in Fennoscandia there are numerous peat deposits. Calcareous rocks are rare, so the buffering capacity of the soil is not high enough to prevent acidification in both soil and lakes. Soils and vegetation are fairly sensitive to erosion both in Scotland and in the more northerly or alpine regions of the Nordic Countries. Scotland lies north of latitude 55°N, as does the overwhelming majority of the Nordic region. The climate is cool and maritime, as it is in most parts of the Nordic Countries, but the growing season is longer in Scotland than in any of the Nordic Countries.

Since the ice receded only quite recently in geological terms, all of the plant and animal species found today in Scotland and the Nordic Countries are relative newcomers, having arrived during the short post-glacial period. Post-glacial land uplift and sea-level rise have alternately opened up and then closed off migration routes into Britain or the Scandinavian Peninsula for terrestrial species.

With similar soils, climatic conditions and plant communities, Scotland and the Nordic Countries have many habitats in common, including coniferous forests, coastal heaths and grasslands, and a wide variety of bogs and fens. Mire habitats of various kinds cover 23 per cent of Scotland (Mackey *et al.*, 1998), giving much of the landscape a Fennoscandian appearance. Most of Scotland can be classified as belonging to the boreo-nemoral transitional vegetation zone, although parts of the northern half of the country clearly have boreal features, and the highest mountains belong to the oro-hemiarctic or alpine realm (Ahti *et al.*, 1968).

Scotland's species diversity is similar to that of the Nordic Countries, and many of the same species are found in both Scotland and Scandinavia. The moist climate of both of these regions results in particularly diverse bryophyte communities. While more northerly habitats usually sustain a smaller number of species than those habitats in milder climates, where mosses are concerned, diversity may be greater further north. A total of 1,064 species of mosses and liverworts are found in Norway and 928 species in Scotland, compared to 584 species in Denmark (Hallanaro and Pylvänäinen, 2002). There are even more lichen species than bryophytes.

The coasts of Scotland, Iceland, the Faroe Islands and Norway are very important breeding areas for many seabirds. In recent decades, however, seabird numbers have fallen in Scotland, Norway and Svalbard, although there is no evidence of such a decline in Iceland (Hallanaro and Pylvänäinen, 2002). In winter, the Scottish coast plays host to tens of thousands of birds, including internationally significant numbers of more than 30 species of waders, waterfowl, grebes and divers. Two species of goose link the ecology and cultures of Greenland, Iceland and the west coast of Scotland. A distinct subspecies of the white-fronted goose (*Anser albifrons flavirostris*) and a geographically distinct population of the barnacle goose (*Branta leucopsis*) breed in Greenland and winter in north-western parts of Britain and Ireland. During both spring and autumn migrations these birds stop over in Iceland. The island of Islay in south-western Scotland plays host to 60 to 70 per cent of the total Greenland population of barnacle goose and 30 per cent of the total population of Greenland white-fronted goose (Hallanaro and Pylvänäinen, 2002).

Due to the prevalence of moorland habitats, a large proportion of the world's twite (*Carduelis flavirostris*) population breeds in Norway and Scotland. The willow grouse (*Lagopus lagopus lagopus*), a common species in western and northern parts of Fennoscandia, is paralleled in Scottish moorland habitats by the closely related red grouse (*Lagopus lagopus scoticus*), whose total population is estimated at 200,000 birds, with very high densities locally (Hagemeijer and Blair, 1997).

The levels of human habitation are also similar. Some 5.1 million people live in Scotland today, and the country's average population density (66 inhabitants per km^2) is lower than Denmark's (123 inhabitants per km^2), but higher than those of the other Nordic Countries (e.g. Sweden 22 inhabitants per km^2 and Finland 17 inhabitants per km^2).

3.2 Becoming more different

3.2.1 Diverging flora and fauna

Scotland, like the Nordic Countries, lies on Europe's northern periphery. As well as meaning that human population densities are relatively low, this leaves extensive areas for natural and semi-natural habitats, and their associated fauna and flora. The Nordic Countries and Scotland have indeed become a last resort for many 'wilderness' species. Wolves (*Canis lupus*), for instance, survived in Scotland into the eighteenth century, whereas in England the last wolf was seen as long ago as 1486. Similarly, Britain's last native white-tailed eagles (*Haliaeetus albicilla*) lived in Scotland until the beginning of the twentieth century, when an aged albino female was shot in 1916 in Shetland.

The red squirrel (*Sciurus vulgaris*) is still present in much of Scotland, as well as in the Nordic Countries, but its days may be numbered. In Scotland the presence of the non-native grey squirrel (*Sciurus carolinensis*), a North American species introduced into Britain at the end of the nineteenth century, casts a shadow over the future of the red squirrel. Grey squirrels compete closely with red squirrels, especially in deciduous and mixed woodlands which today make up the overwhelming majority of Britain's forests. Three-quarters of Britain's remaining red squirrels live in Scotland, mainly in pine forests (Mackey, 1995), but even in Scotland the grey squirrels outnumber the reds, and the future for the native species is literally looking 'grey'.

Some wilderness species or game species that still survive in Fennoscandia have become extinct in Scotland during recent millennia: reindeer (*Rangifer tarandus*) disappeared soon after the ice retreated; the elk (*Alces alces*) disappeared some 3,900 years ago; the European beaver (*Castor fiber*) disappeared in the sixteenth century; and the loss of the wolf and white-tailed eagle was mentioned above.

Giving these examples of the loss of notable animals in Scotland does not mean to say that the Nordic Countries have not experienced similar losses, or that many important species have not been on the verge of extinction there, too. The insularity of the British Isles has, however, prevented the return of former native species, while countries in Fennoscandia are not similarly isolated. In Sweden, for example, the once extinct European beaver was able to return, thanks to the survival of a small population in Norway. Likewise, the forest reindeer (*Rangifer tarandus fennicus*), having become extinct in Finland in the late 1800s, has been able to spread back from Russia. Many other small populations have been able to survive in the Nordic Countries because they have received constant reinforcements from neighbouring areas on the other side of national borders.

In addition to preventing the return of lost species to the British Isles, this isolation is also a contributory factor in the relatively high level of endemism in Scotland, where there are more endemic species than in any of the Fennoscandian countries. Because of its special habitats and relative isolation, Scotland has a total of nine endemic, sexually-reproducing vascular plant species, including the Scottish primrose (*Primula scotica*) (Sydes, 1997). Fennoscandia has one endemic vertebrate, the Norwegian lemming (*Lemmus lemmus*). While this species is absent in Scotland, another vertebrate may be classifiable as endemic to Scotland, the Scottish crossbill (*Loxia scotica*). However, the taxonomy of crossbills is still unclear, and recent work undertaken in the United Kingdom suggests that while no genetic distinctions have been isolated between common crossbills (*Loxia curvirostra*), parrot crossbills (*L. pytyopsittacus*) and Scottish crossbills, consistent differences between these three putative species in bill size and call have been observed (Piertney *et al.*, 2000; Summers *et al.*, in press). It is still not clear whether this justifies making them species in their own right, rather than merely subspecies, in which case the Scottish crossbill would join the much longer list of endemic subspecies and endemic forms exclusively found in either Scotland or Fennoscandia. This list includes vertebrates like the ringed seals of Finland's Lake Saimaa (*Phoca hispida saimensis*), and the numerous distinctive fish populations found in various unconnected lakes, as well as red grouse and the various subspecies of reindeer.

3.2.2 Habitat loss and change

The forested areas of both Scotland and the Nordic Countries increased throughout the twentieth century, whereas they had been shrinking over previous centuries, when forests were widely cleared to create pastures and arable land. Deforestation was most extensive in densely populated Denmark, where the climatic and soil conditions were favourable for agriculture, and in Iceland and Scotland, where extensive areas of grazing land replaced the lost woodland. The native forests in these countries have almost all gone. In Iceland about 5 per cent remain, whereas in Denmark and Scotland just 2 and 3 per cent respectively of the former total area of native forest cover is left (Hallanaro and Pylvänäinen, 2002). Native Caledonian pine forests nowadays only cover 1 per cent of their former extent across the Scottish Highlands.

Norway, Sweden and Finland provide a stark contrast in this respect. In all of these countries, native forests still cover most of their original area, and in Finland over two-thirds of the total land area is forested (see Plate 2).

In both Scotland and Denmark, new forests were planted during the twentieth century, and it is intended that the forested area should be further increased in the future. Much of the planting, however, particularly in the earlier days, involved non-native tree species, mainly Continental European and North American conifers, so they cannot be considered as replacing the lost natural ecosystems, even if some new kinds of ecosystems may form. But today, the trend has been reversed, and increasing amounts of deciduous trees of native origin are being planted both in Scotland and Denmark.

In both of these countries non-native trees still outnumber the natives. Scotland's commonest tree today is the Sitka spruce (*Picea sitchensis*), a native of the west coast of North America. Another North American tree, the shore or lodgepole pine (*Pinus contorta*), has also been widely grown in Scotland. The Sitka spruce is also the most common non-European tree species in Denmark. The most widespread non-native tree species in Denmark is, however, the Norway spruce (*Picea abies*), which now makes up nearly a third of the country's forests. Although the Norway spruce is native to Fennoscandia, it never spread naturally to either Denmark or the British Isles (Moen, 1999) after the last glaciation.

Silvicultural practices differ greatly between countries and result in quite different forest landscapes, even where the same tree species are grown. Most of the forest area of Norway, Sweden and Finland could be described as semi-natural woodland, rich in variety and subtlety of detail, while Scotland and Denmark have more monotonous plantations, with trees of the same age and height uniformly spaced across the landscape.

Whereas forests cover only about 15 per cent of the Scottish landscape today, there are more grasslands and heaths or moors than in any of the Nordic Countries. Heather moors in particular are characteristic of the Scottish landscape. The maritime climate of Scotland suits the key species, heather (*Calluna vulgaris*), which requires stable humidity, and is susceptible to heavy frosts. The local soils, being mainly acidic, with podsols in many areas, are also ideal for heather. Where trees are removed from such soils, and the land is not too intensively grazed, heather and other moorland plants can easily become predominant.

In many parts of Denmark, and southern parts of Norway and Sweden, conditions are similarly favourable for heathland to develop, but Scandinavia's remaining heathlands are few and far between. When agriculture became increasingly intensified and mechanised during the twentieth century, heathlands almost completely vanished from the region, as in commercial farming terms they became too outdated and unproductive to justify being grazed any longer. In 1800, when the total area of heathland in Denmark was at its maximum, some 40 to 50 per cent of Jutland was covered by heathlands (Hansen, 1980). By 1950 this figure had fallen to approximately 2 per cent. In the province of Halland in south-western Sweden, heathlands used to cover almost a third of the land a century ago, but nowadays they account for just about 1 per cent of the area (Rosén and Borgegård, 1999).

Scotland's heather moors have been much more widely preserved, although their total area has decreased by over 20 per cent since the 1940s. Today they cover about 15 to 20 per cent of the country, depending on exactly where the dividing line is drawn between heather moor and blanket bog (Miles *et al.*, 1997; Mackey *et al.*, 1998). Heather moors are highly valued in Scotland for producing the abnormally high densities of red grouse annually exploited by hunters. They are also doubly valued in conservation terms, firstly because these ecosystems, with their distinctive flora and fauna, have largely disappeared from continental Europe, and secondly for their many historical and archaeological remains. For these reasons attempts are being made to preserve the Scottish moors through both continued light grazing and, most importantly, regular controlled burning. The seasonal burning conducted since the early 1840s results in a patchwork-like landscape with varying ages of vegetation cover.

The total area of grassland in Northern Europe was probably at its greatest at the end of the nineteenth century, when most of the region's growing population still made their living from farming, and mineral fertilisers and other external inputs were rare. Since those days, grasslands have shrunk drastically in most of the Nordic Countries. Nowadays, grasslands are mainly used by sheep, which are less demanding than cattle in nutritional terms. More grassland indeed remains in regions where sheep-rearing is more common today, such as Iceland, the Faroe Islands and the Norwegian mountains, and in Scotland, where grasslands today cover 28 per cent of the country. In Scotland, the total area of grassland only shrank by 10 per cent between the 1940s and the 1980s (Mackey *et al.*, 1998), while Sweden's grasslands, for example, declined by approximately 50 per cent during the same period (Bernes, 1994). But even in Scotland grassland habitats have changed, as the proportion of enclosed and regularly mown hay meadows has declined dramatically.

The preservation of meadows and other semi-natural habitats is important for many invertebrate species, including bees (Apidae) and other pollinating insects, as well as true bugs (Heteroptera), leafhoppers (Auchenorrhyncha) and other related species. The abandonment of semi-natural pastures and meadowland and the consequent overgrowing of these habitats is considered to be the major threat for 66 per cent of Finland's 241 threatened butterflies and moths (Lepidoptera) (Rassi *et al.*, 2001).

In Scotland most of the more widespread butterfly species seem to be holding their own, or even increasing in numbers (Mackey, 1995), in contrast to their fate in the Nordic Countries. The underlying reasons may be long-term stability in land use practices, and the preservation and maintenance of moorland habitats. It is very likely, however, that Scotland's Lepidoptera were greatly affected by earlier habitat changes, when native forests were cut down and replaced by grassland and moorland. There is recent evidence that some of the scarcer butterfly species, especially those that are associated with more restricted habitats, are declining (Mackey *et al.*, 2001).

3.3 Shared problems, parallels and attitudes

In spite of the various diverging trends and developments in Scotland and the Nordic Countries, the similarities in fauna, flora and habitats are still overwhelming. Since many of the direct pressures on the natural environment are also the same in both regions, it is not surprising that Scotland's list of threatened or declining species is very similar to that of the Nordic Countries in that it includes many birds of prey, the corncrake (*Crex crex*) and the otter (*Lutra lutra*), for example. Shared problems have also arisen from similar mistakes made in Scotland and the Nordic Countries, such as the decision in the 1920s and 1930s to farm American mink (*Mustela vison*), which soon enabled this non-native species to become established in the wild in both regions at about the same time.

The overexploitation of marine resources is a problem shared by most countries with fisheries in the North Atlantic, and particularly in the North Sea. Virtually all of the region's commercially significant fish stocks have been overexploited at some stage, especially during the last 50 years. Fish farming is thought to be compounding these problems in both Scotland and the Nordic Countries, since escaped fish may spread disease and weaken the genetic stock of wild populations. It is estimated that 40 per cent of the salmon (*Salmo salar*) caught around the Faroe Islands in 1990 were originally escapees from fish farms (Jacobsen and Hansen, 1998). Experiments involving tagging suggest that most of these fish were probably from Norwegian fish farms.

Other problems in Scotland have parallels in the Nordic Countries. Just as the Fennoscandian countries are struggling with the overgrazing of the lichen cover by reindeer, Scotland faces a similar overgrazing problem in some areas, with the culprits being red deer (*Cervus elaphus*). Almost a fifth of Europe's red deer live in Scotland (Gill, 1990), and their numbers have been on the increase since the 1950s (see Plate 3). The country's total red deer population amounts to nearly 350,000 animals, with an average density of 6.5 animals per km^2 over their range.

But common problems can also be solved together, as has been exemplified by the white-tailed eagle reintroduction programme, which started in Scotland in 1975 involving eagles brought in from northern Norway. Eighty-two eagles were subsequently released, and in 1985 the first Scottish-bred eaglet for almost a century was reared.

Concerted international action has also led to improvements in both Scotland and the Nordic Countries. The International Convention on Transboundary Air Pollution, for example, has induced better air pollution control throughout Europe, and resulted in diminishing acid precipitation and a change for the better in many Nordic and Scottish lakes, giving hope for the rehabilitation of the populations of some aquatic organisms.

The organisational frameworks for nature conservation in Scotland and the Nordic Countries differ considerably. In the Nordic Countries all major areas to be protected are, as a rule, first acquired by the state, but in Scotland the conservation areas often continue to belong to their original owners. Another obvious difference is that while in most of the Nordic Countries national parks have long played an important role in conservation, none has so far been designated in Scotland, although some 70 National Nature Reserves covering 1.4 per cent of Scotland's total area at least partly fulfil the same functions as national parks elsewhere. About 14 per cent of Scotland can in fact be considered as protected, in terms of the internationally recognised protection categories defined by the International Union for the Conservation of Nature. The figures for the Nordic Countries vary between 8.5 per cent (Sweden and Finland) and about 30 per cent (Denmark).

People's attitudes towards nature are in practice very similar in both regions, although the free right of access to natural areas has not yet been enshrined in Scottish legislation. Levels of environmental awareness and knowledge are also similarly high, although the emphasis may vary between the different countries.

Scotland and the Nordic Countries will share other concerns over the coming years, ranging from minor issues like drawing up the boundaries of Natura 2000 sites along the ever-changing coastlines, to as yet unanticipated wider issues stemming from the need to adapt to climate change. Considering all of the similarities between these two regions, there is plenty of scope for fruitful co-operation in the fields of environmental research, monitoring work, exchanging experiences, and carrying out conservation policies. This chapter itself is an example of this type of co-operation, as it is largely based on the results of a major project that has involved Scotland and the Nordic Countries whose full results have now been published in Hallanaro and Pylvänäinen (2002). All initiatives to facilitate further co-operation between Scotland and the Nordic Countries should be greatly encouraged in the future.

References

Ahti, T., Hämet-Ahti, L. and Jalas, J. (1968). Vegetation zones and their sections in northwestern Europe. *Annales Botanici Fennici*, **5**, 169-251.

Bernes, C. (1994). *Biologisk mångfald i Sverige – en landstudie*. Naturvårdsverket, Växjö.

Gill, R. (1990). *Monitoring the Status of European and North American Cervids*. Global Environment Monitoring System Information Series **8**. United Nations Environment Programme, Nairobi.

Hagemeijer, W.J.M. and Blair, M.J. (ed.) (1997). *The EBCC Atlas of European Breeding Birds: their Distribution and Abundance*. Poyser, London.

Hallanaro, E.-L. and Pylvänäinen, M. (2002). *Nature in Northern Europe – Biodiversity in a Changing Environment*. Nord 2001: 13. Nordic Council of Ministers, Helsinki.

Hansen, V. (1980). Hedens opståen og omfang. In *Danmarks natur 7. Hede, overdrev og eng*, ed. by A. Nørrevang and J. Lundø. Politikens Forlag, København. pp. 9–28.

Jacobsen, J.A. and Hansen, L.P. (1998). *Laksen i havet: Resultater fra et forskningsprosjekt ved Færøyene*. TemaNord 1998:520. Nordisk Ministerråd, Copenhagen.

Mackey, E.C. (ed.) (1995). *The Natural Heritage of Scotland: an Overview*. Scottish Natural Heritage, Perth.

Mackey, E.C., Shaw, P., Holbrook, J., Shewry, M.C., Saunders, G., Hall, J. and Ellis, N.E. (2001). *Natural Heritage Trends: Scotland 2001*. Scottish Natural Heritage, Perth.

Mackey, E.C., Shewry, M.C. and Tudor, G.J. (1998). *Land Cover Change: Scotland from the 1940s to the 1980s*. The Stationery Office, Edinburgh.

Miles, J., Tudor, G., Easton, C. and Mackey, E.C. (1997). Habitat diversity in Scotland. In *Biodiversity in Scotland: Status, Trends and Initiatives*, ed. by L.V. Fleming, A.C. Newton, J.A. Vickery and M.B. Usher. The Stationery Office, Edinburgh. pp. 43–56.

Moen, A. (1999). *National Atlas of Norway: Vegetation.* Norwegian Mapping Authority, Hønefoss.

Piertney, S.B., Summers, R.W. and Marquiss, M. (2000). Microsatellite and mitochondrial DNA homogeneity among phenotypically diverse crossbill taxa. *Proceedings of the Royal Society of London Series B*, **268**, 1511–1517.

Rassi, P., Alanen, J., Kanerva, T. and Mannerkoski, I. (ed.) (2001). *The 2000 Red List of Finnish Species.* Ministry of the Environment and Finnish Environment Institute, Helsinki.

Rosén, E. and Borgegård, S.-O. (1999). The open cultural landscape. In *Swedish Plant Geography*, ed. by H. Rydin, P. Snoeijs and M. Diekmann. Acta Phytogeographica Suecica 84, Uppsala. pp. 113–134.

Summers, R.W., Jardine, D.C., Marquiss, M. and Rae, R. (in press). The distribution and habitats of crossbills *Loxia* spp. in Britain, with special reference to the Scottish crossbill *Loxia scotica*. *Ibis.*

Sydes, C. (1997). Vascular plant biodiversity in Scotland. In *Biodiversity in Scotland: Status, Trends and Initiatives*, ed. by L.V. Fleming, A.C. Newton, J.A. Vickery and M.B. Usher. The Stationery Office, Edinburgh. pp. 89–103.

4 LAND COVER MAP 2000: A DATA RESOURCE FOR SCOTLAND

G.M. Smith and R.M. Fuller

Summary

1. The Land Cover Map 2000, a key part of the Countryside Survey 2000, records 26 classes of land cover, on a field-by-field scale, with a minimum mappable unit of 0.5 ha, throughout the United Kingdom.

2. Spatial segmentation of satellite images provided a structured picture of the landscape with 'vector' polygons delineating land parcels, treated as 'objects' in a geographical information system. The cover in each land parcel was distinguished using the spectral reflectance data, with additional knowledge-based corrections.

3. Each land parcel carries information about its size, shape, source data, spectral character, lineage, land cover in or around 1998 and a measure of heterogeneity.

4. The map shows Scotland's unique character in a UK context. The information can thus contribute to the sustainable management of the Scottish environment.

4.1 Introduction

The Land Cover Map of Great Britain (LCMGB), produced between 1990 and 1992, formed a land cover census at the national scale (Fuller *et al.,* 1994). It recorded 25 land cover types, on a 25 m grid. The LCMGB has had more than 400 users and was aggregated to a 1 km grid format for incorporation into the Countryside Information System (CIS). More recently, LCMGB was converted to the CORINE Land Cover format, contributing the British component to this European land cover map and database (Brown *et al.,* in press), which maps 44 land cover and land use types with a minimum mappable unit of 25 ha.

Pixel-based analyses, as used for LCMGB, impose an unrealistic structure on the landscape and can lead to a range of erroneous effects which reduce accuracy and utility. Pixels within areas assumed to be 'thematically homogeneous' do not necessarily give the same results due to data noise, atmospheric effects and natural variation of the surface. Pixels on boundaries or containing features smaller than the pixel size may give erroneous results as their spectral information is received from mixed surface types. The results of pixel-based methods therefore have a speckled appearance which can be misleading. Intensively used landscapes might more realistically be mapped as parcels: fields, woods, water bodies and urban areas. In semi-natural environments, the boundaries between land parcels may be less distinct and more difficult to map. In a similar way as cartographic representation generally delineates distinct areas within semi-natural environments of a supposedly uniform character, so areas with uniform spectral characteristics can be identified in remotely sensed images.

The Land Cover Map 2000 (LCM2000) was part of the Countryside Survey 2000 (CS2000), a major audit of the British countryside, which also involved detailed field survey observations within 569 1 km survey squares for Great Britain and Northern Ireland (Haines-Young *et al.,* 2000). The LCM2000 was designed to complement the sample based field survey of CS2000. The production of the LCM2000 was funded by a consortium of nine government bodies whose policy and/or operational remits required sound information on the status and trends in natural resources. The LCM2000 aimed both to update and to upgrade the LCMGB and therefore adopted a parcel-based approach (Plate 5) for the analysis of remotely sensed images and the storage of results (Smith *et al.,* 1998; Smith and Fuller, 2001). The LCM2000 provides up-to-date information to supersede (where details are adequate) the 1988 air-photo-based Land Cover of Scotland (Anon., 1993).

4.2 Land Cover Map 2000

The LCM2000 (Smith and Fuller, 2000; Fuller *et al.,* in press) was based on multi-temporal satellite images; summer images to separate crop types and winter images to identify permanently vegetated areas and their deciduous or evergreen character. The dates of image acquisition aimed to match the CS2000 field survey of summer 1998 (with winter data from 1997/98). Due to poor weather conditions over several years, images were acquired between 1996 and 2001.

Practical difficulties prevented the use, at the national scale, of existing Ordnance Survey land parcel vector data. Land parcels were instead generated by image segmentation which identified spectrally similar areas, which were amalgamated as polygons to produce vector land parcels. It was then necessary to 'train' the classification algorithm using data for areas of known cover; this was objectively based on individual land parcels. The operator then compared training areas, grouped them into spectral subclasses, rejected anomalous examples and selected training parcels and other examples for validation.

The parcel-based classification treated the land parcel as an entity in analyses of remotely-sensed data. To avoid mixed-edge pixels and to remove within-parcel variability, boundary pixels were excluded and core pixels were aggregated to give mean values per spectral band. The classification analysed the values in a conventional maximum likelihood algorithm, comparing these with training statistics and recording the probabilities for the five most likely subclasses.

Ancillary data, such as elevation and soil sensitivity, were attached to the land parcels from a range of raster, vector and point sources. Knowledge-based corrections, based on the ancillary data and internal context, were used to correct the initial classification results. All the ancillary data and results were held as attributes of the land parcels.

The LCM2000 data were compared with the CS2000 field survey data by calculating correspondence between the two data sets at the 569 field survey 1 km squares. Tables of agreement, or 'correspondence matrices', were constructed by direct overlay of datasets in the GIS (a separate matrix for each 1 km square). Matrices were then combined to give assessments for the UK. The accuracy, once legitimate differences of scale and timing are taken into account, was about 85 per cent. Problems, where present, concerned broad habitat definitions based on species contents and/or contexts which were nor discernible from spectral and available ancillary data. The most evident discrepancies were between semi-natural and improved grasslands and between bog and heathland or moor. It is envisaged that users with better ancillary data (e.g. on peatland maps) will refine the basic classifications with their own additional site-specific knowledge.

4.3 LCM2000 products

The LCM2000 (Plate 6) is a vector GIS database which provides comprehensive UK cover, structured into approximately 6.6 million land parcels. The LCM2000 classification scheme delivered 16 target land cover types which were subdivided into 26 subclasses and subdivided again into 72 variant classes. These classes were selectively aggregated to generate widespread examples of 'broad habitats' (Jackson, 2000), defined to help meet conservation objectives of the UK's Biodiversity Action Plan (UK Biodiversity Steering Group, 1995) and the UK's obligations under the European Union's Habitats Directive (Commission of the European Communities, 1997). The classification scheme also meets much wider user needs, for example by giving greater detail on farming practices (arable and horticulture is subdivided into three subclasses and then 22 variants) and urbanisation (built up areas and gardens is subdivided into two subclasses and then three variants). Each land parcel holds an extensive range of attributes (Plate 7) that can be interrogated and analysed.

From the LCM2000 database, standard products are derived with a subset of attributes appropriate to different applications. These products will be available for the whole country or user-defined areas. Additional outputs are available, such as 25 m raster products and summary datasets giving percentage cover and cover-dominance per 1 km square (including datasets suitable for the CIS (Howard *et al.*, 1994)).

4.4 Conclusions

The LCM2000 provides much more than just an update of the LCMGB. Parcel-based approaches have taken land cover mapping from the analysis of an arbitrary grid of pixels to the consideration of 'real world' objects and their place in a structured landscape. The LCM2000 products therefore address the needs of users more closely. Processing information, results and contextual data are attached to each land parcel, forming a much richer information source than conventional pixel-based classifications. The LCM2000 provides information for environmental analysis, and can form the framework for future data collection and integration.

The LCM2000 records Scotland's land cover and broad habitats in a UK context (Table 4.1). It shows that only about 30 per cent of Scotland is intensively used for building, farming or forestry, compared with a UK average of nearly 60 per cent. Mountain, moor and heath (which includes bogs on deep peat) occupy over half the landscape and contribute nearly 60 per cent of the UK total for this range of habitats.

In a landscape which is predominantly unenclosed semi-natural land, the construction of an objectively-based record of structure and pattern combined with attribute data on habitats is a particularly important contribution to policy, planning and sustainable management of landscape. In its own right and through integration with other data, LCM2000 will underpin many aspects of environmental research, policy and planning. It will serve the needs of non-governmental organisations, the utilities and commerce. Potential uses of the data include taking stock of habitats, understanding environmental processes, modelling and predicting change, planning environmental management and monitoring its success. The areas of application include air and water quality, climate change, hydrology, nature conservation, health and hazard assessment, agriculture, forestry, impact assessments, and local, regional and national planning.

Table 4.1. Scotland's broad habitats in a UK context as recorded by the Land Cover Map 2000. Note, for clarity the broad habitats have been aggregated as follows: semi-natural grass and bracken (neutral, calcareous and acid grass, bracken, fen and marsh swamp); mountain, heath and bog (dwarf shrub heath, bog, montane habitats and inland bare ground); coastal (supra-littoral rock, supra-littoral sediment, littoral rock and littoral sediment).

Aggregated classes	Area (km²)		Area (per cent)	
	Scotland	UK	Scotland	UK
Broadleaved/mixed woodland	2,687	15,600	3.4	6.3
Coniferous woodland	8,454	13,540	10.9	5.5
Arable and horticultural	7,342	57,630	9.4	23.4
Improved grassland	10,326	59,073	13.3	23.9
Semi-natural grass and bracken	15,110	41,600	19.4	16.9
Mountain, heath and bog	30,786	38,892	39.5	15.8
Water (inland)	1,420	2,771	1.8	1.1
Built-up and gardens	1,483	16,637	1.9	6.7
Coastal	290	945	0.4	0.4
Total	77,898	246,688	100.0	100.0

Aknowledgements

Land Cover Map 2000 was funded by a consortium of nine government departments and agencies. The production team also included Jane Sanderson, Ross Hill, Andy Thomson, Nigel Brown, France Gerard, Matthew Hall and Alastair Graham.

References

Anonymous (1993). *The Land Cover of Scotland 1988. Final Report.* Macaulay Land Use Research Institute, Aberdeen.

Brown, N.J., Gerard, F.G. and Fuller, R.M. (in press). Mapping land use classes within the CORINE Land Cover Map of Great Britain. *Cartographic Journal.*

Commission of the European Communities (1997). Council Directive 97/62/EC of October 1997 adapting to technical and scientific progress Directive 92/43/EEC on conservation of natural habitats and of wild fauna and flora. *Official Journal of the European Communities,* No. L305/42.

Fuller, R.M., Groom, G.B. and Jones, A.R. (1994). The Land Cover Map of Great Britain: an automated classification of Landsat Thematic Mapper data. *Photogrammetric Engineering and Remote Sensing,* **60**, 553-562.

Fuller, R.M., Smith, G.M., Sanderson, J.M., Hill, R.A. and Thomson, A.G. (in press). The UK Land Cover Map 2000: construction of a parcel-based vector map from satellite images. *Cartographic Journal.*

Haines-Young, R.H., Barr , C.J., Black, H.I.J., Briggs, D.J., Clarke, R.T., Cooper, A., Dawson, F.H., Firbank, L.G., Fuller, R.M., Furse, M.T., Gillespie, M.K., Hill, R., Hornung, M., Howard, D.C., McCann, T., Morecroft, M.D., Petit, S., Sier, A.R.J., Smart, S.M., Smith, G.M., Stott, A.P., Stuart, R.C. and Watkins, J.W. (2000). *Accounting for Nature: Assessing Habitats in the UK Countryside.* Department of the Environment, Transport and the Regions, London.

Howard, D.C., Bunce, R.G.H., Jones, M. and Haines-Young, R.H. (1994). *Development of the Countryside Information System. Countryside 1990 series, volume 4.* Department of the Environment, London.

Jackson, D.L. (2000). *Guidance on the interpretation of the Biodiversity Broad Habitat Classification (terrestrial and freshwater types): definitions and the relationships with other habitat classifications.* Joint Nature Conservation Committee Report No. 307.

Smith, G.M. and Fuller, R.M. (2000). Land Cover Map 2000: more than just an update. *The Society of Cartographers Bulletin*, **33**, 13-16.

Smith, G.M. and Fuller, R.M. (2001). An integrated approach to land cover classification: an example in the Island of Jersey. *International Journal of Remote Sensing*, **22**, 3123-3142.

Smith, G.M., Fuller, R.M., Amable, G., Costa, C., Devereux, B.J., Briggs, J., Murfitt, P., Cowan, L. and Hobman, E. (1998). CLEVER-Mapping: classification of environment with vector- and raster mapping. Unpublished report.

UK Biodiversity Steering Group (1995). *Biodiversity: the UK Steering Group Report. Volume 1: Meeting the Rio Challenge.* HMSO, London.

PART TWO

SCOTLAND'S LAND, AIR AND WATER

PART TWO

SCOTLAND'S LAND, AIR AND WATER

It is widely accepted that sustainable development must be underpinned by good quality data. A strong argument is made by Dunion *et al.* (Chapter 20) for high level integrative indicators of sustainability in Scotland. Their argument appears compelling when reviewing the abundance and diversity of environmental data which are presented in the eleven chapters of Part 2.

A repeated message, however, is that as we begin better to understand the complex interactions between people and their environment then gaps in essential data are exposed. There is an increasing need for trend analysis using longer time-series of data to determine whether our activities are creating benefit or harm.

These problems are immediately encountered by Birnie *et al.* (Chapter 5) who find evidence of some significant damage to Scotland's land surface and soil quality. They argue that improved strategic monitoring is required to determine the extent and severity of harm. Land use changes have been a major factor in the decline and occasional recovery of specific habitats and species and it appears that the UK Biodiversity Action Plan is beginning to show some dividends. In setting themselves the task of determining the likely contribution of future agricultural trends in contributing to sustainable development, they encounter the common problem of scale with a broadly optimistic outlook being compromised with concerns in some specific areas of Scotland. Birnie *et al.* comment on the role of surprise events, such as foot and mouth disease, as drivers of change and Holbrook and Hall (Chapter 6) appropriately identify the potential for the introduction of non-native species to create a negative impact on indigenous flora and fauna.

Fowler *et al.* (Chapter 7) provide a convincing illustration of the connectedness of the environment and of human impact by considering the effect, predominantly on soil quality, of the legacy of polluting atmospheric emissions producing very widespread acidification and eutrophication and a consequent disturbance of natural flora. Recent international agreements and regulation are steadily reducing emission loads but it will be many decades before full recovery is a realistic prospect. More worryingly, ammonia emissions remain stubbornly high. Long-distance transport and photochemical reactivity of volatile organic compounds can generate damaging levels of ozone, particularly in rural upland areas where habitats are, in any case, fragile. Again it is emphasised that further monitoring data are required. McDonald *et al.* (Chapter 8) extend the argument to heavy metals which have been, and continue to be, emitted to the atmosphere and deposited on the land surface irrespective of national boundaries. Although validation through improved strategic monitoring, also called for by Birnie *et al.* (Chapter 5), is required, it is predicted that concentrations in soil in some areas may be damaging.

Scotland enjoys an abundance of rivers and lochs which provide multiple services including amenity, recreation, fisheries, a resource for water supply and waste discharge, and rich and varied habitats. Doughty *et al.* (Chapter 9) conclude that many historical point source pollution impacts from industry and sewage have been controlled. However, significant problems remain due to diffuse pollution resulting from widespread causes such as application of fertilisers, spreading of wastes on land, spraying of pesticides, atmospheric deposition, and wastewater overflows. The degradation of habitats through human activities, such as river engineering, drainage works, impounding and bankside land use, is more difficult to quantify as data are generally sporadic and short-term. The resulting impacts on aquatic species are also difficult to determine with certainty although Bennion *et al.* (Chapter 10) are able to use palaeolimnological techniques to investigate long-term impacts of a range of pollutants on community structure. These studies show that significant impacts are readily observable, even in lochs which would normally be considered unpolluted. On a positive note, improvements over recent years are also evident.

Doughty *et al.* (Chapter 9) also argue that the future of Scotland's aquatic heritage lies in the hands of its own people. A shift in public and organisational attitudes, allied to a growing understanding of pollution and ecosystem dynamics, allows a high degree of self-determination and Lassière (Chapter 11) presents a convincing example of the ensuing benefits. Both economic and social revival are stimulated by the re-opening of the Forth & Clyde and Union Canals in Central Scotland. A biodiversity action plan drives habitat improvements and species recovery in these slow flowing and nutrient rich waters.

Saunders *et al.* (Chapter 12) turn their attention to the marine environment where significant advances have been made in reducing polluting discharges. Coastal and estuarine water quality has significantly improved, with a resulting and demonstrable increase in faunal diversity. However, the difficulties in determining the optimal balance within the concept of sustainable development is perhaps exemplified by the case of marine fish farming, a highly successful industry in some of the most economically fragile areas of Scotland. It is an industry that brings employment and wealth to isolated communities but also generates adverse environmental impacts, some of which may not be fully understood. In addition, stocks of some wild, commercially exploited, marine fish are dangerously depleted. These major issues remain to be resolved within a regulatory framework which can, and does, provide ecological protection to designated sites but does not, as yet, provide the holistic approach required.

The general improvement in marine waters is exemplified by Dobson's case study (Chapter 13) which reveals that inputs of mercury to the Forth Estuary have declined, resulting in lower concentrations in biota. Malcolm *et al.* (Chapter 14) also report encouraging declines in organochlorine concentrations in gannet eggs. However, in both cases it is clear that marine systems take many decades to recover fully due to long residence times of persistent pollutants.

Finally, Baxter and Hutchinson (Chapter 15) suggest that the Atlantic salmon is a useful indicator of the overall state of both the marine and freshwater environments since it is a widespread species in Scotland and migrates between the North Atlantic feeding grounds and upper river catchment spawning beds. This being the case, then despite many environmental improvements reported in Chapters 5 to 14, we must remain seriously concerned about the causes of the rapid and substantial reduction of the salmon population. This decline appears to be driven by several factors, possibly including climate change, degradation of physical habitat and the spread of parasites from marine aquaculture.

The aquatic environment has benefited from sustained protection through legislation over the past 50 years and yet changing pressures of diffuse pollution and physical habitat deterioration remain significant. A new generation of regulation, exemplified by the Water Framework Directive, seems set to drive forward further improvements by requiring more holistic planning at the catchment scale and by setting environmental objectives rather than by establishing fixed numeric standards for an ever increasing range of parameters. This modern approach to regulation should provide a valuable platform for promoting sustainable development and improving stakeholder and community involvement.

5 THE LAND RESOURCES OF SCOTLAND: TRENDS AND PROSPECTS FOR THE ENVIRONMENT AND NATURAL HERITAGE

R.V. Birnie, J. Curran, J.A. MacDonald, E.C. Mackey, C.D. Campbell, G. McGowan, S.C.F. Palmer, E. Paterson, P. Shaw and M.C. Shewry

Summary

1.   Scotland's landscape has evolved in response to the complex interactions of geological processes over millennia and through the more recent impacts of human activity. This chapter seeks to illustrate the present condition of Scotland's non-renewable and renewable land resources from a sustainability point of view. A framework for understanding the social and environmental processes that might drive future changes is developed and illustrated using agricultural change as a case study.

2.   The underlying geological and soil resources of Scotland are non-renewable and subject to a range of pressures. Many of the subsequent impacts are irreversible and, arguably, non-sustainable. There is a lack of data relating to soil quality. For most issues, in particular the deposition and accumulation of pollutants, no systematic monitoring is carried out. It is suggested that soils should be afforded the same level of environmental protection as water and air, backed up with appropriate monitoring.

3.   The major drivers of land use change have been related to changes in the technologies of farming and forestry, and to urban growth. Significant changes in both area and intensities of use from the late 1940s to the late 1980s are reflected in habitat and species declines. Land use policy reforms, particularly from the late 1980s onwards, are reflected in some recent signs of habitat preservation and diversification. The effectiveness of Biodiversity Action Plans has yet to be fully assessed; however, there are some early successes.

4.   In rural Scotland the prospects are for long-term trends towards agricultural intensification in areas with production advantages. In other areas with high amenity, priorities will continue to shift towards satisfying environmental objectives. The remaining intermediate areas, with currently high levels of dependency on agricultural employment, are particularly exposed to land use changes. New forms of geographically separated agri-industrial landscapes and conservation landscapes may emerge.

5.   Our analysis suggests that the pre-eminence of social and economic forces in driving change in the short term (i.e. ten years) may mean that, despite Scotland moving towards a more sustainable position when judged nationally, there may be significant regional disparities. The fundamental question is whether we are prepared to trade-off environmental gains in some places with environmental losses in others.

5.1 Introduction

5.1.1 Background and objectives

Within a relatively small land area (approximately 78,000 km²), Scotland displays considerable geological diversity – the heritage of some three billion years of Earth history. The main geological components of Scotland came together around 400 million years ago and their margins are marked by the boundary faults that define the Highlands to the north, the Southern Uplands to the south, and between them the lower-lying Midland Valley. Geomorphological processes, principally glaciation during the Pleistocene, have operated on this geological basement of Scotland to produce the physical landscape of the present day. In general, the west and north are characterised by erosional landscapes. These are typified by highly dissected mountain massifs with high rainfall and acidic mineral or peat soils. The eastern lowlands and the Midland Valley are characterised by depositional landscapes underlain by glacial tills or fluvio-glacial deposits. These typically form a lower-lying, more undulating topography with lower rainfall and less acidic soils.

The geographic distribution of the major soil types also reflects the post-glacial vegetation history of Scotland. The climax vegetation over much of the eastern lowlands is oak-dominated broad-leafed woodland. In the west and north, woodland still forms the climax vegetation but with different species dominating, principally birch (*Betula* spp.) and Scots pine (*Pinus sylvestris*).

It is probable that Scotland supported hunter/gatherer communities soon after the ice retreated. These communities could have used fire for clearing vegetation. However, it is most likely that the first systematic use of fire and tools for woodland clearance was associated with early Neolithic farmers and that these practices continued for around 6,000 years. Whilst the early reasons for woodland clearance would have been related to the needs of agriculture, building materials and fuel wood, during historical times clearance and woodland management were also strongly associated with industrial needs. Both the Industrial and Agricultural Revolutions of the eighteenth and nineteenth centuries placed new demands on the non-renewable (e.g. minerals, soils) and renewable (e.g. wood) land resources, and led to the development of significant new resource-based industries like coal mining, quarrying and large scale, organised agriculture. These created new 'industrial' landscapes typified by those of mineral workings in the Midland Valley, arable farming in the eastern lowlands and livestock farming in the west and north.

Until the mid-twentieth century it was generally assumed that the exploitation of natural resources could be justified on the basis of the social and economic benefits that it provided. However, more recently issues like climate change and concepts of sustainability have led us to question this assumption. This chapter therefore aims to bring together a range of information about the land resources of Scotland and in particular that related to the drivers of change. Data have been obtained from a wide range of primary and secondary sources and therefore it must be recognised that the analyses could contain unknown biases and errors.

The objectives are to establish the present condition of the land resources of Scotland, both non-renewable and renewable, and to identify possible changes that might affect their sustainable use in the future. It is impossible to cover all aspects of the land resources of Scotland either in terms of the resources themselves or the identification of future changes. Examples are presented on stock, condition and trends, and a framework is developed for assessing potential impacts of future changes. Agricultural change is used as a case study. The overarching question to address is whether Scotland is currently moving towards, or away from, the sustainable use of land resources.

5.1.2 Definitions

Land can be defined in several ways. Narrow definitions limit its meaning to rock and soil whilst other definitions extend it to include biological dimensions. Still wider definitions are sometimes employed, where 'land' conveys the sense of a whole dynamic system, in which both biophysical and human land management components are coupled. Together they are considered in terms of managed ecosystems or socio-ecosystems (Holling, 1995). Although this chapter focuses on stock and condition, latter sections, on the causes of future environmental changes, include a systematic treatment of the socio-economic aspects.

5.1.3 Sustainability: the concept of natural capital

Sustainability thinking underpins many of the policies of the current United Kingdom (UK) government, the Scottish Executive, and their respective agencies. Despite this, the concept is still poorly defined in practical terms. J.P.G. Webster (pers. comm.) used a helpful financial metaphor to point out that income is that which can be consumed, in a given period, leaving the consumer as well off at the end as the beginning, i.e. capital is conserved. In the context of sustainability, J.P.G. Webster extended the concept of capital to include natural, man-made, human and social stocks. Collectively they represent aggregate capital. Sustainability is therefore concerned with the conservation of aggregate capital. This definition allows such widely differing dimensions as natural resources, human skills, technologies, and institutions to be considered. Within this broad framework this chapter considers the condition of selected elements of the natural capital of Scotland and only therefore supports an assessment of environmental sustainability. It remains a challenge to put together a full sustainability assessment.

5.1.4 Tests of environmental sustainability

Two tests are applied to determine whether the trend over a 50 year time period in any of the natural capital stocks is moving either away from or towards environmental sustainability. The first is reversibility. This is whether any decrease in stock can be reversed or mitigated, at reasonable cost. The second is severity. This concerns rates and directions of change, and the impacts of changes at immediate and distant scales in both geographical and temporal senses.

5.2 Non-renewables

5.2.1 Background

Scotland's geological materials and soils comprise a non-renewable resource which form an integral part of the landscape and support the vegetation, habitats and agriculture upon which humans and wildlife depend. The chemical, physical and biological properties of soils enable many essential ecosystem functions. These can include the provision of a growth medium for vegetation, the regulation of water flow, and the transformation and degradation of pollutants. Soils contain a large biological diversity that is associated with essential functions of biogeochemical cycling of carbon, nitrogen and other compounds.

However, soils are subject to a wide range of anthropogenic pressures (RCEP, 1996; SEPA, 2001), ranging from the deposition of pollutants to the physical removal of soil.

There has been much recent debate concerning the concept and measurement of soil quality. This is complicated because of the spatial heterogeneity of soil, and the lack of understanding of many processes, particularly biological, in relation to its function. However, a set of soil quality indicators has recently been published (Loveland and Thompson, 2001) which will form a part of any future soil protection strategy.

Because of their relatively long formation times, soils are considered as a non-renewable resource. Although soils are continually undergoing pedogenesis, many of the pressures result in irreversible impacts affecting their sustainable use. These pressures are examined in terms of development, including urbanisation, and agricultural practices. Our analyses are summarised in Table 5.1.

5.2.2 Development

Development can generate a range of pressures at a number of scales from local to international. Such pressures can involve physical damage, sealing or removal of soil and rock; practices which are inherently unsustainable. However, 'new' capital may sometimes be created through, for example, the restoration of quarries and can result in significant biodiversity benefits.

A wide range of chemical pollutants is emitted, leaked or spilt, and the soil is the ultimate sink for many of these. Emissions to the atmosphere result in deposition to land of a range of compounds that acidify or cause eutrophication. These can have a negative impact on soil quality as well as on the wider environment. In addition, the response of soil to climate change has the potential to have a significant impact on all aspects of land.

Urbanisation: Urbanisation carries with it a number of environmental problems including sealing of the soil resource, change to habitats and also associated energy costs caused by increased reliance on transport. In 1996, 2,056 km² (2.6 per cent) of Scotland's land area was classified as urban (Scottish Office, 1998). The number of households rose by 18 per cent (332,000) between 1981 and 1999 and projections suggest that by 2012 there will be 2.43 million households, an increase of 12 per cent (see www.scotland.gov.uk/stats/envonline/menu0.asp). There was over 53,500 km of public road in 1999 (Scottish Executive, 2000a). However, the rate of new road construction has decreased in recent years despite the number of cars increasing to 2.13 million in 1999, an increase of 26 per cent in 10 years. The area of industrial holdings has increased from 6,003 ha in 1985 to 7,786 ha in 1995 (Scottish Office, 1998). No future projections are available and these would be highly dependent on both future economic growth and government policies particularly regarding the redevelopment of brown-field sites.

Between 1947 and 1988 the area of built land increased by an estimated 46 per cent, mainly on improved grassland and arable farmland (Mackey *et al.*, 1998). Figure 5.1 shows the net loss of agricultural land between 1970-71 and 1999-2000. The principal conversion was to forestry although this has decreased in recent years. Between 1970 and 1999, 25,339 ha were converted to recreational use, 25,217 ha to roads, housing and industry and 9,481 ha to mineral workings. Land managed for formal recreation (e.g. playing fields and golf courses) also increased, by around 138 per cent. The loss of land to development poses a significant threat to sustainability given the small proportion of high quality agricultural

Table 5.1. Sustainability tests applied to the non-renewable components of the land resource. Trends are indicated as increasing (↑), decreasing (↓), or ambivalent (↕) and might be reversable or capable of restoration/mitigation (✔) or not (✘). Environmental impacts are high (H), medium (M) or low (L), and components are assessed as becoming more sustainable (☺), unchanged (☺), or becoming less sustainable (☹). ? indicates that the result is unknown or cannot be assessed.

Category	Trend (amount)	Reversibility	Restoration/ Mitigation	Environmental Impact		Future trend (up to 2050)	Becoming more or less sustainable?	Comments
				primary	secondary			
Industrial development Development rate								
– housing	↑	✘	✔	H	M	↑	☹	
– roads	↑	✘	✔	H	M	↑	☹	Although the area covered by roads is increasing, the rate of road building has decreased.
– industrial holdings	↑	✘	✔	H	M	↑	☹	No Scottish target exists for the development of housing on brownfield land.
Abandonment of land	↕	✔	✔	M	L	→	☹	PPC Regulations should ensure the restoration of industrial sites post-closure.
Mining	↑	✘	✔	H	L	↔	☹	
Amount of waste going to landfill	→	✘	✔	H	H	→	☺	National Waste Strategy
Point source chemical pollution	?	✘	✔	M	M	→	☺	PPC Regulations should ensure no future local soil contamination

Category	Trend (amount)	Reversibility	Restoration/ Mitigation	Environmental Impact primary	secondary	Future trend (up to 2050)	Becoming more or less sustainable?	Comments
Diffuse chemical pollution								
– acidification	→	✓	✗	H	H	→	☺	Very little is known about recovery from acidification. It is expected that recovery rates will be very slow (although unknown for peats?).
– eutrophication	←?	?	✗	H	H	→	☺?	No trend data exist to assess whether or not these compounds are accumulating in soils remote from sources.
– heavy metals	?	✗	✗	L	L	→?	☺?	
– POPs	?	✗	✗	L	L	→?	☺?	
– radioactivity	→	✓	✗	L	L	→	☺	
Climate change	←	✗	✗	M	H	←	☹	
Agricultural practices								
Erosion	←	✗	✓	M	M	→	☺	Trend data based on increasing pressures not measured events.
Rate of peat loss	→	✗	✗	H	M	→	☺	
Fertilisers	↔	✓	✓	M	H	→	☺	
Pesticides	←	?	?	M	M	←	?	
Wastes to land	←	✗	✗	M	M	←	☹	Potentially sustainable if soil protection is taken into account.

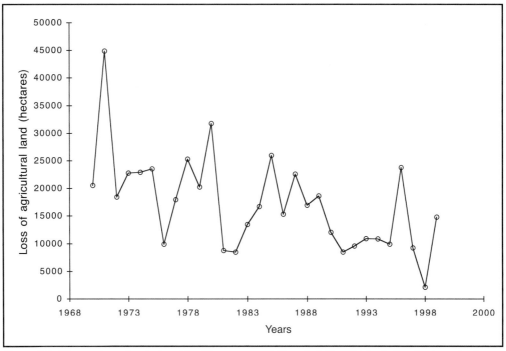

Figure 5.1. The net loss of agricultural land between 1970-71 and 1999-2000 (excluding land previously not measured) (taken from Scottish Office (1998)).

land that exists in Scotland. It is therefore of concern that the recent Agricultural Strategy suggested that the protection afforded prime agricultural land be removed (Scottish Executive, 2001a).

Land abandonment: Industrial activity over the last 200 years has produced an estimated 11,683 ha of vacant and derelict land, equivalent to some 5,000 individual sites (Scottish Executive, 2000a). The majority of vacant and derelict sites in Scotland are concentrated in the Central Belt, with North Lanarkshire (18 per cent), City of Glasgow (13 per cent) and West Lothian (10 per cent) Council areas having the highest proportions. The principal former use of derelict land is mineral extraction and of vacant land is agriculture. Although the total extent has decreased in recent years, derelict land is still being created in significant quantities. Of the 600 ha of land reclaimed in 2000, the largest proportion (20 per cent) was in Glasgow City. The most common new use of derelict land was for residential purposes. It should be noted that some derelict and vacant sites have value for nature conservation and urban green space. Under the recently introduced Pollution Prevention and Control (Scotland) Act 1999, regulated industries will be required to return sites to their original condition on cessation of activities, thereby preventing the creation of further derelict land.

Mining: Mining has resulted in a range of environmental impacts including soil contamination, water pollution from drainage, and changed landscape character. Mineral resources, such as coal and sand, are non-renewable. The amount of coal and shale produced decreased from over 2,000,000 t in 1985 to approximately 500,000 t in 1996 (Scottish Office, 1998). The method of mining also changed with the number of deep coal mines decreasing from over 200 in the 1950s to only one in 2001. In contrast, opencast coal mining has expanded to over 60 operations, with subsequent impacts on the landscape. The extraction of igneous rock has shown a steady increase.

Landfill: Landfill is the primary disposal route for waste in Scotland, accounting for over 90 per cent of waste. The amount of waste produced and subsequently going to landfill steadily rose from 4,530,000 t in 1986 to 18,800,000 t in 1994 (Scottish Office, 1998). A small decrease between 1997 and 1998 was a result of a reduction in construction and demolition material. In 1998, 12 million tonnes of waste was landfilled, comprising 3 million tonnes of household waste, 2 million tonnes of commercial waste and 7 million tonnes of industrial waste (SEPA, 1999). The Scottish Environment Protection Agency (SEPA) currently licenses 263 landfill sites in Scotland. There is a range of environmental impacts associated with landfilling in addition to the irreversible loss of natural resources: the release of methane, the contamination of soils, surface and groundwaters by leachate, and local odour and litter problems. A principal target of the European Commission's Directive on Landfill of Waste is to reduce the amount of biodegradable municipal waste going to landfill by 65 per cent by 2016 and SEPA has recently published a strategy which sets out a sustainable integrated waste management system.

Point source chemical pollution: Chemically contaminated land can represent a potential risk to the environment and human health. Typical sources of contamination include mining, metal smelters, oil refineries, gas works, the textile industry and chemical works. The nature and extent of chemically contaminated land in Scotland is not yet known accurately. However, new regulations, under Part IIA of the Environmental Protection Act 1990, are in place to address this. It is estimated that 3,545 ha, or about one quarter of the total vacant and derelict area, was either suspected or known to be contaminated in 2000. The known types of contaminants include arsenic, asbestos, chromium, coal, copper, nickel, zinc, cyanides, gases, phenols and sulphates. Coal is the most common contaminant, affecting 539 ha, followed by asbestos on 235 ha.

Radioactive contamination of soil has come mainly from former industrial processes such as luminising using radium, gas mantle manufacture, phosphate manufacture and use, metal ore refining and various other industrial and medical uses of radioisotopes. The legacy left by industrial manufacturing of radioactive products and by-products is such that the nature and total extent of radioactively contaminated land in Scotland is unknown. Regulations are being prepared under Part IIA of the Environmental Protection Act 1990 to address this.

Transboundary chemical pollution – acidification: Major reductions in the emission of acidifying compounds have occurred over the last two decades. Their emission and deposition are described by Fowler *et al.* (Chapter 7). Reductions in deposition of nitrogen have not been as great as those of sulphur. Acid deposition has been shown to have serious impacts on the health of soil, vegetation and freshwater ecosystems. Many soils in Scotland, especially upland soils, are shallow and overlay acidic parent material. These soils have limited base cation exchange or buffering capacity, and are sensitive to acidification from acid deposition. Plate 8 shows both the exceedance of the critical load of acidity for soils and the projected exceedance in 2010. The largest input of acidity occurs over Dumfries and Galloway, the west-central Highlands and the eastern Cairngorms. The critical load is exceeded in 89 per cent of the land area. However, it should be noted that the contribution of deposited nitrogen to acidification is not clear and when the effect of ammonia is excluded then the area falls to just over 50 per cent. Reductions in emissions by 2010 following the United Nations Economic Commission for Europe's Second Sulphur Protocol are expected to result in the area exceeded decreasing to 78 per cent.

The recovery of soils and freshwaters from acidification can be extremely slow and spatially variable, depending on the release of base cations from soil minerals. Models have predicted that current agreed sulphur reductions will have only a marginal beneficial effect on the recovery of soils and surface waters in Scotland (European Geophysical Society, 1998). Increased acidity has been measured in both peat and forest soils. Soil chemical changes, including increased acidity, have been recorded over a 40 year period in a coniferous plantation in north-eastern Scotland (Billett *et al.*, 1988). Peat acidification has been found to be correlated with acid deposition (Skiba *et al.*, 1989). However, recent results from the Countryside Survey's Measurement and Assessment of Soil Quality (MASQ) component indicate there has been an increase in pH of acid soils in the UK (Haines-Young *et al.*, 2000). The reasons for this increase are not yet clear.

Nitrogen deposition contributes to soil and water eutrophication as well as to acidification and can lead to vegetation change in nutrient poor environments. In addition, N deposition can also lead to elevated emission of nitrous oxide from soil (Skiba *et al.*, 1998).

Transboundary chemical pollution - heavy metals: Heavy metals are emitted to the atmosphere from a range of sources including coal combustion, road transport, metal smelting and waste incineration. Modelled deposition rates of heavy metals show Scotland at the low end of the range found across Europe (www.nilu.no/projects/ccc/). Concentrations in mineral soil profiles from National Soils Inventory (NSI) sites have been measured, based on a 10 km grid across Scotland (Paterson, 1999). Chromium, nickel, copper, zinc, cadmium and lead showed a wide range of concentrations, often two orders of magnitude, reflecting the influence of soil parent material and anthropogenic inputs. Heavy metal concentrations have also been measured in upland organic soils across four east to west transects from the north of the country to the south (www.macaulay.ac.uk/tipss/index.html). The smallest metal concentrations were observed in the most northerly transect and the largest across the Central Belt, reflecting industrial sources and transport.

Transboundary chemical pollution - persistent organic pollutants: Industrial processes can result in the release of a range of persistent organic pollutants including dioxins, furans, polychlorinated biphenyls (PCBs) and polyaromatic hydrocarbons (PAHs). It has been estimated that most of the UK environmental burden of PCBs (93.1 per cent), dioxins and furans (95 per cent) is associated with soils (Harrad and Jones, 1992; Harrad *et al.*, 1994), and soils are thought to be the main source of PCBs released back to the UK atmosphere (Harrad *et al.*, 1994). Soil has also been identified as an important PAH reservoir (Wild and Jones, 1995). Modelled deposition rates of PCBs show that rates in Scotland, at 100 to 1,000 mg per km^2 per year, are at the low end of the range observed across Europe, although an analysis in Scotland of surface organic horizons in soil profiles has indicated that greater concentrations of PCBs are observed in these soils relative to other UK studies (Bracewell *et al.*, 1993). Deposition rates of dioxins and furans in urban and rural environments are estimated to be 10.2 mg per km^2 per year and 4.2 mg per km^2 per year respectively (Duarte-Davidson *et al.*, 1997).

For PAHs, an analysis of contemporary and archived (1951-1974) soil samples showed no significant trends in concentrations (Lead *et al.*, 1997). Total PAH concentration in Scotland ranged between 20 and 3,800 mg per kg at rural locations. For dioxins and furans typical concentrations have been estimated at between 1.4 mg per kg and 4.7 mg per kg for urban and at 3.3 mg per kg for rural soils (Creaser *et al.*, 1990; Duarte-Davidson *et al.*, 1997).

Transboundary chemical pollution – radioactivity: Fallout from the Chernobyl nuclear accident was one of the most widespread sources of radioactivity deposition to land. In 1986 restrictions on the movement and slaughter of sheep were placed on over 2,000 farms. In 1999 only 20 farms, in East Ayrshire, East Renfrewshire and Stirlingshire, remained under control. Recent observations have shown a decline in levels of caesium-137 in soils (Hird *et al.*, 1996).

Climate change: Over the next century Scotland's climate is expected to become warmer by between 2° and 3°C and wetter, with annual rainfall increasing by 20 per cent (Scottish Executive, 2001b; Kerr and Ellis, Chapter 16). An increase in flooding is likely to extend the area from the present 4.2 per cent of the Scottish mainland that currently lies within the modelled 1 per cent annual flood risk envelope. The impact of climate change on soil quality is uncertain. Changes in the soil moisture regime are likely to have significant impacts on the range and location of agricultural crops, with drought impacting on crop growth and soil wetness impacting on harvesting and ploughing. Microbial processes are particularly sensitive to changes in soil temperature and moisture.

Soils play an important role in the emission and uptake of greenhouse gases. The Scottish Climate Change Programme (Scottish Executive, 2000b) estimated that emissions from the agriculture, forestry and land use sectors contributed 8.5 million tonnes of carbon or 36 per cent of the total in 1995. Agricultural soil is the largest source of nitrous oxide in Scotland, estimated to contribute 60 per cent of the total source strength (U. Skiba, pers. comm.). Soil can act as both a source and sink for methane, depending on aeration status. Both land use change and the input of nitrogen fertilisers affect the amount of methane taken up by soils. The average reduction across Scotland in the rate of methane uptake in agricultural compared to forest soils has been estimated to be 50 per cent (Dobbie and Smith, 1996). Under anaerobic conditions, such as those found in peatlands, the decomposition of organic matter leads to methane formation. In Scotland, it has been estimated that the largest sources of methane are landfill sites and livestock (www.aeat.co.uk/netcen/airqual/), but peatlands such as the Flow Country in Caithness, the largest expanse of blanket bog in Europe, contribute a significant 17 per cent to the methane budget (Fowler *et al.*, 2000). An estimated 69 per cent of the carbon stored in soil occurs in Scotland (Milne, 1998). Land use change, such as the conversion of forests or grassland to arable use, can result in soils becoming a net source of carbon dioxide to the atmosphere.

5.2.3 Land Management

Agriculture has a dominant influence on the land resource with nearly 80 per cent of the land in Scotland being classified as agricultural. Many agricultural activities have the potential to degrade the soil resource, unless best practice techniques are adopted. Pressures such as overgrazing and increased mechanisation may lead to soil erosion, soil compaction and loss of organic matter. Fertiliser and pesticide application can impact soil quality and may result in the leaching of pollutants to surface and ground waters.

Erosion: Soil erosion has been recorded in a wide range of environments, from the Cairngorm Plateau to the arable farms of East Lothian. However, there has been no systematic survey or monitoring and it is often difficult to attribute a specific causation. Conditions on agricultural soil which exacerbate erosion include fields with little or no crop cover, compacted soils, inappropriate cultivation of steep slopes, removal of hedgerows and shelter belts, and the changes from spring to winter cropping. Soil erosion can also result from forestry practices. Soil losses following storm events result typically in between 1 and 2 t per ha, although losses of up to 80 t per ha have been recorded (Grieve and Hipkin, 1996).

Soil erosion in the uplands is also of concern. A survey in 1995 (Grieve *et al.*, 1995) concluded that a significant degradation of the peatland resource was occurring, reaching 20 per cent in the Monadhliath Mountains. The most severely eroded areas were found in the eastern Southern Uplands and eastern Grampians along with evidence of land management pressure such as grazing and burning. Overgrazing increases the risk of soil erosion. Sheep and deer numbers have increased in recent years (see section 5.3.7). Recreational activities can also result in localised erosion. In the Cairngorms, for example, footpath widening affected up to 72 m per km^2 (Grieve *et al.*, 1995). A recent study detailed trends in some of the factors influencing soil erosion rates (Davidson and Grieve, 2001) including increased grazing, human trampling, skiing and visitor numbers.

Peat loss: Peatlands are an important resource in Scotland, both for their conservation and environmental value. They are under threat from commercial extraction for horticulture, drainage, overgrazing, pasture improvement and forestry, although recent changes in their conservation status have reduced the risk of loss. It has been estimated that a 21 per cent reduction in the area of mire (fen and bog) occurred between the 1940s and the 1980s (Mackey *et al.*, 1998). The most affected area was the Borders. Raised bogs are found in the Central Belt and the Grampian coastal plain. No completely natural vegetation exists on lowland raised bogs today and of an estimated 27,892 ha only 2,515 ha (9 per cent) of raised bog exhibit near-natural vegetation (Lindsay and Immirzi, 1996). Scotland has over 1 million ha of blanket bog, approximately 10 per cent of the world's coverage. The total extent of blanket bog that has been degraded is not known although it has been estimated that forestry has had the largest impact with nearly 130,000 ha, over 12 per cent, being affected (Lindsay and Immirzi, 1996).

Fertilisers: Agricultural intensification since the Second World War has resulted in large increases in crop yields in part due to increased reliance on inorganic fertilisers and pesticides. The use of these chemicals can impact on soil quality through changes in soil biodiversity and nutrient cycling, and potential pollution of surface and groundwater (see Doughty *et al.*, Chapter 9). In addition, the use of nitrogen fertilisers can result in elevated emission of the greenhouse gas nitrous oxide from soil. Nitrogen applications to agricultural land were fairly stable between 1986 and 1999 at 116 to 129 kg per ha. In contrast to nitrates, phosphorus is relatively immobile in soil, being strongly adsorbed to soil particles, so that pollution of surface waters mainly occurs through transport of soil particles by erosion. Application rates of inorganic phosphorus were also stable between 1986 and 1999 at 20 to 45 kg per ha. However, it has been estimated that most agricultural land is over-supplied with phosphorus (Edwards and Withers, 1998) and this has led to a build-up of phosphorus in soils (Tunney *et al.*, 1997) and to the transport of dissolved as well as particulate phosphorus into surface and ground waters.

Pesticides: Over 450 pesticides comprising insecticides, molluscicides, fungicides, herbicides, growth regulators and seed treatments are currently approved for application to arable and horticultural land (MAFF *et al.*, 1998). Concern has been expressed that the repeated use of pesticides may lead to accumulation in soil and to damaging effects on the environment. Although soil acts as a sink for the majority of pesticides, with soil properties and biota determining their persistence and fate, a recent study (PEWG, 2000) found no systematic surveys of pesticide residues in soil or their impacts on soil quality. Pesticides can enter watercourses in surface run-off, damaging aquatic ecosystems and polluting drinking water. They may also affect non-target species directly and predators indirectly, either by eliminating their food sources or by accumulation in their fat resources.

The amount of pesticide applied to arable crops in Scotland increased from 4,847 t in 1982 to 7,767 t in 1998. The majority (nearly 80 per cent) is sulphuric acid applied to potato crops as a desiccant prior to harvesting. The observed increase was due to a greater proportion of the potato crop being treated in recent years. Other pesticides decreased slightly over the period, possibly reflecting factors such as the use of lower dose, but biologically more active, substances and the use of Integrated Crop Management plans (PEWG, 2000). Although not strictly defined as a pesticide, over 2 million litres of sheep dip chemicals (either organophosphorus compounds or synthetic pyrethroids) were disposed to sacrificial land in 1999 (SEPA, 2001).

Waste application to land: Organic wastes, such as sewage sludge, industrial and agricultural wastes, applied to land can have beneficial effects on soil quality. Many wastes contain significant quantities of nitrogen, phosphorus and organic matter that can improve fertility and soil condition. However, wastes can contain potentially polluting compounds such as heavy metals, organic compounds and pathogens.

It is reported (Scotland and Northern Ireland Forum for Environmental Research, 1999) that 96 per cent of organic waste applied to land in Scotland is agricultural waste (15 million t), comprising manures, slurries and silage effluent, which is exempt from regulatory control. In 1996-1997, 185,000 wet t of sewage sludge, or 19 per cent of the total produced, was recycled to land; this is expected to rise to over 858,000 wet t by 2005 to 2006 as a result of additional sewage treatment and the ban on sludge dumping at sea under the Urban Waste Water Treatment Directive. At present, sewage sludge is applied to just over 4,000 ha of agricultural land at 597 sites. Most sludge is recycled to arable farmland (2,815 ha, 378 sites) and a smaller amount to pasture (1,389 ha, 219 sites) (Gendebien *et al.*, 1999). The most common industrial wastes applied to land in Scotland include distillery waste, blood and gut content from abattoirs and paper waste, for which SEPA records a total 368,000 wet t applied to land in 1998.

5.3 Renewable resources

Scotland's native plants and animals generally colonised from the south and across the European land bridge as the ice sheets receded from around 15,000 years BP (before present). Scotland's distinctive biogeography, its climate, topography, geology and soils, and its history of land and resource use, are reflected in its landscape and wildlife. The industrialisation of Scotland and the reorganisation of agriculture from around the end of the eighteenth century shaped the modern-day landscape. Medieval cultivation patterns, such as rig and furrow features, are testament to a longer history of land use that has removed, obscured and buried earlier components (RCAHMS, 1994). Subsequent advances in farming, forestry and urban development, particularly since the mid-twentieth century, have in turn stamped their mark upon the landscape. It is these more recent trends that are considered here, with reference to the summary assessments of landscape and wildlife in Tables 5.2 (habitats) and 5.3 (species). In general, reported increases or decreases are those which are statistically significant ($p<0.05$) or, in the case of species range and abundance, show at least a 10 per cent or more change between two time periods.

5.3.1 Soil

As a mainly unseen component of the landscape and wildlife, soil is essential for maintaining Scotland's biodiversity and ecosystem services (Usher, 1996). Soil ecosystems are particularly important for the decomposition of dead organic matter and for the recycling of nutrients on which plant productivity, and ultimately animal life, depends. Soil organisms have a key role to play in developing and maintaining soil structure, in nutrient cycling and in interactions with plant roots. Parts of the soil biota are important for the restoration of ecosystem functions by decomposing polluting chemicals (Usher, 1996).

The productivity of soils is often a function of reclamation, cultivation and manuring over the last 400 years. In the past century, however, the link between local organic materials and soil making has been broken (Smout and Davidson, 1996). Where there is a mismatch between land management and soil properties, the environmental functions provided by the soil may be diminished or lost (Taylor, 1995; Bullock and Thompson, 1996; Puri *et al.*, 2001). Land use change and pollution can have large impacts on soil biota, and particularly species richness (Usher, 1996). Changes in soil properties and processes can also impact upon sensitive plants and water bodies (Paterson, 2000). However, a lack of trend data on soil properties impedes the assessment of sustainable land use practices (SEPA, 2001).

5.3.2 Habitat diversity

Land use and development pressures have been the main drivers of change in Scotland's land cover over recent decades (Mackey *et al.*, 1998). In 1988, three-fifths of Scotland's land cover could still be regarded as semi-natural, following a decline of 17 per cent over the previous four decades (SNH, 2001a). Conifer plantation on habitats such as acid grassland, mire, heather moorland and former woodland accounted for 81 per cent of the decline. Pasture improvement, on acid grassland and heather moorland, accounted for a further 13 per cent (Plate 9).

For biodiversity action planning and monitoring, the UK and surrounding seas have been classified into 37 broad habitats (Jackson, 2000). Of the 18 terrestrial habitats that occur in Scotland, 16 were sufficiently widespread to be reported in the latest Countryside Survey (Haines-Young *et al.*, 2000). The two habitats that increased significantly between 1990 and 1998 were 'fen, marsh & swamp' by 19 per cent, and 'broad-leaved, mixed & yew woodland' by 9 per cent (Figure 5.2).

A break point in land cover change appears to be evident from around 1990, following

Table 5.2. Sustainability tests applied to renewable components of land resource: habitats (based on Mackey *et al.*, 2001). Trends are indicated as having increased (↑), bi-directional or no change (↕), or decreased (↓). Prospects for reversing unfavourable trends or for restoration/mitigation are assessed as feasible (✔) or not feasible (✗). Ecological impacts of possible future scenarios are outlined. Components are assessed as potentially becoming more sustainable (☺), or potentially becoming less sustainable (☹), apparently unchanged or mixed (☺), or change clearly established between first and last year, but no clear evidence for a trend (C), or change probable but not fully-established (c), or change indicated but not well-established (c). Statistical significance was tested where possible (at the 5 per cent level).

Category	Trend (range/extent/abundance)	Reversibility	Restoration/Mitigation	Ecological Impact		Reliability of trend	Becoming more or less sustainable?	Comments
				primary	secondary			
Habitat diversity	↓ past declines in semi-natural habitats have slowed but not necessarily stopped	✔ notably through habitat conservation	✔ habitat enhancement/restoration	positive: where wildlife communities and populations are restored	positive: where ecological functions are restored	C	☺	c. 1947-c. 1988 (Mackey et al., 1998) • Semi-natural and long-established decreased in extent by 17 per cent. 1990-1998 (Haines-Young et al., 2000) • Weak evidence of declines/declines arrested. • Fen, marsh and swamp expanded by 19 per cent. • Broadleaved, mixed and yew woodland expanded by 9 per cent.
Forest and woodland networks	↓ restoration of habitat diversity and enhancement of landscape character through forest and woodland networks	✔ negative impacts of former blanket afforestation are being reversed	✔ habitat enhancement/restoration through new planting and restructuring	positive: woodland is a species rich habitat	positive: woodland contributes to the restoration of ecological functions and opportunities for recreation	C	☺	Trends (Forestry Commission data). • 1984-1999: native woodland extent increased by 34 per cent. • 1988-1998: 275 km² of native pine woods established through Woodland Grant Scheme funding. • 1995-2000: 31 km² native woodland established by natural regeneration: 26.8 km² broadleaves and 4.6 km² Scots pine.

Category	Trend (range/extent/abundance)	Reversibility	Restoration/ Mitigation	Ecological Impact primary	Ecological Impact secondary	Reliability of trend	Becoming more or less sustainable?	Comments
								Forecast • 1994 and 2005: native pinewood to increase by 305 km^2 over 1994 area. • 1999 and 2015: priority broadleaved woodland types to increase by 72 km^2 over 1999 area. *Woodland birds* • c.1970-c.1990 (from British Trust for Ornithology data): 10 woodland species contracted in range and 11 expanded. • 1994-1999 (Noble *et al*, 2000): 5 of 14 widespread woodland species increased in abundance, one species declined.
Arable and mixed farmland habitats	continuing trend towards intensification and specialisation	possible future changes in the structure of farm support	habitat restoration, e.g. Rural Stewardship Scheme	positive: where wildlife communities and populations are restored	positive: where ecological functions are restored	C	☺	*c. 1947-c. 1988* (Mackey *et al*., 1998) • Arable area increased by 11 per cent and became more dominant in the east • *1990-1998* (Haines-Young *et al.*, 2000) • No significant overall change. *Mixed farming* • 23 per cent decline in mixed farming between 1987 and 1999 (ag. census). • 23 per cent reduction in crofters between 1960 and 1985 (RSPB and SCU, 1992).

Category	Trend (range/extent/abundance)	Reversibility	Restoration/Mitigation	Ecological Impact		Reliability of trend	Becoming more or less sustainable?	Comments
				primary	secondary			
								• No significant overall change. *Mixed farming* • 23 per cent decline in mixed farming between 1987 and 1999 (ag. census). • 23 per cent reduction in crofters between 1960 and 1985 (RSPB and SCU, 1992).
Grassland habitats	continuing trend towards intensification and specialisation (→)	possible future changes in the structure of farm support (✔)	habitat restoration, e.g. Rural Stewardship Scheme (✔)	positive: where wildlife communities and populations are restored	positive: where ecological functions are restored	C	⊗	*c. 1947-c. 1988* (SNH 2001e) • Rough grassland area decreased by 10 per cent. • *1990-1998* (Haines-Young et al, 2000) • No significant overall change. *Other indicators* • Hay production declined by 34 per cent and silage production increased by 8 per cent between 1991 and 2000 (ag. census). • Three farmland birds declined in abundance between 1994 and 1999 (Noble et al, 2000). • Corncrake singing males increased by 33 per cent between 1993 and 1999 (RSPB pers. comm.).
Heath and moorland habitats	evidence of continuing decline in heather moorland (→)	improved moorland management and reduced grazing pressure (✔)	reduced N enrichment from air pollution (✔)	positive: where semi-natural habitat structure restored	positive: where wildlife communities and populations are restored	C	⊗	*c. 1947-c. 1988* (Mackey et al, 1998) • Heather moorland reduced by 23 per cent. • Blanket mire reduced by 21 per cent.

Category	Trend (range/extent/abundance)	Reversibility	Restoration/ Mitigation	Ecological Impact primary	Ecological Impact secondary	Reliability of trend	Becoming more or less sustainable?	Comments
								• *1990-1998 (McGowan et al, 2001)* • Weakly significant 5 per cent decline in dwarf shrub heath. • No significant change in extent of bog.
Montane habitats	→ restricted and under threat, with further uncertainties from climate change	✗ difficult to reinstate fragile ecosystems	✓ sensitive management of recreational pressures; reduced N enrichment from air pollution; reduced grazing where appropriate	negative: potential loss of scarce habitats	negative: potential impacts on dependent species	c	☹	Highly restricted in extent; vulnerable to excessive trampling and grazing, air pollution and climate change.
Coastal habitats	→ much of the coast remains relatively unaltered, but a host of pressures come together at some parts of the coast	✗ pressures are unlikely to diminish	✓ sensitive management of coastal ecosystems	positive: where dynamic coastal processes are safeguarded	positive: where ecosystem functions are safeguarded	c	☺	10 per cent of coast directly affected by urban or industrial use (Ritchie, 1999). Climate and sea level changes will affect some coasts.
Settlements and green space	→ continuing development pressures	✗ continuing expansion of built-up land	✓ creativity in the planning and management of urban green space	positive: where green space planning becomes integral to development	positive: where urban ecosystems are protected	c	☺	Continuing development pressure requires careful management to conserve and enhance tranquillity and green space.

Table 5.3. Sustainability tests applied to renewable components of land resource: species (based on Mackey *et al.*, 2001). Trends are indicated as increased (↑), bi-directional or no change (↕), or decreased (↓). Reliability of change or trend between specified years is indicated as an increasing (or decreasing) trend established (T), change clearly established between first and last year, but no clear evidence for a trend (C), change probable but not fully-established (c), or change indicated but not well-established (c). Statistical significance was tested where possible (at the 5 per cent level). Trends are indicated as a favourable trend (☺), trend mixed or unclear (☺), or unfavourable (☹).

Category	Trend (range/abundance)	Feasibility of managing/ reversing current trends	Reliability of trend	Favourable trend?	Comments
Breeding land birds	↕ 50 per cent showing little change in range, but notable declines among farmland species	Habitat restoration feasible (e.g. Rural Stewardship Scheme), but trends depend on broad-scale policies relating to farming, forestry and upland use.	C	☺ all species ☹ farmland spp.	*Geographical range* • 1968/72-1988/91 (BTO data for Scotland) 124 species surveyed; 24 increased and 38 decreased. Reduced range for 60 per cent of farmland birds. *Abundance* • 1994-1999 (Noble *et al.*, 2000): 57 species surveyed; 12 increased and nine decreased.
Wintering wildfowl and waders	↑ many species showing sustained increases	High populations sustainable if hunting restrictions maintained, and through habitat management, but climate change may lead to geographic shift in some populations and loss of estuarine habitats.	T	☺	*Wildfowl* • 1966-1998 (Wildfowl and Wetlands Trust data) data for 18 native species wintering in Scotland; 12 increased and four decreased. *Waders* • 1969/70-1998/99 (Atkinson *et al.*, 2000) winter count data for 11 wader species; 10 increased and one declined in abundance.
Mammals	↓ more species declining than increasing	Declines due to wide range of factors, including habitat loss, degradation, disturbance, pollution effects and introduced species. Hence difficult to manage or reverse.	c	☹	Of 26 native mammal species assessed by The Mammal Society (1999), 11 thought to be declining and seven increasing in population size.

Category	Trend (range/abundance)	Feasibility of managing/reversing current trends	Reliability of trend	Favourable trend?	Comments
Butterflies	↔ but scarce species in decline	Targeted habitat enhancement/restoration possible for selected species. Effects of climate change difficult to predict.	C	☺	28 butterfly species resident in Scotland (Asher *et al.*, 2001); five (scarce species) contracted in recent decades and five (common and widespread species) expanded; two potentially vulnerable species are data deficient.
Rare and endemic plants	→ more populations declined than increased	Targeted habitat enhancement/restoration possible for selected species. Effects of climate change difficult to predict.	C	☹	45 threatened/endemic vascular plant species surveyed in Scotland between 1990 and 1996: 18 had at least 10 per cent fewer populations than had been found before 1990 and 14 had more.
Non-native plants	↔ geographical range of most species relatively stable	Need to control invasive plants that suppress native biodiversity, but success limited or unlikely where non-natives well-established.	c	☹	826 non-native plant species introduced into Scotland by the 1950s (Welch *et al.*, 2001); 104 increased and 13 decreased in range by 1987–88.
Threatened wildlife	↔ more species declined than increased, but majority unchanged	Protective legislation more likely to succeed in combination with habitat management/restoration.	c	☺	Of 111 species given legal protection and for which trend data available in 1997 (SNH, 2001d), 18 thought to be increasing and 40 decreasing. 51 showed little change.
Priority (BAP) habitats and species	→ by definition, priority habitats and species are scarce or declining	Biodiversity Action Plans identifying targets and costed actions are in place. However, in a recent review of 20 BAP bird species in Scotland, at least 16 were thought unlikely to achieve their targets.	c	☹	• 41 BAP priority habitats in Scotland (Jones *et al.*, 2001); four showed signs of recovery, five still declining. • 186 BAP priority species assessed; three recovered, eight showed signs of recovery, 47 thought to be declining, 16 lost from Scotland prior to BAP.

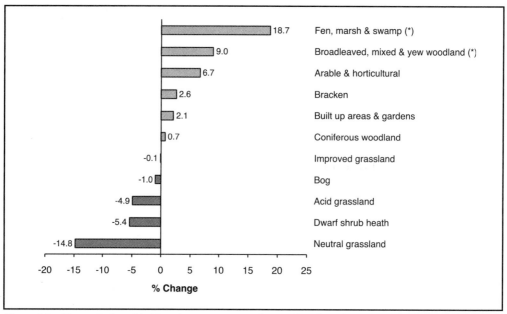

Figure 5.2. Change in broad habitats between 1990 and 1998, based on data in Haines-Young *et al.* (2000). An asterisk indicates statistical significance with *p*<0.05.

new wildlife legislation and reforms to both agriculture and forestry policy during the 1980s. Especially noteworthy was the changed structure and composition of forest and woodland during the 1990s, in marked contrast with previous decades.

5.3.3 Forest and woodland networks

Having been reduced to less than 5 per cent of Scotland's land area by the early 1900s, forest and woodland had expanded to around 17 per cent by 2001. Conifer afforestation between the 1940s and the 1980s played a large part in this, mainly on blanket mire, rough grassland and heather moorland in the uplands, and within former broad-leaved woodland in the lowlands (SNH, 2001b).

The rough pastures and heather moorlands of the uplands have become a zone of survival for archaeological features. Nevertheless, in a case study of part of Dumfriesshire, forestry dating from the 1960s occupied 50 per cent of land that was not under cultivation, leaving a relatively small area unaltered (RCAHMS, 1997). The uplands are also characterised by expansive tracts of blanket mire, where high rainfall and low temperatures have inhibited the decay of bog vegetation over millennia. Their importance for wildlife, landscape and carbon storage became more widely recognised in the late 1980s (Stroud *et al.*, 1987; Lindsay *et al.*, 1988), leading to a cessation of afforestation on deep peat.

During the 1990s and subsequently, opportunities have been taken to restructure conifer plantations in order to protect and restore landscape and archaeological features. Greater emphasis on broad-leaved planting and local progeny of seed is leading to the restoration of habitat diversity, connectivity and the naturalness of woodland. A 9 per cent expansion of broad-leaved, mixed and yew woodland between 1990 and 1998 contrasts with a 26 per cent decline in broad-leaved woodland over the previous four decades. The area of native woodland in Scotland increased by one third between 1984 and 1999 (SNH, 2001c). The area of farm woodland recorded in the June Agricultural Census doubled between 1991 and 2000. Five out of 14 widespread woodland birds increased in abundance between 1994 and 1999 (Noble *et al.*, 2000).

5.3.4 Arable habitats and mixed farmland

Intensification and specialisation have transformed the appearance and structure of lowland farmland (SNH, 2001d). Over recent decades, the west has become more dominantly pastoral and the east has become more dominantly arable. Hedgerows, which can be important for food and shelter to invertebrates, birds, mammals, amphibians and reptiles, were reduced by half between around 1947 and 1988 (Mackey *et al.*, 1998). No further evidence of change in overall hedgerow length was detected between 1990 and 1998 (Haines-Young *et al.*, 2000).

As mixed farming declined, according to the agricultural census by 23 per cent between 1987 and 1999, so the function of hedgerows as stock barriers in previously mixed farming landscapes has diminished. A decline in small-scale mixed farming in the north-west of Scotland is evident from a 23 per cent reduction in the number of crofters between 1960 and 1985, reduced tillage and replacement of cattle grazing by sheep (RSPB and Scottish Crofters Union, 1992). Such changes are likely also to signal declines in the mosaic of habitats that have been sustained by mixed farming systems.

5.3.5 Arable weeds

These are the most threatened group of plants in the British flora, and declined in frequency of occurrence between 1930 to 1960 and 1987 to 1988 (Rich and Woodruff, 1996). There was no clear evidence of change from the 1990 to 1998 Countryside Survey (McGowan *et al.*, 2001).

5.3.6 Grassland habitats

Rough grassland decreased by 10 per cent between 1947 and 1988, mainly due to afforestation and grassland improvement (SNH, 2001e). An estimated reduction of 16 per cent in the extent of calcareous grassland in the marginal uplands between 1990 and 1998 was due mainly to its conversion to more intensively managed grassland. On the other hand, a 19 per cent expansion of fen, marsh and swamp seemed due in part to reduced or abandoned grassland drainage in wetter areas (McGowan *et al.*, 2001). According to the agricultural census, hay production declined by 34 per cent and silage production increased by 8 per cent between 1991 and 2000. Stocking rates, based on units of livestock per hectare of grassland, increased by 7 per cent across Scotland between 1987 and 1999 (FPD Savills, 2001).

5.3.7 Heaths and moorland habitats

Conditions are optimal for the development of heather moorland in Scotland (Thompson *et al.*, 1995a). Sporting estates flourished from the 1870s onwards, but their economic value has declined since the 1930s. Fewer gamekeepers to manage the sporting interest, rising sheep numbers and falling standards of burning have resulted in a decline in the heather (*Calluna vulgaris*) cover upon which grouse (*Lagopus lagopus*) rely (Watson and

Lance, 1984). Between the 1940s and 1980s, heather moorland was reduced by about 23 per cent through afforestation and conversion to rough grassland (Mackey *et al.*, 1998). Weaker evidence (*p* less than 0.1) suggests that a further decline of 5 per cent between 1990 and 1998 was associated mainly with forest cover or canopy closure and conversion to grassland (McGowan *et al.*, 2001).

Within dwarf shrub heath habitats, a slight decline in stress-tolerant species, and an increase in competitive species between 1990 and 1998, point to a decline in habitat quality (McGowan *et al.*, 2001). Nutrient enrichment from airborne pollution may be a causal factor, but the conversion of heather moorland to grass-dominated vegetation has been shown to be driven principally by grazing (Hartley, 1997). Moderate to low grazing levels tend to maximise plant and animal diversity (Milne *et al.,* 1998). In northern Scotland, sheep numbers are thought to have increased by about 50 per cent between 1875 and 1966 (Harding *et al.*, 1994). More widely, they appear to have increased by 32 per cent between 1950 and 1990 (Fuller and Gough, 1999). Sheep numbers in Less Favoured Areas rose by 18 per cent between 1982 and 1998, as sheep displaced cattle. Red deer (*Cervus elaphus*) are thought to have almost doubled in number between 1959 and 1989, to around 300,000 head (Staines *et al.,* 1995). Declines in populations of red grouse, black grouse (*Tetrao tetrix*), hen harrier (*Circus cyaneus*) and ring ouzel (*Turdus torquatus*) between the 1970s and 1990s have been attributed, at least in part, to heavy grazing (Thompson *et al.*, 1995b).

5.3.8 *Montane habitats*

Montane environments are among the least altered in Scotland. Their arctic-alpine communities of plants and animals echo Scotland's post-glacial past. Nevertheless, they are vulnerable to disturbance by, for example, excessive trampling, climate change and air pollution. Nitrogen enrichment, together with grazing pressure, has been implicated in declines in the extent and quality of montane heaths dominated by the moss *Racomitrium lanuginosum* (Baddeley *et al.*, 1994). Increased tissue nitrogen, associated with air pollution during the twentieth century, has been shown to pose a threat to snowbed bryophyte communities (Woolgrove and Woodin, 1996a and 1996b).

5.3.9 *Coastal habitats*

Much of the Scottish coast remains relatively unspoiled, hosting large numbers of species and distinctive habitats such as sand dune, machair, saltmarsh, shingle, sea cliff, hard shore, sandy shore and intertidal flats (SNH, 1997). It is a naturally dynamic environment of erosion and accretion in which continuous processes of habitat creation and ecological succession are vital to maintaining species richness (Usher, 1999). Climate and sea level changes are likely to affect parts of the coast.

Settlement, industry and power generation have located mainly in the coastal lowlands and in places have built out from, or engineered the stabilisation of, the coast. There, a host of social, economic and environmental pressures come together (Sankey, 1999). Compared with the late eighteenth century, by the late 1980s it was estimated that about 8 per cent of Scotland's coast had been physically modified (Ritchie and McLean, 1988). By the late 1990s, some 10 per cent of the coastline was affected by intensive urban or industrial use (Ritchie, 1999). The visual impact and perception of development on the coast can be considerable (David Tyldesley and Associates, 1999).

5.3.10 Settlements and green space

From 1947 to 1988, the area of built-up land increased by an estimated 46 per cent (SNH, 2001f), often on the most fertile soils. Since the 1990s, emphasis has been placed on vacant and derelict land for re-development or restoration. Although the number of households rose by 18 per cent between 1981 and 1999 (Landrock *et al.*, 2001), the Countryside Survey detected no clear evidence of urban expansion; by 1998 it was estimated that built-up land covered 3.1 per cent of Scotland (Haines-Young *et al.*, 2000).

Too little is known about the composition and quality of urban green space, for example in terms of its spatial structure and extent, its connectivity for movement on foot or by bicycle, particularly into areas of relative tranquillity, its accessibility for relaxation and recreation, and its value for wildlife. Where it is known, green space comprises around 10 to 40 per cent of the major Scottish towns and cities and contributes greatly to the quality of life within them.

Tranquillity in the countryside refers to quietness and visual calm. Although landscaping and tree screening can enhance tranquillity locally, for example, the trend in recent decades has been of increased disturbance. A pilot study around the A96 corridor between Aberdeen and Inverness (Ash Consulting Group, 1998) showed that tranquillity was reduced throughout 45 per cent of the study area between the mid-1960s and the mid-1990s (Figure 5.3).

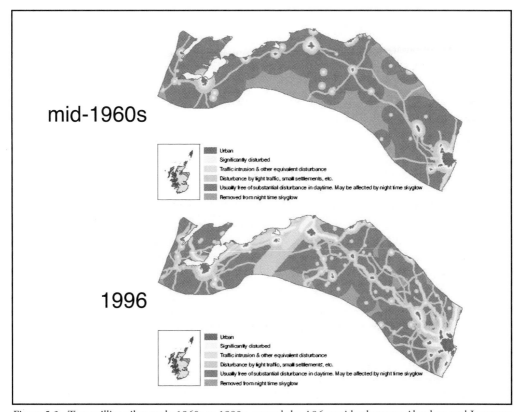

Figure 5.3. Tranquillity pilot study 1960s to 1990s, around the A96 corridor between Aberdeen and Inverness (based on Ash Consulting Group, 1998).

5.3.11 *Species diversity: birds*

From breeding bird atlas projects, the geographic ranges recorded for about half of Scotland's terrestrial and freshwater bird species showed little change between around 1970 and 1990. However, almost one third of species, including 60 per cent of farmland birds, showed a marked reduction in range size (SNH, 2001g). Reversing long-term declines in common farmland and woodland birds is a 'headline' indicator of UK sustainable development (DETR, 1999). Corncrake (*Crex crex*) and corn bunting (*Miliaria calandra*) declines in grassland and arable habitats were especially marked in Scotland. Those, together with range contractions among other species with varied ecological requirements suggested a number of causal factors at work. Amongst those most commonly identified were the loss of nest sites, a switch from spring to autumn sowing with reduced winter seed availability, hedgerow removal, the shift from hay to silage production, conversion of rough grazing to improved grassland, the effects of pesticides and herbicides on food availability, and the possible effects of agricultural intensification on populations of small mammal prey.

Between 1994 and 1999, 12 out of 57 widespread breeding bird species showed a significant increase in abundance, nine showed a significant decrease, and 36 showed no significant change (Noble *et al.*, 2000). The population sizes of the majority of wintering wader and wildfowl species increased by 10 per cent or more between the 1960s and 1998 (Atkinson *et al.*, 2000). Geese increased markedly, having benefited from reduced persecution and improved feeding opportunities on agricultural grasslands (SNH, 2001h).

5.3.12 *Species diversity: mammals*

The Scottish populations of more than one third of 26 native land mammal species for which estimates have been made are thought to be in decline (Mammal Society, 1999). The red squirrel (*Sciurus vulgaris*) and water vole (*Arvicola terrestris*) have decreased in population and range size throughout Great Britain, and are consequently priority species for biodiversity action. Habitat loss and pollution are considered to be the commonest threats to mammals other than bats. Overgrazing has affected the mountain hare (*Lepus timidus*), pygmy shrew (*Sorex pygmaeus*) and field vole (*Microtus agrestis*), and stubble burning has affected the wood mouse (*Apodemus sylvaticus*).

5.3.13 *Species diversity: butterflies*

Of 28 butterfly species currently resident in Scotland, 16 are considered to be habitat 'generalists' or use habitats that are very widespread, and 12 are regarded as habitat 'specialists'. The geographic ranges of the majority of resident Scottish butterfly species appear to have been relatively stable (Asher *et al.*, 2001). However, 42 per cent of 'habitat specialists' contracted in range in recent decades, associated with the destruction or deterioration of their scarce habitats. None of the generalist species contracted and 31 per cent expanded northwards, benefiting from warmer weather conditions (see Usher, Chapter 18).

5.3.14 *Species diversity: plants*

Of 79 rare or endemic plant species with few Scottish populations prior to 1990, around 30 per cent had fewer and around 30 per cent had more populations when resurveyed in 1990-96 (SNH, 2001i).

Non-native vascular plants have become established throughout Scotland, but particularly in southern and central areas, reflecting their origins in parks and gardens, from which they have spread, for example, into woodlands (184 species), grasslands (301 species), upland habitats (15 species) and freshwater habitats (14 species). Most are thought not to have increased in range in recent decades, but of 58 that did expand between the 1950s and 1988, 31 are thought to have a medium or high adverse impact on native species (Welch *et al.*, 2001).

5.3.15 *Threatened wildlife*

Native species at risk is a 'core' indicator for reporting on Sustainable Development in the UK (DETR, 1999). Of 111 Scottish species given legal protection and for which trend information was available in 1997, 36 per cent were thought to be declining (SNH, 2001j). The 16 per cent of protected species that were thought to be increasing included the pine marten (*Martes martes*), which began its recovery before gaining statutory protection, and the European otter (*Lutra lutra*) and peregrine falcon (*Falco peregrinus*), which have benefited from tighter controls on water pollution and insecticide use.

Some successes have been achieved in re-establishing breeding populations of species that had become extinct in Scotland, such as the red kite (*Milvus milvus*) and the white-tailed eagle (*Haliaeetus albicilla*) (SNH, 1995). Raptors in general have benefited from tighter controls on insecticide use, but many continue to be suppressed by persecution (Scottish Executive, 2001c).

Priority habitats for conservation action under the Biodiversity Action Plan (DoE, 1994) are habitats for which the UK has international obligations; they are habitats at risk from high rates of decline or which are rare, habitats which may be functionally critical, and habitats which are important for priority species. Priority species are those which are globally threatened or which have declined by at least 50 per cent in the UK over the past 25 years (UK Biodiversity Steering Group, 1995). By 2001, there were action plans for some 45 habitats and 391 species in the UK. Of those, 41 habitats and 221 species either

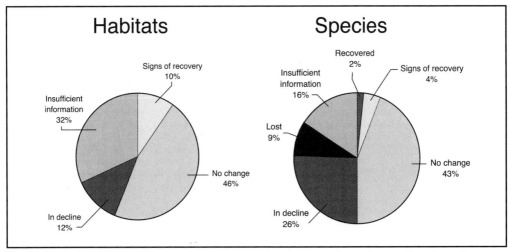

Figure 5.4. Biodiversity Action Plan priority habitats and species assessed in early 2001 (based on information in Jones *et al.* (2001)).

occur in, or have recently been lost from Scotland (Usher, 2000). A recent review by the Joint Nature Conservation Committee and the Scottish Biodiversity Group (Jones *et al.*, 2001) suggested that among the 41 BAP priority habitats occurring in Scotland, four had shown signs of recovery and five appeared to be declining. Of 186 BAP priority species assessed, three were thought to have recovered and eight showed signs of recovery. Some 47 species were thought still to be declining and 16 species had been lost from Scotland prior to the establishment of the BAP programme (Figure 5.4). Of 20 BAP priority bird species occurring in Scotland, at least 16 are considered unlikely to achieve their plan targets (Mackey *et al.*, 2001).

5.4 Overview of current trends in non-renewable and renewable stocks

Scotland's rich land resources are vital to both its biogeographical identity and its sustainable development. The latter can be considered in terms of fostering a healthy environment and vibrant rural economy, improving the quality of life in towns and the countryside, and ensuring Scotland's continued attractiveness for tourism and economic investment. Human welfare and livelihood, and the natural heritage, are intimately linked. Natural heritage trends reflect the complexity of the world around us, and the ways in which we interact with it. It gives people pleasure and opportunities for enjoyment.

The state of the natural heritage and the ways in which it is managed reflects changing economics and technological advance, societal preferences, policy objectives and legal obligations. The natural heritage will continue to evolve through land management and through factors outwith direct management control such as climate change. Sustainable responses to changing preferences and priorities should seek land-use solutions which

- maximise natural diversity and biogeographical distinctiveness;
- conserve and enhance ecosystem functions on land, in soils and within fresh waters; and
- take account of landscape character and the capacity of different landscape types to accommodate a changing balance or intensity of land use, for example from settlement and transport, energy generation and associated infrastructure, primary production and mining, or recreation.

There will be a continuing need to monitor such changes through time, to adapt policies to changing conditions, and to assess the effectiveness of actions aimed at the conservation and enhancement of the natural heritage.

5.5 Causes of future rural land use and environmental changes

5.5.1 Background and focus

We have chosen to focus here on possible changes in Scottish agriculture and their potential impacts over the next 25 years. Agriculture is used as a specific case study, partly because it is the predominant land use over 80 per cent of the country, and partly because changes in agriculture are known to have significant impacts on other natural resource stocks which include soils, species, habitats and landscapes. It is hoped that the framework we apply to the example of agriculture may be usefully applied to other change contexts, for example the extraction industries.

A number of conceptual frameworks have been developed for systematically identifying the drivers of environmental change. The most familiar is the Pressure-State-Response (PSR) framework and its variants. These have been largely developed and applied in the context of 'State of the Environment Reporting' (Stanners and Bourdeau, 1995). Recently, Geist and Lambin (2001) developed a similar framework, but one intended specifically for the systematic identification and description of the factors which drive land use change (i.e. an expansion of the 'pressure' component of the PSR framework). In their framework they distinguish between proximate and underlying drivers of change. Proximate causes are "near-final or final human activities that directly affect environment", whereas underlying causes are "the fundamental forces that underpin the more obvious or proximate causes". They see the proximate causes (e.g. agricultural changes) as operating at a local level, whilst the underlying ones operate both directly at the local level and indirectly from the national or international levels (e.g. cultural, policy, institutional, demographic, economic and technological factors). A key feature of their framework is the recognition of the importance of pre-disposing environmental factors (e.g. land characteristics and land tenure) as well as key trigger events (e.g. fires, pests and social disorder). Because Geist and Lambin's (2001) framework was developed from an analysis of case studies of land use change, we have used it here as the framework for identifying some of the main factors which might drive agricultural and related environmental change in rural Scotland over the next 25 years (Figure 5.5).

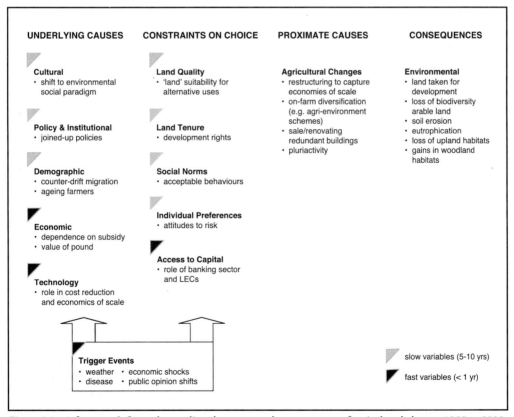

Figure 5.5. A framework for understanding the causes and consequences of agricultural change, 1980 to 2000.

5.5.2 *Underlying causes of change*

Cultural factors: A useful perspective on the cultural factors influencing environmental change (Dunlap and Van Liere, 1978, 1984) focuses on the concept of 'dominant social paradigms'. This refers to the existence within society of 'common values, beliefs and shared wisdom about the physical and social environment'. This is a general world-view that operates very broadly within society and 'forms the core of a society's cultural heritage'. During the period post-1945, the predominant social paradigm in the UK was one that reflected commitments to individualism, technology and growth - the technocentric paradigm. This broadly equates to the period during which productivist views of agriculture predominated and were reinforced by their policy and institutional settings.

It is hypothesised that this dominant social paradigm is reflected in the prevailing social trends and the ways in which the countryside is used (this broadly equates with the concept of a cultural landscape). Commitment to the technocentric paradigm in the period 1945-80 supported the development of a productivist agricultural landscape where machinery replaced labour in the arable farming areas and labour was also shed in the livestock farming areas. Both had effects on the environment and natural heritage through field amalgamations and eutrophication of soils and waters on the one hand, and reductions in grazing management inputs on the other (see section 5.3). Likewise, in the forestry sector the emphasis was on the expansion of the commercial softwoods principally through the planting of exotic species. This led directly to the loss of semi-natural habitats including remnant native woodlands and indirectly to both soil and water acidification (see section 5.2.2). Both were associated with continued rural depopulation and the loss of both human and social capital (e.g. loss of traditional skills, closure of rural schools). The outcome was a specialised productivist landscape where the agricultural and forestry elements were commonly spatially separated and the social and environmental consequences of intensification or extensification were generally ignored.

In the period post-1980, the growing awareness of environmental pollution and global change led to increasing social commitment to a new environmental paradigm (Dunlap and Van Liere, 1978) and a related interest in environmentally-friendly agricultural practices. However, it has to be noted that not all groups within society will subscribe to the prevailing world-view (Dunlap and Van Liere, 1984), and there are significant cohort effects. This is especially true within farming because of its long-term nature and traditions of inheritance.

If the commitment to an environmental world-view is inversely related to a person's age (Arcury and Christianson, 1990), then it is likely that this is a slowly changing variable, taking decades to change. Therefore it is likely that the environmental paradigm will remain as UK society's predominant world-view over the next 20 to 30 years. This will act to reinforce current public attitudes towards the environment, safe food and biosecurity. The countryside is likely to remain desirable on 'quality of life' grounds and pressure will remain on agricultural industry to produce safe food without damage to the environment.

Policy and institutional factors: If highly specialised productivist landscapes are the cultural landscapes of a time when commitment to the technocentric paradigm dominated UK society's world-view, then it follows that the developing commitment to the new environmental paradigm post-1980, both within UK society and the related European institutions, should be creating the elements of a new cultural landscape in Scotland. A direct indication is the proportion of Scotland that has now been formally designated as being of natural heritage interest and, more recently, the designation of National Parks. Likewise, within the Common Agricultural Policy, the emergence of specific agri-environment support schemes like the Environmentally Sensitive Area Scheme, the Countryside Premium Scheme and the new Rural Stewardship Scheme, all reflect similar environmental concerns.

The rural policy agenda is complicated at present by the multiplicity of institutions and the lack of a single identifiable rural policy (Ward, 2000). We are currently in a transitional phase, moving from a policy arena dominated by sectoral interests, to one where the focus is on 'joined-up policies'. Agriculture has lost its place as the principal economic concern, being replaced by concerns about service industries like tourism, about community support, and about the environment. It is likely that the move towards more integrated departments of Rural Affairs or Rural Development will continue. Increasingly the agenda will include issues of social equity and justice, concerning access to employment, housing, health and educational services. It is unlikely that existing planning policy (i.e. with its focus on development control) will change, although the role of planning may be extended to include other land uses (e.g. forestry), especially where they impinge on issues like water supply and waste disposal.

One critical issue is the extent to which the European Union (EU) can continue to support 'agriculture'. With further expansion of the Union, planned for 2005, imposing budgetary constraints, and with pressure being applied by the World Trade Organisation to reduce product support within the EU, further reform of the Common Agricultural Policy (CAP) is likely to mean a more rapid shift towards payments for environmental and social benefits and an overall decrease in the total public support. If this is the case, then there will be increasing pressure for Scottish farmers to produce at world prices and this will have significant structural effects with associated selective impacts on habitats and species. On the positive side, where it is uneconomic to continue farming, more land might be released into conservation management or be more extensively managed. On the negative side, current trends for field amalgamations and loss of landscape structure in areas with production advantages might be accelerated.

Demographic factors: The Scottish Rural Life Report (Scottish Office, 1992) and its subsequent update (Scottish Office, 1996) showed that the proportion of the population living in rural Scotland fell from 1801 to 1971. Since then it has been growing mainly as a result of in-migration, reflecting generally higher levels of mobility in UK society. For predominantly rural areas, out-migration appears to show a sharp rise in the 16 to 20 age group (leaving for employment or education) whereas in-migration is dominated by the 20 to 40 age group and those of retirement age. These patterns indicate a growing but ageing population. Many of the in-migrants originate from other parts of the UK. In five of the then Scottish Districts (Berwickshire; Annandale and Eskdale; Stewartry; Badenoch and Strathspey; and Kincardine and Deeside), the 1991 Census of Population indicated that between 20 and 30 per cent of the residents had been born outside Scotland. These patterns reflect areas with rising employment and/or those that are scenically attractive and also attractive in terms of access to services (e.g. Skye and Lochalsh, Badenoch and Strathspey, and the Borders districts). These trend data indicate that the social composition of the rural population is changing in relation to the lifestyle choices of both the 20 to 40 age group and those of retirement age. Both this and the longer-term demographic evidence accords with the view of a shift in the predominant social paradigm. The countryside is now seen as a place of service provision and consumption (e.g. of amenity) rather than production. Ironically those electing to move into rural areas are most likely to be committed to the environmental paradigm whereas the existing farming community in these areas is most likely, given an average age of over 55, to be committed to the technocentric paradigm.

With the national population falling, and an ageing demographic structure, it is likely that the trend for in-migration to rural Scotland will increase over the next 25 years, particularly through retirement. It is likely that this will reinforce the current patterns of rural population growth, and demands for housing, in those areas with high scenic amenity and access to local services. In areas without these attractions, particularly those with currently high dependencies on primary sector employment, there are likely to be net losses of population. The human and social capital of rural Scotland will continue to change or continue to be lost. Land management skills associated with agriculture will be replaced by an increasing number of conservation managers.

Global environmental change: The forecast impacts of global climate change vary considerably within Scotland (Scottish Executive, 2001b). A longer growing season should promote higher output and perhaps the introduction of new production crops. However, these advantages may be offset to different degrees, depending on location, due to more variable and intense rainfall, increased risks of both floods and droughts, abundance of pests, and damaging wind events. Climate predictions suggest that there will be increasing divergence between the resulting agricultural and land management practices of the western and eastern zones.

Economic factors: Whilst UK economic policy may continue to focus on the control of inflationary pressures, much will depend on the strength of the currency. This particularly affects access to international markets for food products and the viability of the Scottish tourist industry. If it is assumed that the UK joins the euro zone, and the pound weakens in value, then the terms of trade for Scottish agriculture, forestry and tourism will all improve. However, much will also depend on global economic cycles. It is clear that fluctuations in exchange rates have a major controlling effect on the viability of many of the economic enterprises in rural Scotland and these feed through to environmental changes.

Technological factors: The machinery, breeding and chemical technologies of farming have developed rapidly throughout the period since 1945. If we assume that the demand and prices for food and fibre products will remain relatively static over the next 25 years, but costs of inputs, particularly labour, continue to rise, then profitability can only be maintained by reducing costs. There are a number of ways of doing this. These include improving use-efficiencies (as in precision agriculture methods or through biotechnology), sharing capital equipment (through machinery rings or contracting), and increasing the economies of scale through expansion. Some of these technological improvements have very clear environmental benefits, for example the use of precision farming methods and integrated pest control. Others are much more problematic. Larger machines require bigger fields, and bigger units farmed with larger machines sometimes mean that field operations are carried out at sub-optimal times that may exacerbate problems like soil erosion or nutrient losses. Other problematic technical innovations include the further development of genetically modified crops and livestock. These may continue to meet with strong consumer opposition on both environmental and biosecurity grounds.

5.5.3 *Proximate causes of environmental change: agricultural change*

These underlying drivers of change set the context for present and future changes in Scottish agriculture. These are well summarised both by the Scottish Executive (2001a) and by an Aberdeen Research Consortium report (University of Aberdeen and Macaulay Land Use Research Institute, 2001). Accordingly they are only briefly summarised here.

Against a background of declining economic importance (4 per cent of gross domestic product (GDP) in 1973 to 1.4 per cent GDP in 1998), declining employment importance, increasing average age and increasing dependence on public subsidy support, one of the major features to emerge is that the larger farming businesses are gradually becoming 'de-linked' from their local surroundings. The Aberdeen Research Consortium report points out that "the drive towards ever more efficient production processes and higher levels of output has meant that farmers are increasingly dependent on distant markets for both their inputs and outputs and, more recently, labour" (p.10). The report also points out that there is a countervailing trend with other farm businesses, where new types of linkages are being developed (e.g. non-food land based activities and off-farm pluriactivity). Over the period 1990 to 2000 there has been an increase in the proportion of pluriactive farm households from 60 per cent to 77 per cent.

In common with many other agricultural regions in Europe, these changes continue to be accompanied by structural changes through amalgamations, or increasing farm area through renting land. This is leading to the creation of a dualistic structure in Scottish farming. On the one hand, there are farm businesses that are capital intensive, technology-based, focusing on production for specific markets (e.g. supermarkets), or vertically integrated to provide opportunities for value-added products. On the other hand, there is an increasing number of farmers who are part-time and depend upon both farming and other employment for their income. Even at present we are unclear about the effect of this dualistic structure in terms of associated environmental impacts, and more research is needed. We are also uncertain about its effect in the future given that it is likely to involve a different cohort of farmers. It is conceivable that pluriactivity will enable the smaller family-farm units to persist, and this may have beneficial effects in terms of maintenance of habitat structure and diversity. Farmers on these small units may also be more willing to adopt agri-environment or farm woodland support measures since these afford some medium term security in income. On the other hand, such farmers could also be more inclined to rent out some or all of their land, effectively enabling their neighbours to increase the scale of their operations. This might lead to the same negative environmental effects in terms of habitat and species losses. It is an interesting question whether farmers renting land are more or less inclined to adhere to best environmental management practice. This leads into a wider consideration of the impact of ownership and tenurial arrangements in relation to future agricultural changes in Scotland.

5.5.4 *Constraints on land use change: land ownership and land tenure*

Two further factors have a profound influence on environmental change in much of rural Scotland. These are the concentrated pattern of land ownership and land tenure arrangements. Whereas there are some 33,000 main agricultural holdings in Scotland of more than 1 ha, and an additional 17,685 registered crofts, covering around 75 per cent of the land area (Egdell, 1999), it has to be acknowledged that much of rural Scotland is not owned by farmers but is instead managed by tenant farmers or crofters. Throughout the nineteenth century over 90 per cent of Scotland was owned by around 1,500 landowners. This remarkable concentration of land ownership was reduced through the twentieth century, principally through major state interventions in the land market (e.g. by the Forestry Commission, Department of Agriculture and Fisheries for Scotland and Ministry of Defence). Nonetheless, by 1970 over 64 per cent of the country was still held by just over 1,700 owners, with just 17 owners accounting for 10 per cent of the land (Wightman, 1996).

The environmental, social and economic consequences of the highly concentrated pattern of land ownership in rural Scotland remains a contentious subject and lies at the heart of the ongoing debate on land reform. Many of the large estates in the Highlands and Islands have been traditionally managed as sporting estates with farming or secure crofting tenancies. Others are managed 'in hand' and combine farming, forestry, recreational and other enterprises. Estates have also been purchased by 'not for profit' organisations like the National Trust for Scotland, the Royal Society for the Protection of Birds and the John Muir Trust, principally for conservation purposes. Management objectives vary from estate to estate, and between different areas of Scotland. With so few landowners it is not sensible to generalise, other than to say that management styles are highly individualistic and tend to change dramatically from one owner to the next (MacGregor, 1994).

While high turnover of estate owners in some areas, and the pre-eminence of individual interests, exposes both land and people to inconsistency in long-term management objectives, the effects are localised and highly variable. More universal effects are found in the nature of agricultural tenancies themselves. Some 35 per cent of Scottish farms are worked under agreements (Wightman, 1996) which limit the scope of the tenant's property rights and therefore their management options. The most obvious example concerns woodlands; if a tenant farmer plants a tree it is not owned by him or her but by the landowner. Less obvious examples concern restrictions on the use of farm buildings that might, for example, exclude the running of a tourist enterprise. Land reform proposals, that affect farming tenancies and the rights of tenant farmers to buy, could have far reaching implications for future environmental as well as socio-economic changes in rural Scotland. Here the interplay between government policies on land reform, agriculture and the environment is difficult to forecast. The evidence from the twentieth century is that remarkably little has happened in terms of redistribution of land ownership, and on this basis it would be somewhat reckless to predict radical changes in the next 25 years. However, radical changes may still occur in relation to particular trigger events.

5.5.5 *Trigger events*

The role of particular events in triggering change must not be underestimated. One of the ideas proposed by Holling (1995) is that slowly changing variables, for example an ageing population of farmers or gradual climate shifts, interact with rapidly changing event variables (such as the 2001 foot and mouth disease outbreak in the UK) to cause in some situations very rapid and profound changes in the whole socio-ecosystem. Whilst trigger events are hard to predict accurately, it may be argued that some characteristics predispose a system to rapid change. This predisposition is related to the concepts of risk and resilience and together these provide a valuable way of assessing exposure to change. Increasing dependency on public funding support, the emergence of near monopolies (e.g. in the dairy sector and in certain areas of the processing chain), and the pre-eminence of big supermarkets as buyers, are all indicative of a system that is becoming less diverse, with less redundancy and less resilience.

Recent challenges to Scottish agriculture include disease (bovine spongiform encephalopathy, foot and mouth disease and *E. coli* 0157), poor terms of trade due to the strong pound, and falling subsidy support through shifts in EU policy to rural development. Collectively these represent a major challenge to the technocentric paradigm. Further, a survey by Lloyds TSB Scotland, reported in *Scotland on Sunday* on 14 May 2000, indicated that by 2005 the number of working farms in Scotland would fall by a further 8 per cent, and that over half of those that remained (52 per cent) will have no successors in place. Taken together, these economic and demographic changes indicate that the Scottish countryside is entering a period of unprecedented changes in both its societal context, and in the ways that it will be owned and managed.

5.6 The geography of future agricultural and related environmental changes in rural Scotland

It is evident that Scottish agriculture is increasingly exposed to rapid changes as a result of external shocks: these may be financial (e.g. in relation to currency fluctuations or rapid change in subsidy regimes), legislative (e.g. changes in the conditions of agricultural tenancy agreements, biosecurity legislation, pollution control) or environmental (e.g. weather or disease). This exposure to change is not spread uniformly across Scotland. As broad generalisations the three following statements may hold true.

First, in areas with production advantages, for example the eastern coastal lowlands, smaller units will become increasingly uneconomic. Although some farmers will adopt a pluriactive strategy and continue farming on a part-time basis, generally the outcome will be farm amalgamations resulting in fewer and larger agricultural units operating on a capital-intensive basis (i.e. highly dependent on large machines and contract labour). The environmental consequences are likely to continue the pattern of association between productivist agriculture and environmental disbenefits, including loss of landscape and habitat diversity and structure, and increased risk of soil erosion and nutrient enrichment. Both legislation, for example the Nitrates Directive, and new forms of delivering agri-environment support, possibly through Land Management Contracts, will be critical to mitigating these impacts.

Second, in areas with environmental advantages, that may either be within the metropolitan travel-to-work areas or in areas with both high scenic amenity and access to services (e.g. Skye and Lochalsh, Badenoch and Strathspey, and parts of the Borders) there will be less pressure for structural changes. This is due to several factors, such as the possible focus of agri-environmental support payments through shifts from headage to area-based payments, the opportunities for on-farm diversification and non-farm employment, a buoyant market for small farms in response to in-migrant lifestyle choices, a market for high conservation value land through purchases by conservation and amenity trusts, and a trend for 'new' estate owners to commit to environmental objectives. Taken together, these will reinforce the existing trend for these areas to be managed primarily for environment and natural heritage objectives.

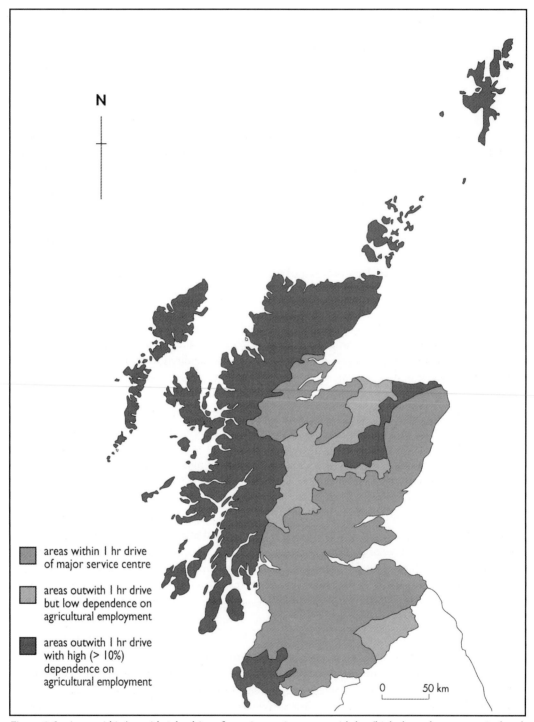

N

areas within 1 hr drive
of major service centre

areas outwith 1 hr drive
but low dependence on
agricultural employment

areas outwith 1 hr drive
with high (> 10%)
dependence on
agricultural employment

0   50 km

Figure 5.6. Areas within/outwith 1 hr drive of a major service centre with low/high dependency on agricultural employment.

Third, the most problematic areas are those with neither production nor environmental advantages, the so-called 'middle countryside'. These are areas outside the metropolitan travel-to-work areas, with relatively poorer access to services (e.g. health, education), and which may currently have a high dependency on the agricultural sector for employment. These fragile areas (Copus *et al.*, 1998) include parts of Banff and Buchan, Caithness, Orkney, Shetland, the Outer and Inner Hebrides, the west coast peninsulas and parts of Dumfries and Galloway. In some of these areas, surplus agricultural land has previously been converted to commercial forestry. Under current forestry policy, many of the more suitable areas will qualify under existing farm woodland schemes. In areas where this is not appropriate, it is likely that surplus agricultural land will result in the adoption of more extensive forms of land management, and there is considerable opportunity for environmental gains. However, these have to be counter-balanced with inevitable socio-economic losses.

Figure 5.6 provides an illustration of the potential patterns of change based on accessibility and dependency on agricultural employment. Clearly the actual geography of the changes will be more complex and involve many of the individual farmer's or land owner's behaviours discussed above. The patterns we forecast represent less of a 'sea change" in the countryside of Scotland and more a continuation of long established trends in increased mechanisation, declining agricultural employment and continued farm structural adjustment. Nonetheless, the geographic impacts of these changes suggest that we are continuing along a trajectory of an even more specialised countryside than we have at the moment - with arable production being the imperative in the eastern lowlands, intensive livestock production in parts of the west and south, and the environment and natural heritage being the imperatives elsewhere. As a consequence, the negative and positive impacts associated with these changes will also be geographically separated.

The above forecast does not provide a vision of Scotland's rural landscapes of 2025 being environmentally sustainable everywhere. Whilst at an all-Scotland level we may well be judged as moving towards environmental sustainability in relation to agricultural land use, it is clear that we will appear to be making trade-offs between different areas. We suspect that these trade-offs will be made implicitly rather than explicitly. However, the question is whether we want to deliver environmental benefits in all places or whether we are prepared to continue to trade-off environmental gains in one place with environmental losses in another. If the former, then the key issue is how best to adapt legislation and incentives to enable us to shift on to this change pathway rather than the one we have outlined here. The key challenge appears to be achieving environmentally sustainable land management in areas with intensive arable or livestock farming.

Acknowledgements
The authors would like to thank the following individuals who contributed to this chapter either through provision of data, helpful discussions or constructive comments on the text: Dr Inge Aalders, Dr Jenny Bellamy, Dr Rob Burton, Mr Andy Dalziel, Mr Alistair Geddes, Mr Rob Morris, Dr Scot Mathieson, Dr Deb Roberts, Prof Mark Shucksmith, Mr Alan Sibbald, Dr Ute Skiba, Prof Ken Thomson, Mr Willie Towers and Dr Paula Woolgar. The authors would also like to acknowledge the constructive comments provided by two anonymous referees. While the views expressed remain those of the authors, they are

pleased to acknowledge that much of the work reported here was funded by the Scottish Environment Protection Agency, Scottish Natural Heritage and the Scottish Executive Environment and Rural Affairs Department.

References

Arcury, T.A. and Christianson, E.H. (1990). Environmental worldview in response to environmental problems: Kentucky 1984 and 1988 compared. *Environment and Behaviour*, **22**, 387-407.

Ash Consulting Group (1998). A96 Aberdeen–Inverness tranquil areas study. Unpublished report.

Asher, J., Warren, M., Fox, R., Harding, P., Jeffcoate, G. and Jeffcoate, S. (2001). *The Millennium Atlas of Butterflies in Britain and Ireland*. Oxford University Press, Oxford.

Atkinson, P.W., Austin, G.E., Burton, N.H.K., Musgrove, A.J., Pollitt, M. and Rehfisch, M.M. (2000). WeBS Alerts 1998/99: changes in numbers of wintering waterbirds in the United Kingdom at national, county and Special Protection Area (SPA) scales. British Trust for Ornithology Research Report No. 239.

Baddeley, J.A., Thompson, D.B.A. and Lee, J.A. (1994). Regional and historical variation in the nitrogen content of *Racomitrium lanuginosum* in Britain in relation to atmospheric nitrogen deposition. *Environmental Pollution*, **84**, 189-196.

Billet, M.F., Fitzpatrick, E.A. and Cresser, M.S. (1988). Long term changes in the acidity of forest soils in North East Scotland. *Soil Use and Management*, **4**, 102-106.

Bracewell, J.M., Hepburn, A. and Thomson, C. (1993). Levels and distribution of polychlorinated biphenyls on the Scottish land mass. *Chemosphere*, **27**, 1657-1667.

Bullock, P. and Thompson, T.R.E. (1996). Towards a strategy for the sustainability of the soil resources of the UK. In *Soils, Sustainability and the Natural Heritage*, ed. by A.G. Taylor, J.E. Gordon and M.B. Usher. HMSO, Edinburgh. pp. 281-294.

Copus, A.K., Gourlay, D., Chapman, P. and Shucksmith M. (1998). *Small Area Data Sources for Socio-Economic Typologies of Rural Scotland*. Scottish Office Central Research Unit, Edinburgh.

Creaser, C.S., Fernandes, A.R., Harrrad, S.J. and Cox, E.A. (1990). Levels and sources of PCDDs and PCDFs in urban British soils. *Chemosphere*, **21**, 931-938.

David Tyldesley and Associates (1999). Landscape character vignettes. Unpublished report.

Davidson, D.A. and Grieve, I.C. (2001). Trends in soil erosion. Unpublished report.

Davidson, D.A. and Smout T.C. (1996). Soil change in Scotland: the legacy of past land improvement processes. In *Soils, Sustainability and the Natural Heritage*, ed. by A.G. Taylor, J.E. Gordon and M.B. Usher. HMSO, Edinburgh. pp. 44-54.

Department of the Environment (1994). *Biodiversity: The UK Acton Plan*. HMSO, London.

Department of the Environment, Transport and the Regions (1999). *Quality of Life Counts: Indicators for a Strategy for Sustainable Development for the United Kingdom. A Baseline Assessment*. DETR, London.

Dobbie, K.E. and Smith K.A. (1996). Comparison of CH_4 oxidation rates in woodland, arable and set aside on the rate of methane uptake by surface soils in Northern Europe. *Atmospheric Environment*, **30**, 1005-1011.

Duarte-Davidson, R., Sewart, A., Alcock, R.E., Cousins, I.T. and Jones, K.C. (1997). Exploring the balance between sources, deposition and the environmental burden of PCDD/Fs in the UK terrestrial environment: an aid to identifying uncertainties and research needs. *Environmental Science and Technology*, **31**, 1-11.

Dunlap, R.E. and Van Liere, K.D. (1978). The new environmental paradigm. *Journal of Environmental Education*, **9**, 10-19.

Dunlap, R.E. and Van Liere, K.D. (1984). Commitment to the dominant social paradigm and concern for environmental quality. *Social Science Quarterly*, **65**, 1013-1028.

Edwards, A.C. and Withers, P.J.A. (1998). Soil phosphorus management and water quality: a UK perspective. *Soil Use and Management*, **14**, 124-130.

Egdell, J.M. (1999). *Agriculture and the Environment. Scottish Environment Audits No. 2.* Scottish Wildlife and Countryside Link, Perth.

European Geophysical Society (1998). *Hydrology and Earth System Sciences, Special Issue: The DYNAMO Project*, 375-577.

Fowler, D., Hargreaves, K., Skiba, U. and Bower, K. (2000). Direct measurement of the UK source strength of radiatively trace gases. Department of the Environment, Transport and the Regions, London.

FPD Savills (2001). Trends in agricultural land use in Scotland. Unpublished report.

Fuller, R.J. and Gough, S.J. (1999). Changes in sheep numbers in Britain: implications for bird populations. *Biological Conservation*, **91**, 73-89.

Geist, H.J. and Lambin, E.F. (2001). What Drives Tropical Deforestation? A Meta-analysis of Proximate and Underlying Causes of Deforestation Based on Subnational Case Study Evidence. LUCC International Project Office, University of Louvain, Louvain.

Gendebien, A., Carlton-Smith, C., Izzo, M. and Hall J.E. (1999). UK sewage sludge survey. Environment Agency R&D Technical Report P165.

Grieve, I.C. and Hipkin, J.A. (1996). Soil erosion and sustainability. In *Soils, Sustainability and the Natural Heritage*, ed. by A. Taylor, J.E. Gordon and M.B. Usher. HMSO, Edinburgh. pp. 236-248.

Grieve, I.C., Davidson, D.A. and Gordon, J.E. (1995). Nature, extent and severity of soil erosion in upland Scotland. *Land Degradation and Rehabilitation*, **6**, 41-55.

Haines-Young, R.H., Barr, C.J., Black, H.I.J., Briggs, D.J., Bunce, R.G.H., Clarke, R.T., Cooper, A., Dawson, F.H., Firbank, L.G., Fuller, R.M., Furse, M.T., Gillespie, M.K., Hill, R., Hornung, M., Howard, D.C., McCann, T., Morecroft, M.D., Petit, S., Sier, A.R.J., Smart, S.M., Smith, G.M., Stott, A.P., Stuart, R.C. and Watkins, J.W. (2000). *Accounting for Nature: Assessing Habitats in the UK Countryside*. Department of the Environment, Transport and the Regions, London.

Harding, N.J., Green, R.E. and Summers, R.W. (1994). *The Effects of Future Changes in Land Use on Upland Birds in Britain*. Royal Society for the Protection of Birds, Edinburgh.

Harrad, S.J. and Jones, K.C. (1992). A source inventory and budget for chlorinated dioxins and furans in the United Kingdom environment. *The Science of the Total Environment*, **126**, 89-107.

Harrad, S.J., Stewart, A.P., Alcock, R., Boumphrey, R., Burnett, V., Duarte-Davidson, R., Halsall, C., Sanders, G., Waterhouse, K., Wild, S.R. and Jones, K.C. (1994). Polychlorinated biphenyls (PCBs) in the British environment: sinks, sources and temporal trends. *Environmental Pollution*, **85**, 131-146.

Hartley, S.E. (1997). The effects of grazing and nutrient inputs on grass-heather competition. *Botanical Journal of Scotland*, **49**, 315-324.

Hird, A.B., Rimmer, D.L. and Livens, F.R. (1996). Factors affecting the sorption and fixation of caesium in acid and organic soils. *European Journal of Soil Science*, **36**, 1-34.

Holling, C.S. (1995). What barriers? What bridges? In *Barriers and Bridges to the Renewal of Ecosystems and Institutions*, ed. by L.H. Gunderson, C.S. Holling and S.S. Light. Columbia University Press, New York. pp. 3-34.

Jackson, D.L. (2000). Guidance on the interpretation of the biodiversity broad habitat classification (terrestrial and freshwater types): definitions and the relationship with other habitat classifications. Joint Nature Conservation Committee Report No. 307.

Jones, A., Bain, C., Easton, C. and Ramsey, J. (2001). Report of working group into analysis of lead partner reporting. Unpublished report.

Landrock, J., Hawkins, J., Simcox, H., Smolka, Z. and Kelly, F. (eds.) (2001). *Key Scottish Environment Statistics*. Scottish Executive, Edinburgh.

Lead, W.A., Steinnes, E., Bacon, J.R. and Jones, K.C. (1997). PCBs in UK and Norwegian soils. Spatial and temporal trends. *Science of the Total Environment*, **193**, 229-236.

Lindsay, R.A., Charman, D.J., Everingham, F., O'Reilly, R.M., Palmer, M.A., Rowell, T.A. and Stroud, D.A. (1988). *The Flow Country: the Peatlands of Caithness and Sutherland.* Nature Conservancy Council, Peterborough.

Lindsay, R.A. and Immirzi, C.P. (1996). An inventory of lowland raised peat bogs in Great Britain. Scottish Natural Heritage Research, Survey and Monitoring Report No. 78.

Loveland, P.J. and Thompson, T.R.E. (eds) (2001). Identification and development of a set of national indicators of soil quality. Environment Agency R&D report P5-053/2/TR.

MacGregor, B.D. (1994). Owner motivation and land use change in north west Sutherland. Unpublished report.

Mackey, E.C., Shaw, P., Holbrook, J., Shewry, M.C., Saunders, G., Hall, J. and Ellis, N. (2001). *Natural Heritage Trends: Scotland 2001.* Scottish Natural Heritage, Perth.

Mackey, E.C., Shewry, M.C. and Tudor, G.J. (1998*). Land Cover Change: Scotland from the 1940s to the 1980s.* The Stationery Office, Edinburgh.

MAFF, Fertiliser Manufactures Association and the Scottish Office (1998). *The British Survey of Fertiliser Practice 1997.* The Stationery Office, London.

Mammal Society (1999). *The State of British Mammals.* The Mammal Society, London.

McGowan, G.M., Palmer, S.C.F., French, D.D., Barr, C.J., Howard, D.C. and Smart, S.M. (2001). Trends in broad habitats: Scotland 1990-1998. Unpublished report.

Milne, J.A., Birch, C.P.D., Hester, A.J., Armstrong, H.M. and Robertson, A. (1998). The impact of vertebrate herbivores on the natural heritage of the Scottish Uplands - a review. Scottish Natural Heritage Review No. 95.

Milne, R. (1998). Land use change and forestry atmospheric CO_2 emissions and removals UK and Scotland. In *A Climate Change Mitigation Strategy for Scotland, Workshop Report*, ed. by ESRC Global Environmental Change Programme. The Scottish Office, Edinburgh. pp. 6-7.

Noble, D.G., Bashford, R.I. and Baillie, S.R. (2000). The Breeding Birds Survey 1999. British Trust for Ornithology Research Report No. 247.

Paterson, E. (1999). Contents of organic matter and potentially toxic elements in the mineral soils of Scotland. Unpublished report.

Paterson, E. (2000). Development of a framework for soil monitoring for state of the natural heritage reporting. Unpublished report.

Pesticides in the Environment Working Group (2000). *Monitoring of Pesticides in the Environment.* Environment Agency, Bristol.

Puri, G., Willison, T. and Woolgar, P. (1999). The sustainable use of soil. In *Earth Science and the Natural Heritage: Interactions and Integrated Management,* ed. by J.E. Gordon and K.F. Leys. The Stationery Office, Edinburgh. pp. 190-196.

Rich, T.C.G. and Woodruff, E.R. (1996). Changes in the vascular plant floras of England and Scotland between 1930-1960 and 1987-1988: the BSBI monitoring scheme. *Biological Conservation*, **75**, 217-229.

Ritchie, W. (1999). The environmental impact of changing uses on the North Sea littoral of Scotland. In *Denmark and Scotland: the Cultural and Environmental Resources of Small Nations,* ed. by G. Fellows-Jensen. Royal Danish Academy of Sciences and Letters, Copenhagen. pp.103-122.

Ritchie, W. and McLean, L. (1988). UK. Scotland. In *Artificial Structures and Shorelines*, ed. by H.J. Walker. Kluwer, Dordrecht. pp. 127-135.

Royal Commission on the Ancient and Historical Monuments of Scotland (1994). *South-east Perth: an Archaeological Landscape*. HMSO, Edinburgh.

Royal Commission on the Ancient and Historical Monuments of Scotland (1997). *Eastern Dumfriesshire: an Archaeological Landscape*. The Stationery Office, Edinburgh.

Royal Commission on Environmental Pollution (1996). *19th Report: Sustainable Use of Soil*. HMSO, London.

Royal Society for the Protection of Birds and Scottish Crofters Union (1992). *Crofting and the Environment: A New Approach*. RSPB, Edinburgh.

Sankey, S. (1999). The Scottish Coastal Forum: an independent advisory body to government. In *Scotland's Living Coastline*, ed. by J.M. Baxter, K. Duncan, S.M. Atkins and G. Lees. The Stationery Office, London. pp. 123-131.

Scotland and Northern Ireland Forum for Environmental Research (1999). *A User's Guide to Research on Application of Organic Wastes to Land*. Report SR4624/3.

Scottish Environment Protection Agency (1999). *National Waste Strategy: Scotland*. SEPA, Stirling.

Scottish Environment Protection Agency (2001). *State of the Environment: Soil Quality Report*. SEPA, Stirling.

Scottish Executive (2000a). *Statistical Bulletin Environment Series: Scottish Vacant and Derelict Land Survey 1999*. Government Statistical Service, Edinburgh.

Scottish Executive (2000b). *Scottish Climate Change Programme Consultation*. The Stationery Office, Edinburgh.

Scottish Executive (2000c). *The Rural Stewardship Scheme*. The Stationery Office, Edinburgh.

Scottish Executive (2001a). *A Forward Strategy for Scottish Agriculture: a Discussion Document*. Scottish Executive Environment and Rural Affairs Department, Edinburgh.

Scottish Executive (2001b). *An Exploration of Regional Climate Change Scenarios for Scotland*. Central Research Unit, Edinburgh.

Scottish Executive (2001c). *The Nature of Scotland: a Policy Statement*. Scottish Executive, Edinburgh.

Scottish Natural Heritage (1995). *Species Action Programme*. Scottish Natural Heritage, Perth.

Scottish Natural Heritage (1997). *Coasts: Scotland's Living Landscapes*. Scottish Natural Heritage, Perth.

Scottish Natural Heritage (2001a). Natural heritage trends: land cover 1947-1988. Semi-natural habitats. Information & Advisory Note No. 124.

Scottish Natural Heritage (2001b). Natural heritage trends: land cover 1947-1988. Forests and woodlands. Information & Advisory Note No. 125.

Scottish Natural Heritage (2001c). Natural heritage trends: forest and woodland. Native woodland. Information & Advisory Note No. 139.

Scottish Natural Heritage (2001d). Natural heritage trends: land cover 1947-1988. Enclosed farmland. Information & Advisory Note No. 126.

Scottish Natural Heritage (2001e). Natural heritage trends: land cover 1947-1988. Mountain, moor and heath. Information & Advisory Note No. 127.

Scottish Natural Heritage (2001f). Natural heritage trends: land cover 1947-1988. Developed habitats. Information & Advisory Note No. 128.

Scottish Natural Heritage (2001g). Natural heritage trends: species diversity. Breeding bird species. Information & Advisory Note No. 133.

Scottish Natural Heritage (2001h). Natural heritage trends: species diversity. Wintering bird species. Information & Advisory Note No. 134.

Scottish Natural Heritage (2001i). Natural heritage trends: species diversity. Plant species. Information &

Advisory Note No. 130.

Scottish Natural Heritage (2001j). Natural heritage trends: species diversity. Species given legal protection. Information & Advisory Note No. 136.

Scottish Office (1992). *Scottish Rural Life: a Socio-economic Profile of Rural Scotland.* Scottish Office Central Research Unit, Edinburgh.

Scottish Office (1996). *Scottish Rural Life Update: a Revised Socio-economic Profile of Rural Scotland.* HMSO, Edinburgh.

Scottish Office (1998). *The Scottish Environment Statistics.* Government Statistical Service, Edinburgh.

Skiba, U., Cresser, M.S., Derwent, R.G. and Futty, D.W. (1989). Peat acidification in Scotland. *Nature,* **337,** 68-69.

Skiba, U., Sheppard, L.J., Pitcairn, C.E.R., Leith, I., Crossley, A., Van Dijk, S., Kennedy, V.H. and Fowler, D. (1998). Soil nitrous oxide and nitric oxide emissions as indicators of elevated atmospheric N deposition rates in semi-natural ecosystems. *Environmental Pollution,* **102,** 457-461.

Staines, B.W., Balharry, R. and Welch, D. (1995). The impact of red deer and their management on the natural heritage in the uplands. In *Heaths and Moorland - Cultural Landscapes,* ed. by D.B.A. Thompson, A.J. Hester and M.B. Usher. HMSO, Edinburgh. pp. 294-308.

Stanners, D. and Bordeau, P. (eds) (1995). *Europe's Environment: the Dobris Assessment.* European Environment Agency, Copenhagen.

Stroud, D.A., Reed, T.M., Pienkowski, M.W. and Lindsay, R.A. (1987). *Birds, Bogs and Forestry: the Peatlands of Caithness and Sutherland.* Nature Conservancy Council, Peterborough.

Taylor, A. (ed.) (1995). Environmental problems associated with soil in Britain: a review. Scottish Natural Heritage Review No. 55.

Thompson, D.B.A., Hester, A.J. and Usher, M.B. (eds) (1995a). *Heaths and Moorland: Cultural Landscapes.* HMSO, Edinburgh.

Thompson, D.B.A., MacDonald, A.J., Marsden, J.H. and Galbraith, C.A. (1995b). Upland heather moorland in Great Britain: a review of international importance, vegetation change and some objectives for nature conservation. *Biological Conservation,* **71,** 163-178.

Tunney, H., Breeuwsma, A., Withers, P.J.A. and Ehlert, P.A.I. (1997). Phosphorus fertiliser strategies: present and future. In *Phosphorus Loss from Soil to Water,* ed. by H. Tunney, O.T. Carton, P.C. Brookes and A.E. Johnston. CAB International, Wallingford. pp. 177-203.

UK Biodiversity Steering Group (1995). *Biodiversity: the UK Steering Group Report. Volume 2: Action Plans.* HMSO, London.

University of Aberdeen and Macaulay Land Use Research Institute (2001). *Agriculture's Contribution to Scottish Society, Economy and Environment: A Literature Review for the Scottish Executive Rural Affairs Department and CRU.* Scottish Executive, Edinburgh.

Usher, M.B. (1996). The soil ecosystem and sustainability. In *Soils, Sustainability and the Natural Heritage,* ed. by A.G. Taylor, J.E. Gordon and M.B. Usher. HMSO, Edinburgh. pp. 22-43.

Usher, M.B. (1999). Scotland's coastal biodiversity: what, where and when? In *Scotland's Living Coastline,* ed. by J.M. Baxter, K. Duncan, S.M. Atkins and G. Lees. The Stationery Office, London. pp. 173-189.

Usher, M.B. (ed.) (2000). *Action for Scotland's Biodiversity.* Scottish Executive, Edinburgh.

Ward, N. (2000). Actors, institutions and attitudes to rural development: the UK national report: Research Report to the World-Wide Fund for Nature and the Statutory Countryside Agencies of Great Britain. Unpublished report.

Watson, A. and Lance, A.N. (1984). Ecological aspects of game shooting and upland conservation. *ECOS,* **5,** 2-7.

Welch, D., Carss, D.N., Gornall, J., Manchester, S.J., Marquiss, M., Preston, C.D., Telfer, M.G., Arnold, H. and Holbrook, J. (2001). An audit of alien species in Scotland. Scottish Natural Heritage Review No. 139.

Wightman, A. (1996). *Who Owns Scotland*. Canongate, Edinburgh.

Wild, S.R. and Jones, K.V.K. (1995). PAHs in the UK environment: a preliminary source inventory and budget. *Environmental Pollution*, **88**, 91-108.

Woolgrave, C.E. and Woodin, S.J. (1996a). Current and historical relationships between the tissue nitrogen content of a snowbed bryophyte and nitrogenous air pollution. *Environmental Pollution*, **91**, 283-288.

Woolgrave, C.E. and Woodin, S.J. (1996b). Effects of pollutants in snowmelt on *Kiaeria starkei*, a characteristic species of late snowbed bryophyte dominated vegetation. *New Phytology*, **133**, 519-529.

6 NON-NATIVE SPECIES IN SCOTLAND

Julian Holbrook and Jeanette Hall

Summary

1.   There are at least 988 terrestrial and freshwater non-native species in Scotland. Vascular plants made up nearly 80 per cent of all species listed.

2.   Only 155 species have become naturalised (self maintaining). About 80 species may be considered problematic.

3.   Non-native species occur in all of the main habitat types, but the greatest number of species are found in man-made, urban and woodland habitats.

4.   Control programmes exist only for a small number of non-native species.

6.1 Non-native species

Non-native species are those introduced to a place either deliberately or accidentally by humans (see Table 6.1). Non-native species are also referred to as 'introduced' or 'alien' species. Some have major effects on the natural heritage and may also have economic costs and land use implications. Increased trade, travel and the development of new crops are increasing the chances of more species being introduced. Climate change may lead to the arrival of new species as their ranges adapt to altered climatic conditions.   Greater understanding of the number of non-native species found in Scotland, how they arrive, their impact and how they might be controlled is required to inform policy development. In 1998, recognising this need, Scottish Natural Heritage commissioned an audit of alien species in Scotland.

Table 6.1. Categories of species status (Usher, 1999).

Category	Explanation
Native	Species present in Scotland without human assistance. Most have migrated into Scotland since the last Ice Age.
Formerly native	Species that no longer occur naturally, but which are known (or presumed) to have occurred naturally at some time in the past.
Non-native	Species introduced, deliberately or accidentally, by humans.
Locally non-native	Species introduced beyond their natural geographical range within Scotland.
Long-established	Species that were introduced by humans a long time ago, but which have now become part of the 'natural' food chain.
Recently arrived	Species whose recent occurrence has been associated with human activity, for example through changes in agricultural practices, or through climate change, probably caused by human activities.

The potential problems caused by non-native species have been recognised within the UK's biodiversity process. It is interesting to note that the report on the first five years of that process states "We welcome the Government's announcement of a fundamental review of the policy relating to the control of non-native species" (Anon., 2001, p. 71). This audit in Scotland will undoubtedly contribute to that review.

6.2 The audit

The audit (Welch *et al.*, 2001) listed all of the terrestrial and freshwater non-native species known to occur in Scotland and provided basic facts about these species, such as their origin, manner of introduction, current distribution in Scotland, trends in abundance, habitats affected and ratings for their current and future impacts. There are at least 988 non-native species and detailed information is available in the audit for 945 of these. The total consists of 824 vascular plants, six bryophytes, two fungi, 13 mammals, 49 birds (but only eight breeding species), one amphibian, 16 fish, 22 insects in better-known groups, 50 molluscs and five other invertebrates. It is likely that the invertebrate totals are underestimates and it was not possible to attempt a systematic review of fungi. A review of non-native species in the marine environment has been given by Eno *et al.* (1997).

Almost half of the non-native species originated in Europe, of which a fifth were introduced from other parts of the British Isles. Large numbers also originated in the Americas and Asia. Most vascular plants were introduced to the wild as garden escapes or outcasts. Many others were introduced deliberately, mostly for horticulture or forestry. Other important modes of origin were accidental carriage in grain imports and seed mixes. Almost 40 per cent of animals were introduced accidentally in soil (e.g. slugs and other invertebrates). Another 25 per cent were introduced deliberately, mostly for sporting purposes (e.g. birds and fish), and a small number escaped from collections or arrived on shipping or in timber. It is not known how some 27 per cent of animal species arrived in Scotland.

We have defined 'problem species' as those which have an adverse impact on the natural heritage of a 'moderate' or 'highly' significant nature. There are 76 such species. Around 78 per cent of these are vascular plants, the rest being mostly either mammals, fish or invertebrates.

Non-native species occur in all the main types of habitats (see Figure 6.1), being most numerous in man-made habitats, e.g. arable land and waste ground. Woodland has the largest number of problem species, illustrating how greatly this habitat has been modified by human activity. Although there are fewer introduced species in fresh waters, they can spread rapidly and may be very costly or even impossible to control.

Non-native species may lead to a range of impacts upon Scotland's biodiversity (see Table 6.2). Half of the non-native species have little impact on the natural heritage beyond their presence in habitats otherwise composed largely of native species (see Figure 6.2). Of the 76 problem species, 34 per cent are thought to be competitors and 41 per cent cause habitat damage.

Nearly 80 per cent of non-native species have shown little or no change in abundance in Scotland in recent decades (see Figure 6.3). Sixty-five species showed significant increases, including 33 per cent of all naturalised species and 50 per cent of all problem species. Only about 2 per cent showed a decrease. Most of the species that have become widespread have

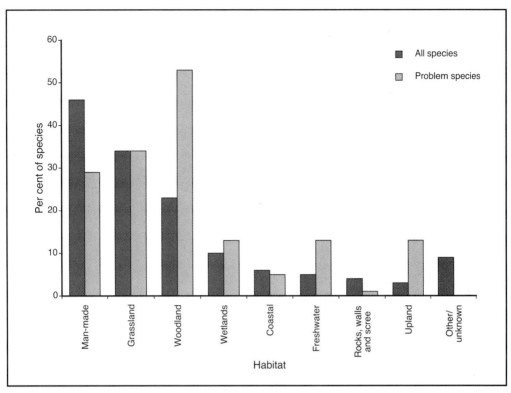

Figure 6.1. The proportion of the 945 non-native species and the 76 problem species found in different habitats. The data are derived from Welch *et al.* (2001).

Table 6.2. Examples of the types of impact on Scotland's biodiversity of non-native species.

Impact	*Examples*
Competition	Breeding Canada geese (*Branta canadensis*) are aggressive towards native wildfowl and may compete with them for nest sites. Competitive plants, such as Himalayan balsam (*Impatiens glandulifera*), grow so tall or so vigorously that other species are lost from communities.
Habitat damage	The litter or shade produced by some species can prevent the growth of others. The dense shade cast by rhododendron (*Rhododendron ponticum*) eliminates ground vegetation, and prevents regeneration of tree species.
Ecosystem disruption	In Loch Lomond, ruffe (*Gymnocephalus cernua*), which are benthic feeders, are now the main prey of pike (*Esox lucius*) and heron (*Ardea cinerea*), which used to feed mainly on powan (*Coregonus lavaretus*) and roach (*Rutilus rutilus*), which are pelagic feeders. This has led to fundamental changes in the flow of energy through the ecosystem.
Predation	American mink (*Mustela vison*) have eliminated populations of water vole (*Arvicola terrestris*) in many areas and threatened populations of ground nesting birds by preying on eggs and young.
Hybridisation	Sika deer (*Cervus nippon*) threaten the genetic integrity of native red deer (*Cervus elaphus*) through hybridisation.

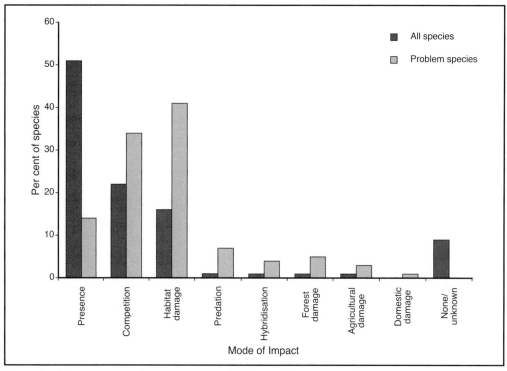

Figure 6.2. The proportion of non-native species leading to different types of impacts.

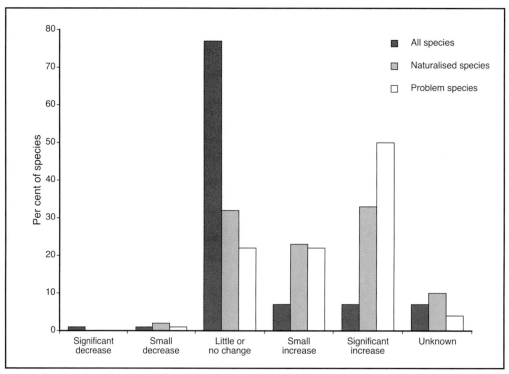

Figure 6.3. Trends in abundance of non-native species in Scotland (1950s-late 1980s).

four basic attributes: they come from areas with similar climates to the regions they have colonised; they reproduce and disperse well; they are competitors, able to do well in widespread habitat types; and they have good defences against herbivory and carnivory.

6.3 Conclusions

The audit provides a unique overview for Scotland and is believed to be the first comprehensive report of its kind in Europe. There are probably no sizeable areas of Scotland now entirely free of introduced species. A selective approach to eradicating or controlling non-native species seems to be the most pragmatic option. Initial prevention of species introductions is more effective than trying to control them afterwards.

There are four main requirements for tackling non-native species. First, it is important to identify which species require control, which are beyond control and which are benign or insufficiently problematic to need controlling. Second, increasing public awareness of the potential threats from the introduction and release of non-native species, and of the difficulty of controlling species once they have got into the wild, is increasingly essential as so many programmes for controlling non-native species will require inputs from a wide section of society. Third, government, its agencies and the voluntary sector will need to develop policy frameworks, guidance and advice. Finally, it will be essential to implement co-ordinated control programmes at local and national levels; non-native species cannot be successfully controlled in one part of the country if they are not controlled in the rest of the country, unless the control is targeted at island populations.

Acknowledgements

We wish to acknowledge both the team at the Centre for Ecology and Hydrology and SNH colleagues who contributed towards the audit.

References

Anonymous (2001). *Sustaining the Variety of Life: 5 Years of the UK Biodiversity Action Plan.* Department of the Environment, Transport and the Regions, London.

Eno, C.N., Clark, R.A. and Sanderson, W.G. (eds.) (1997). *Non-native Marine Species in British Waters: a Review and Directory.* Joint Nature Conservation Committee, Peterborough.

Usher, M.B. (1999). Nativeness or non-nativeness of species. SNH Information and Advisory Note No. 112.

Welch, D., Carss, D.N., Gornall, J., Manchester, S.J., Marquiss, M., Preston, C.D., Telfer, M.G., Arnold, H. and Holbrook, J. (2001). An audit of alien species in Scotland. Scottish Natural Heritage Review No. 139.

7 AIR POLLUTION AND ATMOSPHERIC DEPOSITION IN SCOTLAND: ENVIRONMENTAL AND NATURAL HERITAGE TRENDS

D. Fowler, G.G. McFadyen, N.E. Ellis and W.G. MacGregor

Summary

1. The atmosphere over Scotland contains a range of pollutants as gases and particles which have the potential to damage fauna and flora. The current regional threat to the natural heritage of Scotland is largely from the pollutants responsible for acidification, eutrophication, and ground level ozone (sulphur dioxide, nitrogen oxides, ammonia and volatile organic compounds).

2. The pollutants are emitted from sources within Scotland and from elsewhere in Europe, and, in the case of ozone, precursor gases emitted from sources throughout the industrial northern hemisphere contribute substantially to ecosystem exposure in Scotland.

3. Long-range transport of air pollutants to and from Scotland requires control measures which operate across the main source areas for the pollutant deposition and exposure. The international protocols developed to control the pollutants responsible for acidification, eutrophication and ground level ozone apply throughout Europe and the most recent (Gothenburg) protocol will reduce annual emissions of the major pollutant gases.

4. The potential effects from these pollutants have been assessed using Critical Loads methods for deposited pollutants and Critical Levels for ambient exposure.

5. The exceedance of Critical Loads for soil acidification in Scotland has been estimated for the period 1995 to 1997 to be 85 per cent, but this will decline to 35 per cent by 2010 due to reduced emissions and deposition.

6. The exceedance of Critical Loads for eutrophication in Scotland has been estimated to range from 2 per cent for acid grassland to 76 per cent for coniferous woodland and will decline by only approximately 15 per cent by 2010.

7. For ground level ozone, the exceedance of Critical Levels implies a potential for widespread adverse effects on crops and semi-natural vegetation across Scotland. However, a flux based approach, currently in development, may yield a quantitative assessment of risk. Reductions in the emissions of volatile organic compounds and nitrogen dioxide by 2010 will reduce ozone exceedances, but a steady increase in the background concentration over the following decades, due to emissions throughout the northern hemisphere, may pose a substantially larger long-term threat to vegetation in Scotland, especially in the uplands.

7.1 Introduction

The pollutants which determine air quality in Scotland include the gases sulphur dioxide (SO_2) and the nitrogen oxides (NO and NO_2) from combustion processes, ammonia (NH_3) from agriculture and volatile organic compounds (VOC) from motor vehicles and industrial processes. A range of metals, mostly in particulate form, are emitted by combustion and other industrial processes. Particles are also formed within the atmosphere through oxidation of the primary pollutant gases such as SO_2 and NO_2, to SO_4^{2-} and NO_2^- respectively. The oxidation processes occur in the gas phase and in cloud droplets, and on aerosol surfaces by heterogeneous mechanisms (Wayne, 1985). These pollutant gases and aerosols are the primary cause of the three major regional air pollution problems,

- acidification of terrestrial and aquatic ecosystems (SO_2, H_2SO_4, SO_4^{2-}, NO_2, HNO_3, NO_3^-, NH_3, NH_4^+),
- eutrophication of terrestrial ecosystems (NO_2, HNO_3, NO_3^-, NH_3, NH_4^+), and
- ground level ozone (O_3) effects on human health, semi-natural vegetation and crop plants (NO, NO_2, O_3, VOC).

This chapter is comprised of three main sections. The first describes the sources of the pollutants and the development of controls to reduce the impact of pollutants on Scotland's natural heritage (and human health). The second section considers the deposition of pollutants in Scotland, identifying the major sources, within Scotland and elsewhere in Europe, to illustrate both the international character of many of the air quality issues and the need to develop control strategies appropriate to the scale of the problem. The final section considers the effects of pollutant exposure and deposition on the natural heritage across Scotland.

In assessing the ecological effects of the deposited pollutants, the Critical Loads approach, which is widely applied in pollution effects research and for policy development in Europe, has been used in this chapter. By applying these methods, it is possible to quantify the spatial distribution of the individual pollution threats throughout Scotland, primarily described in section 7.3. The Critical Load is defined as 'a quantitative estimate of exposure to one or more pollutants below which significant harmful effects on sensitive elements of the environment do not occur according to present knowledge'. Concentrations in the air can be similarly defined using Critical Levels. The Critical Level is defined as 'the concentrations in the atmosphere above which direct adverse effects in receptors such as plants, ecosystems or materials, may occur according to present knowledge' (NEGTAP, 2001).

7.2 Emissions

The links between air quality, health and environmental quality underpin the range of initiatives, policies and legislation that currently control emissions from major sources. These controls have their origins in the industrial revolution, with the first formal legislation, the Alkali Works Act of 1863, resulting from the rapid industrialisation of the eighteenth and nineteenth centuries. This was accompanied by the establishment of an Alkali Inspectorate to ensure that 95 per cent of 'offensive' emissions should be arrested, predominantly from the emerging chemical industry. This legislation resulted in a significant reduction of the United Kingdom's hydrochloric acid emissions. The concept of Best Practicable Means (BPM) to prevent emissions was introduced in 1874 and the controls extended to all potentially polluting industries. A statutory emissions limit was also introduced for hydrogen chloride.

Advances in technology, urban growth and an increasing need for energy supplies compounded the potential to pollute the atmosphere and in response a number of Acts and control measures were introduced during the first half of the twentieth century. Despite these, however, some of the worst air pollution incidents and associated fatalities occurred and environmental impacts such as acidification became apparent.

Although the Alkali Inspectorate was given additional statutory controls over industrial emissions, the pervading problem was smoke and sulphur emissions from domestic chimneys. As urbanisation continued, a resultant five-day smog incident in London in 1952 led to the first Clean Air Act in 1956, which was amended in 1968. The 1993 Clean Air Act updated the previous acts and enabled the control of dust, grit and smoke from domestic and commercial sources through regulation of fuel type, chimney height and prohibition of dark smoke emissions and allowed the designation of 'smokeless zones' where urban pollution problems were greatest. Scottish local authorities have therefore monitored smoke and SO_2 at numerous sites since the 1960s and their records show a marked decline in annual averages, especially in urban areas.

The recognition of the effects of acid deposition in Scandinavia in the 1970s (Anon., 1972) brought about a change in the focus of air pollution policy from local health effects to acidification and long-range transport of pollution. This led to the development of International Conventions on Transboundary air pollution across the whole of Europe. The first International Convention to limit emissions of acidifying gases in Europe was the '30 per cent club' (the 1st Sulphur protocol) in which countries agreed to a 30 per cent reduction in sulphur emissions. The United Kingdom (UK) did not sign this protocol, but ironically met the emission reduction target by the specified date (1993). Further protocols, which the UK signed, followed for sulphur (1998), VOC (1991, 1997), heavy metals (1998) and Persistent Organic Pollutants (POPs) (1998). The latest protocol brings many of these pollutants together within the Gothenburg Protocol (1999) to control the pollutants which cause acidification, eutrophication and ground level ozone problems. A brief review of the development of international protocols to regulate these pollutants is provided by NEGTAP (2001).

During the latter part of the twentieth century, there were increases in emissions of other pollutants. These resulted from societal changes such as urbanisation, rising energy demands and improved standards of living. In particular these led to large increases in transport-related emissions from road vehicles, especially in urban areas. This resulted in largely uncontrolled emissions of NO_x, VOC, CO and particulates as UK transport policy focused primarily on safety and alleviating nuisance rather than environmental impact.

The introduction of the Environmental Protection Act (1990) and the Environment Act (1995) provided an integrated approach to reducing air pollution from significant industrial sources and enabled control of a wider range of pollutants than previously; the main instruments used to regulate pollutant emissions from large sources being the Integrated Pollution Control (IPC) (1990) and Integrated Pollution Prevention and Control (IPPC) (2000) Regulations. There was also a major step forward in local air quality management through the introduction of the Government's National Air Quality Strategy (NAQS) in 1996. The NAQS resulted in a more strategic and integrated approach to air quality management, including the recognition of transport impacts for the first time.

Emissions inventories are essential policy and regulatory tools because they identify the type and location of air pollutant sources. Informed in this way, policy developers can devise and implement emission reduction strategies, based on model simulations of the concentration and deposition footprint of emissions at local and regional scales. The success of the policies can then be assessed from air quality trends and future inventories.

The direct measurement of all pollutant emissions is impractical and most data are estimated on a sectoral basis as described below. Accurate emission data for Scotland are only readily available for the largest point sources, such as large combustion plants, which currently represent around 60 per cent of Scottish SO_2 and 30 per cent of NO_x emissions. From 2003, additional point source emission data should become available from the Scottish Environment Protection Agency's (SEPA's) pollutant emission register which focuses on those sectors subject to the new Scottish Pollution, Prevention and Control Regulations.

Inventory methods combine the actual and estimated emission data from individual sources and sectors to provide national emission estimates. This is currently undertaken annually at the UK level to form the National Atmospheric Emissions Inventory (NAEI) (NEGTAP, 2001). Emissions estimates are prepared as follows. For each process that releases atmospheric pollutants, an emission factor is determined that relates how much pollutant is emitted for a set level of activity (for example, the sulphur content per tonne of fuel). This is then combined with a measure of the activity of the source (for example, the amount of fuel used per year) to calculate the annual emission. Such inventories are subject to considerable uncertainty which arises from the uncertainty associated with sectoral emission factors and activity measures. The Scottish emission data described in this chapter were extracted from the NAEI 1 x 1 km UK emission maps for 1999. This process suggested that Scottish emissions were 9.1 per cent, 8.5 per cent, 11.3 per cent and 16.9 per cent of the UK's emissions of SO_2, NO_x, NH_3 and VOCs respectively, for that year. Though the percentages for SO_2 and NO_x are similar to Scotland's share of the UK population, those for NH_3 and VOCs are significantly larger. The importance of oil and gas extraction and processing facilities in Scotland's industrial base is reflected in it being almost twice as large a source of VOCs when expressed on the basis of the Scottish population.

The percentages above were applied to UK emission data for 1990 to 1999 to provide a provisional 10-year dataset for Scotland. Although the NAEI reports on the emissions from a wide range of source categories, this chapter uses fewer categories for clarity. Clearly, these data are subject to a range of uncertainties. The UK NAEI quotes values of ±10 to 15 per cent for SO_2 and ±30 per cent for NO_x and VOCs. No confidence limits are quoted for ammonia which is likely to be the least certain.

7.2.1 Sulphur dioxide

Sulphur dioxide (SO_2) is a soluble, colourless, pungent and acidic pollutant formed during the combustion of fuels containing sulphur. Following release to the atmosphere, it may be directly deposited (dry deposition) to soil or vegetation but can be oxidised by gas phase reaction to sulphuric acid, which rapidly condenses or is taken up by existing particles, or to sulphate in liquid phase reactions in cloud or rain. The removal process, both in the atmosphere and at terrestrial surfaces, is affected by the presence of ammonia. Thus the different pollutants influence each other, so that policies to control one pollutant may strongly influence the atmospheric behaviour of other pollutants. The atmospheric oxidation of SO_2 is also influenced by oxidizing agents, such as hydrogen peroxide in cloud water. Aerosols are deposited much more slowly than gases, which increases the atmospheric lifetime of (and hence area affected by) pollutants present in the aerosol phase. Since they can be present in multiple forms, the emissions are frequently quoted as a mass of sulphur, e.g. thousands of tonnes of sulphur (kT(S)).

The principal source of emitted SO_2 in Scotland is the combustion of fossil fuels in large industrial boilers and heating units (Plate 10). Electricity generation, which now accounts for approximately 60 per cent of SO_2 emissions in Scotland, is the most significant sector. Combustion of coal and oil in other industries, along with some refinery processes, are the most significant contributors to the remainder (Table 7.1). Emissions from transportation represent only around 1 per cent of the total SO_2 released.

`Table 7.1. Scottish emissions of major pollutants (k Tonnes). Source: National Environmental Technology Centre, and the Centre for Ecology and Hydrology, Edinburgh.

	1990	*1999*	*Percentage of UK emissions (1999)*
SO_2-S	170	55	9
NO_x-N	70	42	8
NH_x-N	32	32	11
VOC	441	297	16
CO	590	388	8
PM_{10}	48	20	10

The UK's emissions of SO_2 peaked in 1970 and, as shown in Figure 7.1, have declined by almost 70 per cent since 1990. They are now approaching levels required under the United Nations Economic Commission for Europe's Second Sulphur Protocol for 2010. Scottish emissions are expected to have followed a similar trend and to have shown a similar distribution across source categories to that for the whole UK in 1999. The total emissions shown in Plate 8 are considered to be a good approximation for Scotland in recent years but less so for the earlier years in which the source distribution, and, in particular domestic emissions, were much more important.

During the next decade, Scottish, UK and European legislation – primarily IPPC, the revised Large Combustion Plant (LCP) and the National Emission Ceiling (NEC) Directives – should lead to further reductions in SO_2 emissions. The latter will limit the UK's 2010 sulphur emissions to 312 kT(S) and the Scottish total will be approximately 26 kT(S).

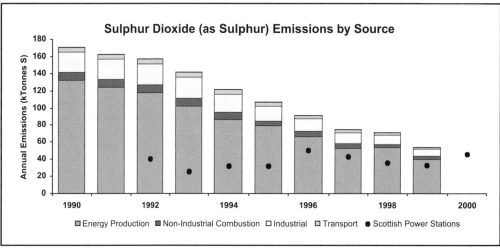

Figure 7.1. Emission of sulphur dioxide in Scotland for the major source categories.

7.2.2 *Nitrogen oxides*

Oxidised nitrogen refers to several atmospheric species but only two are emitted into the atmosphere by human activity, namely nitric oxide (NO), a colourless gas formed during high temperature combustion of fuels, and nitrogen dioxide (NO_2).

Oxides of nitrogen are emitted primarily as NO during combustion, and, except in the most polluted cases, are rapidly converted to NO_2 by reaction with ozone. NO and NO_2 are rapidly inter-converted in the atmosphere during the day and are generally referred to as NO_x, the sum of NO and NO_2. Emissions are usually quoted as NO_2 or, as in this chapter, as a mass of nitrogen (e.g. kT(N)).

NO_x contributes to acidification through the direct deposition of NO_2 and through the formation of nitric acid from NO_2 in the atmosphere. Deposition of nitric acid and other oxidation products of NO_2 is an important sink for NO_2. Oxidised nitrogen compounds also increase the acidity of rain and cloud water and nitrate can enter the aerosol phase and react with ammonium in solution. The oxides of nitrogen also play an essential role in the photochemical reactions that lead to low-level ozone formation. Sunlight can split NO_2 to form NO and oxygen atoms, which combine with molecular oxygen to produce ozone. The oxidation of NO to NO_2 without consuming ozone, which is carried out by a number of reactive compounds in the sunlit atmosphere, is thus the dominant source of ozone in the lower atmosphere. In addition, NO_2 can directly damage crops as well as contribute to eutrophication of ecosystems.

Road transport is the largest source of NO_x emissions, now accounting for around 56 per cent of the Scottish total. Electricity generation is the next largest (contributing around 21 per cent), with the remainder from other large-scale industrial combustion processes, the domestic and commercial sectors and other mobile sources such as aircraft. The spatial distribution of sources which is shown in Plate 11 is similar to that for the UK. The validity of the value for total Scottish emissions decreases for earlier years as does our confidence in the distribution across individual source sectors. However, the comparison with data collected for emissions from the main Scottish power station shows reasonable agreement with the estimate for this sector.

UK emissions of NO_x peaked in 1990 and have declined during the last decade by approximately 40 per cent. A substantial fraction of the reduced emissions of NO_x from transport can be attributed to the requirement to fit catalytic converters to new cars along with increased regulation of emissions from heavy goods vehicles. The overall reduction has occurred despite the concurrent increase in road and air transport. In the case of industrial input, the reduction is associated with environmental regulation coupled with availability of improved technologies such as low-NO_x burner systems and the change of fuel use from coal to gas.

During the next decade, Scottish, UK and European legislation – primarily the IPPC, the revised LCP and the NEC Directives – should lead to further reductions in NO_x emissions. The latter will limit the UK's 2010 NO_x emissions to 1,167 kT which is equivalent to 359 kT(N) and the Scottish emissions in 2010 will be approximately 30 kT(N).

7.2.3 Ammonia

Ammonia is a highly soluble, basic gas emitted mainly from biological sources. It dissolves readily in cloud and rain droplets to form ammonium ions. Evaporation of the droplets can lead to the formation of aerosol and in the aerosol phase, ammonium is less easily removed by deposition and is the form of reduced nitrogen which is subject to long range transport. Ammonia impacts on the environment in two ways; it contributes to the eutrophication of terrestrial ecosystems directly and to acidification (when converted to nitrate by biological processes).

The spatial distribution of NH_3 is shown in Plate 12. As this pollutant is emitted largely from agricultural sources, and especially from intensive livestock farming, the emissions are primarily rural, and are concentrated in the livestock producing areas of Scotland. Agriculture now contributes around 80 per cent of Scottish emissions; of this, animal waste contributes almost 90 per cent with the remainder coming from the application of nitrogen fertilizers either directly or from plants and decomposing vegetation. This sector has a similar dominance for the UK as a whole and the total emissions for Scotland, based on the 1999 proportion, are likely to be a reasonable estimate, within the inherently large uncertainty estimated for this pollutant.

Emissions from intensive agriculture, where large quantities of animal waste are spread on the land over a short period, are proportionately larger than those from grazing animals where the nitrogen is more readily taken up by plants and soils. It is not yet clear what effect the recent outbreak of foot and mouth disease has had on Scottish ammonia emissions. The number of animals culled may be balanced by the number of animals that otherwise would have been exported or slaughtered. Other waste sources, including human, landfill, waste treatment, domestic pet and wildlife waste account for a further 11 per cent. Combustion is the only other significant source with 6 per cent coming from catalytic converters and 1 per cent from combustion in residential combustion sources. A further 1 per cent is contributed from industrial sources. There have been no major changes in emissions from agricultural animal waste although there has been a small reduction in other agricultural emissions. Only road transport shows a rise because of the increased use of catalytic converters, which produce NH_3 when faulty or run at low temperature.

During the next decade, Scottish, UK and European legislation – primarily the IPPC and the NEC Directives – should reduce NH_3 emissions. The former will introduce pollution control techniques to the intensive pig and poultry sectors while the latter will limit the UK's 2010 ammonia emissions to 297 kT. However, the emission reductions agreed to date are small, amounting to a reduction of 11 per cent of the 1990 total by 2010. With the known uncertainties in NH_3 emissions, such reductions are unlikely to lead to measurable reductions in deposition or effects.

7.2.4 Volatile organic compounds

For the purposes of this chapter, VOCs are defined as all organic compounds (other than methane) arising from human activities, which evaporate readily and contribute to air pollution. VOCs are oxidised in the atmosphere to carbon dioxide and water vapour although some have degradation products with longer lifetimes than the parent compounds and may be removed by deposition.

Although there are concerns over the direct health and environmental effects of some VOCs, their most important role is in the formation of secondary pollutants, in particular ground level ozone through reactions with nitrogen oxides in the presence of sunlight. The capacity for ozone formation varies between different VOCs and is quantified by their 'photochemical ozone creation potential' (POCP) (PORG, 1997).

Major sources of Scottish VOCs include industrial solvents (which now account for around 35 per cent of emissions), whisky distillation (17 per cent or 50 kT per year) and oil and gas refining. The spatial distribution in VOC emissions, shown in Plate 13, suggests that transport sources account for a substantial fraction of Scottish emissions, with the main transport routes clearly visible on the emission map. Approximately 30 per cent of Scottish emissions of VOCs originates from road transport. While the total emissions may be reasonable estimates for Scotland, the distribution across source sectors is known to be inaccurate, even for the most recent year.

Emissions have declined by 35 per cent since 1990 from industrial solvent based industries in particular. The nature of regulation in this sector has resulted in the development of, and continuing move towards the use of, water-based substances. Transportation emissions have also decreased as a result of the increased use of catalytic converters in cars and the impact of regulations relating to recovery of petrol vapour within distribution systems. Fuel switching from petrol to diesel is another potential factor in the downward trend.

During the next decade, Scottish, UK and European legislation – primarily the IPPC, the NEC and the Solvent Emissions Directive – should lead to further reductions in VOC emissions. This will limit the UK's 2010 VOC emissions to 1,200 kT and the Scottish emissions will then be approximately 156 kT.

7.2.5 Ambient concentrations of the major pollutant gases

Currently, the air concentrations of SO_2 in Scotland range from annual mean values of 15 to 20 mg per m^3 in city centres to very small values (<1 mg per m^3) throughout rural areas of Scotland north of the central lowlands (Plate 14). In all rural areas, including the central lowlands, concentrations are small relative to thresholds for effects on vegetation, and hence only very sensitive lichen species are at risk from the current concentrations. However, the much larger concentrations of the twentieth century leave a legacy of historical effects which are considered later in the chapter. Concentrations of NO_2 are substantially larger than those of SO_2 throughout Scotland, and in the central lowlands annual mean values range from 10 to 20 mg per m³, with larger values in urban centres, largely derived from traffic sources. The traffic sources also lead to a marked pattern of the major trunk roads in surface concentrations (Plate 15). In general, concentrations of NO_2, like those of SO_2, decline towards the north and west from peak values in urban centres and the central lowlands. Ammonia concentrations also show patterns of declining values towards the north and west of the country, but in this case, are largest in the rural areas containing the major livestock production. Thus the intensive areas for cattle, pig and poultry production are clearly evident in the ammonia concentration field (Plate 16).

7.2.6 Ozone

Ground level ozone arises largely from photochemical production within the troposphere from the emissions of VOC and NO_x. The production is relatively slow, with daily production contributing 10 to 20 ppb (parts per billion) of additional O_3 in regional polluted air on sunny, warm days. Thus the daily production of ozone in a photochemical smog in northern European conditions is typically 20 ppb or so each day as the air is slowly advected over the industrial regions of Europe. The winds bringing such plumes to Scotland are not common, and peak concentrations in Scotland seldom exceed 80 ppb. The number of occasions during a typical summer of O_3 concentration exceeding 60 ppb, which is the threshold for effects on sensitive humans, is generally less than ten and typically five. However, vegetation has been shown to be sensitive to concentration exceeding 40 ppb and exceedances of 40 ppb are much more frequent because this level lies close to the background concentration of 20 to 25 ppb. The most commonly applied measure of the

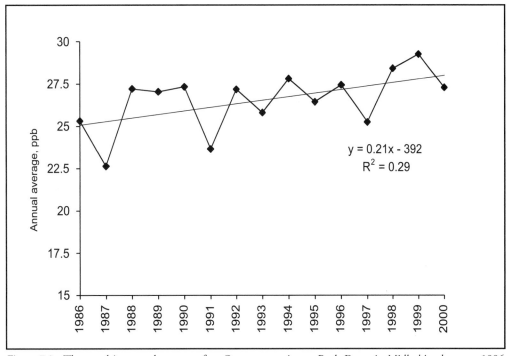

Figure 7.2. The trend in annual mean surface O_3 concentration at Bush Estate in Midlothian between 1986 and 2000.

potential for damage to vegetation by ozone is the AOT40, which is the accumulated exposure of terrestrial surfaces to concentrations in excess of 40 ppb (PORG, 1997). The accumulated exposure to 40 ppb for crop plants and semi-natural vegetation in Scotland shows exceedances of critical levels (3,000 ppb h) over substantial areas of Eastern Scotland (Plate 17), and especially over the higher ground.

The introduction of controls on NO_x and VOC emissions has reduced peak concentrations throughout the UK, and for Scotland peak values were typically 20 to 30 ppb smaller during the last five years than they were in the 1980s. This improvement in air quality in Scotland benefits human health, especially as potentially damaging concentrations are now quite rare. However, the background concentration has been steadily increasing and in southern Scotland has been increasing at about 0.2 ppb per annum during the last 14 years (Figure 7.2). With this increase in background concentration, the mean concentrations are quite rapidly approaching values which have been shown to be damaging to vegetation. A model projection of the background concentration increases suggest that by 2050 the UK will experience mean concentrations larger than 40 ppb, even though peak values will by then be smaller than current ones. The net effect of the declining peak concentrations and increasing mean values on crops and semi-natural vegetation is unknown. The basis for effects assessment is currently under review as briefly discussed in section 7.4.2 and in more detail by NEGTAP (2001).

7.3 Deposition of pollutants in Scotland

The gases SO_2, NO_2, HNO_3, NH_3, and O_3 are all absorbed by terrestrial surfaces (dry deposition) but at different rates. Rates of dry deposition are determined by the chemical reactivity (and solubility) and by rates of turbulent transport from the atmospheric boundary layer to the absorbing surfaces (Figure 7.3). Dry deposition rates are largest for the reactive and water soluble species HNO_3 and NH_3 and smallest for NO_2, but for all pollutant gases, dry deposition represents a major sink for the gas. In the absence of other processes removing the pollutant gases from the atmospheric boundary layer, dry deposition

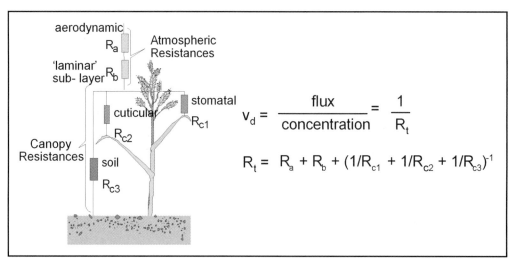

Figure 7.3. A schematic representation of the resistance analogue of surface-atmosphere exchange of pollutant gases and its relationship with deposition velocity (V_d).

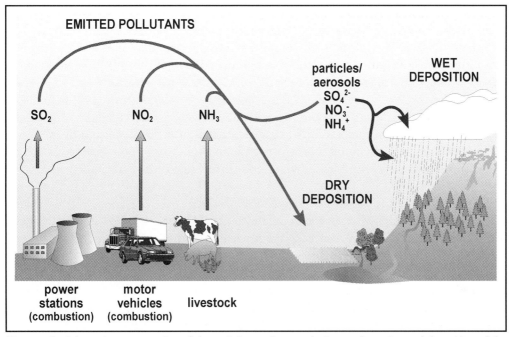

Figure 7.4. Schematic representation of the emission and atmospheric transformation and deposition of the major pollutants SO_2, NO_2 and NH_3.

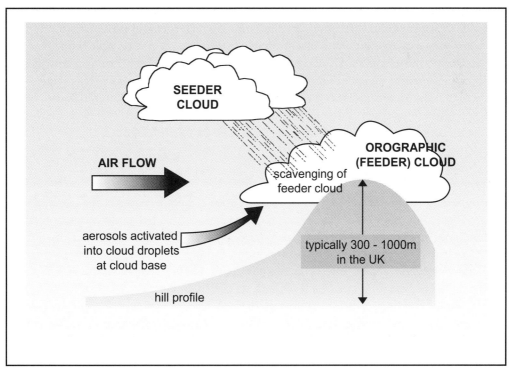

Figure 7.5. The seeder-feeder process by which boundary layer pollutants are efficiently removed from the atmosphere over the uplands of Scotland by rain.

would limit the atmospheric lifetime to between 0.1 and 3 days for NH_3 and NO_2 respectively. However, there are other processes removing the pollutant gases. Oxidation of SO_2 and NO_x to SO_4^{2-} and NO_3^- also leads to particle formation, as all of the oxidized SO_2 is transformed to aerosol particles, and a substantial fraction of the NO_3^- is also present as aerosol. These aerosols are dry deposited slowly, and are removed from the atmosphere primarily by rain (Figure 7.4). Rainfall is the dominant removal mechanism for sulphur and total nitrogen (oxidized and reduced) in Scotland. The seeder-feeder washout of hill cloud is a particularly efficient process for scavenging aerosols over the Scottish uplands (Figure 7.5) and the deposition patterns show the maximum annual deposition in the areas of high rainfall, as shown in the deposition map of non-marine sulphur in Scotland (Plate 18).

7.3.1 Atmospheric mass budgets for S and N over Scotland

The emission of sulphur in Scotland in the mid-1990s of 93 kT(S) was of a similar magnitude to the combined wet and dry deposition within the country, amounting to 87 kT(S) (Figure 7.6(a)). Thus, even with a substantial atmospheric import of sulphur totalling 39 kT(S) annually from elsewhere in the UK and continental Europe, the emissions and deposition are closely matched.

For oxidized nitrogen, the emissions of 51 kT(N) are greater than the deposition of 36 kT(N), so that Scotland is a net exporter of oxidized nitrogen, amounting to 15 kT(N), and representing about a third of emissions (Figure 7.6(b)). In contrast to sulphur and oxidized nitrogen, the atmospheric budget of reduced nitrogen (Figure 7.6(c)) shows Scotland to be a substantial net importer, with deposition within the country of 68 kT(N) exceeding emissions by about a factor of two. These deposition totals show only the country budgets, and provide no guide to the environmental effects, or their location. The detailed presentation of each of the components of the acidifying or eutrophying deposition is not possible with the space constraints of this chapter. However, the deposition map for total nitrogen provides an important example of the spatial distribution pattern in Scotland (Plate 19). The figure shows the potential nitrogen deposition on woodland within each 5 km x 5 km grid square of the country, with maximum values in the central lowlands, the north-east and south-west Scotland, with deposition values in the range 30 to 40 kg N per ha annually.

7.4 Natural heritage trends

7.4.1 Introduction

It is important to consider atmospheric pollution impacts both in terms of the concentration in air as well as the deposition. Each species and each ecosystem has a tolerance threshold for atmospheric concentration or deposited loads beyond which adverse effects occur. Detrimental effects include plant physiological process responses and physical damage, leading to a decline in productivity and viability. Effects on an individual species can reduce species diversity.

The value presented as a critical level for a specific pollutant (e.g. for SO_2 or NO_2) and a target organism (e.g. a plant species) is defined empirically on the basis of field or laboratory data. For critical loads, both empirical and theoretical approaches have been adapted for acidification of soils and freshwaters. Critical loads have been widely applied in the development of abatement strategies for Europe to maximise environmental protection for investment in control measures. This has led to a rapid development of the methods to define critical loads and an extensive literature (Posch *et al.*, 2001).

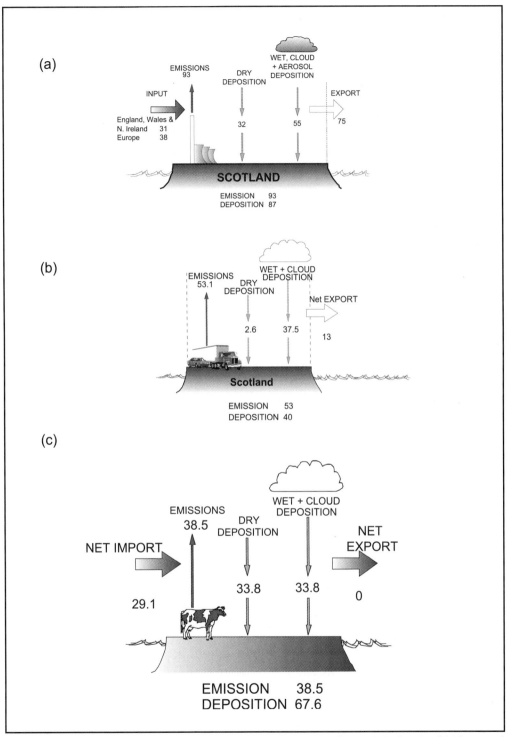

Figure 7.6. (a) The annual atmospheric sulphur budget over Scotland for 1994 (in kT S). (b) The annual atmospheric budget over Scotland in 1996 for oxidized nitrogen (in kT N). (c) The annual atmospheric budget over Scotland in 1996 for reduced nitrogen (in kT N).

7.4.2 Ecological consequences of air pollution

Acidification: The deposition of pollutants, which lead to soil and freshwater acidification, may induce disruptions in the biogeochemical cycling of nutrients through changes in pH and chemical reactivity. Base-rich soils are less susceptible to acidification as the presence of base cations, such as magnesium and calcium, buffer incoming acidity. Over time, high levels of incoming acidity increase the leaching of base cations and the availability of aluminium and iron cations. The release and subsequent leaching of base cations can deprive vegetation and soil organisms of essential minerals. Acidification of base-poor soils releases aluminium ions which are directly toxic. Heavy metals such as manganese and lead may also be released. The presence of such heavy metals in peat soils in Scotland has been observed (Tipping *et al.*, 2001). Where nitrogen is deposited as ammonia or ammonium, soil acidification is accelerated by nitrification and root ammonium uptake. Further, soil water draining from acidified soils may acidify freshwaters and have direct effects on freshwater species, including diatoms and invertebrates, and may also have indirect effects on birds and mammals dependent on these ecosystems.

Eutrophication: A number of upland soils across Scotland are naturally nutrient-poor and their ecosystems harbour species adapted to such conditions, such as on montane heaths. The addition of nitrogen from the atmosphere therefore acts as a fertiliser. Nitrogen deposition can also be directly toxic to some species, such as some mosses and lichens (Press *et al.*, 1986; Gordon *et al.*, 2001), whereas other species can be outshaded by species exploiting the more fertile conditions. Consequently there are changes in species communities, usually with a decline in the number of species. An increased nitrogen concentration within the tissues of such vegetation also leads to a different pattern of herbivory which can lead to a greater frequency of pest outbreaks, and an increase in sensitivity to frost and drought.

Ozone: At present, the effect of ozone on ecosystems is more difficult to quantify. Ozone has been shown to reduce the productivity of crop and semi-natural species in closed chambers and open–top chambers. The measurements show that the exposure expressed as AOT40 significantly reduces the yields of sensitive cultivars of wheat with 3,000 ppbh, and that the yield declines linearly with increasing dose above this threshold (Fuhrer *et al.*, 1997). However, the conditions within the open-top chambers differ from those in the field such that simple extrapolation from the open-top chamber results probably overestimates the magnitude of the yield reduction (NEGTAP, 2001). The most recent evidence suggests that observed yield reductions are the consequence of a flux in excess of the plant's capacity to detoxify the stomatal uptake of ozone. These findings suggest that, to quantify the effects of ozone in the field, stomatal fluxes need to be quantified in field conditions and the relationship between stomatal uptake and reductions in dry matter production established. The development of a flux-based approach to assess ozone effects on vegetation is in progress and may provide the basis for a quantitative assessment of regional effects of ozone on crops and semi-natural vegetation (NEGTAP, 2001).

7.4.3 Critical load and level impacts on natural and semi-natural habitats of Scotland

Acidification: It is estimated that during the 1990s, acidifying inputs across Scotland exceeded the critical loads for over half of the 1 km Ordnance Survey grid squares for a variety of habitats (Fowler *et al.*, 2002) (Table 7.2). Being naturally acidic, it is not

Table 7.2. The percentage of 1 km squares (rounded to nearest whole number) within which acidity critical loads are exceeded (1995-1997), according to the presence of that habitat in the square (ammonia deposition has not been included). Source: Fowler *et al.* (2002).

Habitat	Percentage of 1 km squares with exceedance	Number of 1 km squares used to determine exceedance
Peatland	88	41,042
Acid grassland	87	37,929
Heathland	63	38,675
Deciduous woodland	62	4,643
Coniferous woodland	53	14,436

surprising that peatlands and acid grasslands should be among the most affected habitats with an estimated 88 per cent and 87 per cent, respectively, of 1 km squares within which they occur receiving acidifying inputs above their critical load. The largest areas of exceedance occur throughout the central and southern areas of Scotland, concurrent with highest levels of acid deposition (Fowler *et al.*, 2002) (Plate 20).

Eutrophication: The extent of exceedance of critical loads of eutrophying inputs during the 1990s varied greatly according to the habitat. Calcareous grassland is not considered to be at risk from current levels of nutrient nitrogen deposition whereas the ground flora of coniferous and deciduous woodlands (upon which the woodland critical loads are based), and oligotrophic waters, are estimated to be in exceedance of critical loads in two-thirds or more of the 1 km grid squares within which they occur (Fowler *et al.*, 2002) (Table 7.3). The largest exceedances of critical loads for nutrient nitrogen for woodland ground flora occur across extensive areas of the lowlands in southern, central and north-east Scotland, being very similar for both coniferous and deciduous woodlands (Plate 21). Peatlands and heathlands are no less sensitive to nutrient nitrogen deposition but occur less extensively in high deposition areas.

Table 7.3. The percentage of 1 km squares (rounded to nearest whole number) within which nutrient nitrogen critical loads are exceeded (1995-1997), according to the presence of that habitat in the square. Source: Fowler *et al.* (2002).

Habitat	Percentage of 1 km squares with exceedance	Number of 1 km squares used to determine exceedance
Coniferous woodland	76	15,459
Deciduous woodland	75	12,579
Oligotrophic waters	65	49,925
Peatland	45	49,625
Heathland	19	54,125
Acid grassland	2	72,200

Ozone: Between 1986 and 1998, ozone concentrations exceeded critical levels for crops (based on experimental investigations) and for semi-natural vegetation across 30 per cent of Scotland, with some of the largest exceedances in the eastern uplands.

7.4.4 Observed effects of acid deposition on ecosystems across Scotland

Lichens have been recognised as good indicators of the quality of air, in particular, for concentrations of sulphur dioxide (e.g. Gilbert, 1970; Hawksworth and Rose, 1970). Lichens, like mosses and liverworts, are particularly sensitive to acidification because they obtain their nutrients directly from precipitation and do not have a protective cuticle. Distribution maps of the lichen *Lobaria pulmonaria* show that it has disappeared from sites in eastern Scotland around Edinburgh and Glasgow since 1960 (Looney and James, 1988). This was also true for a number of moss species which occurred in fewer 1 km squares across Scotland from 1950, particularly where the concentration of sulphur dioxide in the air was greater than 5 mg per m^3. For example, the moss *Antitrichia curtipendula* has disappeared from 47 per cent of sites in which it occurred before 1950, and where the modelled average air sulphur dioxide concentration was greater than 5 mg per m^3 (Table 7.4).

Table 7.4. Relationships between the percentage of sites lost since 1950 where the presence of moss has been recorded, categorised according to the predicted SO_2 concentration in a 10 km^2 grid square for 1987-1991. Source: adapted from Fowler *et al.* (2002).

Moss species	*Percentage of sites lost since 1950*	
	Sites with 0-5 µg per m^3 SO_2	*Sites with greater than 5 µg per m^3 SO_2*
Antitrichia curtipendula	8.5	47.0
Cryphaea heteromalla	16.7	19.5
Grimmia orbiculare	50.0	66.7
Leucodon sciuroides	29.0	50.0
Orthotrichum speciosum	18.0	23.0
Ulota hutchinsiae	3.3	41.4
Ulota coarctata	33.3	73.3

Skiba *et al.* (1989) concluded that the pH of peatlands across Scotland was related to the level of acid deposition with high levels of deposition (greater than 0.8 kg H$^+$ per ha per yr) occurring where dystrophic peats had low pH values (below pH3). Although this was a spatial correlation, there are examples of sites for which pH levels were shown to have decreased over time. For example, an upland site in Grampian managed as a heather-dominated rough grazing pasture and receiving no fertiliser, showed an increase in exchangeable hydrogen throughout all soil horizons (i.e. decreasing pH), in the order of 100 to 400 per cent, between 1956 and 1997 (Miller *et al.*, 2001). At this site, availability of magnesium in the humic layer decreased by 78 per cent and calcium by 100 per cent (Miller *et al.*, 2001).

Many freshwater systems in Scotland received high levels of acid deposition, particularly between 1930 and 1970. The pH of the water in a number of lochs fell below pH6, some lochs in the south-west being as low as pH4.4 (Battarbee *et al.*, 1988; Harriman *et al.*, 1995). By 1995-1997, deposition of acidifying pollutants to freshwaters by sulphur and nitrogen compounds resulted in exceedance of the critical load for acidity of freshwaters in 12 per cent of the areas examined (Mackey *et al.*, 2001). These areas coincided with high wet deposition rates, i.e. west central Highlands, south-west Scotland, the Cairngorm mountains and the Southern Uplands. A number of diatom, invertebrate and fish species were reduced in abundance or lost from particular sites (Battarbee *et al.*, 1988; Harriman *et al.*, 1995; Soulsby *et al.*, 1997). However, as sulphur emissions declined, particularly during 1980-1985 and into the 1990s, a number of acid-sensitive diatom species have returned (Battarbee *et al.*, 1988; Harriman *et al.*, 1995; Soulsby *et al.*, 1997).

Acidification of water courses was also linked to a decline in the distribution of bird species that feed on aquatic invertebrates. For example, the distribution of the dipper (*Cinclus cinclus*) declined between 1970 and 1990, disappearing from some parts of Galloway (Gibbons *et al.*, 1993). The decline was linked to a lowered abundance and biomass of aquatic invertebrates, such as mayfly nymphs and caddisfly larvae (Vickery, 1991; Gibbons *et al.*, 1993). A reduction in the availability of calcium-rich prey as a result of acidification has led to thinner bird egg shells which has raised the mortality of the chicks of a number of invertebrate- and fish-eating birds (Green, 1998).

The loss of invertebrate, fish and amphibian species from freshwater systems has had a knock-on effect to predators, such as the otter (*Lutra lutra*). Areas without otters during the 1990s were confined to southern and central Scotland, the Firth of Forth, and the south-west, i.e. where areas of high exceedance of critical loads of acidity occurred (Green and Green, 1997). The level of exceedance of acidification was related to a decline in both otter distribution and abundance, with otters absent from 61 per cent of km squares where acid deposition exceeded critical loads.

7.4.5 Observed effects of eutrophication in ecosystems across Scotland

Using data from the Countryside Surveys (Barr *et al.*, 1993; Haines-Young *et al.*, 2000), McGowan *et al.* (2001) examined the evidence of eutrophication in Scotland. Between 1990 and 1998, a greater number of species more suited to fertile conditions (such as the foxglove, *Digitalis purpurea*, and purple moorgrass, *Molinia caerulea*) occurred within lowland raised bogs, blanket bogs and dwarf-shrub heath across Scotland, whilst the overall number of species declined by 6 to 7 per cent in the latter. This is consistent with experimental observations which have shown losses of moss and lichen species where nitrogen has been added (e.g. Carroll *et al.*, 1999).

The increase in the nutrient status of upland soils has been used to explain observed increases in grasslands at the expense of heaths and moorland in the Scottish uplands. This is particularly true of the moss *Racomitrium lanuginosum* in arctic-alpine heaths which has declined by 75 to 95 per cent over the last century (Thompson and Baddeley, 1991) because of differential growth rates between species under high nitrogen inputs. In non-grazed exclosures, the addition of atmospheric nitrogen has been found to encourage heather growth over the shade-intolerant mat-grass (*Nardus stricta*) and other grasses (Hartley, 1997). This indicates that grazing can have as large an effect as deposition of airborne nitrogen. However, opening up of the heather canopy may occur due to pest damage encouraged by the higher nitrogen content of heather foliage and therefore also indirectly encourage grass growth. Again this may also occur under high grazing regimes.

Changes in botanical diversity within coniferous woodlands across Scotland suggest that eutrophication, but not acidification, has occurred with a significant shift towards species more suited to fertile conditions (McGowan *et al.*, 2001). The coniferous woodlands analysed included native pine woodlands as well as Sitka spruce plantations, so the shift to species of more fertile conditions is likely to have been caused by both airborne nitrogen deposition and the addition of fertiliser. However, no changes in species composition, soil fertility or pH for broadleaved/mixed woodlands were observed (McGowan *et al.*, 2001).

The nitrogen content of heather (*Calluna vulgaris*) and moss species including woolly fringe moss (*Racomitrium lanuginosum*), increased during the twentieth century (Pitcairn *et al.*, 1995; Woolgrove, 1994). The tissue nitrogen content of *R. lanuginosum* reflected the magnitude of the atmospheric inputs, being least in north-western Scotland and greatest (as much as six-fold greater) near to urban centres in northern England (Baddeley *et al.*, 1994). This regional difference was less marked during the nineteenth century when nitrogen concentrations were lower (Baddeley *et al.*, 1994). With greater precipitation and larger NH_4^+ and NO_3^- concentrations at higher altitudes, it is not surprising that nitrogen tissue content is also larger at elevated sites (Baddeley *et al.*, 1994; Hicks *et al.*, 2000; Leith *et al.*, 1999).

Increased levels of foliar nitrogen have been related to increased frequencies of pest outbreaks. During the latter part of last century, winter moth (*Operophtera brumata*) outbreaks on *Calluna vulgaris* increased in frequency across Scotland (Kerslake *et al.*, 1998). The frequency of heather beetle (*Lochmaea suturalis*) outbreaks on *Calluna vulgaris* has also increased (A. MacDonald, pers. comm.).

Critical levels of atmospheric nitrogen for vegetation are exceeded in very few areas of Scotland. Whilst those for NO_x are restricted to urban centres and major roads, those for NH_3 are limited to the vicinity of large intensive livestock farms. Concentrations of ammonia decline rapidly over distances of tens of metres from the source although, within this area, ammonia significantly affects ground flora composition, even within woodlands. For example, there are increases in the abundance of nitrophilous species such as the Yorkshire fog grass (*Holcus lanatus*) and rosebay willowherb (*Chamerion angustifolium*) close to sources of ammonia (Pitcairn *et al.*, 1998). Reduced nitrogen dominates the atmospheric nitrogen input to semi-natural ecosystems and will continue to do this for the foreseeable future.

7.4.6 *Effects of ozone on ecosystems across Scotland*
Ozone damage has not yet been observed on any semi-natural ecosystem in the field in Scotland. However, observations of plants in experimental systems indicate that sensitive cultivars of indicator species are damaged by ambient concentrations in the range of those currently experienced across Scotland. The extensive data for open-top chamber experiments for both crop and semi-natural species also show effects at AOT40 values within the range of those observed in the air across Scotland (e.g. PORG, 1997; NEGTAP, 2001; Bergmann *et al.*, 1995; Thwaites, 1996).

7.4.7 Future prospects

Between 1995/97 and 2010, the predicted area for which critical loads for acidity for soils are exceeded, is expected to decline by 12 per cent (Mackey *et al.*, 2001). Areas that will still remain in exceedance include large tracts of the west central highlands, south-west Scotland, and north-east Grampian, the latter being particularly affected by deposition of ammonia and ammonium. Peatlands are expected to experience a decrease in the area of exceedance by 2010. However, acidified peatland may take several decades to recover to a more usual pH of about 4 (Skiba *et al.*, 1989).

The reduction in emissions of acidifying pollutants by 2010 is estimated to produce a 67 per cent decline in exceedance of freshwater acidification. Like soils, the areas of exceedance will be areas of high wet deposition, namely Galloway and the west central highlands. In both these regions, however, the magnitude of the exceedance will be small relative to values for 1995-1997 (Mackey *et al.*, 2001). The recovery of acidified freshwaters will be delayed by the release of sulphur adsorbed by soils, with the recovery of the composition of freshwater biota, such as diatoms, possibly taking decades (Battarbee *et al.*, 1988).

Reductions in the emissions of nitrogen oxides to be achieved by the year 2010 are predicted to lead to a 37 per cent decrease in the area of exceedance of the critical loads for nutrient nitrogen (Mackey *et al.*, 2001). However, the decline in the fertility of ecosystems that have undergone eutrophication is expected to be slow and the re-appearance of species associated with less fertile conditions is also expected to be either very slow or unlikely to occur in the absence of management.

By 2010, it is expected that emissions of the main ozone precursors across the UK will decline by 20 to 30 per cent from 1997 values, and that the area of critical levels exceedance may decline by about 20 per cent across Scotland (NEGTAP, 2001). However, global mean ozone concentrations are expected to increase. With the highest annual mean concentrations found in upland areas, which are already stressed by the deposition of other atmospheric pollutants, it is difficult to predict the effect of increases in the background concentrations of ozone on upland ecosystems. With increasing ambient carbon dioxide levels and warmer minimum temperatures tending to encourage vegetative growth, the net effect of such climate change impacts with ozone damage are difficult to predict. However these upland locations and the semi-natural plant communities present, are the focus for effects assessment (NEGTAP, 2001). This work will require further field and laboratory experiments. Ground-level ozone therefore poses a long-term, but as yet unquantified, threat to semi-natural ecosystems across Scotland.

7.5 Conclusions

This chapter has highlighted the particular characteristics of the pollution climate in Scotland and the ecosystems at risk. Assessments of this kind are necessary to develop appropriate control measures. With emissions projected to decline over this decade, ambient concentrations and deposition rates of some pollutants are also expected to decline.

However, trends over the last 20 years indicate that the rate of decline of deposition is not as rapid as those of emissions, due to non-linearities in the spatial patterns of emission and deposition. Observations made on Scottish lochs identify areas where critical levels and loads were exceeded early in the last century, and where the water chemistry reveals the first stages in the process of recovery. However, it is expected that recovery of acidified ecosystems will take many decades. The decline in areas receiving excessive nitrogen input may be much slower than the reduction in sulphur and acidity, particularly if ammonia emissions remain uncontrolled. Areas that have undergone eutrophication may also take even longer to recover than the acidified areas, the effects of nutrient nitrogen being persistent where nitrogen is retained in the soil-plant system. Where nutrient nitrogen is mobilised, the speed of recovery of the ecosystem may well depend upon the longevity of the dominant vegetation.

Increasing global background tropospheric ozone concentrations may pose the greatest long-term threat to vegetation across Scotland. At present, the precautionary principle would lead us to suggest reducing levels of ozone precursors, especially given the proximity of the current background concentration across the country to the threshold for adverse effects. Such action would, however, require collective reductions in ozone precursors throughout the Northern Hemisphere, which poses a major challenge for environmental protection in the coming decade.

Acknowledgements
Thanks to Justin Goodwin of AEA Technology, Abingdon, for supplying the emissions data used to determine trends and apportion sources to Scotland, Julian Holbrook, Angus Macdonald, Andrew Coupar and Jon Foot for discussions about the natural heritage implications and Ulrike Dragosits and Mhairi Coyle for supplying maps and figures.

References
Anonymous (1972). *Air Pollution across National Boundaries. The Impact on the Environment of Sulphur in Air and Precipitation. Sweden's Case Study for the United Nations Conference on the Human Environment.* Swedish Royal Ministry for Foreign Affairs and the Royal Ministry of Agriculture, Stockholm.

Baddeley, J.A., Thompson, D.B.A. and Lee, J.A. (1994). Regional and historical variation in the nitrogen content of *Racomitrium lanuginosum* in Britain in relation to atmospheric nitrogen deposition. *Environmental Pollution*, **84**, 189–196.

Barr, C.J., Bunce, R.G.H., Clarke, R.T., Fuller, R.M., Firse, M.T., Gillespie, M.K., Groom, G.B., Hallam, C.J., Horning, M., Howard, D.C and Ness, M.J. (1993). *Countryside Survey 1990 Main Report.* Department of the Environment, London.

Battarbee, R., Flower, R.J., Stevenson, A.C., Jones, V.J., Harriman, R. and Appleby, P.G. (1988). Diatom and chemical evidence for reversibility of acidification of Scottish lochs. *Nature,* **332**, 530–532.

Bergmann, E., Bender, J. and Weigel, H. (1995). Growth response and foliar sensitivies of native herbaceous species to ozone exposure. *Water, Air and Soil Pollutants*, **85**, 1437-1442.

Carroll, J.A., Caporn, S.J.M., Cawley, L., Read, D.J. and Lee, J.A. (1999). The effect of increased deposition of atmospheric nitrogen on *Calluna vulgaris* in upland Britain. *New Phytologist*, **141**, 423-431.

Fowler, D., Dragosits, U., Pitcairn, C., Sutton, M., Hall, J., Roy, D. and Weidemann, A. (2002). Deposition of acidity and nitrogen and exposure of terrestrial surfaces to ozone in Scotland; mapping critical loads, critical levels and exceedances. Scottish Natural Heritage Research, Survey and Monitoring Report No. 169.

Fuhrer, J., Skarby, L. and Ashmore, M.R. (1997). Critical levels for ozone effects on vegetation in Europe. *Environmental Pollution,* **97**, 91-106.

Gibbons, D.W., Reid, J.B. and Chapman, R.A. (1993). *The New Atlas of Breeding Birds in Britain and Ireland: 1988–1991.* T & A D Poyser, London.

Gilbert, O.L. (1970). A biological scale for the estimation of sulphur dioxide pollution. *New Phytologist*, **69**, 629–634.

Gordon, C., Wynn, J.M. and Woodin, S.J. (2001). Impacts of increased nitrogen supply on high Arctic heath: the importance of bryophytes and phosphorous availability. *New Phytologist*, **149**, 461-471.

Green, R. and Green, J. (1997). *Otter Survey of Scotland 1991-1994*. The Vincent Wildlife Trust, London.

Green, R.E. (1998). Long-term decline in the thickness of eggshells of thrushes, *Turdus* spp., in Britain. *Proceedings of the Royal Society London*, **B265**, 679–684.

Haines-Young, R.H., Barr, C.J., Black, H.I.J., Briggs, D.J., Bunce, R.G.H., Clarke, R.T., Cooper, A., Dawson, F.H., Firbank, L.G., Fuller, R.M., Furse, M.T., Gillespie, M.K, Hill, R., Hornung, M., Howard, D.C., McCann, T., Morecroft, M.D., Petit, S., Sier, A.R.J., Smart, S.M., Smith, G.M., Stott, A.P., Stuart, R.C., and Watkins, J.W. (2000). *Accounting for Nature: Assessing Habitats in the UK Countryside*. Department of the Environment, Transport and the Regions, London.

Harriman, R., Morrison, B.R.S., Birks, H.J.B., Christie, A.E.G., Collen, P. and Watt, A.W. (1995). Long term chemical and biological trends in Scottish streams and lochs. *Water, Air and Soil Pollution*, **85**, 701-706.

Hartley, S.E. (1997). The effects of grazing and nutrient inputs on grass-heather competition. *Botanical Journal of Scotland*, **49**, 317-326.

Hawksworth, D.L. and Rose, F. (1970). Qualitative scale for estimating sulphur dioxide air pollution in England and Wales using epiphytic lichens. *Nature*, **227**, 145–148.

Hicks, W.K., Leith, I.D., Woodin, S.J. and Fowler, D. (2000). Can the foliar nitrogen concentration of upland vegetation be used for predicting atmospheric nitrogen deposition? Evidence from field studies. *Environmental Pollution*, **107**, 367-376.

Kerslake, J.E., Woodin, S.J. and Hartley, S.E. (1998). Effects of carbon dioxide and nitrogen enrichment on plant-insect interaction: the quality of *Calluna vulgaris* as a host for *Operophtera brumata*. *New Phytologist*, **140**, 43-53.

Leith, I.D., Hicks, W.K., Fowler, D. and Woodin, S.J. (1999). Differential responses of UK upland plants to nitrogen deposition. *New Phytologist*, **141**, 277-289.

Looney, J.H.H. and James, P.W. (1988). Effects on lichens. In *Acid Rain and Britain's Natural Ecosystems*, ed. by M. Ashmore, N. Bell and C. Garretty. Imperial College Centre for Environmental Technology, London. pp. 13-25.

McGowan, G.M., Palmer, S.C.F., French, D.D., Barr, C.J., Howard, D.C. and Smart, S.M. (2001). Trends in broad habitats: Scotland 1990-1998. Unpublished report.

Mackey, E.C., Shaw, P., Holbrook, J., Shewry, M.C. Saunders, G., Hall, J. and Ellis, N.E. (2001). *Natural Heritage Trends: Scotland 2001*. Scottish Natural Heritage, Perth.

Miller, J.D., Duff, E.I., Hirst, D., Anderson, H.A. and Bell, J.S. (2001). Temporal change in soil properties at an upland Scottish site between 1956 and 1997. *The Science of the Total Environment*, **265**, 15–26.

National Expert Group on Transboundary Atmospheric Pollution (NEGTAP) (2001). *Transboundary Air Pollution: Acidification, Eutrophication and Ground-level Ozone in the UK*. Department for Environment, Food and Rural Affairs, London.

Pitcairn, C.E.R., Fowler, D. and Grace, J. (1995). Deposition of fixed atmospheric nitrogen and foliar nitrogen content of bryophytes and *Calluna vulgaris*. *Environmental Pollution*, **88**, 193-205.

Pitcairn, C.E.R., Leith, I.D., Sheppard, L.J., Sutton, M.A., Fowler, D., Munro, R.C., Tang, S. and Wilson, D. (1998). The relationship between nitrogen deposition, species composition and foliar nitrogen concentrations in woodland flora in the vicinity of livestock farms. *Environmental Pollution*, **102 (S1)**, 41-48.

Photochemical Oxidants Review Group (PORG) (1997). *Ozone in the UK: Fourth Report of the Photochemical Oxidants Review Group.* Department of the Environment, Transport and the Regions, London.

Posch, M., de Smet, P.A.M., Hettelingh, J.-P. and Downing R.J. (2001). Modelling and Mapping of Critical Thresholds in Europe. RIVM Report No. 259101010. National Institute of Public Health and the Environment (RIVM), Bilthoven, The Netherlands.

Press, M.C., Woodin, S.J. and Lee, J.A. (1986). The potential importance of an increased nitrogen supply to the growth of ombrotrophic *Sphagnum* species. *New Phytologist,* **103**, 45-55.

Skiba, U., Cresser, M.S., Derwent, R.G. and Futty, D.W. (1989). Peat acidification in Scotland. *Nature,* **337**, 68–69.

Soulsby, C., Turnbull, D., Hirst, D., Langan, S.J. and Owen, R. (1997). Reversibility of stream acidification in the Cairngorm region of Scotland. *Journal of Hydrology,* **195**, 291–311.

Thompson, D.B.A. and Baddeley, J.A. (1991). Some effects of acidic deposition on montane *Racomitrium lanuginosum* heaths. In *The Effects of Acid Deposition on Nature Conservation in Great Britain,* ed. by S.J. Woodin and A.M. Farmer. Nature Conservancy Council, Peterborough. pp. 17–28.

Thwaites, R. (1996). The effects of tropospheric ozone on calcareous grassland communities. Unpublished PhD thesis, Imperial College, London.

Tipping, E., Smith, E.J., Hughes, S., Lawlor, A.J., Lofts, S., Simon, B.M., Stevens, P.A., Stidson, R. and Vincent, C.D. (2001). Metals in ombrotrophic peats across Scotland. Scottish Natural Heritage Research, Survey and Monitoring Report No. 129.

Vickery, J. (1991). Breeding density of dippers *Cinclus cinclus,* grey wagtails, *Motacilla cinerea,* and common sandpipers, *Actitis hypoleucos* in relation to the acidity of streams in south-west Scotland. *Ibis,* **133**, 178–185.

Wayne, R.P. (1985). *Chemistry of Atmospheres.* Oxford University Press, Oxford.

Woolgrove, C.E. (1994). Impacts of climate change and pollutants in snowmelt on snowbed ecology. Unpublished PhD thesis, University of Aberdeen.

8 MODELLING HEAVY METAL DEPOSITION ACROSS SCOTLAND

A.G. McDonald, E. Nemitz, U. Dragosits, M.A. Sutton and D. Fowler

Summary

1. Heavy metal emission and deposition to the UK generally, and to Scotland in particular, have been neglected. Only recently have spatially disaggregated inventories and deposition maps become available.

2. Scotland is a net importer of most of the heavy metals. Although subject to considerable uncertainty, typically 20 per cent to 40 per cent of the heavy metal deposition in Scotland is from internal sources.

3. Recent work to develop a critical loads approach suggests that soils in some areas of Scotland exceed critical loads. Such estimates require validation from much higher quality emission inventories and a network of deposition measurement stations.

8.1 Introduction

Heavy metals of major concern include arsenic (As), cadmium (Cd), chromium (Cr), copper (Cu), lead (Pb), nickel (Ni), selenium (Se), vanadium (V) and zinc (Zn). These metals are mostly emitted by industrial and fuel combustion processes, such as vehicles, power stations and steel works. Once deposited, toxic metals can accumulate in water bodies, vegetation and soils, such as peat (Tipping *et al.*, 2001), which can seriously affect fauna and flora. While the primary concern is the effect on soils and biota, heavy metals can also enter the food chain, leading to potentially serious effects on human health, including the impairment of the nervous and immune systems. It is important, therefore, to understand the processes controlling the deposition of heavy metals and to derive heavy metal deposition maps at a spatial resolution which is appropriate to calculate exceedances of critical loads for heavy metals. The critical load is a measure of environmental sensitivity, defined as the deposition, below which significant harmful effects on sensitive elements of the environment do not occur according to present knowledge. Whilst the critical loads approach is commonly used for acidification and nitrogen (eutrophication) (e.g. NEGTAP, 2001), for heavy metals it is still in its infancy. Combinations of experimental and empirical techniques have been used to improve our understanding of the response of soils and biota to metal deposition (UBA, 1998). The United Nations Economic Commission for Europe Convention on Long Range Transboundary Air Pollution (CLRTAP) specifically targets Cd and Pb in its mapping and critical loads programmes.

8.2 Method

The atmospheric transport model used to calculate the heavy metal deposition is a statistical Lagrangian multi-layer dispersion model (FRAME-HM), originally developed to study the deposition of ammonia (Singles *et al.*, 1998), and adapted for heavy metals. The boundary conditions at the edge of the UK model domain are calculated using a European atmospheric transport model (TERN) (ApSimon *et al.*, 1994), together with a European heavy metal emissions inventory for 1990, adjusted for changes in emissions between 1990 and 1998 (Berdowski *et al.*, 1997).

It is known that the total UK emissions of most heavy metals have been decreasing steadily over the last 30 years (Figure 8.1), but the 1998 'official' National Environmental Technology Centre National Atmospheric Emissions Inventory (Goodwin *et al.*, 2000) was the first to be spatially disaggregated (see www.aeat.co.uk/netcen/airqual). The inventory reports area sources, which are dominated by low-level emissions (e.g. traffic) and point sources (e.g. large industrial plant), which are mostly emitted at an elevated height in the atmosphere, separately. These are injected into the appropriate height layer, using source characteristics obtained from a separate study (Nemitz *et al.*, 1999).

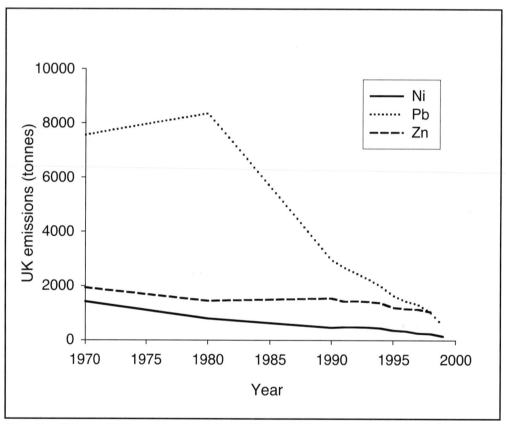

Figure 8.1. UK annual heavy metal emissions from 1970 to 1998 (source: Goodwin *et al.*, 2000).

The model parameters used to calculate deposition, such as wet scavenging ratios and land-use specific dry deposition velocities (V_d), were derived experimentally in UK process studies (Ashmore *et al.*, 2001) (see www.aeat.co.uk/netcen/airqual/reports/metals/Critical_Loads_2000.pdf). In particular, V_d is calculated from a combination of micrometeorological measurements of size-dependence (Nemitz *et al.*, in press), and size-distributions of metals measured in the UK (Allen *et al.*, 2001).

8.3 Results

Table 8.1 shows the deposition of metals within Scotland from Scottish sources, non-Scottish UK sources, and non-UK sources, obtained from the FRAME-HM model, and, for comparison, the Scottish emissions. Non-UK sources make a significant contribution to the total deposition, although no European emission data are available for Se and V. For all metals, slightly more (between 10 per cent and 55 per cent) is deposited across Scotland than is emitted within the country. For comparison, Scotland is a net importer of ammonia and a net exporter of oxidised nitrogen, while the import/export budget of sulphur dioxide is roughly in balance (Fowler *et al.*, Chapter 7).

Table 8.1. 1998 emissions (in tonnes) from Scottish sources (Goodwin *et al.*, 2000), and deposition (also in tonnes) across Scotland from various different sources. There are no European data (n.d.) for Se and V.

Metals	Scottish emissions	Deposition from			
		Scottish sources	Non-Scottish UK sources	Non-UK sources	All sources
As	2.7	1.2	0.9	0.9	3.0
Cd	0.43	0.26	0.24	0.12	0.62
Cr	4.1	1.8	1.5	2.2	5.5
Cu	3.2	1.9	2.0	1.7	5.6
Ni	12.5	11.3	5.4	10.8	27.5
Pb	62.2	27.7	27.7	20.8	76.2
Se	7.0	3.1	2.1	n.d.	> 5.2
V	61.9	26.6	14.3	n.d.	> 40.9
Zn	44.1	28.1	19.1	10.8	58.0

The maps in Figure 8.2 show the total deposition from all sources for selected metals. The deposition fields of As, Cu and Pb roughly follow the pattern of population and traffic densities, while individual point sources (e.g. Grangemouth) dominate the deposition pattern for Cd and Ni. The deposition fields for Scottish, non-Scottish UK and non-UK sources are shown in Figure 8.3 for Ni. Scottish sources dominate the deposition in central Scotland, while long-range transport delivers a significant flux to eastern Scotland. Non-Scottish UK sources mainly affect the deposition in southern Scotland.

8.4 Discussion

The long-range transport of heavy metals from sources outside Scotland leads to a substantial proportion of the deposition across Scotland. In fact, Scotland is a net importer of metals, whereas the UK as a whole is a net-exporter of metals (Ashmore *et al.*, 2001).

A disaggregated emission inventory is available for 1997, and was compiled independently of the National Atmospheric Emissions Inventory, but with slightly different methodology. Trends and inter-year variability due to changing climatic conditions can

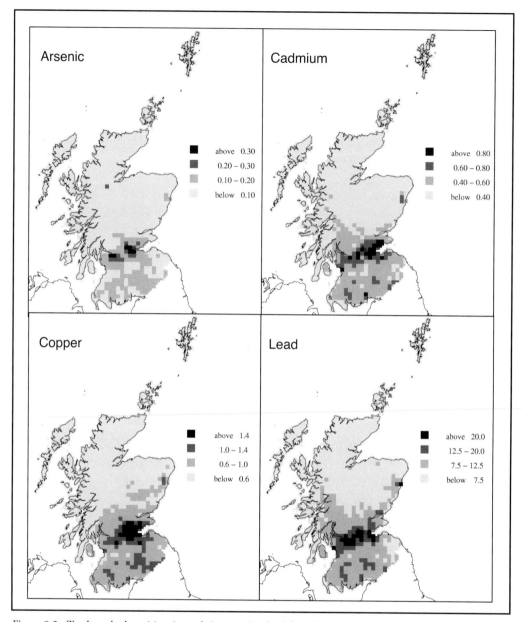

Figure 8.2. Total yearly deposition (g per ha) across Scotland for selected heavy metals.

only be assessed when emission data for later years become available. Emission inventories are likely to be the largest source of error in calculating metal deposition, and current data suggest that these probably underestimate the total emissions. However, since it is known that total metal emissions have declined across Europe, it is very likely that the total deposition of metals across Scotland will also have declined.

At present, the estimation of critical load exceedances is at a very early stage, especially for vegetation. Initial results indicate that in Scotland, there are very few areas where the critical load for soils appears to be exceeded for cadmium, though for lead there appear to

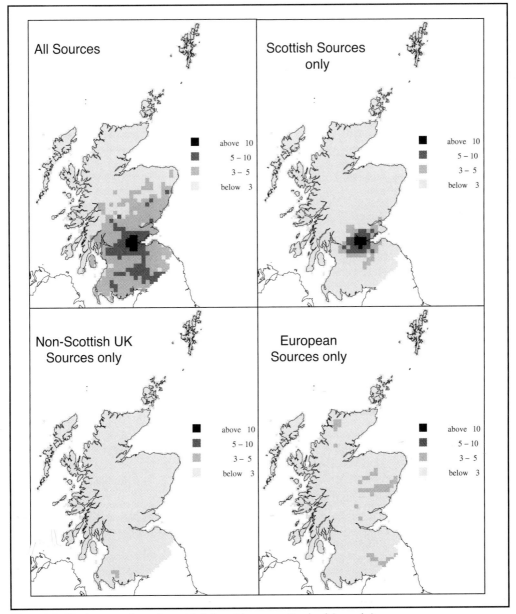

Figure 8.3. Yearly source dependent nickel deposition across Scotland (g per ha).

be some areas of exceedance, mainly in the eastern Highlands and Grampian regions (Ashmore *et al.*, 2001). The critical loads approach is only gradually being extended to other metals, such as As and Hg (mercury). This information, along with the metal deposition data, is of importance to SNH and SEPA, to assist in identifying areas where environmental damage is likely due to the toxic effects of heavy metals.

Future developments to the model, including the use of size-dependent deposition velocities, will improve the deposition estimates. This will improve the estimates of critical load exceedances. There are very few direct measurements of heavy metal deposition in

Scotland (or the rest of the UK). Thus there are few data for model validation. A high quality measurement network is urgently needed to assess the deposition fields presented here.

Acknowledgements

This work was funded by the UK Department for Environment, Food and Rural Affairs, the Scottish Executive, the National Assembly for Wales and the Department of the Environment for Northern Ireland, as well as by the Environmental Diagnostics Programme of NERC.

References

Allen, A.G., Nemitz, E., Shi, J.P., Harrison, R.M. and Greenwood, J.C. (2001). Size distributions of trace metals in atmospheric aerosols in the United Kingdom. *Atmospheric Environment*, **35**, 4581-4591.

ApSimon, H.M., Barker, B.M. and Kayin, S. (1994). Modelling studies of the atmospheric release and transport of ammonia – applications of the TERN model to an EMEP site in eastern England in anticyclone episodes. *Atmospheric Environment*, **28**, 665-678.

Ashmore, M., Colgan, A., Farago, M., Fowler, D., Hall, J., Hill, M., Jordan, C., Lawlor, A., Lofts, S., Nemitz, E., Pan, G., Paton, G., Rieuwerts, J., Thornton, I. and Tipping, E. (2001). *Development of a Critical Load Methodology for Toxic Metals in Soils and Surface Waters: Stage II*. Department of Environmental Science, University of Bradford, Bradford.

Berdowski, J., Baas, J., Bloos, J.P.J., Visschedijk, A.J.H. and Zandveld, P.Y.J. (1997). *The European Atmospheric Emission Inventory of Heavy Metals and Persistent Organic Pollutants*. Umweltbundesamt, Berlin.

Goodwin, J.W.L., Salway, A.G., Murrells, T.P., Dore, C.J., Passant, N.R. and Eggleston, H.S. (2000). *UK Emissions of Air Pollutants 1970–1998*. National Environmental Technology Centre, AEA Technology, Culham.

NEGTAP (2001). *Transboundary Air Pollution: Acidification, Eutrophication and Group-level Ozone in the UK*. CEH Edinburgh, Edinburgh.

Nemitz, E., Fowler, D., Dragosits, U. and Pitcairn, C.E.R. (1999). Data for atmospheric transport and deposition numerical modelling of trace metals. Unpublished report.

Nemitz, E., Gallagher, M.W., Duyzer, J.H. and Fowler, D. (in press). Micrometeorological measurements of particle deposition velocities to moorland vegetation. *Quarterly Journal of the Royal Meteorological Society*.

Singles, R.J., Sutton, M.A. and Weston, K.J. (1998). A multi-layer model to describe the atmospheric transport and deposition of ammonia in Great Britain. *Atmospheric Environment*, **32**, 393-399.

UBA (1998). *Workshop on Critical Limits and Effect Based Approaches for Heavy Metals and Persistent Organic Pollutants*. German Federal Environment Agency (Umweltbundesamt), Berlin.

Tipping, E., Smith, E.J., Hughes, S., Lawlor, A.J., Lofts, S., Simon, B.M., Stevens, P.A., Stidson, R. and Vincent, C.D. (2001). Metals in ombrotrophic peats across Scotland. Scottish Natural Heritage Research, Survey and Monitoring Report No. 129.

9 THE STATE OF SCOTLAND'S FRESH WATERS

C. Ross Doughty, Philip J. Boon and Peter S. Maitland

Summary

1.   The chemical and biological quality of Scottish rivers is high and is continuing to improve. Improvements have been particularly dramatic in the formerly heavily polluted rivers of Central Scotland.

2.   Mean annual flows in rivers across Scotland and the frequency of flood events in western catchments have increased in recent years as a result of climate change.

3.   Extensive monitoring of Scotland's freshwater lochs began only recently and it is too early to discern trends, although some recovery from acidification is apparent. Palaeolimnological studies reveal that over longer timescales many lochs show evidence of eutrophication or acidification.

4.   Assessment of natural heritage trends is hindered by the lack of information on some components of the freshwater biota and the short-term, site-specific nature of most studies. The effect of European legislation has been to focus attention on particular habitats and species, whereas a broader view would be more desirable.

5.   Over the last decade the number of small lowland ponds has increased and riparian vegetation alongside lowland streams has become more dominated by tall woody species. Case studies illustrate the value of historical reconstruction for revealing habitat trends and techniques such as River Habitat Survey are likely to prove invaluable for this purpose in the future.

6.   Human activities have resulted in the loss of many freshwater fish stocks over the last 200 years. The number of freshwater fish species has increased owing to the introduction of alien species and UK species non-native to Scotland, posing a further threat to native stocks. Populations of the globally-threatened freshwater pearl mussel have declined dramatically.

7.   Recovery from domestic and industrial pollution and acidification, together with better forestry management practices and planning controls, give cause for optimism. However, climate change, diffuse pollution, the rapid expansion of fish farming and the introduction of further non-native species pose a continuing threat.

8.   European legislation is having an increasing influence on the conservation and management of Scotland's fresh waters, but local people have a major role to play through, for example, biodiversity initiatives and involvement in implementing the European Union's Water Framework Directive.

9.   Information is needed on little-studied freshwater habitats such as groundwaters and temporary surface waters. Action is required to protect species which are threatened in Scotland, but are not protected by European legislation, and to restore habitats and species which have been lost or damaged. Most importantly, a Scottish freshwater strategy is needed to promote the sustainable development of Scotland's freshwater resources.

9.1 Introduction

Scotland is blessed with an abundance of fresh waters. It has been estimated that the total river length shown on 1:50,000 scale maps is about 100,000 km and the total number of standing water bodies discernible at this scale is around 27,000 (SEPA, 1999). A comprehensive review, including uses and threats to this considerable resource, has been published by Maitland *et al.* (1994). Additional information on pollution and other pressures affecting Scotland's fresh waters has also become available (SEPA, 1999).

In this chapter environmental and natural heritage trends in Scotland's rivers, lochs and other inland waters, particularly over the last few decades, are described, together with the changes that may be expected during the current century. This has proved rather easier for environmental trends because of long-term monitoring by the Scottish Environment Protection Agency (SEPA) and its predecessors. Even here, considerably more information is available for rivers than for lochs and other water body types. General trends in freshwater habitats and species are more difficult to identify because of the lack of long-term datasets, so here only selected examples are provided.

To assess future trends, the ways in which environmental problems affecting fresh waters have been dealt with in the past are considered. Whereas it is acknowledged that past performance is not necessarily a reliable guide to the future, it provides a useful indication of what might be expected in the absence of a major shift in organisational and public attitudes. The future of Scotland's fresh waters is being increasingly determined by decisions made at the European level, but there remains ample scope for the people of Scotland to play a leading role (see Mackey, Chapter 1; Currie, Chapter 2). The European Union's Water Framework Directive, particularly with its emphasis on the involvement of all interested parties in the river basin management process, may provide the catalyst for such a fundamental change in attitudes.

9.2 River and stream quality

9.2.1 SEPA quality classification

SEPA classifies the quality of Scotland's running waters annually. The classification scheme uses chemical (dissolved oxygen, biochemical oxygen demand (BOD), ammonia, iron, pH and soluble reactive phosphorus), biological (macroinvertebrates) and aesthetic (general and sewage-derived litter) components to place river stretches into five quality classes, ranging from A1 (excellent) to D (seriously polluted). The results are used both to report on the overall state of Scotland's rivers and to assess progress towards environmental improvement targets. The scheme is default-based i.e. the overall class is determined by the lowest class of any of the individual components.

In 2000, 91 per cent of Scottish rivers by length were classified as excellent or good (Table 9.1). Compared with 1996, the percentage of rivers in class A1 has fallen slightly, because in the intervening period additional river stretches have been monitored (the scheme assumes that unmonitored stretches are class A1). The percentage of river length classified as poor or seriously polluted fell from 2.6 per cent in 1996 to 1.9 per cent in 2000, representing the removal of 361 km from the two lowest quality classes, equivalent to three times the length of the River Clyde.

The major causes of pollution in Scottish rivers in 1996 were sewage effluent (33.9 per cent of classes B, C and D by length), diffuse agricultural pollution (26.2 per cent),

Table 9.1. River quality classifications in 1996 and 2000, length (rounded to nearest km) and percentage of river in each class (total length classified = 50,254 km; percentages in italics in parentheses).

Year	A1 Excellent	A2 Good	B Fair	C Poor	D Seriously Polluted
1996	37,743 *(75.1)*	8,187 *(16.3)*	3,006 *(6.0)*	1,179 *(2.3)*	138 *(0.3)*
2000	36,477 *(72.6)*	9,405 *(18.7)*	3,417 *(6.8)*	873 *(1.7)*	83 *(0.2)*

acidification (11.7 per cent), urban drainage (11.4 per cent), mine drainage (8.9 per cent) and point-source agricultural pollution (6.3 per cent). Together these accounted for over 98 per cent of downgraded river length (SEPA, 1999). A comparable analysis for 2000 is not yet available, but little change is expected.

Before SEPA was established in 1996, river water quality in Scotland was classified every five years, starting in 1975, although by then some significant improvements in river quality had already been achieved (Hammerton, 1994). Unfortunately it is difficult to compare classification results from 1975 with the present because the methods of classification have changed over the years. For example, before 1996, the biological component was reported separately from the chemical one. Also, very different methods were used to derive the biological classification in 1975, 1980 and 1990 (there was no biological classification in 1985). River quality can be reclassified by applying current methods to historical data, but difficulties arise because, for example, invertebrate identification has improved owing to the development of better keys and quality control has become much tighter. The aesthetics component of the classification was not introduced until 1997.

Despite these problems, biological quality at selected sites in 1980 and 2000 has been compared using the biological component of the current SEPA river classification scheme (Table 9.2). In doing so it has been assumed that the physical characteristics of the sites have not changed significantly. These sites are all on formerly heavily polluted rivers in the Central Belt and have improved mainly as a result of sewage treatment upgrades or the

Table 9.2. Changes in biological quality of selected polluted rivers, 1980 to 2000. The classes are A2 = good, B = fair, C = poor and D = seriously polluted.

River and location	1980 Class	2000 Class
River Clyde, Tidal Weir	D	C
River Kelvin, Balmuildy Bridge	C	A2
Allander Water, downstream Milngavie	C	A2
White Cart Water, Crookston	C	A2
North Calder Water, Carnbroe	D	B
South Calder Water, Motherwell	D	A2

closure of polluting industries. The improvement in the condition of the South Calder Water at Motherwell following upgrades in sewage treatment and the closure of Ravenscraig steelworks is particularly striking. It is likely that some of the observed improvements have resulted from higher dilution of polluting discharges by increasing river flows related to climate change (Curran and Robertson, 1991).

Since 1994, chemical and biological data collected by SEPA from eight Scottish rivers (Allt a'Mharcaidh, Clyde, Cree, Eden, Ewe, Spey, Stinchar and Tweed) have been collated by the UK Environmental Change Network (ECN), a research initiative concerned with the monitoring, analysis and prediction of long-term environmental change. Although this work will eventually provide additional valuable information on quality trends in the rivers concerned, the extent to which these trends will reflect environmental change across Scotland as a whole is debatable.

9.2.2 Countryside Survey 2000

The biological quality of rivers and streams in Scotland has also been assessed using macroinvertebrates as part of Countryside Survey 2000 (CS2000) (Haines-Young *et al.*, 2000). The methodology was similar to that used in the biological component of SEPA's river quality classification scheme.

CS2000 was a Government-sponsored programme to collect information about the stock of broad habitat types in the countryside and their condition, allowing the monitoring of changes over time. The survey was actually carried out in 1998 and involved sampling at about 180 randomly selected sites on small rivers and streams across Scotland. Results were expressed using the Environment Agency's classification scheme in England and Wales which has six classes rather than five. These range from grade a (very good) to grade f (bad), with grades a to d being equivalent to SEPA's classes A1 to C, and grades e and f corresponding to SEPA's class D.

In 1998, 60 per cent of sites were in grades a and b compared with fewer than 40 per cent in the previous Countryside Survey (CS90) in 1990. Improvements were noted in all areas of Scotland, with 63 per cent of sites improving (probability greater than 50 per cent) since 1990, compared with 11 per cent deteriorating and 26 per cent remaining unchanged. While improvements in lowland sites may be attributed to the effects of tighter regulation by SEPA and the former River Purification Boards (RPBs), or investment by the regional water authorities, it is difficult to account for the improvement in upland sites. It has been suggested that the improvement may in fact be the result of poorer than expected results in 1990 owing to a particularly wet spring that year (Haines-Young *et al.*, 2000).

9.2.3 Monitoring of acid rivers

Acidification is one of the main pressures on river quality in Scotland. Acidification is caused by emissions of sulphur (mainly from industry) and nitrogen (mainly from motor vehicles) and is a problem over wide areas of Scotland where geology and soils are base-poor and are unable to neutralise acid deposition. The effects are exacerbated by coniferous afforestation (Morrison, 1994). Information on acidification in Scottish rivers has been collected since 1975 by the Fisheries Research Services (FRS) Freshwater Laboratory, Pitlochry, and since the early 1980s by the RPBs (later SEPA) and from 1988 by the UK Acid Waters Monitoring Network (UKAWMN).

Emissions and deposition of sulphur have declined dramatically since the 1970s, raising expectations of recovery from acidification in affected Scottish rivers and streams. Indeed there is now a growing body of evidence to support chemical recovery from acidification in several parts of Scotland. This evidence takes the form of reductions in non-marine sulphate concentrations, and, at some sites, increases in pH and alkalinity. However, evidence for biological recovery is patchy (Anonymous, 2001).

SEPA has been examining long-term macroinvertebrate data from acid streams in south-west Scotland for evidence of biological recovery. At most sites, no clear evidence of recovery has been found. Trends are difficult to detect because of between-year variations in the occurrence and abundance of acid-sensitive species. These variations may reflect differences in the frequency and intensity of acid episodes or may be related to climatic variations. However, there are indications of recovery at a few sites such as the River Tarf and the River Doon (Figure 9.1). Recovery is most likely to be detected at sites of intermediate acidity. It may be some time before the more acid sites recover sufficiently to permit recolonisation by acid-sensitive species.

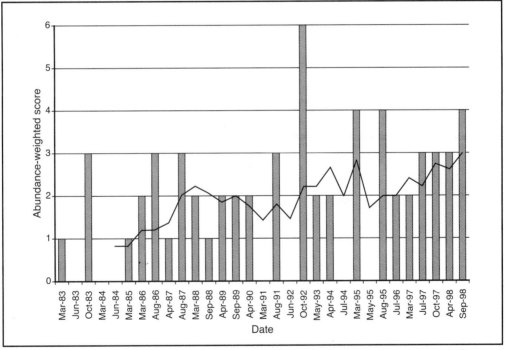

Figure 9.1. Acid-sensitive invertebrates in the River Doon below Loch Doon, 1983 to 1998 (with five-point moving average).

9.2.4 Fish populations

Although macroinvertebrates are the most commonly used group of organisms for assessing the quality status of Scottish rivers, fish populations can also be used for this purpose. Atlantic salmon (*Salmo salar*) disappeared from many rivers in central Scotland during the nineteenth century as a result of increasing pollution from industry and the growing human population. Their well-documented recolonisation of many of their former haunts over the last 30 years is a clear indication to scientists and the public alike of improving river quality (Mackay and Doughty, 1986; Gardiner and McLaren, 1991; see also Baxter and Hutchinson, Chapter 15). Key factors in the return of salmon have been improvements in sewage treatment and the decline of traditional polluting industries.

Additional evidence for improvements in river quality is provided by records of pollution-related fish kills. Detailed records of fish kills are available for the former Clyde RPB area since 1978. These show the frequency of fish kills rising to a peak in the mid-1980s followed by an overall decline, although with year-to-year fluctuations (Figure 9.2). Agricultural pollution (particularly silage and slurry) was the major cause of fish kills during this period, accounting for 43 per cent of all incidents. The numbers of fish kills caused by agriculture, industry, water treatment and poaching with toxic chemicals have all declined. The number attributable to sewage discharges has remained at a constant, but low level.

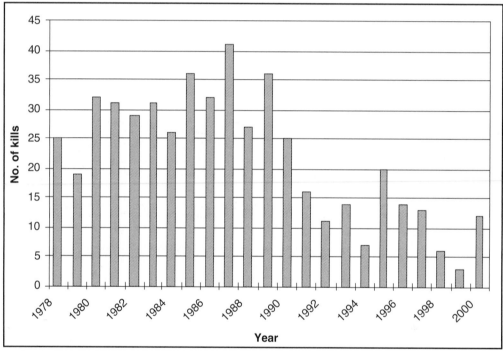

Figure 9.2. The number of pollution-related fish kills in western Scotland (former Clyde River Purification Board area), 1978 to 2000.

9.3 River flow

SEPA operates a network of 311 primary river flow gauging stations covering much of mainland Scotland. Many of the gauges on larger rivers have been in operation for several decades, providing a long continuous flow record. Virtually no information exists for the Scottish islands. The major pressures on river flow are surface water and groundwater abstraction and flow regulation, for example for hydroelectric power generation or water supply. The extent of flow regulation in Scotland and its environmental effects have been reviewed by Gilvear (1994). SEPA has no classification scheme for river water quantity comparable to that for river water quality, although this is being addressed through current research (SEPA, 1999).

Analysis of long-term flow records has revealed increasing annual flows over the period 1969 to 1988 in rivers draining to the Clyde Estuary (Curran and Robertson, 1991), a trend that has continued to the present (Figure 9.3). Other Scottish catchments such as the Nith, Teviot, Tay, Findhorn and Aberdeenshire Dee also experienced increasing mean annual flow between 1970 and 1989. Increased flows were observed in all seasons apart from in the Dee where there was a slight decrease in winter (Smith and Bennett, 1994). As well as increases in mean flows, the frequency of major floods has increased in more westerly catchments (Black, 1996). The fact that rivers in different areas of Scotland have experienced these changes suggests that the cause is climatic rather than catchment-related. The observed trends have significant implications for the future management of water resources, water quality and flood defence.

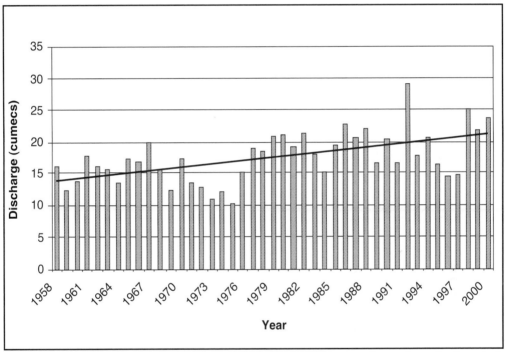

Figure 9.3. River Clyde at Hazelbank Q_{50} flow 1958 to 2000 with linear trend. The Q_{50} flow is that flow which is exceeded for 50 per cent of the time.

9.4 Loch quality

9.4.1 SEPA quality classification

Until the late 1980s, the RPBs regarded Scotland's freshwater lochs as being generally unpolluted with a few notable exceptions (e.g. Loch Leven and Kinghorn Loch). Only a few lochs (e.g. Loch Lomond and Loch Dee) were routinely monitored. RPB priorities centred on the control of significant point discharges, very few of which were made directly to lochs. With increasing awareness of acidification-related damage, land-use changes, concerns about eutrophication effects (e.g. risks to public health from potentially toxic blue-green algal blooms) and a marked increase in the use of lochs for aquaculture, this view began to change.

In 1994, RPB scientists devised a classification scheme for lochs based principally on modelled changes in nutrient and acidification status compared with a theoretically derived historical baseline state. The presence of toxic substances in concentrations exceeding environmental quality standards was also used as a classification criterion. In 1995 this scheme was used for the first time to classify the quality status of Scotland's largest lochs (Fozzard *et al.*, 1999). The four-class scheme is based on water chemistry, but with a provision to allow the use of biological information to modify the class where such information exists.

Of the 176 lochs assessed, which included almost all with a surface area of more than 1 km[2], 84 per cent showed no evidence of significant human impact and could be described as being in good or excellent condition. Only three lochs were classified as poor or seriously polluted (Table 9.3).

Table 9.3. Lochs classification in 1995 and 2000, with the number and percentage of lochs in each class[1].

Year	Class 1 Excellent/ good	Class 2 Fair	Class 3 Poor	Class 4 Seriously Polluted
1995	148 (84.0%)	25 (14.2%)	2 (1.1%)	2 (0.6%)
2000[2]	141 (80.1%)	32 (18.3%)	2 (1.1%)	2 (0.6%)
2000[3]	149 (75.3%)	44 (22.2%)	4 (2.0%)	1 (0.5%)

1. Where individual basins of large lochs have been classified separately, they have been treated as if they were separate lochs.
2. Includes lochs classified in both 1995 and 2000.
3. Includes lochs classified for the first time in 2000.

A further survey was carried out in 2000 on those lochs classified in 1995, plus an additional 22 lochs of particular interest (e.g. for conservation reasons or because they were known to be at risk from activities such as fish farming). Of those lochs classified in both 1995 and 2000, there was a slight reduction in the number which could be described as good or excellent and a concomitant increase in the number categorised as fair. When the additional 22 newly classified lochs were included, the shift from excellent/good quality was accentuated (Table 9.3). This was perhaps not unexpected given that many of the lochs classified for the first time in 2000 were included because they were known or suspected to be affected by pollution to some degree. As the quality classification of lochs began so recently, it is too early to draw conclusions as to possible trends, but further analysis will be undertaken when sufficient data have been gathered to justify it.

The major causes of quality downgrading in Scottish freshwater lochs were found to be nutrient enrichment (arising from agriculture, sewage effluent, forestry, fish farming and urban drainage) and acidification (SEPA, 1999). In 2000, 40 lochs were downgraded because of nutrient (phosphorus) enrichment, eight because of acidification and one as a result of toxic (trace metal) pollution.

Data collected by SEPA from five lochs (Davan, Dee, Katrine, Kinord and Lomond) are submitted to the ECN. Information on two further lochs (Leven and Lochnagar) is provided by the Centre for Ecology and Hydrology and the UKAWMN respectively. As for the ECN river sites, the information is likely to reveal more about quality trends in the individual waters concerned than for Scottish fresh waters in general.

9.4.2 *Monitoring of acid lochs*

As for rivers, information on acidification in Scottish lochs has been collected by the FRS Freshwater Laboratory, Pitlochry, the RPBs and subsequently SEPA, and UKAWMN. Monitoring by UKAWMN began in 1988 at six Scottish lochs and includes measurements of water chemistry, epilithic diatoms, macroinvertebrates, fish and aquatic macrophytes. Five lochs (Lochnagar, Loch Chon, Loch Tinker, Loch Grannoch and the Round Loch of Glenhead) are significantly acidified.

Data for the period 1988 to 1998 have been analysed (Monteith and Evans, 2000). During this time emissions of sulphur and deposition of non-marine sulphur declined by more than 50 per cent and UK emissions of nitrogen oxides fell by 14 per cent. There is no clear evidence of a general recovery from acidification over this period. In Lochnagar, non-marine sulphate concentrations have declined, but acidity has increased owing to an increase in nitrate concentrations. Alkalinity and pH have increased in Loch Chon and there are signs of recovery in the biota, but as non-marine sulphate and nitrate have not declined, the improvements cannot yet be ascribed to reduced emissions. At all Scottish and most other UK sites, dissolved organic carbon concentrations have increased, possibly because of climatic changes.

Information from other sources provides a clearer indication of recovery from acidification in some Scottish lochs. Although UKAWMN data for the Round Loch of Glenhead fails to show a clear trend, a large reduction in non-marine sulphate concentrations and a small rise in pH is evident when earlier data collected by the FRS Freshwater Laboratory since 1979 are taken into account (Monteith and Evans, 2000). This conclusion is supported by palaeolimnological studies in which historical pH has been reconstructed from fossil diatoms in loch sediment cores (Battarbee *et al.*, 1988; Allott *et al.*, 1992). In five other Galloway lochs (Enoch, Valley, Neldricken, Narroch and Grannoch) non-marine sulphate declined significantly between 1978 and 1994 with the greatest change in the mid-1980s, coinciding with the period of greatest decline in sulphur deposition (Harriman *et al.*, 1995).

9.4.3 *Palaeolimnological studies*

Work on the palaeolimnology of Scottish lochs has been reviewed by Battarbee and Allott (1994). Additional palaeolimnological studies have recently been completed at 31 sites on 29 Scottish lochs selected either because of their high conservation value or because they were known or suspected to be under threat from nutrient enrichment or acidification (Bennion *et al.*, 2001, Bennion *et al.*, Chapter 10).

Historical total phosphorus concentrations and pH were reconstructed from diatom remains in sediment cores. Nutrient enrichment was evident at 19 sites and acidification at seven. One loch showed indications both of acidification and recent enrichment. Only two sites showed no evidence of either. At the remaining two sites the results were inconclusive owing to poor preservation of the diatoms (Table 9.4).

Table 9.4. Environmental change in Scottish lochs as assessed from palaeolimnology (adapted from Bennion *et al.*, 2001). The impacts are recorded as A = acidification, E = eutrophication, I = inconclusive, and N = no change.

Loch	Impact	Onset of change (approx.)	Comments
Awe (N basin)	E	1976	
Awe (S basin)	E	1970	
Butterstone	E	1960	
Carlingwark	E	pre-1900	
Castle (Lochmaben)	E	1900	
Castle Semple	E	1900	
Chon	A	1850	Indications of recent improvement
Davan	E	1900	
Dee	A	1850	
Doon	A	1850	
Doon	E	1950	
Earn	E	1985	
Eck	A	1870*	
Einich	A	1850	
Eye	E	1600	
Grannoch	A	1860*	
Harray	E	-	Core chronology unclear
Kilbirnie	E	1915	
Kinord	I	-	Possible eutrophication since 1982
Leven	E	1850	Indications of improvement since 1985
Lomond (N basin)	E	1950	
Lomond (S basin)	E	1960	
Lowes	E	1730	Changes more marked since 1940
Lubnaig	N	-	
Maree	N	-	
Menteith	E	1920	Changes more marked since 1980
Mill (Lochmaben)	E	1900	Changes more marked since 1970
Muick	A	1850	
Rannoch	I	-	Probably no change
Shiel	A	1850	
Skene	E	1820	Changes more marked since 1938
Ussie	E	1950	

* Date of core base

9.5 Quality of other water bodies

The quality of Scotland's 200 km of canals is assessed by SEPA using its river classification scheme and the results are not normally reported separately. Only the chemical and aesthetic components of the scheme are used for classification as the biological component is not applicable to canals. In 1996, 131 km of canal were classified as being of less than good quality (46 km fair, 82 km poor and 3 km seriously polluted) (SEPA, 1999). These downgraded stretches were mostly on the lowland canals of the Central Belt, with the major causes of downgrading being pollution from urban drainage, agriculture and sewage.

There have been few systematic surveys of the quality of smaller water bodies and none which provides national coverage. As part of the Operation Brightwater initiative, ponds and lochans in the former Central Region were surveyed between 1990 and 1992 (Lassière, 1993). Although the purpose of this work was primarily to assess conservation value, 15 of the 195 waters assessed experienced water quality problems (turbidity or eutrophication) and a further ten suffered from dumping of litter and domestic refuse. Jeffries (1991) surveyed 42 natural and artificial forestry ponds in central and south-west Scotland. Problems were noted at 29 ponds, of which the most common were infilling, overgrowing and acidification.

Information on the overall quality of groundwaters in Scotland is poor and virtually nothing is known about the biota. In the past, monitoring has been limited mainly to groundwaters used for potable supply, which form only a small proportion (3.5 per cent) of the total potable resource and are of necessity of high quality (SEPA, 1999). Groundwater quality is threatened by agriculture, urbanisation, waste disposal to landfill and land contaminated by historical industrial use. There is as yet no classification system available for groundwater quality comparable with those for surface waters and proposals for a strategic groundwater monitoring network have been implemented only within the last two years.

9.6 Natural heritage trends: problems and issues

The natural heritage interest of Scotland's fresh waters encompasses a broad range of categories. Not only does it include the whole array of freshwater habitats, species, and ecological and geomorphological processes that have traditionally been the province of 'nature conservation', but also aesthetic and recreational aspects. This chapter concentrates on trends in habitats and species as this is where the main emphasis has been placed in data collection, and it is the principal area of interface between Scottish Natural Heritage (SNH) and SEPA.

The linkages between people and nature are perhaps nowhere as clearly marked as they are for fresh waters, whether through the degree of impact that humans exert on rivers and lakes or the appeal that they have as places for recreation. Describing the characteristics and importance of the fresh waters of Scotland (e.g. Maitland *et al.*, 1994) is, however, an easier task than identifying freshwater natural heritage trends. There are two principal problems associated with identifying trends.

First, despite the importance of fresh waters in the landscape of Scotland, there are still many fundamental gaps in knowledge that hinder the identification of genuine 'trends' in data. For example, there have been few attempts to record invertebrate assemblages in lochs, perhaps due to the fact that the biological water quality of lochs is not systematically monitored (using invertebrates) as it is for rivers. Some extensive datasets have been compiled, most notably on standing water macrophytes through programmes of survey by SNH (and previously by the Nature Conservancy Council) during the 1980s and 1990s.

Even here, though, the 3,182 lochs for which botanical data are available represent fewer than 12 per cent of the total number of standing waters in Scotland marked on 1:50,000 maps. More comprehensive, longer-term studies on Scottish fresh waters are often site-specific, such as the River Endrick (Maitland, 1966, 1996; Doughty and Maitland, 1994) and Loch Leven (see the extensive reference list in Bailey-Watts, 1994) and whilst extremely valuable they can only provide a limited insight into more general freshwater trends.

The network of biological recording groups throughout the UK is a useful means of gathering data on the distribution of various groups of plants and animals. For freshwater organisms, some recording groups have been in operation for long enough to be capable of detecting species trends. Yet while there are well-developed recording schemes for freshwater Coleoptera, Odonata, Ephemeroptera and Heteroptera, other major invertebrate groups such as Plecoptera are not well covered.

The European Union's Habitats Directive has proved to be a significant impetus for biological survey and research, and for supporting nature conservation throughout the UK, but in some ways it has proved to be a double-edged sword. Much of the work of bodies such as SNH has been directed at selecting Special Areas of Conservation (SACs) for habitats and species listed on the Directive's Annexes I and II, respectively. By definition, these are habitats and species that, at the level of the European Union, are threatened or in decline. Table 9.5 lists the freshwater habitats and species covered by the Directive that occur in Scotland, and this illustrates a two-fold effect on the information base for Scottish fresh waters. On the one hand, the incomplete reflection of Scottish river types in Annex I

Table 9.5. Freshwater habitats and species occurring in Scotland and listed in Annexes I and II of the EC Habitats Directive (habitat names are in accordance with the formal EC descriptions).

Annex I habitats

Oligotrophic waters containing very few minerals of Atlantic sandy plains with amphibious vegetation: *Lobelia*, *Littorella* and *Isoetes*

Oligotrophic to mesotrophic standing waters of plains to subalpine levels of the Continental and Alpine Region and mountain areas of other regions, with vegetation belonging to *Littorelletea uniflorae* and/or *Isoeto-Nanojuncetea*

Hard oligo-mesotrophic waters with benthic vegetation of *Chara* formations

Natural eutrophic lakes with *Magnopotamion* or *Hydrocharition*-type vegetation

Dystrophic lakes

Floating vegetation of *Ranunculus* of plain and sub-mountainous rivers

Annex II species

Slender naiad (*Najas flexilis*)

Freshwater pearl mussel (*Margaritifera margaritifera*)

Atlantic salmon (*Salmo salar*)

Twaite shad (*Alosa fallax*)

Allis shad (*Alosa alosa*)

Brook lamprey (*Lampetra planeri*)

River lamprey (*Lampetra fluviatilis*)

Sea lamprey (*Petromyzon marinus*)

('Rivers with *Ranunculus*' is the only Annex I river habitat identified as occurring in the UK) has tended to shift the emphasis away from the totality of Scotland's river resource. On the other hand, it has focused survey and ecological study on a few particular species of importance such as salmon, sea lamprey (*Petromyzon marinus*) and freshwater pearl mussel (*Margaritifera margaritifera*). This is an approach that equates rarity or vulnerability with importance, and whilst there is certainly a case for conserving these species at a UK or a European level, freshwater conservation needs to be far broader in its outlook.

The second problem in identifying freshwater natural heritage trends is related to time scales. Long-term datasets are few and far between, and often comprise little more than a few snapshots in time making the interpretation of real 'trends' extremely difficult. The programme of 'site condition monitoring' which SNH has recently begun should help in this respect, as it will provide long-term, standardised data for all of the 'designated freshwater features' on Sites of Special Scientific Interest (SSSIs) and SACs.

Data interpretation is also critically important, and wrong conclusions can be drawn by defining as a trend something that is simply part of a longer-term cycle or pattern. This is well illustrated by the extensive work carried out by the Tweed Foundation to determine which areas of the catchment produce spring salmon (Campbell, 1998). Radio-tracking in the River Tweed between 1994 and 1996 showed that the Ettrick Water was the most important area of the catchment, compared with the upper Tweed where no spring salmon were captured. However, an analysis of historical records shows quite a different picture. At the beginning of the twentieth century, Ettrick Water produced few, if any, spring salmon, whereas the upper Tweed did for a period of about 20 years in the 1940s and 1950s. Campbell (1998) concluded that without this longer, historical perspective, the significance of the present salmon stock structure could have been misinterpreted.

In the absence of a comprehensive overview of Scotland's freshwater natural heritage and the way it has changed over time, some specific examples are now presented by way of illustration.

9.7 Trends in freshwater habitats

Fresh waters (certainly the larger ones) rarely disappear entirely, and changes over time are usually more related to *quality* rather than to *area*, especially in terms of water pollution, physical habitat structure, and riparian land-use.

9.7.1 Countryside Survey 2000

The recent completion of CS2000 has provided an opportunity to investigate not only the 'stock' of fresh waters in Scotland, but also various aspects of their condition (Haines-Young *et al.*, 2000). For the purposes of reporting, the results from CS2000 are interpreted mainly in terms of the 'broad habitats' in the UK Biodiversity Action Plan (UK Biodiversity Steering Group, 1995). There are only two freshwater 'broad habitats' – 'Rivers and Streams' and 'Standing Waters and Canals'. Some of the key objectives for these habitats set out by the UK Biodiversity Steering Group include the encouragement of appropriate management of freshwater habitats and their adjacent land, the maintenance of appropriate hydrological regimes, and a reduction in nutrient enrichment (UK Biodiversity Steering Group, 1995; UK Biodiversity Group, 1998).

The results from CS2000 confirm that in all three 'Environmental Zones' in Scotland (Zone 3, Lowlands; Zone 4, Intermediate uplands and islands; Zone 5, True uplands) the areas and numbers of water bodies over the past decade have remained more or less stable. However, the numbers of small lowland ponds (defined as 0.25 to 2 ha, usually holding water for at least four months of the year) show a small increase (5 per cent). Ponds are important habitats for a wide range of animals and plants and, as small habitats, are especially susceptible to impacts such as agricultural pollution, acidification and species introduction. The small increase in lowland ponds contrasts with an estimated 7 per cent decline in numbers between the 1950s and 1980s (Swan *et al.*, 1994). Haines-Young *et al.* (2000) concluded that whilst new ponds may not compensate ecologically for the loss of old ones, they may sometimes represent important aspects of conservation value.

A comparison of streamside vegetation data from CS90 and CS2000 shows that there has been a significant increase in the growth of tall, woody plants alongside lowland streams in Scotland, in common with rivers and streams elsewhere in Britain. In general, a riparian zone with varied and well-developed vegetation is a positive feature, offering benefits to aquatic systems such as increased bank stability, controls on water temperature and hydrology, enhanced energy input, and the provision of habitats both for terrestrial and aquatic organisms. However, as Haines-Young *et al.* (2000) pointed out, an increase in tall, competitive species alongside streams may have adverse effects on other plant species whose streamside location provides a refuge from threats elsewhere.

9.7.2 *Determining trends through historical reconstruction*

Techniques of historical reconstruction, based usually on old maps or aerial photographs, are beginning to yield useful information on the way that specific fresh waters have changed over time. A good example is a recent study by Gilvear (2000) who investigated concerns that the bed of the River Spey (upstream of Newtonmore) is aggrading as a result of changes in the upper catchment. The study specifically addressed a perception by landowners that the morphological diversity of the river channel has been reduced, and whether such changes were the result of the construction and management of the Spey Dam. This dam was completed in 1942 for hydroelectric generation, and forms part of a wider network of river transfer and regulation. The results indicated that channel capacity in the Spey has been reduced owing to a 50 to 80 per cent reduction in river width, coupled with sediment accumulation on the river bed, and the author concluded that these changes have occurred in response to flow regulation by the Spey Dam. Conversely, the regulation of the Spey downstream from the dam has brought about a reduction in the frequency and magnitude of flood flows.

Whilst the results from this work are useful both in confirming the perceptions of local landowners and in documenting habitat change brought about by flow regulation, they are unlikely to lead to any realistic proposals for habitat restoration. In contrast, the recent identification of habitat trends in the River Tummel (Perthshire) has shown both the value of historical reconstruction in identifying change, and the potential that simple changes in river management can have on conservation value (Parsons and Gilvear, submitted).

The Tummel is a moderately large river (40 to 50 m wide, mean flow 70 m^3 per second), with a channel that was confined by flood embankments during the eighteenth and nineteenth centuries to assist agricultural development. In 1903, however, the embankments were abandoned owing to the expense of repeatedly repairing them. The study by Parsons and

Gilvear (submitted) investigated long-term change in valley floor landforms and vegetation patch dynamics over the 100 years since then, using previous studies of historical maps coupled with analyses of aerial photographs. A comparison of a section of the river corridor between 1946 and 1994 showed extensive increases in habitat diversity, from 11 to 20 land-cover types and from 26 to 61 vegetation patches. The authors concluded that simple changes in river management and land-use practices could result in re-establishment of the nature conservation value of similar river corridors in Europe without active restoration efforts.

9.7.3 Baselines for defining future trends: the development of new techniques

The development of new techniques in data recording and evaluation is likely to play an important role in tracking future change in freshwater habitats. For example, field methods such as River Habitat Survey (RHS) are already producing a baseline for future comparison (Raven *et al.*, 1997). This system has been developed by the Environment Agency in England and Wales and is now used throughout the UK. A standard field survey method is used to produce an inventory of physical features and thereby to assess the state of river habitats. The degree of degradation and the quality of habitat features can be determined by comparing the surveyed site with similar sites held in a UK-wide database. Interrogation of the database allows the user to produce tables and maps showing the location of individual river features. For example, a database query on the distribution of RHS sites in Scotland with extensive bank resectioning produced the map shown in Figure 9.4. In future, time-series analysis from RHS should enable trends in river habitat quality to be detected and displayed.

9.8 Trends in freshwater species

Although some trends in freshwater species occurrence have been identified, it is difficult to put together a coherent picture of overall change. Nevertheless, the two examples below – a broad-scale overview of Scottish freshwater fish, and the specific example of the globally threatened freshwater pearl mussel (*Margaritifera margaritifera*) – give a flavour of some of the changes that have occurred and some of the causes for concern that such changes elicit.

9.8.1 Freshwater fish

With the exception of salmon and sea trout (*Salmo trutta*), relatively little monitoring of freshwater fish has been carried out, so few data are available on current trends. However, there is no doubt that hundreds of fish communities and individual stocks of fish have been lost from Scotland's fresh waters over the last 200 years, largely due to human activities.

Severe domestic and industrial pollution removed all fish from the lower reaches of some rivers (e.g. Clyde, Carron and Leven in Fife) and migratory species from their middle and upper reaches because of the pollution barrier to migration. Acidification (in places exacerbated by blanket afforestation) has eliminated the entire fish populations of many lochs and streams in base-poor upland areas (e.g. Galloway). Sparling (*Osmerus eperlanus*), formerly recorded from at least 16 rivers in southern Scotland, is now found in only three of them (Cree, Tay and Forth) as a result of overfishing and pollution. Populations of Arctic charr (*Salvelinus alpinus*), a species for which Scotland is a stronghold in Europe, have disappeared from most of their southern sites (Lochs Grannoch, Dungeon, St Mary's and Leven) and are continuing to do so further north (e.g. Heldale Water) (see Figure 9.5).

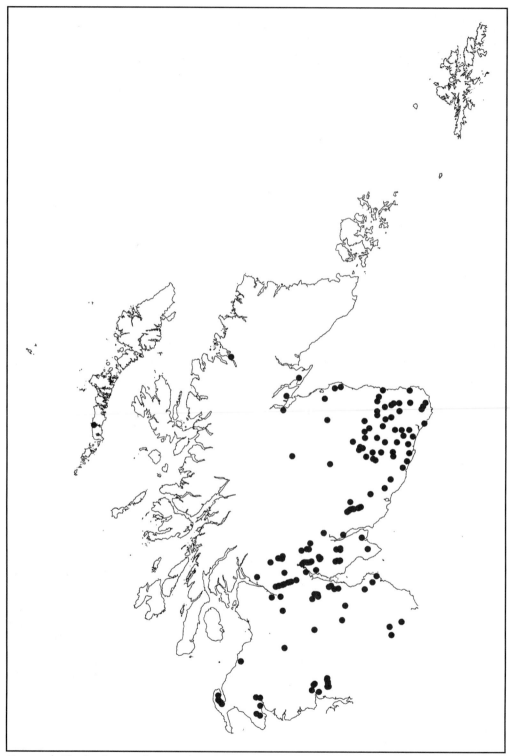

Figure 9.4. The distribution of River Habitat Survey (RHS) sites in Scotland where extensive bank resectioning has been recorded.

Figure 9.5. Loch Eck, a major Site of Special Scientific Interest for its native fish community, and the only water in Scotland where powan (*Coregonus lavaretus*) and Arctic charr (*Salvelinus alpinus*) occur together (photo: P.S. Maitland).

Other species, for which data are more fragmentary but which appear to have suffered significant decline over the last 100 years, include migratory species – sturgeon (*Acipenser sturio*), allis shad (*Alosa alosa*), twaite shad (*Alosa fallax*), river lamprey (*Lampetra fluviatilis*), sea lamprey and eel (*Anguilla anguilla*) – as well as entirely freshwater species such as brook lamprey (*Lampetra planeri*) and nine-spined stickleback (*Pungitius pungitius*).

Despite the widespread reduction in fish stocks, the overall number of freshwater fish species in Scotland has risen slowly to its present total of 42 since the last Ice Age. Far from being a success story, this increase in species richness is partly the result of expansions of species native to Britain but non-native to Scotland (e.g. dace (*Leuciscus leuciscus*), chub (*Leuciscus cephalus*) and bream (*Abramis brama*)), as well as the introduction into Scotland of species non-native to the UK (e.g. orfe (*Leuciscus idus*), rainbow trout (*Oncorhynchus mykiss*)). Alien species frequently exert strong competitive pressure on native species, and this has been especially apparent with the introduction of ruffe (*Gymnocephalus cernuus*) into Loch Lomond. The loch has high conservation value, not least as a result of the presence of powan (*Coregonus lavaretus*) (Figure 9.6) within a diverse fish community (Maitland, 1991). The known predation by ruffe on the eggs of powan represents a severe threat to its population.

Figure 9.6. Powan (*Coregonus lavaretus*) native in Scotland only to Loch Lomond and Loch Eck (photo: P.S. Maitland).

Perhaps not surprisingly, the decline of economically important stocks of salmon and sea trout has led to far louder cries for action than for other freshwater fish species. There are some encouraging signs of improvement with common and widespread species returning to systems which are recovering from organic pollution (e.g. salmon and river lamprey to the River Clyde) or acidification (e.g. brown trout (*Salmo trutta*) to Loch Neldricken).

However, the continued threat of disease, competition and predation from the further spread of fish species within Scotland and from outside is a matter of great concern.

9.8.2 Freshwater pearl mussel

The freshwater pearl mussel lives in cool, nutrient-poor, mildly acidic streams, partly or wholly buried in sand or gravel. Mussels are usually long-lived, and it is not uncommon to find specimens more than 100 years old.

Pearl mussel populations of international importance are now few and far between: in Canada, Russia and north-east Scandinavia; in Bavaria and adjacent parts of the Czech Republic and Austria; in Scotland, and possibly Eire (Young *et al.*, 2001). There are very few countries now that can compare with Scotland in terms of pearl mussel population size and viability. Despite that, Scotland's freshwater pearl mussels can hardly be said to be flourishing. The main threats have come from pollution, nutrient enrichment, channel engineering, and exploitation by pearl fishermen.

In recognition of the problems facing this species, and the general consensus that Scotland is especially important as its remaining stronghold, SNH commissioned a survey of all rivers in Scotland with historical records of pearl mussel. The results of the survey, carried out between 1996 and 1999, showed the full extent of pearl mussel decline (Tables 9.6 and 9.7). Out of the 155 Scottish rivers where pearl mussels were recorded historically, only about one-third remain reproductively viable, or 'functional'. Moreover, fewer than 20 per cent of those functional populations had densities reported as 'common' or 'abundant'.

More recently, a drastic reduction in the numbers of juvenile salmonids, on which pearl mussel larvae depend, has also been implicated in pearl mussel decline, especially in north-west Scotland (Cosgrove *et al.*, 2000; Hastie and Cosgrove, 2001). Although the evidence is circumstantial, there is a marked inverse relationship between the numbers of sea trout caught and the number of pearl mussel population extinctions (Figure 9.7; Hastie and Cosgrove, 2001).

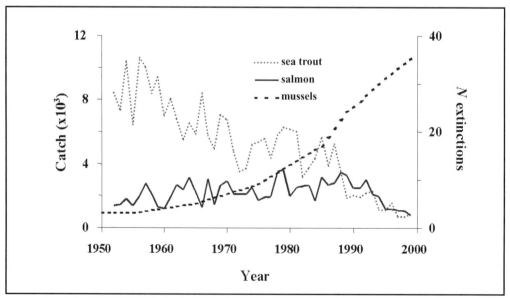

Figure 9.7. Coincidental declines of salmon, sea trout and pearl mussels in north-west Scotland, 1950 to 2000 (reproduced from Hastie and Cosgrove (2001), with permission). The graphs indicate the rod catches of salmon and sea trout, and the estimated number of pearl mussel population extinctions.

Table 9.6. The status of *M. margaritifera* populations (1996-1999) in 155 Scottish rivers with historical pearl mussel records.

Mussel population status	Number of rivers	Percentage
Extinct	58	37
Not currently viable	43	28
Functional	52	34
Unknown	2	1

Table 9.7. The relative abundance of pearl mussels in the remaining functional *M. margaritifera* populations in Scotland (1996-1999).

Relative abundance	Number of rivers	Percentage
Rare	19	37
Scarce	23	44
Common	2	4
Abundant	8	15

9.9 Prospects

As many researchers have discovered, ecological forecasting is notoriously difficult, primarily due to the large number of variables involved, as well as ignorance of many of them and how they may interact. A good example is the population explosion following the introduction of a few ruffe to Loch Lomond and the complex and unforeseen changes which took place there as a result. No-one predicted these at the time the first ruffe were discovered. In contrast, scientists have made predictions in the past which turned out to be true but were ignored by the authorities concerned. Two factors are clear, however, in relation to future prospects: first, lessons can be learned from past experience and from the results of scientific research, and, second, many of the prospects for future change in Scotland's fresh waters and their biota depend largely on human decisions and activities (Maitland *et al.*, 1994) and thus should be controllable.

9.9.1 Positive aspects

After a century of decline in water quality due to domestic and industrial pollution, and the subsequent loss of numerous species of invertebrates and fish from many of Scotland's rivers, the situation has been reversed since the 1960s thanks to the work of the RPBs and subsequently SEPA. Waters such as the Rivers Clyde and Carron, which had lost their entire migratory fish populations (some 50 per cent of native species in the river) and were virtually fishless in their lower reaches, have recovered to the point that salmon, and other migratory species such as the river lamprey, are now returning to them. In the River Forth, improvements in water quality during the 1980s led to the return of the sparling, which had disappeared two decades earlier, and a substantial population of this threatened species is now present there. Given time, it seems likely that the full complement of native species will be restored naturally to these and other formerly polluted waters. Thus it seems reasonable to predict that, given continued support to the activities of SEPA, point-source pollution will continue to decrease and the biodiversity of Scotland's rivers will improve.

Atmospheric pollution giving rise to acid precipitation has caused major damage to aquatic biota in various parts of the world including Scotland. Salmonid fish are particularly vulnerable, but many other fish species have been affected. A survey of fish populations in several areas of Scotland (Maitland *et al.*, 1987) showed that in the last few decades of the twentieth century, brown trout and Arctic charr were affected in acidified lochs, whilst salmon had been eliminated from several upland streams. Invertebrate populations too had lost their diversity at many acidified sites. One of the most characteristic effects of acidification on fish populations is the failure of recruitment of new age classes into the population. This is manifest in an altered age structure and reduction in population size, with decreased intra-specific competition for food and increased growth or condition of survivors. To anglers, the fish stock then appears to 'improve' because larger fish are caught, albeit in lower numbers. With no recruitment, year by year, the population contains fewer and fewer fish until eventually it dies out.

However, with the industrial recession towards the end of the twentieth century and greater attention to preventing the release of acidifying material to the atmosphere, it is clear that atmospheric pollution has decreased and some acidified waters are recovering naturally. Thus waters such as Loch Enoch and Loch Valley in Galloway and streams in the Loch Ard Forest which had become acidified and fishless are now becoming less acidic and fish are returning naturally or, in some cases, are being restocked (Anonymous, 1997). Future natural restoration of these and many other acidified waters may be expected, provided that input of acidifying chemicals to the atmosphere continues to be reduced. However, the rate of recovery is difficult to predict and is likely to be influenced by other factors such as climate change and changes in land use.

The impact of coniferous afforestation and forestry practice on freshwater habitats in Scotland and elsewhere has exacerbated the effect of acid deposition and caused much concern in other ways during the second half of the twentieth century. The effects of each stage of the forestry cycle - ground preparation, tree planting to canopy closure, the maturing crop and felling - may have a localised impact on fresh waters (Maitland *et al.*, 1990). Afforestation can affect both the hydrology and the chemistry of streams with subsequent changes in flora and fauna. Changes in hydrology and ambient water temperatures tend to make conditions in streams more extreme for most biota. Turbidity decreases plant growth through reduced light penetration and subsequent siltation damages habitat structure. Increased nutrients alter plant communities and cause problem crops of algae in streams and lakes. Acidification of watercourses affects the composition of their plant and invertebrate communities and completely eliminates fish in some cases. Other vertebrates, such as amphibians and birds, may also disappear.

Fortunately, the impact of afforestation on Scotland's fresh waters has decreased substantially in recent years, largely due to major changes in forestry practices, particularly the implementation of the *Forests and Water Guidelines* (Forestry Commission, 1993). The new schemes include better forest design (with more deciduous trees), less ditching, the blocking of ditches which lead directly to streams, planting well back from watercourses, and no planting on areas prone to acidification. The improvement in associated waters is already noticeable and likely to continue as older forests are felled and new, ecologically sensitive, planting takes its place.

Thanks to a much greater awareness of environmental issues in the last decade, new engineering schemes which may affect fresh waters are now subject to much greater scrutiny at the planning stage, usually involving some form of Environmental Impact Assessment (EIA). Thus, with improved planning and EIAs, and the application of the Precautionary Principle, new schemes should have less impact in the future, though a balance must always be found between the scientific importance of each site and social needs, both local and national. Some previous engineering schemes, which would not be acceptable nowadays, clearly need reviewing and modification. A good example is the hydro-electric scheme associated with the upper River Garry in Perthshire, where the river bed is dry for much of the year and native fish communities, including salmon, have been eliminated. The compensation water provided at many engineering schemes (mostly for hydro-electric and water supply) is inadequate and - worse - is frequently denied at critical times. Thus, particular care is needed where older schemes are being repaired or altered - a good example being the current proposal to abstract more water from Loch Einich, which is a Ramsar site lying within the Cairngorms National Nature Reserve. Thus the future of important fresh waters in Scotland affected by engineering schemes is somewhat debatable, and will only be secure with appropriate planning, construction techniques and subsequent monitoring which gives full consideration to environmental issues.

Tourism plays an increasing role in the economy of Scotland and this trend is likely to continue. There is no doubt that part of the attraction of Scotland is its magnificent scenery, within which thousands of clean, clear lochs and rivers are an important element. The sporting value of extensive populations of salmon, sea trout and brown trout, and other freshwater fish species, is also a considerable draw for many tourists. Thus there is an economic element in the desire to maintain high water quality and diverse native wildlife. Continuing growth in tourism, however, needs to be planned with care to ensure that Scotland's finite resources are not threatened by unsuitable levels of exploitation.

9.9.2 Negative aspects

In contrast to point source pollution, the diffuse pollution emanating from agriculture and some other types of land use has proved more difficult to control. The eutrophication of many lochs and some lowland rivers persists, with associated ecological change and loss of natural biodiversity. A good example is Loch Leven, where input from agricultural runoff, exacerbated by pollution from local domestic and industrial sources, caused an almost complete collapse of the aquatic community during the twentieth century. This resulted in a massive change from a macrophyte dominated system with a wide variety of invertebrates to an algal community, with frequent blooms, and a species-poor invertebrate community dominated by midge larvae and worms (Maitland and Hudspith, 1974). After intensive research (largely completed during the early 1970s) and the belated development of a catchment management plan (precipitated not by the conclusions from research but by the embarrassment caused by a massive algal bloom on the notorious 'scum Saturday' in June 1992), conditions appear slowly to be returning to normal. However, relatively little is being done for many other waters affected by eutrophication and it seems reasonable to predict that diffuse pollution will persist as a problem for many years. Indeed it has been predicted that by 2010, diffuse agricultural pollution will be the most important cause of river pollution in Scotland (SEPA, 1999). Only sensible active catchment management will restore natural biodiversity to many of Scotland's important lochs and rivers. In particular, massive changes in agricultural practices will be needed if substantial improvement is to take place. Rivers may be expected to respond quickly to such changes, but improvement in lochs will be much slower due to the storage of nutrients in their sediments. It is therefore vital that those lochs which are currently unpolluted but are thought to be at risk from eutrophication receive adequate protection.

Fish farming is another source of pollution both in freshwater lochs and in sea lochs. During the early 1980s, concern was expressed by a number of scientists over the rapid development of cage farming and three areas of impact forecast - pollution, disease and parasites, and escapes of farmed fish (Maitland, 1985). By the early 1980s farmed fish were quite different genetically from the Scottish wild stocks, having been interbred with fish from Norway, Iceland and other countries. Unfortunately, although all the forecasts have proved to be correct, fish farming was allowed to expand without restraint but with many consequent problems. The salmon farming industry continues to expand in spite of the shortage of suitable new sites and the trend towards farming new species is likely to bring new problems.

There is increasing evidence that human activities of various kinds are altering the atmosphere to such an extent that global warming may create major climatic changes over the next few centuries. The most certain changes seem to be a rising sea level and a general rise in atmospheric temperatures, especially at high latitudes. Changes in precipitation, wind and water circulation patterns are also likely but their nature is uncertain. These changes are highly likely to affect Scotland's fresh waters and their communities and a number of scenarios are possible. Everywhere there is likely to be a shift of southern species to the north and a retreat northwards of northern species. In the open sea, changing temperature and circulation patterns are likely to affect pelagic, demersal and migratory species such as salmon. Along the coast and in estuaries increased sea levels will create many changes to shallow water systems and produce problems for humans in low-lying areas. In fresh waters, changes related to altitude are likely to parallel latitudinal changes, with coldwater species moving into higher cooler waters and their place being taken in the lowlands by warmwater species. In rich lakes in summer there will be an increasing tendency to hypolimnetic anaerobic conditions, with consequent 'summer kill'; there will be less freezing in winter and so a lesser tendency to 'winter kill' in these lakes. If the observed trend towards increasing river flows and frequency of flood events in western catchments continues, washout of redds may further deplete declining salmon stocks in west coast rivers. Apart from political and practical measures to reduce the amounts of greenhouse gases entering the atmosphere, aquatic biologists can improve understanding and subsequent planning by developing existing monitoring programmes, devising ecological experiments, implementing conservation plans for threatened species, controlling northward movement of undesirable species, analysing existing data and developing better models.

One bleak aspect of the future of many fresh waters is the permanent and irreversible change caused by the numerous alien species which have been introduced and are now well established. Some of the most notorious include Canadian pondweed (*Elodea canadensis),* American signal crayfish (*Pacifastacus leniusculus),* ruffe from England and American mink (*Mustela vison).* One of the best studied examples of these is the ruffe which was unknown in Scotland until it was discovered in Loch Lomond in 1982 (Maitland *et al.,* 1983). The original introduction is assumed to have been some years earlier through the discarding of livebait by anglers from England. Since then, the population has exploded (Adams and Maitland, 1998) and caused massive shifts in many aspects of the ecology of the loch. In addition, at least a further five fish species have been introduced and are now established in Loch Lomond. Lack of action by the former Scottish Office is at least partly responsible for the ease with which many of the fish species have been imported and introduced (Maitland, 1987). It is hoped that legislation, at present proposed by the Scottish Executive Environment and Rural Affairs Department (SEERAD), can be implemented soon to prevent future disasters of this kind from taking place. Whilst many forms of impact can be removed and biodiversity restored, this is not the case with most alien species which, once established, are virtually impossible to eliminate.

9.9.3 Issues

The main driving forces for the future are political decisions concerning the environment taken at world (e.g. climate change), Europe (e.g. EU Directives), United Kingdom (e.g. Wildlife and Countryside Act), Scotland (e.g. the current Green Paper on freshwater fish) and local council (e.g. Local Biodiversity Action Plans (LBAPs)) levels. European legislation in particular is now a strong steering force for the way in which Scotland's fresh waters are conserved and managed. Thus the Bern Convention and the Habitats Directive are having an impact in relation to the protection of habitats and species, with the Wildlife and Countryside Act giving a measure of protection to several aquatic plants, fish, birds and mammals. The present creation of SACs should help to safeguard another four fish species. The current spate of Species Action Plans, Habitat Action Plans and Local Biodiversity Action Plans follows directly from the UK Biodiversity Action Plan (Department of the Environment, 1994). If these measures can get beyond the enormous paper bureaucracy which has arisen around them then collectively they should benefit Scotland's fresh waters and their wildlife. The Green Paper on freshwater fish, at present out for consultation, should, if amended appropriately and implemented, make an enormous difference to freshwater fish and fisheries and the way in which they are managed.

The EU's Water Framework Directive (WFD), which is due to be transposed into Scottish legislation by December 2003, is the most important piece of legislation affecting the management of Scotland's fresh waters since the Rivers (Prevention of Pollution) (Scotland) Acts of 1951 and 1965. The WFD will establish a framework for the enhanced protection and improvement of inland surface waters and groundwaters (also coastal and 'transitional' waters). Its implications are far reaching and include, for example, the need to extend the scope of ecological monitoring to groups other than the aquatic invertebrates which currently form the basis of monitoring programmes and to introduce hydromorphological monitoring for surface waters. Implementation of the WFD will be through River Basin Management Plans, the production and review of which will require the active involvement of a range of organisations and should stimulate action at the catchment level to tackle problems such as diffuse agricultural pollution.

Looking back over the twentieth century, though there were substantial declines in the quality and biota in many of Scotland's fresh waters, many positive things happened, which have borne fruit already and will continue to do so in the future. The Freshwater Biological Association, whose establishment was first mooted at a meeting of the British Association in Glasgow, has been a guiding light in freshwater ecology in Britain since 1929. The formation of the Nature Conservancy in 1949 and the RPBs about a decade later provided a basis for the protection of the environment and its wildlife, aided by the work and campaigning of non-governmental organisations (NGOs) such as the Scottish Wildlife Trust, Royal Society for the Protection of Birds, Friends of the Earth, Worldwide Fund for Nature and Wildfowl and Wetlands Trust. Scottish universities have made, and continue to make, important contributions to freshwater research. There have been many important initiatives by individuals, for example the bathymetric survey of the Scottish lochs (Murray and Pullar, 1910) and the early years of flow gauging of Scottish rivers (McClean, 1933). Recently, the agenda has been dominated by international obligations following European Directives (in particular the Habitats Directive and WFD) and the aftermath of the conference in Rio de Janeiro in 1992, the latter bringing the concepts of biodiversity and sustainability to world attention.

Not all has been sweetness and light, however. Much unnecessary bureaucracy and frequent reorganisation has impeded scientific research and the work of conservation organisations. There has often been delay in initiating research on urgent issues and subsequently in implementing the results of that research to practical effect. There has been a lack of vision and initiative in many quarters, as a result of which many of the important studies have been driven by individuals or NGOs or led by international directives or treaty obligations. Much damage has been done by economic developments which have failed to give proper consideration to the environment. While the long-overdue establishment of national parks in Scotland (initially covering Loch Lomond and the Trossachs, together with the Cairngorms) is to be welcomed, it should be noted that all four aims set out in the National Parks (Scotland) Act are to be accorded equal status. The failure to give priority to conservation over the promotion of recreation and economic development must be viewed with considerable concern.

Though major advances have been made in the last 50 years in the study of the taxonomy, biology and ecology of lochs and rivers in Scotland, there have been relatively few studies of less usual, but sometimes common, habitats - such as ephemeral ponds and streams, subterranean and interstitial waters, high altitude streams and bog pools, moss cascades and other fascinating habitats (Maitland, 1999). It is believed that research on these aquatic systems in the new millennium would reveal much of interest - including new species in otherwise well known geographic areas. In Britain, the original basis for the selection of a range of natural sites worthy of conservation was the *Nature Conservation Review* (Ratcliffe, 1977). Unfortunately, the review dealt only with the larger 'open waters' and none of the more unusual types of water body was considered. Thus, although many are under threat, few have any protection and interesting habitats and species may well be lost without ever being studied. What is needed, for each of these aquatic habitats, is a synoptic programme to describe the extent of the habitat throughout the country and then to sample sites which cover the range of variation - geographic and otherwise. Preliminary research of this nature would help to define the status of the habitats concerned and indicate the range of flora and fauna which they support. It should then be possible to identify some sites worthy of conservation. This would meet one of the major objectives of the UK Biodiversity Action Plan (Department of the Environment, 1994) which is to "continue to designate additional protected areas to deal with acknowledged gaps in the existing coverage, e.g. in relation to freshwater habitats".

Looking forward, it is possible to suggest a number of initiatives which should greatly improve the prospects for Scotland's fresh waters. Sustainable development demands a national freshwater strategy which will encompass all the needs of society and wildlife, with suitable compromises where these are needed. Perhaps the Scottish response to the WFD will give us the basis of such a strategy. However, responsibility for the Scottish environment must not be left entirely to decisions taken in Brussels. For example, considerable effort is at present being spent in giving better protection to species such as the brook lamprey, through the creation of SACs as required by the Habitats Directive. This is admirable, even though there are hundreds of populations of brook lampreys in Scotland, most of which are not under threat. On the other hand, virtually no attention is being given to the sparling, a formerly important commercial species with at least 16 populations, now reduced to three. Surely it is not too much to ask for a Scottish initiative to protect those species which are actually under greatest threat here?

More attention needs to be given to the restoration of lost or damaged habitats and species, both of which require better monitoring. Some of this is already being carried out through aspects of the work of SEPA and SNH, but a more cohesive national programme is needed to ensure that there is no further loss of wildlife. Many fish populations and fisheries are in decline and a proper national framework for their conservation and management is urgently required. Most importantly, environmental education and the need for conservation deserves a much higher profile at all levels from infant schools to universities.

The overall prospects for the future of the fresh waters of Scotland seem to be good, owing to the substantial environmental improvements initiated during the second half of the twentieth century. Yet there is still much to be done. Several, so far intractable, problems remain and must be tackled properly if further deterioration in some aspects of the environment and wildlife is to be halted. Notable among these issues are climate change, agriculture, fish farming and the introduction of alien species. These are challenges which must be met and overcome if the nature and value of Scotland's fresh waters is to be secured for future generations.

References

Adams, C.E. and Maitland, P.S. (1998). The ruffe population of Loch Lomond, Scotland: its introduction, population expansion and interaction with native species. *Journal of Great Lakes Research*, **24**, 249-262.

Allott, T.E.H., Harriman, R. and Battarbee, R.W. (1992). Reversibility of acidification at the Round Loch of Glenhead, Galloway, Scotland. *Environmental Pollution*, **77**, 219-225.

Anonymous (1997). Survival and food selection by Brown Trout in a recovering acid loch. *Freshwater Fisheries Laboratory, Biennial Review 1995-1997*, 32-33.

Anonymous (2001). *FRS Freshwater Laboratory Biennial Review 1999-2001*. Scottish Executive Environment and Rural Affairs Department, Edinburgh.

Bailey-Watts, A.E. (1994). Eutrophication. In *The Fresh Waters of Scotland: A National Resource of International Significance*, ed. by P.S. Maitland, P.J. Boon and D.S. McLusky. John Wiley, Chichester. pp. 385-411.

Battarbee, R.W. and Allott, T.E.H. (1994). Palaeolimnology. In *The Fresh Waters of Scotland. A National Resource of International Significance*, ed. by P.S. Maitland, P.J. Boon and D.S. McLusky. John Wiley, Chichester. pp. 113-130.

Battarbee, R.W., Flower, R.J., Stevenson, A.C., Jones, V.J., Harriman, R. and Appleby, P.G. (1988). Diatom and chemical evidence for reversibility of acidification of Scottish lochs. *Nature*, **322**, 530-532.

Bennion, H., Fluin, J., Appleby, P. and Ferrier, R. (2001). Palaeolimnological Investigations of Scottish Freshwater Lochs. Unpublished report.

Black, A.R. (1996). Major flooding and increased flood frequency in Scotland since 1988. *Physics and Chemistry of the Earth*, **20**, 463-468.

Campbell, R.N.B. (1998). A fisheries management plan for the River Tweed in the Scottish Borders. *Freshwater Forum*, **10**, 2-19.

Cosgrove, P.J., Young, M.R., Hastie, L.C., Gaywood, M. and Boon, P.J. (2000). The status of the freshwater pearl mussel *Margaritifera margaritifera* Linn. in Scotland. *Aquatic Conservation: Marine and Freshwater Ecosystems*, **10**, 197-208.

Curran, J.C. and Robertson, M. (1991). Water quality implications of an observed trend of rainfall and runoff. *Journal of the Institution of Water and Environmental Management*, **5**, 419-424.

Department of the Environment (1994). *Biodiversity. The UK Action Plan*. HMSO, London.

Doughty, C.R. and Maitland, P.S. (1994). The ecology of the River Endrick: present status and changes since 1960. *Hydrobiologia*, **290**, 139-151.

Forestry Commission (1993). *Forests and Water Guidelines: third edition*. HMSO, London.

Fozzard, I., Doughty, R., Ferrier, R.C., Leatherland, T. and Owen, R. (1999). A quality classification for management of Scottish standing waters. *Hydrobiologia*, **395/396**, 433-453.

Gardiner, R. and McLaren, I. (1991). Decline and recovery of salmon in the Central Belt of Scotland. In *Strategies for the Rehabilitation of Salmon Rivers*, ed. by D. Mills. Atlantic Salmon Trust, Institute of Fisheries Management and the Linnean Society, Pitlochry. pp. 187-193.

Gilvear, D.J. (1994). River flow regulation. In *The Fresh Waters of Scotland. A National Resource of International Significance*, ed. by P.S. Maitland, P.J. Boon and D.S. McLusky. John Wiley, Chichester. pp. 463-487.

Gilvear, D.J. (2000). An assessment of reported aggradation within the upper Spey SSSI. Unpublished report.

Haines-Young, R.H., Barr, C.J., Black, H.I.J., Briggs, D.J., Bunce, R.G.H., Clarke, R.T., Cooper, A., Dawson, F.H., Firbank, L.G., Fuller, R.M., Furse, M.T., Gillespie, M.K., Hill, R., Hornung, M., Howard, D.C., McCann, T., Morecroft, M.D., Petit, S., Sier, A.R.J., Smart, S.M., Smith, G.M., Stott, A.P., Stuart, R.C. and Watkins, J.W. (2000). *Accounting for Nature: Assessing Habitats in the UK Countryside*. Department of the Environment, Transport and the Regions, London.

Hammerton, D. (1994). Domestic and industrial pollution. In *The Fresh Waters of Scotland. A National Resource of International Significance*, ed. by P.S. Maitland, P.J. Boon and D.S. McLusky. John Wiley, Chichester. pp. 347-364.

Harriman, R., Morrison, B.R.S., Birks, H.J.B., Christie, A.E.G., Collen, P. and Watt, A.W. (1995). Long-term chemical and biological trends in Scottish streams and lochs. *Water, Air and Soil Pollution*, **85**, 701-706.

Hastie, L. and Cosgrove, P. (2001). The decline of migratory salmonid stocks: a new threat to pearl mussels in Scotland. *Freshwater Forum*, **15**, 85-96.

Jeffries, M. (1991). The ecology and conservation value of forestry ponds in Scotland, United Kingdom. *Biological Conservation*, **58**, 191-211.

Lassière, O. (1993). *Central Region Lochs and Ponds. The Operation Brightwater Survey of Their Status; Past, Present and Future.* University of Stirling, Stirling.

Mackay, D.W. and Doughty, C.R. (1986). Migratory salmonids of the estuary and Firth of Clyde. *Proceedings of the Royal Society of Edinburgh*, **90B**, 479-490.

Maitland, P.S. (1966). *The Fauna of the River Endrick.* Blackie, Glasgow.

Maitland, P.S. (1985). The potential impact of fish culture on wild stocks of Atlantic Salmon in Scotland. *Institute of Terrestrial Ecology Symposium*, **15**, 73-78.

Maitland, P.S. (1987). Fish introductions and translocations - their impact in the British Isles. *Institute of Terrestrial Ecology Symposium*, **19**, 57-66.

Maitland, P.S. (1991). Conservation of freshwater fish in the British Isles: the current status and biology of threatened species. *Aquatic Conservation: Marine and Freshwater Ecosystems*, **1**, 25-54.

Maitland, P.S. (1996). The River Endrick – then and now, monitoring by photography. *Freshwater Forum*, **7**, 7-22.

Maitland, P.S. (1999). New horizons - new species? The invertebrate fauna of unexplored aquatic habitats in Scotland. *Aquatic Conservation: Marine and Freshwater Ecosystems*, **9**, 529-534.

Maitland, P.S., Boon, P.J. and McLusky, D.S. (eds) (1994). *The Fresh Waters of Scotland: A National Resource of International Significance.* John Wiley, Chichester.

Maitland, P.S., East, K. and Morris, K.H. (1983). Ruffe *Gymnocephalus cernua*, new to Scotland, in Loch Lomond. *Scottish Naturalist*, 7-9.

Maitland, P.S. and Hudspith, P.M.G. (1974). The zoobenthos of Loch Leven, Kinross, and estimates of its production in the sandy littoral area during 1970 and 1971. *Proceedings of the Royal Society of Edinburgh*, **74**, 219-239.

Maitland, P.S., Lyle, A.A. and Campbell, R.N.B. (1987). *Acidification and Fish Populations in Scottish Lochs.* Institute of Terrestrial Ecology, Grange-over-Sands.

Maitland, P.S. Newson, M.D. and Best, G.E. (1990). *The Impact of Afforestation and Forestry Practice on Freshwater Habitats*. Nature Conservancy Council, Peterborough.

McClean, W.N. (1933). Practical river flow measurement and its place in inland water survey as exemplified on the Ness (Scotland) basin. *Transactions of the Institute of Water Engineers*, **38**, 233-267.

Monteith, D.T. and Evans, C.D. (2000). *UK Acid Waters Monitoring Network: 10 Year Report.* ENSIS, London.

Morrison, B.R.S. (1994). Acidification. In *The Fresh Waters of Scotland. A National Resource of International Significance*, ed. by P.S. Maitland, P.J. Boon and D.S. McLusky. John Wiley, Chichester. pp. 435-461.

Murray, J. and Pullar, L. (1910). *Bathymetrical Survey of the Fresh Water Lochs of Scotland.* Challenger Office, Edinburgh.

Parsons, H. and Gilvear, D. (submitted). Valley floor landscape change following almost 100 years of flood embankment abandonment on a naturally wandering gravel bed river. *Regulated Rivers*.

Ratcliffe, D.A. (ed.) (1977). *A Nature Conservation Review.* Cambridge University Press, Cambridge.

Raven, P.J., Fox, P., Everard, M., Holmes, N.T.H. and Dawson, F.H. (1997). River Habitat Survey: a new system for classifying rivers according to their habitat quality. In *Freshwater Quality: Defining The Indefinable?*, ed. by P.J. Boon and D.L. Howell. The Stationery Office, Edinburgh. pp 215-234.

Scottish Environment Protection Agency (1999). *Improving Scotland's Water Environment.* Scottish Environment Protection Agency, Stirling.

Smith, K. and Bennett, A.M. (1994). Recently increased river discharge in Scotland: effects on flow hydrology and some implications for water management. *Applied Geography*, **14**, 123-133.

Swan, M.J.S., Cummins, C.P. and Oldham, R.S. (1994). Amphibians. In *The Fresh Waters of Scotland: A National Resource of International Significance*, ed. by P.S. Maitland, P.J. Boon and D.S. McLusky. John Wiley, Chichester. pp 209-223.

UK Biodiversity Steering Group (1995). *Biodiversity: The UK Steering Group Report.* HMSO, London.

UK Biodiversity Group (1998). *UK Biodiversity Group Tranche 2 Action Plans. Volume II – Terrestrial and Freshwater Habitats.* English Nature, Peterborough.

Young, M.R., Cosgrove, P.J. and Hastie, L.C. (2001). The extent of, and causes for, the decline of a highly threatened naiad: *Margaritifera margaritifera*. In *Ecology and Evolutionary Biology of the Freshwater Mussels Unionoidea*, ed. by G. Bauer and K. Wächtler. Springer-Verlag, Heidelberg. pp. 337-357.

10 Environmental Change in Scottish Fresh Waters

H. Bennion, G. Simpson, R.W. Battarbee, N.G. Cameron,

C. Curtis, R.J. Flower, M. Hughes, V.J. Jones, M. Kernan,

D.T. Monteith, S.T. Patrick, N.L. Rose, C.D. Sayer and H. Yang

Summary

1. Recovery of Scottish inland waters from acidification has been patchy over the period 1988 to 1998 despite large UK sulphur emission reductions. Climate variability may confound the expected relationship between sulphur deposition and surface water acidity. Furthermore, nitrogen has been shown to be an important acidifier and continued high N deposition at some sites may contribute to the lack of chemical recovery.

2. Eutrophication has been identified in a number of lowland Scottish lochs across a broad range of loch types. Importantly, ecological change has been detected in large, deep lochs previously assumed to be relatively unimpacted.

3. Mountain lochs, despite their remote nature and lack of catchment disturbance, have received high levels of atmospheric contaminants, especially metals. The on-going release of these pollutants from catchment soils may delay reductions in loadings by decades.

10.1 Introduction

Over the last few hundred years, Scotland's fresh waters have been subject to increasing human pressures resulting in environmental problems such as acidification, eutrophication, increased catchment erosion, and atmospheric contamination from trace metals and persistent organic materials. The potential exacerbating effect of climate change now poses an additional challenge. The recent European Union Water Framework Directive (WFD) has highlighted the need to evaluate change in the ecological status of waters, requiring an assessment of how far present day conditions differ from those expected in the absence of significant anthropogenic influence ('reference conditions' in WFD terminology). However, the lack of background information on chemical and biological conditions prior to the onset of environmental problems makes this difficult. Palaeolimnology is a technique that employs the sediment record to determine past chemistry and biology of lochs before the onset of monitoring programmes (e.g. Battarbee, 1999). Here we summarise the findings of recent research that examines trends in surface water acidification, eutrophication, and contamination of Scottish fresh waters.

10.2 Surface water acidification

Early palaeolimnological work in the Galloway and Trossachs regions highlighted the primary role of acid deposition in the acidification of surface waters in areas of base-poor geology (e.g.

Flower and Battarbee, 1983; Battarbee *et al.*, 1990). This work was instrumental in the introduction of emission reductions policy, and in 1988 the United Kingdom Acid Waters Monitoring Network (UKAWMN) was established to determine the effect of this legislation on the chemistry and biology of 22 acid-sensitive fresh waters. The nine Scottish UKAWMN sites include lochs and rivers from north-west Scotland, the Cairngorms, the Trossachs and Galloway (Monteith and Evans, 2000). Although UK sulphur emissions have reduced substantially over the last decade, the decline in sulphur deposition across Scotland has been slight relative to that experienced in England and Wales, nearer to the main emission sources. Unsurprisingly, therefore, recovery has been identified in only a few Scottish lochs and streams over this period. Where chemical recovery has been detected, desirable though subtle biological responses have also been observed in some sites (Figure 10.1).

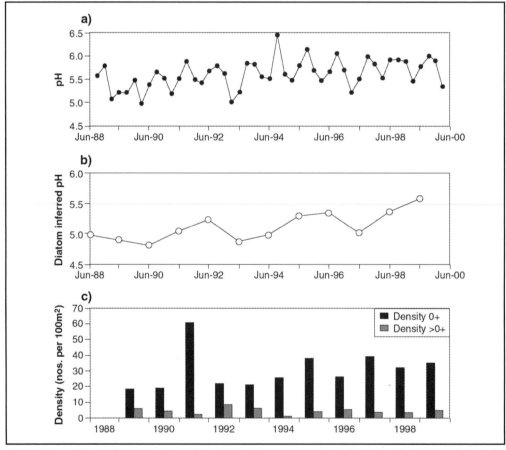

Figure 10.1. Evidence for recent chemical and biological recovery at Loch Chon (1988 to 1998) showing (a) an increase in pH, (b) a change in the loch diatom species composition toward less acid-tolerant species, as indicated by an increase in diatom–inferred pH, and (c) an increase in trout density (0+ = newly recruited fish, >0+ = more than 1 year old; no data for 1988).

Discrepancies between deposition decline and the absence of chemical and biological improvement at some sites have been linked to the influence of the North Atlantic Oscillation (NAO) (Monteith and Evans, 2000). Wet and stormy weather in winter and spring, associated with periods of high NAO, reduces the capacity of catchments to buffer acid pollutants and can also trigger acidic sea-salt episodes (Evans *et al.*, 2001). Both effects can increase the acidity of run-off and may currently be hampering biological recovery. The recent shift toward a greater dominance of the 'high' NAO state and the predicted continuation of this trend by some climate change models, may further impair the expected ecological improvements in acidified upland fresh waters in Scotland. On-going research in north-west Scotland aims to explore these issues.

As part of a wider UK project to examine the spatial extent of surface water acidification, critical loads for fresh waters were mapped for the most acid-sensitive water body in each 10 km grid square in Scotland. This survey found that nitrogen (N) as well as sulphur (S) was contributing to the acidity in many Scottish upland waters especially in Galloway (Allott *et al.*, 1995; Curtis *et al.*, 2000). The First-order Acidity Balance (FAB) model is now used for mapping critical loads and exceedance values in the UK, and recent studies of N dynamics in upland catchments have led to improvements in the formulation of the model (Curtis *et al.*, 2000). FAB modelled requirements for deposition reductions from 1995 to 1997 levels indicate that 26 per cent of the 754 sampled sites exceeded their critical loads for total acidity (S+N deposition). Additional evidence of the importance of N as an acid anion has been provided by monitoring data in several UKAWMN sites in Scotland where N can comprise as much as 50 per cent of acidifying anions. Whereas reductions in S deposition alone could be sufficient to prevent critical load exceedance in 82 per cent of exceeded Scottish fresh waters, N deposition will also have to be reduced to prevent exceedance in 18 per cent of sampled sites. The lack of a reduction in both N deposition and concentrations in certain sites may partially explain the lack of chemical recovery.

Developments in the formulation of the FAB model have also been used to improve chemical (Jenkins *et al.*, 1990) and biological (Juggins, 2001) predictive models, which are being employed to define appropriate recovery targets and to assess the impact of emission reduction policies in attaining these targets. The analogue matching technique (Flower *et al.*, 1997; Simpson, 2001), whereby sedimentary fossil remains in acidified lakes are matched to modern assemblages in other (analogue) lakes, can also be used to set targets for restoration. For example, Simpson (2001) identified lochs in north-west Scotland which may act as 'reference sites' for acidified lochs in Galloway, the Trossachs and other acid sensitive areas of the UK. These are based on comparisons between diatom and cladoceran assemblages in a large dataset of loch surface-sediment samples and pre-disturbance core samples from acid-impacted sites. The former lochs are currently being studied to gain an improved understanding of the ecology of minimally impacted surface waters.

10.3 Eutrophication

To date, the focus of Scottish eutrophication research has been on shallow, productive lochs where the symptoms of enrichment are most visible (e.g. Bailey-Watts, 1994). It is now recognised, however, that factors such as fish farming, forestry fertilisation, agriculture and sewage effluent disposal have enriched a number of the large, deep, oligotrophic lochs.

In a recent palaeolimnological study of 26 Scottish lochs (Bennion *et al.*, 2001), changes in epilimnetic total phosphorus (TP) since 1850 were inferred from diatom transfer functions (e.g. Bennion *et al.*, 1996). Increases in TP concentrations of greater than 5 µg per litre were detected in 19 lochs, and in six of these the increase was more than 20 µg per litre. In a number of the shallow sites, a switch was observed from relatively nutrient-poor conditions with taxa indicative of clear, macrophyte-dominated waters, to highly productive waters dominated by planktonic diatoms, suggesting increased turbidity and potential impacts on macrophytes. Importantly, the study detected ecological change in large, deep lochs, such as Loch Lomond and Loch Awe, previously assumed to be relatively unimpacted. Earlier, in a detailed study of Loch Ness (Jones *et al.*, 1997), highly significant changes in sedimentary diatom composition were observed over the last few decades (Figure 10.2), reflecting an increase in nutrients entering the loch not yet evident in chemical monitoring series. By detecting such changes, these data provide an early warning of potential future problems and can thus guide management.

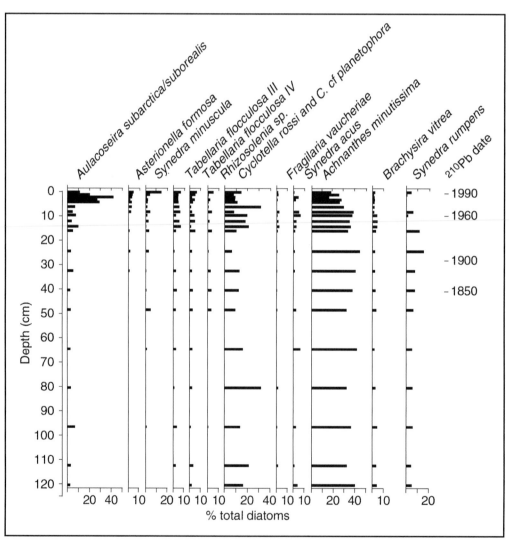

Figure 10.2. Summary diatom diagram of a sediment core from Loch Ness North Basin (Jones *et al.*, 1997). The diatom flora was stable for most of the period represented by the core, being dominated by benthic species such as *A. minutissima*. A marked increase in plankton taxa indicative of more productive waters (e.g. *Aulacoseira* spp. and *A. formosa*) was evident from around 1970. Reproduced with permission from Elsevier.

10.4 Pollution studies at remote, upland lochs

Due to their remote nature, physical characteristics and lack of catchment disturbance, upland lochs often provide a sensitive system for recording the loading and impact of atmospherically transported pollutants. The sediment records of upland lochs are able to provide one of the few means of obtaining long-term pollutant deposition records in these areas. A study on the deposition and fate of mercury (Hg) and lead (Pb) within the loch-catchment ecosystem of Lochnagar, a remote mountain loch, has shown that inputs of available metals are not decreasing despite a reduction of around 80 per cent in industrial emissions since the mid-1970s (Figure 10.3) and this is due to increased catchment inputs (Yang *et al.*, 2002). Further, concentrations of metals in aquatic flora and fauna have been found to reflect these trends. The catchment is known to contain Hg and Pb equivalent to around 400 years of deposition at contemporary levels, and hence the current trend of release from storage, and increased inputs to the aquatic system, could raise metal levels in water and sediment above critical limits for aquatic species, especially benthic feeders. Warmer summer temperatures and higher rainfall as a result of climate change could accelerate the input of metals from the catchment.

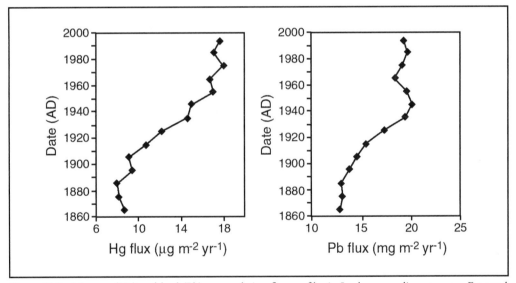

Figure 10.3. Mercury (Hg) and lead (Pb) accumulation flux profiles in Lochnagar sediment cores. Expected declines in metal concentrations following emission reduction have not been observed (see text). Reproduced with permission from the American Chemical Society.

Loch Coire nan Arr and Lochnagar are the focus of research on persistent organic pollutants (POPs). At the former, a reference site in north-west Scotland, the historical record of background concentrations of polyaromatic hydrocarbons and polychlorinated biphenyls is being examined. At Lochnagar, the historical record of toxaphene, a highly toxic pesticide, is the first of its kind outside of North America (Rose *et al.*, 2001). This compound was never produced or used in the UK and hence this study provides evidence for significant long-range transport to remote areas. However, as the main pathway for toxaphene to humans is via fish consumption, the absence of data for areas of Scotland where fish are farmed or routinely caught for consumption raises health concerns. Currently there are no UK Environmental Quality Standards for this pesticide (National Centre for Ecotoxicology and Hazardous Substances, pers. comm.).

10.5 Conclusion

Scottish fresh waters are starting to show signs of chemical and biological recovery from acidification, albeit patchily. There is preliminary evidence, however, that variations in climate may confound the expected relationship between sulphur deposition and surface water acidity. Furthermore, nitrogen has been shown to be an important acidifier and continued high N deposition at some sites may contribute to the lack of chemical recovery from acidification. Eutrophication has been identified at a number of Scottish lochs ranging from large, deep, oligotrophic waters to relatively small, shallow, productive water bodies. While point source nutrient inputs have been substantially reduced over the past 25 years, diffuse sources, which are more difficult to control, have become of greater concern. Indeed, current Scottish Environment Protection Agency projections suggest that diffuse agricultural pollution will be the most important factor affecting water quality in Scotland by 2010. Studies of metals and POPs in Scottish fresh waters are relatively recent and thus the extent of these pollutants and their ecological impacts are currently unknown. Previously deposited pollutants stored in catchments may be released and become bioavailable as a result of climate change; continued research in this field is clearly desirable.

Despite our increased knowledge of environmental change in Scottish freshwater environments, further research and fuller integration of chemical and biological monitoring data, combined with sediment records and mathematical modelling, is urgently needed. The introduction of the UK Biodiversity Action Plans for the lake habitats, mesotrophic lakes and eutrophic standing waters, requires information on lowland lochans, mesotrophic lochs and large, deep oligotrophic loch systems which have received little attention thus far.

In light of the WFD it is now particularly important to underpin European water management policy with aquatic ecology and palaeoecology. Recent methodological developments in palaeolimnology now make it possible to analyse sediments for multiple fossils from different trophic levels (so called multi-proxy studies). For example, the remains of algae (diatoms), macrophytes (aquatic pollen, macrofossils), zooplankton (cladocera), invertebrates (chironomids) and even fish (scales) are all preserved in sediments. When several of these are enumerated together it is then possible to infer past changes in biological structure and establish ecologically meaningful restoration targets based on specific assemblages and indicator taxa (e.g. Sayer *et al.*, 1999). Such techniques could play an important role in defining ecological reference conditions for Scottish lochs as required by the WFD.

Clearly, however, the application of high resolution studies of this type will be restricted to a relatively small numbers of sites. New projects, such as EMERGE (www.mountain-lakes.org/) which includes 30 Scottish upland lochs, are attempting to develop methods of scaling up palaeolimnological results to regional assessments of environmental change. New database developments, notably the inventory of standing waters for England, Wales and Scotland (Environment Agency, unpublished), containing physical, chemical and biological data, will provide for the first time a comprehensive single resource that will be invaluable to scientists and managers in the future management of fresh waters.

Acknowledgements

We acknowledge funding from the CEGB, DoE, DETR, DEFRA, EU, NERC, The Rannoch Trust, The Royal Society, SEPA, SNH and SNIFFER. Figures were produced by the Cartographic Unit, Department of Geography, UCL.

References

Allott, T.E.H., Curtis, C., Hall, J., Harriman, R. and Battarbee, R.W. (1995). The impact of nitrogen deposition on upland surface waters in Great Britain: a regional assessment of nitrate leaching. *Water, Air and Soil Pollution*, **85**, 297-302.

Bailey-Watts, A.E. (1994). Eutrophication. In *The Fresh Waters of Scotland: A National Resource of International Significance*, ed. by P.S. Maitland, P.J. Boon and D.S. McLusky. John Wiley, Chichester. pp. 385-411.

Battarbee, R.W., Mason, J., Renberg, I. and Talling, J. (eds.) (1990*). Palaeolimnology and Lake Acidification*. The Royal Society, London.

Battarbee, R.W. (1999). The importance of palaeolimnology to lake restoration. *Hydrobiologia*, **395/396**, 149-159.

Bennion, H., Juggins, S. and Anderson, N.J. (1996). Predicting epilimnetic phosphorus concentrations using an improved diatom-based transfer function and its application to lake eutrophication management. *Environmental Science and Technology*, **30**, 2004-2007.

Bennion, H., Fluin, J., Appleby, P. and Ferrier, B. (2001). Palaeolimnological Investigation of Scottish Freshwater Lochs. Unpublished report.

Curtis, C.J., Allott, T.E.H., Hughes, M., Hall, J., Harriman, R., Helliwell, R., Kernan, M., Reynolds, B. and Ullyett, J. (2000). Critical loads of sulphur and nitrogen for fresh waters in Great Britain and assessment of deposition reduction requirements with the First-order Acidity Balance (FAB) model. *Hydrology and Earth System Sciences*, **4**, 125-140.

Evans, C., Monteith, D.T. and Harriman, R. (2001). Long-term variability in the deposition of marine ions at west coast sites in the UK Acid Waters Monitoring Network: impacts on surface water chemistry and significance for trend determination. *Science of the Total Environment*, **265**, 115-129.

Flower, R.J. and Battarbee, R.W. (1983). Diatom evidence for recent acidification of two Scottish lochs. *Nature*, **305**, 130-133.

Flower, R.J., Juggins, S.J. and Battarbee, R.W. (1997). Matching diatom assemblages in lake sediment cores and modern surface sediment samples: the implications for conservation and restoration with special reference to acidified systems. *Hydrobiologia*, **344**, 27-40.

Jenkins, A., Whitehead, P.G., Cosby, B.J. and Birks, H.J.B. (1990). Modelling long-term acidification: a comparison with diatom reconstructions and the implications for reversibility. *Philosophical Transactions of the Royal Society of London, series B*, **327**, 209-214.

Jones, V.J., Battarbee, R.W., Rose, N.L., Curtis, C., Appleby, P.G., Harriman, R. and Shine, A. (1997). Evidence for pollution of Loch Ness from the analysis of its recent sediments. *Science of the Total Environment*, **203**, 37-49.

Juggins, S. (2001). The CLAM biological – chemical database: the development and application of biological models to predict taxon distributions from SSWC and MAGIC hydrochemical models. pp. 123-146 in an unpublished report.

Monteith, D.T. and Evans, C.D. (2000). *UK Acid Waters Monitoring Network: 10 Year Report. Analysis and Interpretation of Results April 1988-March 1998*. Ensis, London.

Rose, N.L., Backus, S., Karlsson, H. and Muir, D.C.G. (2001). An historical record of toxaphene and its congeners in a remote lake in Western Europe. *Environmental Science and Technology*, **35**, 1312-1319.

Sayer, C., Roberts, N., Sadler, J., David, C. and Wade, P.M. (1999). Biodiversity changes in a shallow lake ecosystem: a multi-proxy palaeolimnological analysis. *Journal of Biogeography*, **26**, 97-114.

Simpson, G. (2001). Biological targets for recovery from lake acidification: developing the analogue matching procedure. pp. 95-122 in an unpublished report.

Yang, H., Rose, N.L., Battarbee, R.W. and Boyle, J.F. (2002). Mercury and lead budgets for Lochnagar, a Scottish mountain lake and its catchment. *Environmental Science and Technology*, **36**, 1383-1388.

11 CONSERVATION AND RESTORATION CASE STUDY: THE MILLENNIUM LINK

Olivia L. Lassière

Summary

1. The Millennium Link project aims to create a corridor of economic, environmental and social opportunity through the catalyst effect of re-establishing navigation to the Lowland Canals (Forth & Clyde and Union) of Central Scotland which were closed in the early 1960s.

2. A coast to coast and city to city waterway link is being restored through a funding partnership of £78.3 million.

3. The project is based on the principles of sustainable development. The projected long term benefits to Scotland are an additional equivalent of 4,000 new jobs, as well as the increased recreation and leisure amenity along an improved green corridor for both local communities and wildlife.

4. Re-opening the waterways to through boat traffic has involved great engineering innovation and sensitivity to the built and natural heritage of these 200 year-old structures. Use of the ISO14001 standard environmental management systems by major construction contractors and the British Waterways internal environmental appraisal process has ensured full consideration of potential environmental impacts.

5. The wildlife and natural habitat resource of the canal network is unique in Scottish terms where the occurrence of slow flowing, nutrient rich waters is rare. This value is recognised through nature conservation designations, both statutory and non-statutory. A canal-wide Biodiversity Action Plan is currently being developed to guide the protection of wildlife and habitats on an operational waterway network.

6. As we move into a new era for the Lowland Canals further opportunities for sustainable use of the canal network are being considered, including the supply of grey water to industry, generation of hydropower and the development of freight transport.

11.1 Introduction to the Millennium Link project

The Millennium Link project aims to create a corridor of economic, environmental and social opportunity in Central Scotland through the catalyst effect of re-establishing navigation to the Lowland Canals (Forth & Clyde and Union). This model for the improvement of canals in England and elsewhere has been shown to lead to wider regeneration with some notable successes such as in Birmingham (DETR, 2001; Stirling, 2000). Recent government policy documents have highlighted the major role that the UK's waterways can play in sustainable development and the renaissance of our cities and rural areas through innovative use (DETR, 2000).

11.1.1 Canal history

A brief review of the history of the canals of central Scotland will serve to explain how and why the Millennium Link project was conceived. The Forth & Clyde and Union Canals were built as industrial structures. The Forth & Clyde Canal, constructed between 1768 and 1790, was the first ship canal in the world. It offered an alternative to the dangerous shipping route around the north of Scotland by providing a 56 km (35 mile) shortcut between Grangemouth on the Firth of Forth on the east coast and Bowling on the Firth of Clyde on the west coast. The 50 km (31 mile) long Union Canal, which links Edinburgh with Falkirk, was built between 1818 and 1822 to reduce the cost of coal in Edinburgh by linking the capital with the Lanarkshire coal field (Hume, 2000). The canal also provided a route for the transport of stone for construction in Edinburgh. In return, Edinburgh supplied 'night soil' which was used as a fertiliser on the fields outside the city at Ratho.

In their heyday these canals were the 'wet motorways' of central Scotland and provided an important route for goods and people in the days when travelling by road was slow and arduous. In the nineteenth century up to 600,000 tonnes of goods were transported per annum, including agricultural produce, mineral resources, timber, grain, tobacco, sugar, textiles and iron ore (Bowman, 2001). In 1836 over 200,000 people travelled on the canal network, when the journey between Edinburgh and Glasgow took less than seven hours (Lindsay, 1968).

The excellent canal transport routes led to many industries springing up along the canal banks including ship building, iron foundries, engineering plants, distilleries, acid and tar works and munitions factories. Water was supplied to the canals from a series of dedicated supply reservoirs which were built at the time of canal channel excavation. In addition to the transport role, canal water was also used for industry and to supply other facilities such as the Glasgow Royal Infirmary.

By the 1860s, the railway age was at its height and this, along with the subsequent improvements of roads, signalled the death knell of the canals which lost business. Commercial traffic continued on the Union Canal until 1933 when the flight of eleven locks which connected it to the Forth & Clyde Canal was infilled, severing the canal link at Falkirk. With the decline in business, the Lowland Canals fell into disuse and, following public pressure because of safety concerns, the canals were eventually closed to navigation. The Forth & Clyde Canal was closed on 31st December 1962 and the Union Canal was closed in August 1965.

With the canals closed to navigation, the local authorities began improving road linkages across the canals. In three decades, the canals were broken up into a series of shorter sections as a result of over 30 obstructions. These included opening bridges becoming fixed, roads being built at canal bank level prohibiting boat traffic and the flow of water being diverted into culverts. Some 7 km (4.5 miles) of canal were infilled and many public utility services were placed across the canals (Stirling, 2000). On the Forth & Clyde Canal, for example, the construction of the A80 Stirling to Glasgow road and the A803 Kirkintilloch to Glasgow roads effectively split the canal into linear ponds. At these points, the canal was culverted through a series of pipes to maintain the water flow. On the Union Canal the M8 was built directly on top of the canal near Broxburn and the canal channel was completely infilled in Wester Hailes on the western edge of Edinburgh. The map (Plate 22) shows the extent of the canal 'fracture' and the number of obstructions to be removed in order to reopen the canal to through boat traffic. The Monkland Canal, shown in Plate 22, is the principal water feed to the western end of the Forth & Clyde Canal and was not part of the Millennium Link Project.

11.1.2 Birth of the Millennium Link project

The major losers in the post-1962 canal history were the communities which had grown up during the prosperous days of the waterway network. It was these same people who, following 25 years of campaigning along with canal enthusiasts, made a strong case for re-establishing navigation to these historic waterways (Stirling 2000; Davies and MacKinnon, 2001). In the mid-1990s, new funding opportunities from the National Lottery led to the conception of the Millennium Link project in 1994 to restore the two canals from city to city and sea to sea (British Waterways, 1999). A series of applications led to a funding package of £78.3 million being secured which would cover the capital costs of the engineering, dredging and landscaping works required to re-establish navigation to the Lowland Canals.

The funding partnership included the Millennium Commission, Scottish Enterprise, five local enterprise companies, British Waterways, the European Regional Development Fund, seven local Councils and the private and voluntary sectors. British Waterways, the owner and manager of the canal network, was to act as the project manager for the Millennium Link project. With the funding in place the construction phase began in March 1999.

11.1.3 Restoring navigation to the Lowland Canals

Restoring navigation to the Lowland Canals required a massive programme of building, landscaping and dredging works, summarised in Table 11.1. Examples of some of these works are shown in Plates 23 to 25 and Figures 11.1 to 11.5 and 11.7. Overcoming the navigational obstacles has required innovative thinking and clever design (Stirling, 2000; Ballinger, 2000).

Table 11.1. The Millennium Link: summary of works.

Build 38 fixed bridges (29 road and 9 foot)
Build and recommission 13 opening bridges (4 road and 9 foot)
Refurbish 38 masonry bridges, aqueducts and weirs
Dredge 300,000 tonnes of canal sediment
Upgrade 110 km of canal towpath
Build 2 aqueducts and 1 tunnel
Build 5.3 km of new canal channel
Renovate 32 locks, build 9 new locks and build 1 drop lock
Build a boat lifting wheel

The most challenging obstacle to navigation is in Falkirk, requiring the construction of a 1.2 km extension to the Union Canal, three new locks, a canal tunnel under the Antonine Wall, an aqueduct and a boat lifting wheel. The Falkirk Wheel (Plate 23) will transfer 600

Figure 11.1. Cleveden Road Glasgow: January 1999 (a) and May 2001 (b). This bridge in Glasgow now allows for boat navigation and for safe passage of pedestrians and cyclists via the towpath under the bridge.

Figure 11.2. Opening bridge Bonnybridge. A hydraulically operated vertical lifting bridge (b) has replaced the culverted bridge hole (a).

Figure 11.3. Falkirk locks: Lock 4 in August 2000 (a) and May 2001 (b). The lock flight on the Forth & Clyde Canal at Falkirk was fully restored by dredging contaminated sediments, replacing lock gates made with sustainably sourced oak and reinstatement of damaged masonry.

tonnes of boats and water through a 32 m difference in elevation between the two canals. The whole process will take around 15 minutes, which compares favourably with the half day trip through the original lock flight! The wheel is expected to have a considerable impact on tourism in Central Scotland and is already being hailed as a major landmark.

Figure 11.4. Dredging works: before (a) and after (b) the removal of mercury contaminated silts at Polmont, Union Canal.

Figure 11.5. Towpath works: before (a) and after (b) renovation improving the surfacing and accessibility of a traffic free route across the country, and from Glasgow to Edinburgh.

11.2 The Millennium Link and sustainable development

With knowledge of the economic, social and environmental benefits which canal regeneration had brought to run-down areas in England, the bidding process in the mid-1990s involved an assessment of the range of benefits to the communities of central

Economic benefits

Direct:
289 full time equivalent (FTE) construction jobs*.
40 FTE operation and maintenance jobs safeguarded*.
120 FTE tourism jobs: informal recreation and canal users*.
£9.1m pa of spend associated with informal visitors and boaters*.
Indirect:
Development of 5 major and 20 minor visitor sites attracting 2 million visitors and a £32 million spend*.
50 FTE in small to medium sized tourism enterprises e.g shops, chandlers*.
444 FTE in construction of visitor sites*.
465 FTE tourism jobs*.
Development of corridor businesses/housing has potential to accommodate net 2800 FTEs and generate income of £56m*.

For example canal views are estimated to raise the value of a home by 20-30% (Pybus, 2001).

Community benefits

Direct::
70% of construction employment within 30 mile radius of site*.
Scope for 500 canal restoration training places*.
Opportunity to create employment and training initiatives in disadvantaged areas*.
Access improved: increase in informal recreation visits by 1.75m pa*. Access for all groups including elderly and disabled#.
Safe environment away from roads with safety designed in and opportunities for traffic free commuting#.
Opportunities for interpretation and education, close to schools#.
Opportunities for the rehabilitation of young offenders#.
Indirect:
100 FTE in 20 community businesses along the canal*.
Scope for 500 tourist site construction training places*.

For example 70% of the population of Scotland lives within 1 hour drive time of the Lowland Canals.

Sustainable development of Lowland Canals

Environmental benefits

Direct:
Environmental improvements of 120ha of canal/adjacent land*.
Provision of resources to assure the future of the Lowland Canals as an environmental and heritage resource and a long term view of management requirements#.
Restoration of water channel and removal of obstructions to water flow and improvement of water quality#.
Opportunity to deal with contaminated canal sediments#.
Management of canal plant overgrowth which threatens diversity#.
Reinstatement of structures to functional use#.
Renewal of buildings for new uses using current heritage standards#.
Gain an up to date understanding of environmental status of canals through appropriate survey work#.
Indirect:
Build a sense of ownership and partnership with local communities and users based on an appreciation of environmental and heritage value#.
Development of an integrated strategy for recreation and environmental management to establish sustainable patterns of use#.

For example biodiversity action planning will guide the enhancement and protection of the living heritage of the canal network.

Figure 11.6. The Millennium Link: summary of economic, community and environmental benefits. Material is taken from Wood (2000) (*) and British Waterways (1995) (#).

Scotland that would result from reopening the canals. The major benefits identified, both directly of restoring and operating the canals and indirectly through the creation of visitor attractions and business areas along the canal corridor, are summarised in Figure 11.6. The direct benefits were expected by 2001 and the indirect benefits following opening of the canals by 2006 (Wood, 2000).

The model for sustainable development (Figure 11.6) highlights some of the benefits that were identified before work began. The civil engineering part of the project is the key first stage of an exemplar for sustainable development (Stirling, 2000).

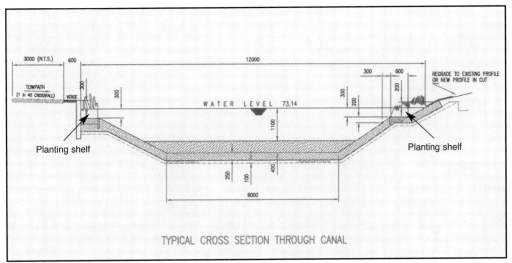

Figure 11.7. Wester Hailes canal channel design, including planting shelves.

11.3 The environmental resource of the canal network

Prior to securing the Millennium Link funding it was recognised that, without continued input of resources to manage and renew the canal network, the environmental value of these man-made assets would decline. Structures would crumble and the channel, valued as a wildlife habitat, would silt up, stagnate and become choked with vegetation and eventually revert to dry land (British Waterways, 1995).

For development to be truly sustainable, effective protection of the environment is essential (DETR, 2001). The following sections describe the environmental resource of the canal network and explain how these resources were taken into account as part of the project. To illustrate this approach, a few examples of best or good practice are given.

11.3.1 Water

The canal network consists of a series of clay lined man-made water channels which are fed with water from a number of dedicated supply reservoirs. Water reaches the canals via several feeder streams and piped sections of the Monkland Canal. Sluices, weirs and locks control flow. The Lowland Canals are unusual in a Scottish context because their waters are slow flowing and of high nutrient status. The Forth & Clyde Canal is a unique water body in Scotland as it crosses two major river catchments, the Forth and the Clyde. The canal network water quality is classified under the Scottish River Classification (SRC) scheme (SEPA, 1999). In 2000, the Forth & Clyde Canal varied between SRC class A2 (Good) and C (poor) along its length and the Union from class B (fair) to class C (poor) (D. Habron, pers. comm.). The main contributor to the poor classifications was the low level of dissolved oxygen which was associated with slow flows, high weed growth and organic enrichment. This problem has been particularly acute in the vicinity of obstructions to navigation where water flow was restricted (Ross *et al.*, 1986).

British Waterways' policy is to achieve class B (fair) or better for recreational and fishery use (British Waterways, 1999). SEPA's target for 2005 is to reduce the overall length of poor and seriously polluted rivers, including canals, by at least 45 per cent (SEPA, 1999).

11.3.2 Habitats

The Lowland canals have a rich diversity of wildlife. Within their cross-section they display an array of habitat types which are a microcosm of the wider environment (British Waterways, 1999). Thirteen habitats have been identified on the canal network, including canal and river channels, waterway banks, towpath verges, hedgerows, cuttings and embankments, built structures, reservoirs, lakes and ponds, dredging tips and historic spoil tips, feeders and streams, reedbeds, adjoining land, field margins and woodlands and scrub (British Waterways, 2000). The wetland habitats are of particular value, especially in Lowland Scotland, where the slow flowing and pond-like conditions of the canals are uncommon (British Waterways, 1995).

The natural heritage value of the canals is reflected in the number of nature conservation designations. Sixteen biological Sites of Special Scientific Interest (Table 11.2) and over 60 non-statutory sites are within 500 m of the Lowland Canal network (channels, feeders and reservoirs). In addition, the Forth & Clyde and Union Canals are the only waters classified as cyprinid in Scotland under the Surface Waters (Fishlife) (Classification) (Scotland) Regulations 1997.

Table 11.2. Sites of Special Scientific Interest on the Lowland canal network, indicated by F&C (Forth & Clyde Canal), M (Monkland Canal) and U (Union Canal).

Site name	Main interest	Local authority	Canal
Bishop Loch	Open water and marsh; woodland	Glasgow City	F&C
Black Loch Moss	Peatland	North Lanarkshire	M
Cadder Wilderness	Woodland	East Dunbartonshire	F&C
Calderwood	Woodland, valley mire	West Lothian	U
Carriber Glen	Woodland	West Lothian	U
Cobbinshaw Moss	Peatland	West Lothian	U
Cobbinshaw Reservoir	Birds, plants	West Lothian	U
Dullatur Marsh	Peatland	North Lanarkshire	F&C
Hawcraig-Glenarbuck	Upland, woodland	West Dunbartonshire	F&C
Hermand Birchwood	Woodland	West Lothian	U
Howierig Muir	Raised bog	Falkirk	U
Inner Clyde	Intertidal mudflats, wintering birds	West Dunbartonshire	F&C
Linlithgow Loch	Birds, plants	West Lothian	U
Philipstoun Muir	Woodland	West Lothian	U
Possil Marsh	Standing water	Glasgow City	F&C
Woodend Loch	Standing water	North Lanarkshire	F&C

The Lowland Canals act as wildlife corridors, bringing the countryside into the town, and are particularly valuable in large conurbations such as Edinburgh and Glasgow. The Lowland Canals' sustainable development strategy identified the Forth & Clyde Canal as one of the most important wildlife corridors in Scotland (Forth and Clyde Canal Joint Advisory Committee, 1995). In urban and rural areas, the canals are valuable foraging areas for wildlife, providing undisturbed habitats in intensively managed and developed surroundings. The canals also link to other sites of nature conservation importance, such as the River Almond (British Waterways, 1995).

11.3.3 Flora

Over 380 plant taxa have been recorded along the canals' channels and adjacent land, not including plants found only in feeders and reservoirs (Scottish Wildlife Trust Environmental Services, 1997). The open water of the canal channel supports a rich diversity of aquatic plants and is more typical of waters in the south of England. Twelve species of *Potamogeton* have been recorded, including the endemic Bennett's pondweed (*Potamogeton* x *bennettii*) and flat stalked pondweed (*Potamogeton friesii*), which has its mainland Scotland stronghold in the canals. Two plant species native to England and rare in Scotland, the frogbit (*Hydrocharis morsus-ranae*) and arrowhead (*Sagittaria sagittifolia*), thrive in the Lowland Canals.

The Lowland Canals are the stronghold for a number of emergent species which are rare or scarce elsewhere in Scotland, including the nationally scarce tufted loosestrife (*Lysimachia thyrsiflora*), reed sweet grass (*Glyceria maxima*) and lesser water plantain (*Alisma lanceolatum*) which thrive in the shallow waters at the canal edge.

At the boundaries of canal land a hedgerow often forms an important living barrier. There are 10.2 km and 6.35 km of hedgerow, mostly hawthorn, on the Union and Forth & Clyde Canals respectively. Embankments and offside areas support woodland and scrub habitat. The towpath areas may support grass species and plants tolerant of trampling. Canal-side buildings support a range of ferns, bryophytes and lichens, some of which grow in the lime rich mortars.

The canals are also home to a number of alien floral species such as Japanese knotweed (*Fallopia japonica*) and Himalayan balsam (*Impatiens glandulifera*) on the embankments, and water fern (*Azolla filiculoides*) in the canal channel.

11.3.4 Fauna

The wide range of habitats and low intensity management on the canal network has allowed a diverse fauna to develop. The water channel of the Forth & Clyde Canal supports an abundant and varied macroinvertebrate fauna dominated by Mollusca, Oligochaeta and hoglice (*Asellus aquaticus*) and a rich cladoceran fauna (Fozzard *et al.*, 1994). Invertebrate species of note include the flatworm *Bdellocephala punctata* which is uncommon in the UK, the leech *Piscicola geometra* which is rare in the west of Scotland and the nationally rare cladoceran *Alona weltneri* (Fozzard *et al.*, 1994). Freshwater sponges, some over 50 cm in diameter have been recorded from submerged debris, locks, lock walls and bridge holes.

The fish communities of the canals are dominated by pike (*Esox lucius*), perch (*Perca fluviatilis*), roach (*Rutilus rutilus*), tench (*Tinca tinca*) and eels (*Anguilla anguilla*) with occasional ruffe (*Gymnocephalus cernua*), stickleback (*Gasterosteus aculeatus*), bream (*Abramis brama*), brown trout (*Salmo trutta*) and carp (*Cyprinus carpio*). Large specimens of pike (11.7 kg, 25lb 12oz) and a Scottish record tench (3.5 kg, 7lb 10oz) have been caught in the Forth & Clyde Canal in recent years.

Smooth (*Triturus vulgaris*) and palmate (*Triturus helveticus*) newts, frogs (*Rana temporaria*) and toads (*Bufo bufo*) breed in the canals and forage in the adjacent habitats.

Reptiles are represented by red-eared terrapins (*Chrysemys scripta*) which are certainly discarded pets.

Fifty-six bird species were recorded along the canals in 1997 (Scott Wilson Resource Consultants, 1997), of which 29 were breeding. Of these, mute swan (*Cygnus olor*), coot (*Fulica atra*), mallard (*Anas platyrhynchos*) and moorhen (*Gallinula chloropus*) were the most common. Away from the water, the grassland, hedgerow, scrub and woodland habitats provide shelter and food for summer visitors like the whitethroat (*Sylvia communis*), as well as other species considered by the Royal Society for the Protection of Birds to be of conservation concern, such as the linnet (*Carduelis cannabina*), grey partridge (*Perdix perdix*) and tree sparrow (*Passer montanus*).

Mammals including otter (*Lutra lutra*), roe deer (*Capreolus capreolus*), fox (*Vulpes vulpes*), badger (*Meles meles*), hedgehog (*Erinaceus europaeus*), mink (*Mustela vison*), bank vole (*Clethrionomys glareolus*), bats (Daubenton's (*Myotis daubentoni*) and pipistrelle (*Pipistrellus pipistrellus*) 55 and 45 kHz) and water vole (*Arvicola terrestris*) frequent the canal network. Recent surveys indicate that despite the presence of suitable habitat the numbers of water voles (*Arvicola terrestris*) are very low. Predation by non-native American mink *(Mustela vison)* is thought to be the main cause for the small and fragmented populations on both canals (Reynolds, 2000).

11.3.5 Landscape

The canal network offers varied landscapes, from the enclosed green wooded corridor of the Union Canal in its rural sections to the industrial and residential urban sections in the larger conurbations.

The Forth & Clyde Canal, a large section of which passes through designated greenbelt land, encompasses five nationally recognised landscape character areas. The high quality rural landscape includes the lowland hill fringes of the Kirkintilloch farmlands, the lowland river landscapes of the Kelvin valley and the Falkirk-Denny urban fringe and the upland regions of the Kilpatrick Hills, Kilsyth Hills and Campsie Fells (British Waterways, 1999). Both in the urban and rural setting, the historic structures and features add to the quality of the canal experience. In the urban setting, particularly in Glasgow, the decaying fabric of the canal and poorly designed buildings detract from the waterway environment (British Waterways, 1999).

The Union Canal also encompasses five nationally recognised landscape character areas. It is predominantly rural in character and designations along the corridor include Greenbelt land, designated Regional Scenic Areas, Area of Great Landscape Value, Outstanding Landscape Quality, and landscapes identified as Countryside/Rural Policy Areas (British Waterways, 1999). The stone bridges and walls, native hedgerow and woodland, and a sense of tranquillity are all distinctive elements of the Union Canal (British Waterways, 1999).

11.3.6 Canal sediments

In some locations, the canal sediments contain elevated concentrations of heavy metals and hydrocarbons which are associated with former canal-side industries, including iron foundries, rubber works, petrol and oil depots, glass works, saw mills and maltings. The most significant contamination of the canal network is in the Redding area of Falkirk where canal sediments contain some of the highest concentrations of mercury compounds of any waterway in the UK. The peak of canal contamination is adjacent to the site of a former detonator factory which used mercury fulminate as a principal raw material (Smith and Lassière, 2000).

The majority of this contamination occurred before the advent of environmental legislation. Over the years the continuous flow of water (0.1 m per sec) has washed the mobile fraction of the contaminants away. The remaining contaminants are largely immobile and confined to discrete stretches of the canal. As a result contaminated sediments have relatively little direct impact on water quality. Nevertheless, removal of sediments is an essential part of the Millennium Link project to provide a navigable depth and to prevent long term spread of contamination (British Waterways, 1995).

11.3.7 Built heritage

The rich built heritage of the Lowland Canals is reflected in numerous designations which give statutory protection to their many historical and architectural features (British Waterways, 1995; Forth & Clyde Canal Society, 2001). The Forth & Clyde and Union Canals are both Scheduled Ancient Monuments (SAMs) and many of the structures, including bridges, locks, basins, canal-side buildings and aqueducts, have either SAM or Listed Building status. The canals also pass through a corridor which has historic links with the Romans. For the majority of its length, the Forth & Clyde Canal closely follows the line of the Antonine Wall, built and abandoned by the Romans in the second century AD (British Waterways, 1995).

11.4 Framework for environmental management

Protection of the environment is at the heart of British Waterways' business approach. In addition to general obligations under national and international environmental legislation, British Waterways has specific environmental duties under the British Waterways Act 1995. When formulating or considering any proposals in relation to its functions, the Act states that British Waterways is obliged to

- further the conservation and enhancement of flora, fauna and geological or physiographical features of special interest;
- have regard for the desirability of protecting and conserving buildings, sites and objects of archaeological, architectural, engineering or historical interest; and
- take into account any effect that the proposals would have on the beauty or amenity of any rural or urban area or on any such flora, fauna, features, buildings, sites or objects.

Following the 1995 Act, British Waterways produced its environmental policy and published an *Environmental Code of Practice* to provide a framework for the appraisal of environmental implications of canal operations. This appraisal assesses nineteen main areas: statutory requirements for consultation (e.g. with Historic Scotland, Scottish Natural Heritage (SNH) and the Scottish Environment Protection Agency (SEPA); advising and consulting local users about the works; phasing of the works; timing of the works; access for users; plants and animals including the presence of protected and valuable species, sites and habitats; fishery; heritage and built environment; landscape; noise; water resources;

pollution; contaminated land; ground disturbance; works access; reinstatement; safety; waste; and sustainability.

The principles of this internal environmental appraisal process were developed for The Millennium Link project to ensure that both British Waterways and external contractors considered environmental issues fully as part of their works. Ecological and landscape surveys were conducted in 1997 to provide background information for both British Waterways and the contractors. These included an assessment of land use along the canal corridor, the vegetation, waterway birds and invertebrates and an overview of the regional landscape character (Scottish Wildlife Trust Environmental Services, 1997; Scott Wilson Resource Consultants, 1997). In 1998 British Waterways compiled a generic list of likely environmental issues for the Millennium Link bridge and channel contracts. For each issue, an appropriate contract clause was written and reference made to published guidance notes and specifications. These included British Waterways' internal advisory publications, such as the *Environmental Bulletin*, and those of external bodies, for example the *Pollution Prevention Guidelines* produced by SEPA and the Environment Agency. Where no previously published guidance was available, new Millennium Link specific guidance was drafted (Table 11.3). This approach was taken to ensure consistency in the delivery of environmental advice during the project.

Table 11.3. Generic advisory materials specifically produced for the Millennium Link project.

Guidance notes on the nature conservation issues associated with the Millennium Link works

Contracting safely

Analytical specifications: sediment, leachability, site monitoring

Disposal of cuttings

Aquatic vegetation, supply, removal and storage

Surface water discharges – procedure for assessment of environmental and hydrological impacts

Bat bricks

Animal drownings and animal ramps

Towpath and offside bank and boundary verge reinstatement

Planting new hedges and hedgerow trees

Guidance notes on limiting the spread of Japanese knotweed

Establishing emergent fringe

Cleaning systems and graffiti removal

Reinstatement of unsurfaced towpaths

Large construction companies were invited to tender for the Millennium Link works, with British Waterways managing the contracts. During the pre-tender phase of the project, the matrix of generic environmental issues and contract clauses was used to identify specific environmental considerations to be written into the contract documents. Every contractor was obliged to have an Environmental Management System following the format of the ISO14001, with regular auditing of the system during the progress of the works. For the 'lifetime' of each contract a generic process of environmental input was followed. This process is described in Table 11.4.

Table 11.4. Process for environmental input to Millennium Link works in 'design and build' contracts. The data are derived from British Waterways (1999).

Stage of process	Actionees	Elements of process
Pre-tender	British Waterways environmental staff	Generic scoping of issues and development of generic advice materials
	Design consultants	Desk study to collate existing environmental information
	British Waterways project manager	Consultation with external bodies e.g. SEPA, SNH, local planning authorities
		Collection of additional data if required
		Development of generic contract clauses
		Production of site specific pre-tender assessments and use of this information to define designs and specifications required in contract documents
Tender	Contractors	Contractors to include design requirements and specifications identified at pre-tender stage in tender documents
	Design consultants	
	British Waterways environmental staff	British Waterways staff to check tenders for inclusion of specified items. Negotiation over points of detail. Inclusion of comments in final submission.
	British Waterways project manager	
Implementation	Contractors	Watching brief and expert input as required/recommended
	British Waterways environmental staff	
	British Waterways project manager	
Monitoring and post-project appraisal	British Waterways environmental staff	Monitoring
		Conclusions and feedback to future projects

To facilitate this process British Waterways employed Glasgow based staff to advise the Millennium Link team on landscape architecture, ecology and other environmental issues. Other British Waterways specialist environmental staff advised on a range of issues including contaminated waste management and water quality modelling.

11.5 Examples of best and good practice

The application of the environmental management framework led to a fuller appreciation of the environmental assets and sensitivities of the canal network. Thus features to be retained or protected at each site were identified and any implications of the timing and duration of the works were considered. In addition, the need and scope for enhancement and mitigation measures were assessed. Table 11.5 gives examples of environmental issues that have been addressed as part of The Millennium Link project.

Table 11.5. Examples of environmental issues addressed during Millennium Link contracts.

Project element	Issues considered	Example from Millennium Link project (location and description)
Design	Process to include opportunities for mitigation and enhancement	**Wester Hailes, Edinburgh: new canal channel and bridges** (Figure 11.7). Shallow margins (planting shelves) of channel edges for planting of marginal vegetation included in design. These in turn will provide nursery areas for fish and nesting sites for birds. Planted areas will be important natural buffers and will absorb the energy of boat wash and reduce the levels of erosion.
		Lathallan Road, new road bridge and canal channel (Plate 24). A small pond and wetland area was created along the old line of the canal.
		Wyndford, new road bridge. Line of bridge wingwall was altered to accommodate water vole habitat.
		Union Canal bridges and milestones (Figure 11.8). Original numbering and lettering style used in replacement stone structures.
Timing	Works to be carried out outside the bird nesting season and planting carried out in the planting season.	**Canal network**. Timing of majority of dredging works over winter.
Site preparation	Vegetation clearance to be limited to area of works and conducted during period September to mid-February.	**Falkirk interchange**. Vegetation on Union Canal extension cut back outwith bird nesting season prior to construction.
	If lengths of canal are drained down fish rescues should be carried out where necessary.	**Canal network**. Fish rescues carried out throughout length of canals provided useful information on population structure.
Environmental protection	Relevant SEPA guidelines should be followed during the construction period.	**Canal network**, Barrier techniques used to prevent along channel migration of sediments at Clydebank and Falkirk. Silt traps used to prevent particulate pollution of the watercourse.
	Minimise disturbance and spread of channel sediments and or water intakes downstream.	During dredging operations oxygen levels were monitored and equipment was on hand to aerate the water if levels fell below acceptable concentrations.
	Protect historic structures and features such as trees and hedges during construction period.	An industrial archaeologist was employed to record the built structure revealed during the construction process (Douglas, 2000)

Project element	Issues considered	Example from Millennium Link project (location and description)
	Vegetation for replanting/ relocation should be stored in accordance with specifications given.	**Falkirk Wheel**. Collection and replacement of soils from Antonine Wall area section of construction site to encourage re-growth of woodland flora.
Waste disposal	Ensure waste generated by the works is removed and disposed of in compliance with Waste Management Regulations.	**Falkirk wheel**. Waste materials were segregated on site for recycling. **Lock 4 to 5, Falkirk**. Stabilised canal sediment used to create moorings thereby reducing volume of material taken to landfill.
Re-use of materials	Where possible, materials such as loose copings should be salvaged and stored.	**Clydebank, canal channel**. Coarser fractions of inert dredged material from shallowed canal channel were used as landscaping material in the Ruchill Community golf course project in Glasgow. **Lock 32 Forth & Clyde**. Stone from Cleveden Road bridge and Balmuildy bridge were used to rebuild Lock 32 in Glasgow. **Falkirk Wheel**. Excavated material was used for construction purposes elsewhere on the site to minimise off-site disposal.
Sustainability	Use recycled or other sustainable materials where possible. Use skilled craftsmen to extend design life of works. Consider the maintenance requirements to ensure long service-life.	**Lock gates: canal network**. New wooden structures on the canal including lock gates and balance beams made from sustainably sourced wood. French oak was used for the new lock gates on the Forth & Clyde Canal in Glasgow and Falkirk. (see Figure 11.3) **Union Canal stone bridges** (Figure 11.9). Historic Scotland approved traditional lime mortar used in bridge reconstruction. Accredited stone masons employed. **Union Canal: dry stone walls**. Accredited craftsmen used to rebuild towpath boundary walls.

11.6 Future management

The construction phase of The Millennium Link Project was concluded at the end of 2001, with the opening of the Falkirk Wheel in spring 2002, restoring full navigation to the Lowland Canal network. The re-opening of the Forth & Clyde Canal in May 2001 and the Wester Hailes section of the Union Canal in Edinburgh in August 2001 were attended by large and enthusiastic crowds, giving an indication of how people value these waterways (Plate 25). The challenge will be to sustain the interest and momentum generated by the

Figure 11.8. Union Canal milestones carved by Historic Scotland stonework apprentices.

Figure 11.9. Union Canal stone bridge under restoration.

project and to realise the full potential for sustainable development in the canal corridor in the coming years. Some of the potential indicators and targets to measure the impact of the Millennium Link are summarised in Figure 11.6. These now need to be developed to reflect sustainable development targets of the Scottish Executive and national UK government (Entec, 2001; DETR, 2001). British Waterways (GB) is currently developing sustainable development indicators and British Waterways (Scotland) intends to tailor these to the Scottish context. Existing environmental monitoring programmes, for example, for water quality, plants and customer usage will need to be extended.

Operational management of the canal network will be undertaken by British Waterways and full consideration of the potential impact of maintenance and future development works on the environmental resource will be given through the use of the corporate *Environmental Code of Practice*. The development of structured long-term plans for management of environmental resources, from woodland to fisheries, will contribute to the environmental sustainability of the canal network. Progress is underway on the development of a biodiversity action plan for the Lowland Canals (Abernethy and Scott, 2001).

British Waterways is committed to developing the sustainable use of canals beyond the immediate geographical extent of the network. For example, British Waterways is currently involved in a Department of Trade and Industry sponsored project examining the potential for the delivery of sustainable water sources for industry at Grangemouth (see www.industrialwaters.co.uk). Integrating with others plans for sustainable development also has the potential to bring benefits. British Waterways has recently been highlighted in the consultation document for *Sustainable Falkirk* for hydropower generation, green transport routes and the development of water based freight transport (Falkirk Council, 2001). West Lothian Council has also identified the Millennium Link project as an action towards sustainable development in their area (West Lothian Council, 2000).

The Millennium Link project has made a major contribution to the renaissance of the Lowland Canals and in the coming years British Waterways plans, through partnership with the wider community, to develop the potential improvements that these waterways can make to the quality of life in Scotland.

Acknowledgements

The author would like to thank the following for provision of images for this paper: George Ballinger, Lisa Kilpatrick, Ian Marr, George McBurnie, Gordon Ramsay and Alex Watson.

References

Abernethy, V. and Scott, M. (eds). (2001). *A Flying Start. Local Biodiversity Action in Scotland*. The Stationery Office, Edinburgh.

Ballinger, G. (2000). New solutions. In *The Millennium Link - the Rehabilitation of the Forth & Clyde and Union Canals*, ed. by G. Fleming. Thomas Telford, London. pp. 79-85.

Bowman, I. (2001). History. In *The Forth & Clyde Canal Guidebook*, ed. by P. Carter. East Dunbartonshire Council, Kirkintilloch. pp. 42-59.

British Waterways (1995). Environment and heritage: Millennium Link. Unpublished report.

British Waterways (1999). Environment and recreation plan. Unpublished report.

British Waterways (2000). *British Waterways and Biodiversity: a Framework for Waterway Wildlife Strategies*. British Waterways, Gloucester.

Davies, R. and Mackinnon, D. (2001). Campaigning for Restoration. In *The Forth & Clyde Canal Guidebook*, ed. by P. Carter. East Dunbartonshire Council, Kirkintilloch. pp. 60-76.

Department of the Environment, Transport and the Regions (2000). *Waterways for Tomorrow.* HMSO, Norwich.

Department of the Environment, Transport and the Regions (2001). *Achieving a Better Quality of Life. Review of Progress Towards Sustainable Development. Government Annual Report 2000.* HMSO, Norwich.

Douglas, G.J. (2000). Recording canal structures for the archive. In *The Millennium Link - the Rehabilitation of the Forth & Clyde and Union canals*, ed. by G. Fleming. Thomas Telford, London. pp. 32-37.

Entec (2001). *Sustainability Indicators for Waste, Energy and Travel for Scotland.* Stationery Office, Edinburgh.

Falkirk Council (2001). *Sustainable Falkirk: a Strategy Contributing to Local Agenda 21 in the Falkirk Council Area. Draft for Consultation.* Falkirk Council, Falkirk.

Forth & Clyde Canal Joint Advisory Committee (1995). *Lowland Canals Sustainable Development Strategy: Nature Conservation Strategy.* Forth & Clyde Canal Joint Advisory Committee , Glasgow.

Forth & Clyde Canal Society (2001). *The Forth & Clyde Canal Guidebook.* East Dunbartonshire Council, Kirkintilloch.

Fozzard, I.R., Doughty, C.R. and Clelland, B.E. (1994). Invertebrates. In *The Fresh Waters of Scotland: a National Resource of International Significance*, ed. by P.S. Maitland, P.J. Boon and D.S. McLusky. John Wiley, Chichester. pp. 171-190.

Hume, J.R. (2000). The canals of Scotland: an historical overview. In *The Millennium Link - the Rehabilitation of the Forth & Clyde and Union Canals*, ed. by G. Fleming. Thomas Telford, London. pp. 1-6.

Lindsay, J. (1968). *The Canals of Scotland.* David and Charles, Newton Abbot.

Pybus, J. (2001). Developing our aquatic assets. *Regeneration and Renewal*, 14 September 2001, 13.

Reynolds, P. (2000). Union Canal water vole survey July-August 2000. Unpublished report.

Ross, S.L., Doughty, C.R. and Murphy, K.J. (1986). Cause, effects and environmental management of a *Lemna* problem in a Scottish canal. In *Proceedings of the European Weed Research Society and Association of Applied Biologists, 7th International Symposium on Aquatic Weeds.* EWRS/AAB. Loughborough. pp. 277-283.

Scottish Environment Protection Agency (1999). *Improving Scotland's Water Environment.* Scottish Environment Protection Agency, Stirling.

Scottish Wildlife Trust Environmental Services (1997). Forth & Clyde Canal and Union Canal; ecological surveys. Unpublished report.

Scott Wilson Resource Consultants (1997). Bird survey Forth & Clyde and Union Canals. Unpublished report.

Smith, N.A. and Lassière, O.L. (2000). Resolving mercury contamination in the Union Canal, Scotland UK. In *The Millennium Link - the Rehabilitation of the Forth & Clyde and Union Canals*, ed. by G. Fleming. Thomas Telford, London. pp. 117-124.

Stirling, J.M. (2000). From decline to a new sustainable future. Project overview, finance and fundraising. In *The Millennium Link - the Rehabilitation of the Forth & Clyde and Union Canals*, ed. by G. Fleming. Thomas Telford, London. pp. 7-14.

Wood, P. (2000). The Millennium Link: economic impact. In *The Millennium Link - the Rehabilitation of the Forth & Clyde and Union Canals*, ed. by G. Fleming. Thomas Telford, London. pp. 51-71.

West Lothian Council (2000). *The West Lothian Council Environmental Programme.* West Lothian Council, Linlithgow.

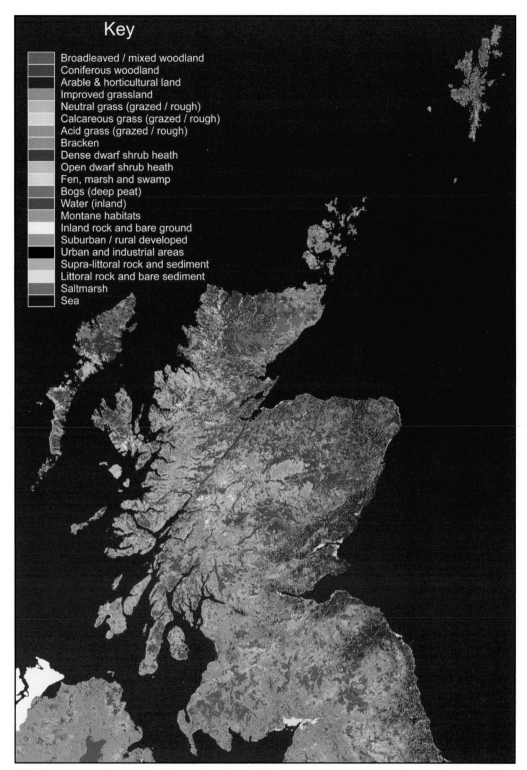

Key

- Broadleaved / mixed woodland
- Coniferous woodland
- Arable & horticultural land
- Improved grassland
- Neutral grass (grazed / rough)
- Calcareous grass (grazed / rough)
- Acid grass (grazed / rough)
- Bracken
- Dense dwarf shrub heath
- Open dwarf shrub heath
- Fen, marsh and swamp
- Bogs (deep peat)
- Water (inland)
- Montane habitats
- Inland rock and bare ground
- Suburban / rural developed
- Urban and industrial areas
- Supra-littoral rock and sediment
- Littoral rock and bare sediment
- Saltmarsh
- Sea

Plate 1.

The Land Cover Map 2000 (the whole of Scotland is shown, together with the northern parts of England and Northern Ireland).

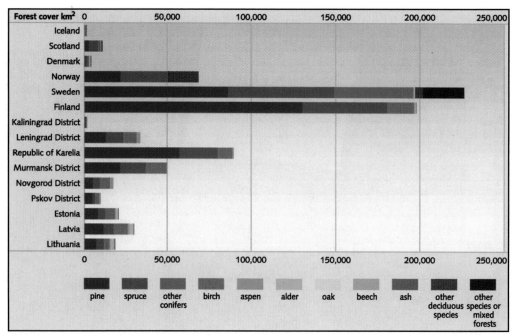

Plate 2.

Forests cover over half of the land in Finland and Sweden, and a good third of Norway, but only about 16 per cent of Scotland, 12 per cent of Denmark and 1 per cent of Iceland. In the Baltic Countries and north-western Russia the proportion of the land under forest varies between these extremes. Coniferous forests naturally dominate over much of the region, but during the twentieth century their area further increased, since commercial forest management favoured conifers over deciduous tree species. The bars are divided according to the areas of forest dominated by different tree species (from Hallanaro and Pylvänäinen, 2002). (Chapter 3)

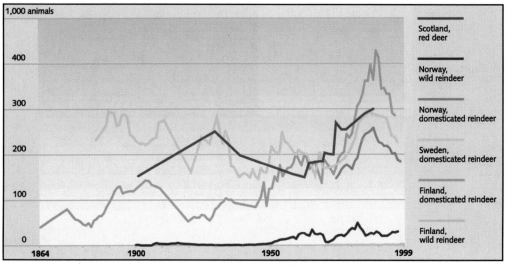

Plate 3.

The present numbers of reindeer in Norway, Sweden and Finland are so large that they are thought to exceed the natural carrying capacity of their pastures. The situation is similar in Scotland where the densities of red deer are as high as those of the reindeer in northern Fennoscandia. The graphs show the trends in the total populations (in thousands) of reindeer and red deer herds (from Hallanaro and Pylvänäinen, 2002). (Chapter 3)

Plate 4.

The Arctic bramble (*Rubus arcticus*) is common in the northern parts of the Nordic nations, but has only very sporadically been found in Scotland. This flower comes from near Kivo, 69° 41′ N in Finland.
(Photo: M.B. Usher)

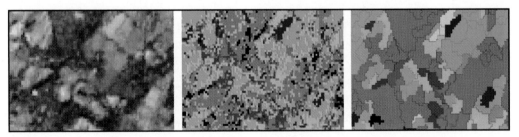

Plate 5.

A comparison of per-pixel and per-parcel mapping. The original image data (left) is a section of Landsat Thematic Mapper data with a pixel size of 25 m and an extent of 2.5 km by 1.5 km. The per-pixel mapping (centre) shows results similar to those achieved by the LCMGB demonstrating a speckled appearance due to image noise and mixed-edge pixels. The per-parcel-mapping (right) shows a more realistic spatial structure while removing the effects of image noise and mixed-edge pixels. (Chapter 4)

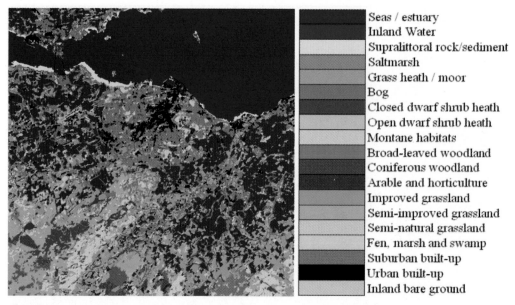

Key to land cover types:

- Seas / estuary
- Inland Water
- Supralittoral rock/sediment
- Saltmarsh
- Grass heath / moor
- Bog
- Closed dwarf shrub heath
- Open dwarf shrub heath
- Montane habitats
- Broad-leaved woodland
- Coniferous woodland
- Arable and horticulture
- Improved grassland
- Semi-improved grassland
- Semi-natural grassland
- Fen, marsh and swamp
- Suburban built-up
- Urban built-up
- Inland bare ground

Plate 6.

An area approximately 33 km square around Edinburgh from the parcel-based LCM2000, with a key to land cover types. (Chapter 4)

Some GIS attributes for the parcel:

Segment ID: *NT061575*
Number of pixels: *239 (= 14.9 ha)*
Core (non-edge) pixels: *165*
Summer image (dominant): *1/8/99*
Winter image: *4/3/97*
Elevation: *249 m*
Slope: *4°*
Aspect: *315°*
Class code: *4.1.4*
Broad Habitat: *Arable*
Subclass: *cereal*
Variant: *wheat*
Probability: *0.7*
Class in 1990: *tilled / arable land*

Plate 7.

An area approximately 10 km square from the parcel-based LCM2000 showing the local parcel structure and examples of some of the GIS attributes used during the production process. Refer to land cover type key in Plate 4. (Chapter 4)

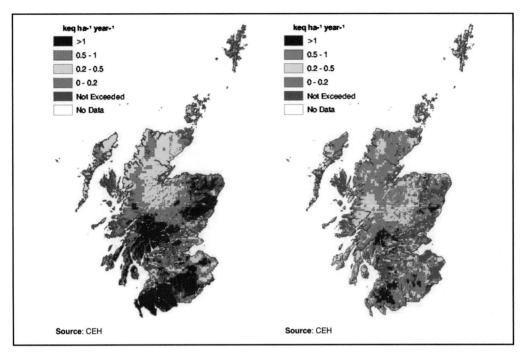

Plate 8.

Critical load exceedances of total acidity for soils, 1995 to 1997 (keq per ha) (at left) and projected critical load exceedances of total acidity for soils in 2010 (keq per ha) (at right). (Chapter 5)

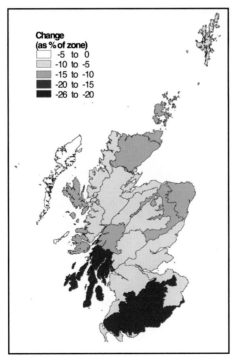

Plate 9.

Semi-natural land cover change, 1947-1988 (based on data in Mackey *et al.*, 1998). (Chapter 5)

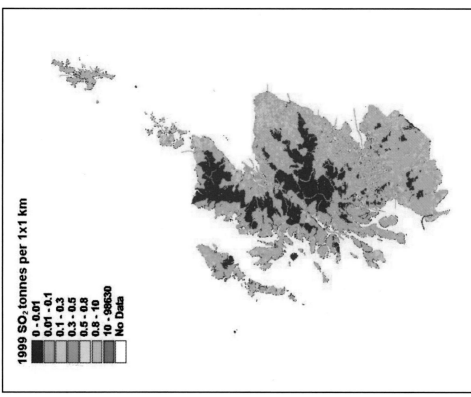

Plate 11.

Spatially disaggregated emissions of NO_x (expressed as NO_2) in Scotland including shipping in inshore waters, at a scale of 1 km x 1 km. (Chapter 7)

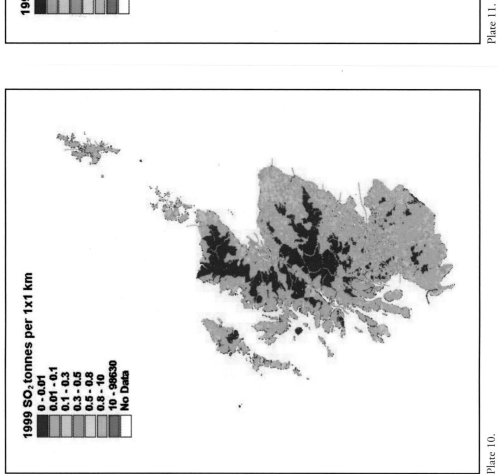

Plate 10.

Spatially disaggregated emissions of SO_2 in Scotland, including shipping in inshore waters, at a scale of 1 km x 1 km. (Chapter 7)

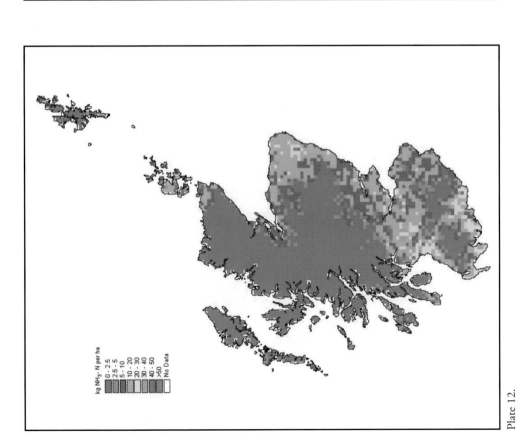

Plate 13.

Spatially disaggregated emissions of VOC in Scotland including inshore waters at a scale of 1 km x 1 km. (Chapter 7)

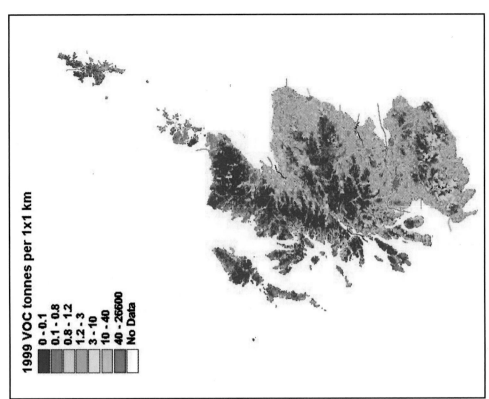

Plate 12.

Spatially disaggregated emissions of NH_3 in Scotland in 1999 at a scale of 5 km x 5 km. (Chapter 7)

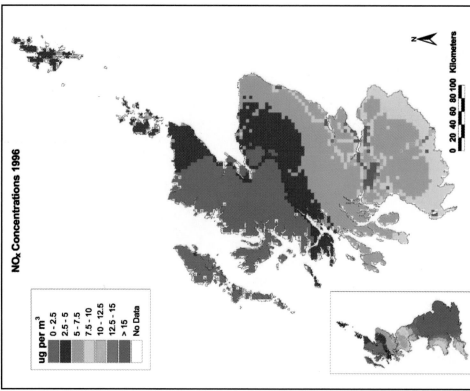

NOx Concentrations 1996

ug per m³
0 - 2.5
2.5 - 5
5 - 7.5
7.5 - 10
10 - 12.5
12.5 - 15
> 15
No Data

0 20 40 60 80 100 Kilometers

N

Plate 15.

Annual average NOx concentrations in Scotland at a scale of 5 km x 5 km.
(Inset is the map including England and Wales for comparison). (Chapter 7)

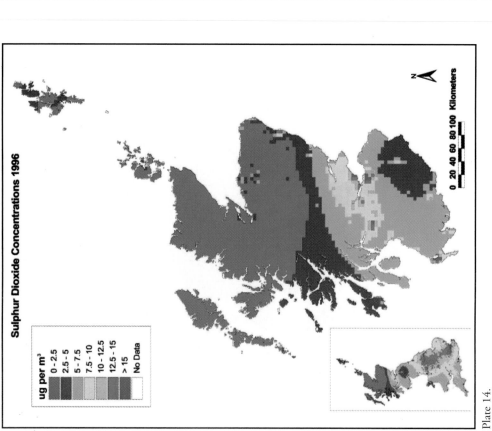

Sulphur Dioxide Concentrations 1996

ug per m³
0 - 2.5
2.5 - 5
5 - 7.5
7.5 - 10
10 - 12.5
12.5 - 15
> 15
No Data

0 20 40 60 80 100 Kilometers

N

Plate 14.

Annual average SO₂ concentrations in Scotland at a scale of 5 km x 5 km.
(Inset is the map including England and Wales for comparison). (Chapter 7)

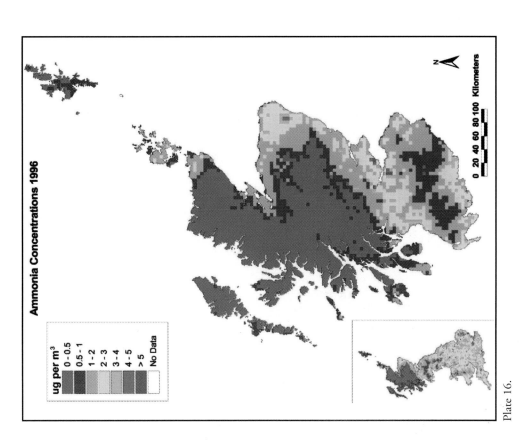

Plate 17.

The accumulated exposure of terrestrial surfaces to O_3 concentrations above 40 ppb between 1 April and 30 June (the AOT40) at a scale of 5 km x 5 km, and inset including England and Wales. (Chapter 7)

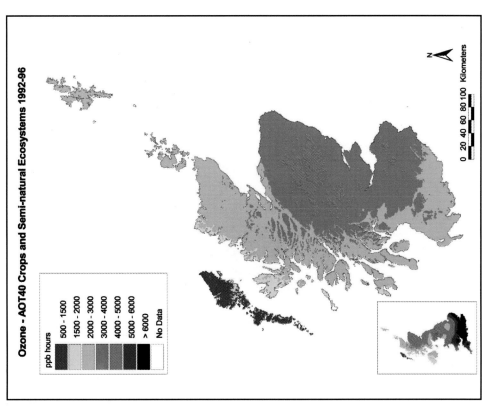

Plate 16.

Annual average NH_3 concentrations in Scotland at a scale of 5 km x 5 km. (Inset is the map including England and Wales for comparison). (Chapter 7)

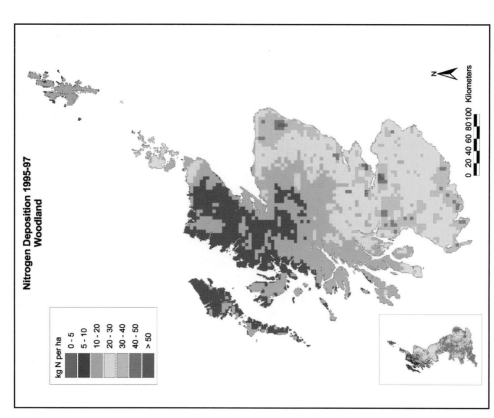

Plate 19.

The annual total deposition of nitrogen to woodland within each 5 km x 5 km of Scotland (insert is the map including England and Wales for comparison). (Chapter 7)

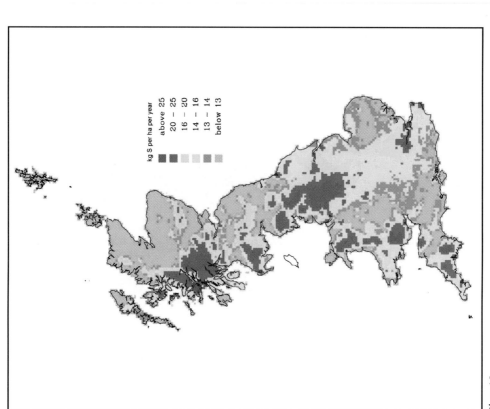

Plate 18.

The total deposition of anthropogenic sulphur in Scotland, England and Wales (including wet, dry and cloud deposition) at a scale of 5 km x 5 km. (Chapter 7)

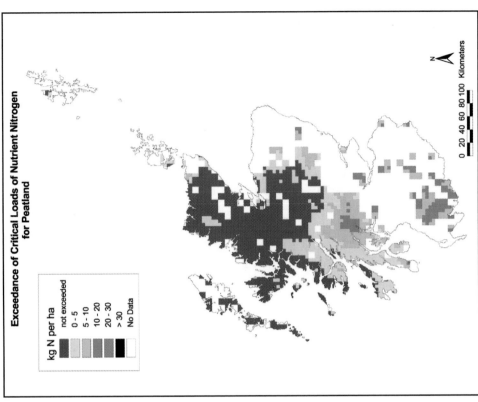

Plate 21.

Exceedance of critical loads of nutrient nitrogen for peatlands in Scotland in 1996, at 10 km x 10 km. (Chapter 7)

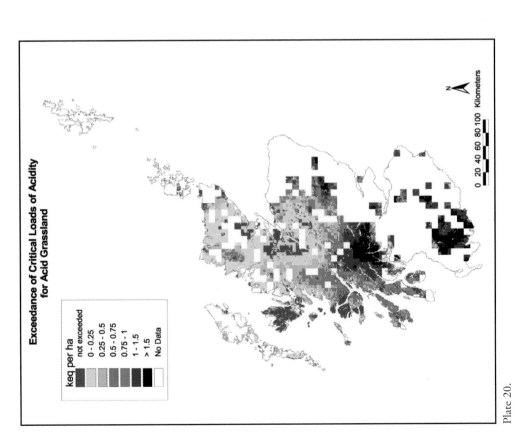

Plate 20.

Exceedance of critical loads for acidity of acid grassland in Scotland in 1996 at 10 km x 10 km. (Chapter 7)

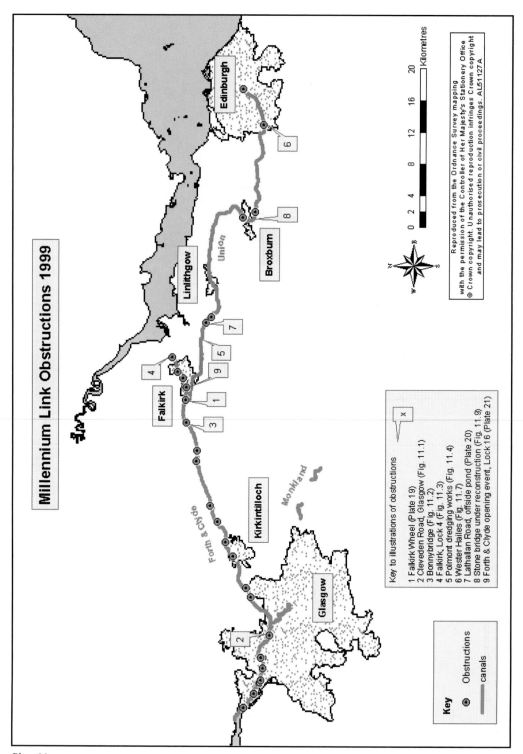

Plate 22.

Obstructions to navigation on the Forth & Clyde and Union Canals in March 1999. (Chapter 11)

(a)

(b)

Plate 23.

The Falkirk Wheel: partly constructed wheel (September 2001) (a) and artist's impression (b). (Chapter 11)

(a)

(b)

Plate 24.
Offside pond created at Lathallan Road Bridge from cut off section of old canal channel in April 2000 (a) and in July 2001 (b). (Chapter 11)

Plate 25.

Forth & Clyde Canal opening event, 26 May 2001, at Lock 16, Falkirk. (Chapter 11)

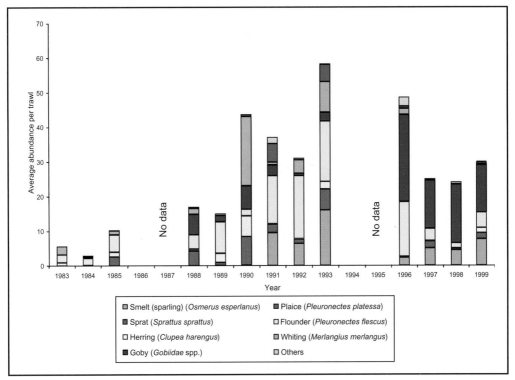

Plate 26.

Trends in the resident fish community in the upper Forth Estuary. (Chapter 12)

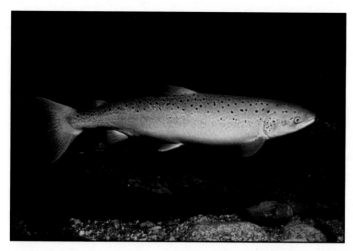

Plate 27.
The Atlantic salmon (*Salmo salar*).
(Photo: Sue Scott) (Chapter 15)

Plate 28.

Changes in precipitation patterns between 1941-1970 and 1961-1990. Derived from Mayes (1996). (Chapter 16)

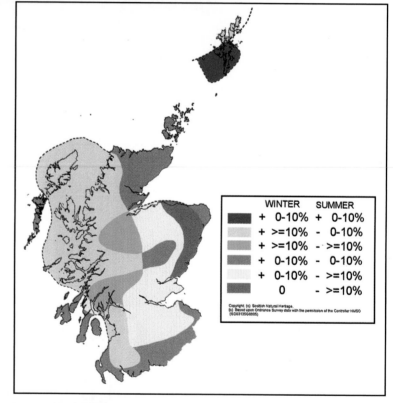

WINTER SUMMER
+ 0-10% + 0-10%
+ >=10% - 0-10%
+ >=10% - >=10%
+ 0-10% - 0-10%
+ 0-10% - >=10%
0 - >=10%

Copyright (c) Scottish Natural Heritage.
(c) Based upon Ordnance Survey data with the permission of the Controller HMSO
(GD03135G0005)

Plate 29.

The holly blue butterfly (*Celastrina argiolus*), one of the species whose geographical range in the United Kingdom expanded sharply in the 1990s. (Photo: M.B. Usher) (Chapter 8)

12 THE STATE OF SCOTLAND'S SEAS AND ESTUARIES

G. Saunders, J. Dobson and A. Edwards

Summary

1.   Scotland's coasts and seas comprise an estimated 53 per cent of the total administrative territory. The Scottish coastline is complex, highly indented and extremely variable in the character and extent of its marine habitats and communities.

2.   The distribution, nature and sensitivity of native marine habitats and species are still not fully documented. There has been increased survey effort over the last 20 years.

3.   Increased statutory control and improved effluent treatment have greatly reduced discharges of anthropogenic contaminants into Scottish coastal seas. Measured environmental concentrations of some pollutants have correspondingly declined.

4.   Estuarine environment quality in the areas of greatest contamination has improved since the 1970s and has been reflected in an increase of faunal diversity.

5.   Coastal water quality has improved as treatment of urban wastewater discharges has been upgraded. This has improved compliance with bacteriological standards at bathing beaches.

6.   Mariculture is a highly successful industry in Scotland but environmental concerns have continued to grow. Organic and other chemical contamination from mariculture is usually highly localised but may remain in sediments for two years.

7.   Knowledge of the status of marine mammals remains variable. Consistent estimates of cetaceans' numbers are few, but declines for some species have been reported. Harbour seal numbers have recovered rapidly and stabilised after the 1988 viral epidemic. The grey seal populations continue to increase.

8.   Stocks of many commercially exploited marine fish species have become dangerously depleted, and there are increasing concerns about the damaging effects of fishing on seabed habitats.

9.   Statutory conservation of Scotland's coasts has been largely achieved through SSSI designation, but protection is limited to the land above the level of Mean Low Water. The UK application of the Habitats Directive has allowed effective conservation protection to be extended to the sublittoral zone.

10. The overall state of Scotland's seas is considered healthy. Areas of historically high anthropogenic contamination are improving. The major ecological issues surrounding marine fisheries, however, remain unresolved.

12.1 Introduction

The surrounding sea is an integral part of Scotland's character, influencing the geography of the coastline by wave action and tidal flows, controlling climate with a complicated convergence of offshore water masses and providing a rich medium in which a considerable array of animal and plant forms flourish. The Scottish coastline is remarkably intricate and variable. To the west, the Atlantic coast is characterised by a highly indented fjordic and fjardic landscape with exposed islands, high sea cliffs and rocky skerries. To the east, the North Sea coast is predominantly low-lying, often supporting sedimentary shores with only intermittent stretches of cliff. This part of the coastline is also less convoluted but is deeply penetrated by five large inlets or firths. Away from the mainland, the three major archipelagos of Shetland, Orkney and the Western Isles all maintain a range of distinctive coastal habitats.

Because of the physical complexity of the boundary between the land and the sea, an accurate estimate of the total length of the Scottish coastline is difficult to determine, but is often stated to be about 11,800 km, representing over 8 per cent of the entire coastline of Europe (Doody, 1999). Advances in computer mapping technology have allowed estimates to be made at greater scales and calculations based on a 1:25,000 scale suggest a revised Scottish coastline length of some 16,491 km (MLURI, 1993). Moreover, a recent additional calculation of the area of sea enclosed within the 12 mile territorial limit returned a figure of 88,597 km^2, suggesting that some 53 per cent of Scotland's administrative territory is essentially marine in nature (Scottish Office GIS Unit, pers. com.).

Human influence on the marine environment is of growing concern throughout the world and, despite a relatively low population density, evidence for the detrimental effects of man's endeavours is not hard to find around Scotland's coasts. Since the arrival of the first human settlers, the sea has maintained a position of supreme importance, as a provider of food, as an effective means of transport, as an important resource for commerce and as a receiver of domestic and industrial wastes.

Here, we address a wide range of issues that are relevant to the current status of Scotland's seas. In doing so, it must be recognised that, in ecological terms, international boundaries are largely meaningless when drawn across a continuous body of water. Hence, in examining some of the problems associated with Scotland's seas some of the information is necessarily drawn from sources with European or even wider perspectives.

12.2 Scotland's marine environment

12.2.1 Marine survey

Scotland's natural marine heritage encloses a sea area greater than that of the rest of the United Kingdom. It is as visually spectacular and varied as the Scottish terrestrial environment, but remains largely hidden from sight and comparatively little studied. Because of the cost and technical challenges of working in the sea our knowledge of species, habitats and communities, particularly those found below the low tide line, is still at an early stage. Davison (1996) and Davison and Baxter (1997) estimated the number of Scottish marine species to be about 8,000 plants, invertebrates and fish, but more than 40,000 if protozoa, bacteria and viruses were included.

Scottish marine survey work, as in the rest of the UK, has not been uniformly distributed, often being concentrated around favoured sites, or close to research or educational establishments. A major expansion of survey activity occurred in the late 1970s and early 1980s (Figure 12.1) and was further accelerated by the establishment of the Marine Nature Conservation Review (MNCR) in 1987. The increased survey effort was sustained into the 1990s partly due to the additional information required to support the implementation of the European Union's Habitats Directive in the UK. Moreover, the early 1980s were a time of increased oil and gas industry activity, with environmental monitoring and sampling, largely of sediments, accompanying all major exploratory and development projects. Although the contribution of purely academic studies should not be underestimated, our current knowledge of the extent and distribution of marine habitats and species comes from a broad network of sources. Even so, the coverage is widely dispersed and patchy, with substantial sections of the north and east coast remaining poorly surveyed (Figure 12.2), either reflecting operational considerations or past selection of what might be considered 'interesting' areas of coastline.

The collation of these data, however incomplete, has revealed a rich and spectacular patchwork of marine communities and habitats. MNCR survey records exist for almost 2,300 of the 8,000 plant, invertebrate and fish species estimated to be present in Scottish waters. Many are common and widely distributed while others are clearly restricted in their distribution due to their dependence on particular conditions, such as those provided by the sheltered west coast sea lochs. This information provides a benchmark in our efforts to mitigate the effects of direct human disturbance and is invaluable in the establishment of baselines, against which the effectiveness of future protection may be judged.

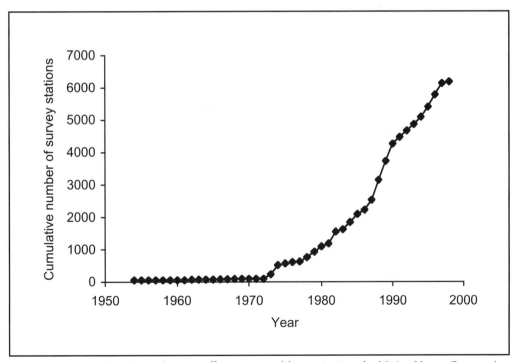

Figure 12.1. Cumulative Scottish survey effort represented by entries into the Marine Nature Conservation Review database.

Figure 12.2. Location of Scottish survey stations held in the Marine Nature Conservation Review database. Note that survey sites near Rockall are not shown.

12.2.2 *Monitoring marine environment quality*

Regular quality controlled monitoring of key aspects of marine condition is required by various pieces of legislation. Scottish tidal waters are protected by a range of European Union Directives, each administered by competent and relevant authorities. The Scottish Environment Protection Agency (SEPA) has a statutory responsibility to protect the tidal waters of Scotland under the 1995 Environment (Scotland) Act. Protection is pursued through the licensing of discharges and the issue of statutory notices. The agency further administers the Dangerous Substances Directive (76/464/EEC), Shellfish Waters Directive (79/923/EEC), Urban Waste Water Treatment Directive (91/271/EEC) and Bathing Waters Directive (76/160/EEC). The Scottish Executive Environment and Rural Affairs Department administers the Food and Environment Protection Act which licenses dredging and dumping activities, the Shellfish Harvesting Directive (91/492/EEC) and the Fisheries Product Directive (91/493/EEC). Scottish Natural Heritage (SNH) is concerned with conservation issues and maintains responsibility for implementation of elements of the Birds Directive (79/409/EEC) and the Habitats Directive (92/43/EEC). The information provided by each of these organisations is used to assess the quality of the estuaries and seas around Scotland.

The River Purification Boards (RPBs – SEPA's predecessors) were responsible after 1960 for new discharges to tidal waters, and from 1965 for all existing discharges. At this time, improvement of river water quality was a priority for the RPBs but domestic and industrial effluent was discharged to tidal waters in an untreated state. The RPBs turned their attention to marine discharges in the 1970s, initiating a programme of discharge improvements and by the mid-1980s only 26.6 per cent of the discharges to the Forth, for example, remained untreated (Collett and Leatherland, 1985). To assist the assessment of water quality, the RPBs developed classification schemes based on chemical and biological criteria. Annual assessments for tidal waters were first produced in 1968 and showed no improvement until after 1975. Separate estuarine and coastal classification schemes, introduced in 1990, showed improvements between 1990 and 1995 when the current schemes were introduced.

The present classification schemes (Tables 12.1 and 12.2) incorporate biological and chemical quality and aesthetic criteria. The estuarine scheme is targeted towards the impact of waste discharges on dissolved oxygen depletion whereas the coastal scheme concentrates on bacterial contamination. There are four quality classes: A (excellent) to D (seriously polluted, the lowest class). A given area is classified by allocating it to the lowest class to which any of its condition criteria conform. This 'default based' classification therefore has focused improvement efforts effectively onto waters in which any single element or group of elements depressed the class.

12.2.3 *Long term trends in estuarine quality*

Out of a total estuarine area of 1,352 km^2, SEPA classifies 810 km^2 within 32 estuaries. The remaining unclassified estuaries are located in areas of low population in the Highlands and Islands and are unlikely to be affected by sewage or industrial pollution. Most of the poor quality waters are located in the Forth and Clyde Estuaries, receiving discharges from large conurbations and industrial complexes. There are also small areas of poor quality near Aberdeen and Inverness. The majority (95 per cent) of estuarine waters was of good quality

Table 12.1. SEPA's estuarine waters classification scheme.

Class	Description	Aesthetic conditions	Fish migration	Resident biota and/or bioassay	Resident fish	Persistent substances (Biota)	Water Chemistry Dissolved oxygen (DO)	UK Red List and EC dangerous substances
A	Excellent	Unpolluted	Water quality allows free passage	Normal	Resident fish community normal	Less than twice national background	Minimum DO >6 mg per litre	100 per cent compliance of samples with EQS
B	Good	May show signs of contamination	Water quality allows free passage	Normal	Resident fish community normal	At least twice national background but not substantially elevated	Minimum DO ≤6 mg per litre but >4 mg per litre	Annual compliance of samples with EQS
C	Unsatisfactory	Occasional observations or substantiated complaints of pollution	Water quality restricts passage	Modified	Resident fish community modified	Substantially elevated but not grossly elevated	Minimum DO ≤4 mg per litre but >2 mg per litre	One or more List II substances fail to comply with EQS. List I and Red List all comply
D	Seriously polluted	Frequent observations or substantiated complaints of pollution	Water quality allows NO passage	Impoverished or severely modified	Resident fish community impoverished	Grossly elevated level	DO ≤2 mg per litre	One or more List I or Red List substances fail to comply with EQS

Table 12.2. SEPA's coastal water classification scheme. For classes A and B all three conditions must be fulfilled; for classes C and D any one condition is sufficient to classify a coastal water in that class.

Class/description	Use-related description	Aesthetic condition	Biological condition		Bacteriological condition		Chemical condition
A Excellent	Fit for all defined uses	Near pristine, uncontaminated	Flora and fauna normal	*and*	Likely to meet quality standards no less stringent than the guideline standards for EC Designated Shellfish and Bathing Waters		
B Good	Fit for all defined uses	Unpolluted but may show signs of contamination	Flora and fauna normal	*and*	Likely to meet quality standards no less stringent than the mandatory standards for EC Designated Shellfish and Bathing Waters	*and*	Likely to meet all quality standards applied as a consequence of the EC Dangerous Substances Directive
C Unsatisfactory	Defined uses may be compromised by the occasional presence of sewage derived material or by moderate organic enrichment	Occasional observations or substantiated complaints of sewage solids, smell nuisance or oil	Flora and/or fauna modified by effluent discharges	*or*	Likely to fail to meet quality standards no less stringent than the mandatory standards for EC Designated Bathing Waters		
D Seriously polluted	Defined uses compromised or prevented by the frequent presence of sewage derived material, or chemical pollutants	Frequent observations or substantiated complaints of sewage solids, smell nuisance or oil	Flora and/or fauna impoverished or absent	*or*	Likely frequently to fail to meet quality standards no less stringent than the mandatory standards for EC Designated Bathing Waters	*or*	Likely to fail any one or more of quality standards applied as a consequence of the EC Dangerous Substances Directive

in 1990 when estuaries were first classified. Of the remaining waters, only 1 per cent were classified as seriously polluted (class D). Although there has been little change in good quality waters since 1990, the percentage of seriously polluted waters had reduced to 0.1 per cent in 1995. It continues to decline with a consequent increase in satisfactory (class C) waters.

The primary cause of downgrading in estuaries is low dissolved oxygen levels in the water, which inhibits the passage of migratory fish and modifies the resident fish community. Lack of dissolved oxygen in the Forth and Clyde Estuaries accounts for approximately 40 per cent of poor quality waters. Improved effluent treatments have reduced discharges of organic wastes, quantified by their measured biochemical oxygen demand (BOD), and have improved dissolved oxygen status in the Forth, Clyde and Eden Estuaries.

As an example, there is a well-documented depression in dissolved oxygen in the upper Forth Estuary (Balls *et al.*, 1996; Collett, 1961; Dobson, 1997; Griffiths, 1987). The consumption of oxygen in the upper estuary is a natural phenomenon which results from degradation of organic matter suspended in the water column. The Forth is a turbid estuary, with the maximum zone of turbidity in the upper estuary where concentrations of suspended solids are particularly high due to the action of tidal currents. The intensity of this turbidity maximum varies in response to tidal range and river flow. Oxygen consumption in the turbidity maximum is a natural process, exacerbated by the presence of organic wastes. In the Forth, the extent and duration of the dissolved oxygen depression has reduced as discharges have declined (Figures 12.3 and 12.4), but still varies considerably because of fluctuating environmental factors.

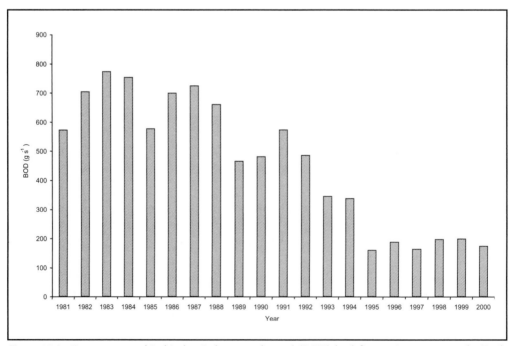

Figure 12.3. Long-term trend in biochemical oxygen demand (BOD) load from point sources to the Forth Estuary.

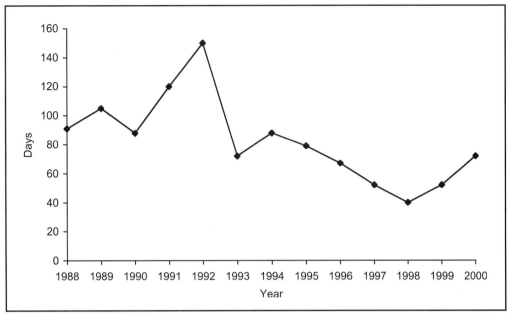

Figure 12.4. Number of days that the minimum dissolved oxygen (DO) fell below 4.5 mg per litre in the Forth Estuary.

During these improvements, regular scientific trawling of the upper estuary has provided information on the resident fish community (Plate 26). The data reveal an increase in average abundance in the 1990s compared to the 1980s. The return of smelt (*Osmerus eperlanus*) to the upper Forth in the 1990s may also indicate improved water quality.

The second most significant factor that downgrades estuarine quality is poor aesthetics – often sewage related litter. This tends to occur where screening of storm overflows from sewage treatment works is inadequate and it accounts for about 2 per cent of poor quality waters. The water authorities are addressing this by upgrading sewage treatments to comply with the requirements of the Urban Waste Water Treatment Directive.

Elsewhere in Scotland, about 0.5 per cent of estuarine areas have been downgraded because of the modification of the benthic fauna by organic inputs. Two examples of this are Kinneil mudflats in the Forth and Barcaldine in Loch Creran, Argyll. The effluent from an oil refinery at Kinneil modified local fauna and caused an abiotic zone nearby. Improvements in effluent treatment with particular pollution loading reduction in 1990 increased the number of species in the mudflat and the abiotic zone has disappeared (Figure 12.5) (McLusky and Martins, 1998).

Marine kelps were processed at Barcaldine on Loch Creran to produce alginates for about 50 years before closure of the plant in 1997. Considerable quantities of macerated and diced seaweed waste were discharged over this period, initially to the shore and, from 1975, via a short subsea outfall at about 15 m depth. The solids had a high organic content and BOD, and in the low currents they settled locally, accumulating on the seabed over a significant area of the bay. Here they decomposed slowly, resulting in the release of noxious odours such as hydrogen sulphide. Such waste affected the susceptible community of benthic invertebrate organisms living in and feeding on the sediment such that the number

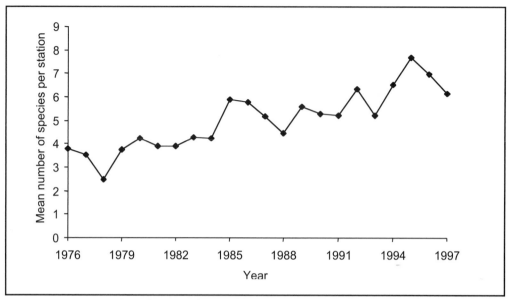

Figure 12.5   Mean number of species of benthic infauna at Kinneil Mudflats in the Forth Estuary (after McLusky and Martins, 1998).

of species was substantially reduced. Biological monitoring of this community since the late 1980s shows that the number of species recorded in the zone impacted by the discharge is smaller than the number of species recorded further offshore (Figure 12.6). The area of the impacted zone decreased from within 600 m of the outfall in 1989 to within 300 m in 1992 as production declined, but there was no further reduction in the impacted area until the plant closed. Further surveys have shown an increase in the number of species in the impacted zone since 1997 although the sea bed has not yet fully recovered..

The River Ythan has a low-lying catchment, with approximately 90 per cent of its area under agriculture. Growths of green macroalgae, principally *Enteromorpha* species, have increased in both abundance and spatial extent within the estuary (Raffaelli *et al.*, 1999). Long-term chemical monitoring data of the river and its tributaries show that nitrogen inputs to the estuary have been increasing over decades (Balls *et al.*, 1995; MacDonald *et al.*, 1995; Pugh, 1993). The catchment is now designated as a Nitrate Vulnerable Zone under the Nitrates Directive. Other similar eastern estuaries are being studied to determine the extent of problems arising from nutrient enrichment along this coastline. Mathieson and Atkins (1995) suggested, from observations of the extent of algal mats in 1981 and 1991, that the Montrose Basin was showing signs of eutrophication. Further studies have shown, however, that there is considerable interannual variation in *Enteromorpha* growth in the basin and that there is no demonstrable increasing trend (Dobson and Park, in press).

Other criteria appear in the classification scheme. Downgrading of about 1 per cent of estuarine areas is linked to environmental concentrations of discharged chemicals listed in the Dangerous Substance Directive. The Forth and Clyde Estuaries receive the greatest anthropogenic inputs of metals in Scotland because they are where most of the population and industry are found. Nevertheless, metal levels in the water of these estuaries are well below national estuarine environmental quality standards and are lower than those recorded

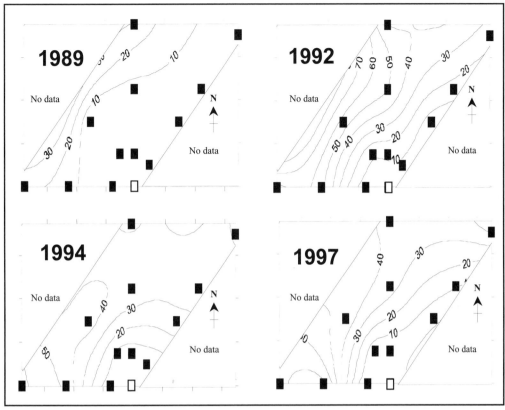

Figure 12.6. Contour chart of the number of species at Barcaldine 1989-1997. Black boxes show sampling sites and graduations mark 200 m intervals. The open box at the bottom of each panel indicates the origin of the effluent.

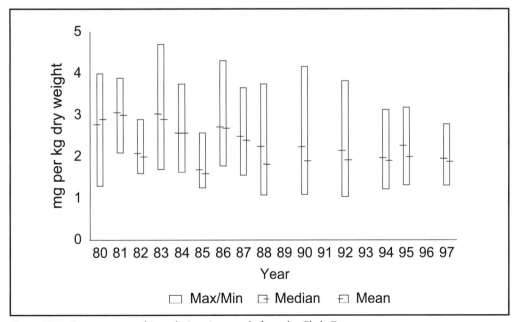

Figure 12.7. Long-term trend in cadmium in mussels from the Clyde Estuary.

in industrialised estuaries in England (Balls *et al.*, 1997). Reductions in point source discharges of these substances have been achieved through effective regulation and effluent treatment; this has been reflected in a lowering of body burden of trace metals in the mussel *Mytilus edulis* (Dobson, 2000; Miller, 1999) (Figure 12.7).

12.2.4 Long term trends in coastal quality

The SEPA classification scheme has hitherto only been applied to the mainland coastline but a planned expansion, incorporating the Outer Hebrides, Orkney and Shetland, will take account of the impact of mariculture in these areas.

The majority of the coastline (92 per cent) was classed as good quality (classes A and B) when coastal waters were first classified in 1990. Improvements in coastal water quality between 1990 and 1995 increased the percentage of good quality coastline to 96 per cent. This was achieved through the introduction of long sea outfalls and treatment for sewage discharges to coastal waters, both of which reduced bacteriological contamination of beaches. The percentage of good quality coastline did not increase between 1995 and 2000, but further improvements are expected in 2005 following the Urban Waste Water Treatment Directive deadline for improvements to discharges by the end of 2000. Scottish water authorities have provided secondary treatment for large discharges to fulfil the requirements of the Urban Waste Water Directive. This has resulted in further reductions in bacteriological contamination, especially at designated bathing beaches (Figure 12.8)).

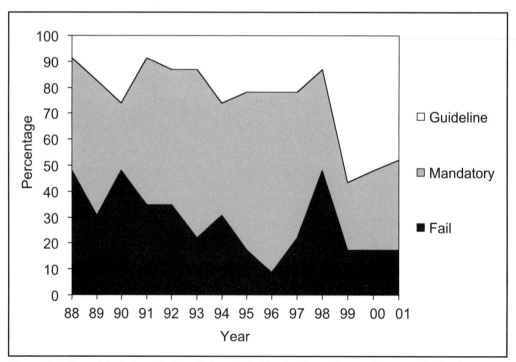

Figure 12.8. Bacteriological standards at designated bathing beaches. The mandatory standard is that 95 per cent of samples should not exceed 10,000 total coliforms and 2,000 faecal coliforms per 100 ml. The guideline standard is that 80 per cent of samples should not exceed 500 total coliforms and 100 faecal coliforms per 100 ml, and that 90 per cent of samples should not exceed 100 faecal streptococci per 100 ml.

The Bathing Waters Directive sets a mandatory standard of 10,000 total coliforms per 100 ml of which no more than 2,000 per 100 ml should be faecal coliforms in 95 per cent of samples. The number of beaches achieving this standard has increased and there has also been an increase in the number of beaches achieving the more stringent guideline standard of 500 total coliforms per 100 ml and 200 faecal coliforms per 100 ml. The guideline standard also specifies that 90 per cent of samples should not exceed 100 faecal streptococci per 100 ml. The trend was interrupted in 1998 by exceptionally wet weather during the bathing season which resulted in an increase in the discharge of sewage from storm overflows and riverine discharges.

Two important historic discharges ceased in the late 1990s: sewage sludge from Edinburgh and Glasgow was dumped at sea until 1998 but this practice stopped in compliance with the Urban Waste Water Treatment Directive. Frequent monitoring of the dumping grounds showed a greater impact at the Firth of Clyde Garroch Head (Glasgow) site which was less dispersive than the two North Sea sites used by Edinburgh. The dumping ground at Garroch Head was contaminated by persistent organochlorine compounds (Kelly and Balls, 1995) and the benthos modified by the organic input. Recent studies have shown that the benthos has improved since the dumping stopped. Sludge disposal off the Firth of Forth had no discernible ecological impact, presumably because of the biodegradability and low concentration of persistent contaminants in the dumped material.

12.2.5 Trends in water quality

To date, national and European legislation directed towards regulating traditional point source discharges has successfully reduced the extent of polluted tidal waters. Where inputs of organic waste and persistent substances have been reduced, the environment has shown signs of recovery. These are encouraging trends. Nevertheless, problems associated with more diffuse pollution remain. Foremost are bacterial and nutrient contamination issues.

Diffuse inputs of faecal coliforms are under investigation as the probable cause of failures to meet the standards of the Bathing Waters Directive in places where point source discharges have largely been eliminated (Centre for Research into Environment and Health, 1999).

Monitoring results for the Firth of Forth have shown no trend in the concentrations of coastal nutrients or chlorophyll over the past 20 years (Dobson *et al.*, in press), whereas a local problem has been recognised in the catchment and estuary of the River Ythan. A recent and more general review of nitrogen inputs to tidal waters has shown rivers to be the major source with relatively minor inputs from point source discharges.

Looking to the future, the Water Framework Directive (WFD) will replace and complement many existing directives and will provide a framework in which good ecological status is actively sought for all waters other than those heavily modified for essential services. Present policies of tolerating no deterioration in classification status will continue, as will control of point sources. In contrast to past legislation, the WFD maintains a more explicit focus on diffuse inputs from agricultural and urban runoff, requiring some adjustments of emphasis relating to monitoring and control.

12.3 Mariculture

Clean waters and a widespread availability of wave-sheltered sites have made Scotland a particularly attractive location for the farming of both finfish and shellfish. Commercial salmon farming began in Scotland in 1969 with the establishment of the first farms near

Aberdeen and at Loch Ailort, while modern shellfish culture became established around the mid-1980s. From the outset, the industry was hailed as environmentally sympathetic: it potentially provided relief for the heavily exploited wild fish stocks while producing a healthy, high value product raised within its natural environment. Few predicted the success of the industry in Scotland and its eventual dominance of the economy of the western, north-western and island coastal communities. In 1979, just over 1,000 t of wild salmon were available for market, but only 510 t of farmed fish were produced (Anon., 2000). Growth in production was slow until the mid-1980s, when financial incentives stimulated a major expansion of the industry (Figure 12.9). In 2000, almost 130,000 t of farmed salmon were produced from 346 marine farm sites around Scotland (Fisheries Research Services, 2001). Production of shellfish has similarly grown but on a much smaller scale, rising to over 1,000 t of mussels (the main species) in 2000.

Currently, almost all sea lochs with conditions suitable for mariculture have at least one installation, prompting concerns for the impacts on the local seabed, aesthetic degradation of the landscape, nutrient enrichment of coastal waters, and interactions with wild populations. Salmon farming in particular has attracted much criticism, with disease outbreaks and interactions with wild salmon populations stimulating major controversy in recent times (see Baxter and Hutchinson, Chapter 15). In some cases, the seabed beneath salmon cages is contaminated with uneaten food and faecal material, together with pharmaceuticals, pesticides and chemical antifoulants applied to the cage structure. Evidence suggests that these areas of contamination are highly localised and may be minimised by careful site selection. Contamination may persist, however, for as much as two years after the removal of the cages (Pearson and Black, 2001). At present, the siting of every new mariculture installation in Scotland undergoes consultation involving both SEPA and SNH. The potential for damage to the environment is rigorously examined case by case, and advice is given using the best available information. Fish farms are granted discharge consents by SEPA that may limit annual production, number and size of cages and the quantities of chemicals that may be used. There have been recent improvements in benthic sediment quality around some marine cage fish farms following the revocation of consents and the implementation of extensive self-monitoring programmes.

Shellfish production in Scotland is small compared to other European countries. The main species are mussel (*Mytilus edulis*), Pacific oyster (*Crassostrea gigas*), scallop (*Pecten maximus*) and queen scallop (*Aequipecten opercularis*) with production concentrated on the west coast, particularly in Argyll. Shellfish production relies on natural phytoplankton in the water. Some of the planktonic species that constitute food for shellfish produce toxins that are subsequently concentrated within the shellfish flesh. Consumption of shellfish containing these toxins may cause paralytic shellfish poisoning (PSP), amnesic shellfish poisoning (ASP) or diarrhetic shellfish poisoning (DSP) characterised by headaches, nausea, diarrhoea and respiratory paralysis.

Monitoring shellfish for the toxins responsible for PSP began after an outbreak in 1968 hospitalised several people in north-east England and south-east Scotland. The programme was extended in 1999 to include ASP. Many of the shellfish production sites were closed during 2000 because of the presence of toxins. Concern has been expressed that nutrients released from salmon farms may be related to an increase in the frequency of toxic algal blooms. Further long-term monitoring is needed to establish if blooms of toxic algae are increasing in reality, or merely as a result of the greater intensity of monitoring. Other possible causes such as climate change, natural variability, the effects of fisheries, pollution and global transfers of harmful species may also be implicated and require further investigation.

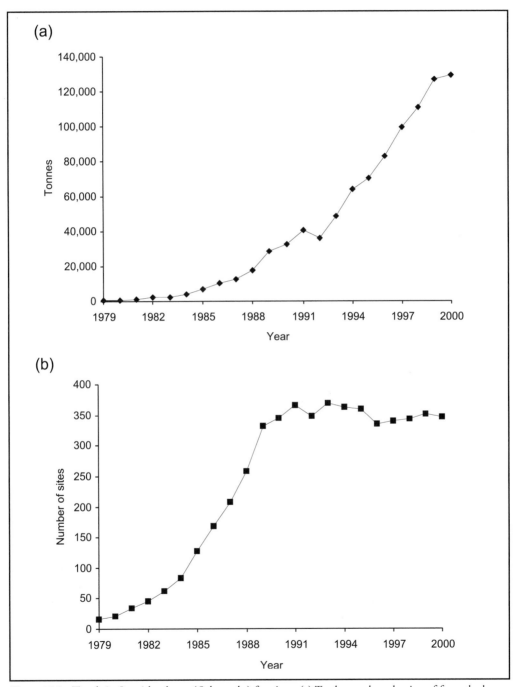

Figure 12.9. Trends in Scottish salmon (*Salmo salar*) farming. (a) Total annual production of farmed salmon. (b) Number of registered active salmon farm sites (source: Fisheries Research Services, 2001).

The increase in dissolved inorganic nitrogen concentration in the waters surrounding fish farms has been modelled (Gillibrand and Turrell, 1997). Recent box modelling of 111 lochs and voes (Davies, 2001) predicts an increase in nitrogen of less than 2 µmol per litre in all except nine lochs, and less than 0.3 µmol per litre in the majority. These are conservative estimates that would be less were it possible to model all the possible water exchange mechanisms between coastal waters and lochs. They suggest that a few fish farms may create minor localised enrichment relative to natural levels, but that mariculture-derived inputs remain comparatively low when viewed alongside other sources (Davies (2000) estimated 5 to 6 kt per annum from aquaculture, whereas total inputs from rivers and sewage would be 67 and 20 to 30 kt per annum respectively). From this viewpoint, direct connection with any real increase in harmful algal blooms cannot reliably be demonstrated and such increases must be considered within the context of observed long-term natural changes in the Atlantic phytoplankton.

12.4 Marine fisheries

Finfish and shellfish have been harvested in Scottish coastal waters for many centuries. Early exploitation probably developed out of necessity, since the greater part of the country - especially the hill and mountain areas - is of limited productivity. Over several centuries the availability of this abundant and relatively reliable food source was a major factor in the settlement of the greater proportion of the population in coastal areas (Coull, 1996).

During medieval times the catching and processing of fish, notably herring (*Clupea harengus*), became an important feature of Scottish culture and trade (Cushing, 1988) and the commercial exploitation of fish and shellfish stocks remains a major contributor to Scotland's economy today. In 2000, total live weight landings of fish and shellfish by UK vessels into Scotland amounted to 307,700 t valued at £261.5 million (Scottish Executive, 2001). Although England, Wales and Northern Ireland maintain a fishing fleet, Scotland remains at the centre of UK fishing activity with over 66 per cent of all UK landings made in Scottish ports (Scottish Executive, 2001).

In recent times, marine capture fisheries throughout the world have entered a state of crisis with many stocks severely depleted or exploited to the brink of collapse. The western European fisheries are among the oldest but have been under mounting pressure since the beginning of the twentieth century. As demand increased and technology provided ever more reliable methods for the preservation of catches, fishing vessels became larger and progressed from sail through steam to diesel power, vastly increasing their range, catching capacity and efficiency. Consequently, most Atlantic and North Sea fish stocks are now thought to be fully exploited and the majority is considered to be outside safe biological limits (Table 12.3).

The waters surrounding Scotland have traditionally been rich in commercially valuable species and have supported some of the most intensive fishing effort in the world. Detailed studies of UK and international fishing effort in the North Sea show that grounds presently subjected to the greatest intensity of otter trawling lie to the north-east of the UK, largely comprising areas off the east and north-east Scottish mainland and east of the Shetland Islands (Greenstreet *et al.*, 1999a; Jennings *et al.*, 1999; Jennings *et al.*, 2000). The nature of the fishery as defined by the type of fishing gear has changed within the last 30 years. The use of demersal gears, such as otter and beam trawls – targeting species such as cod (*Gadus morhua*), haddock (*Melanogrammus aeglefinus*) and plaice (*Pleuronectes platessa*) –

Table 12.3. The status of fish (and shellfish) stocks in the waters surrounding Scotland in 2000 (Source: ICES, 2001). The comments for saithe and monkfish relate to both the North Sea and West of Scotland as the populations are assessed as a single stock. Similarly, the comments for mackerel and hake relate to the assessment of a single stock in all three sea areas. A dash indicates the absence of a fishery or no information available.

Species	*North Sea*	*West of Scotland*	*Irish Sea*
Herring (*Clupea harengus*)	Outside safe biological limits	Status unknown	Status uncertain
Cod (*Gadus morhua*)	Outside safe biological limits	Outside safe biological limits	Outside safe biological limits
Haddock (*Melanogrammus aeglefinus*)	Outside safe biological limits	Outside safe biological limits	Outside safe biological limits
Whiting (*Merlangius merlangus*)	Outside safe biological limits	Outside safe biological limits	Outside safe biological limits
Saithe (*Pollachius virens*)	Within safe biological limits		-
Norway pout (*Trisopterus esmarki*)	Within safe biological limits	Status unknown	-
Sandeel (*Ammodytes marinus*)	Within safe biological limits	Status unknown	-
Monkfish (*Lophius piscatorius*)	Outside safe biological limits		-
Mackerel (*Scomber scombrus*)		Outside safe biological limits	
Plaice (*Pleuronectes platessa*)	Outside safe biological limits	-	Within safe biological limits
Sprat (*Sprattus sprattus*)	Status uncertain	-	-
Hake (*Merluccius merluccius*)		Outside safe biological limits	
Megrim (*Lepidorhombus whiffiagonis*)	-	Within safe biological limits	-
Sole (*Solea solea*)	Outside safe biological limits	-	Within safe biological limits
Pink shrimp (*Pandalus borealis*)	Status uncertain	-	-
Norway lobster (*Nephrops norvegicus*)	Exploited at sustainable levels	Exploited at sustainable levels	Exploited at sustainable levels

has increased slowly throughout the North Sea since the mid-1970s (Jennings *et al.*, 1999), while the pursuit of pelagic species, predominantly mackerel (*Scomber scombrus*) and herring, with seine nets has decreased (Greenstreet *et al.*, 1999a).

Catch quotas were first implemented in the North Sea in the mid-1970s. The European Commission now manages exploited stocks through the Common Fisheries Policy (CFP, established in 1983), acting jointly with Norway in the case of shared stocks. The International Council for the Exploration of the Sea (ICES) provides annual scientific advice on the status of all of the important commercial species. Catch levels are subsequently decided by the Council of Ministers and catch quotas are duly allocated to Member States. Clearly, the primary objective is the maintenance of these resources at a level at which they can be harvested sustainably. The scale and ecological complexity of such an undertaking, combined with inevitable political pressures have, however, proved to be major obstacles and the maintenance of stable population levels remains elusive.

Limited success can be claimed for some species, for example North Sea herring (Figure 12.10), where a dramatic population decline in the 1960s and early 1970s was detected and

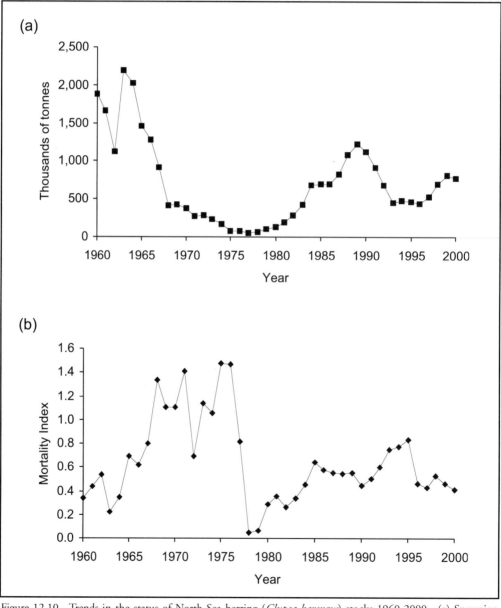

Figure 12.10. Trends in the status of North Sea herring (*Clupea harengus*) stocks 1960-2000. (a) Spawning stock biomass. (b) Fishing mortality (source: ICES, 2001).

reversed with the initiation of a fishing ban in 1977. The ban continued until 1983, by which time a recovery appeared to be in progress. By 1996 exploitation had again increased to a level where measures had to be reintroduced to reduce fishing mortality (ICES, 2001). This 'reactive' approach appears to work, since North Sea herring stocks, although currently considered outside safe biological limits, are again showing signs of recovery.

In contrast, demersal stocks, notably cod (Figure 12.11), have continued to decline despite successive reductions in catch quotas. This is probably a reflection of fundamental differences in the selectivity of pelagic and demersal fishing gears. Pelagic species are

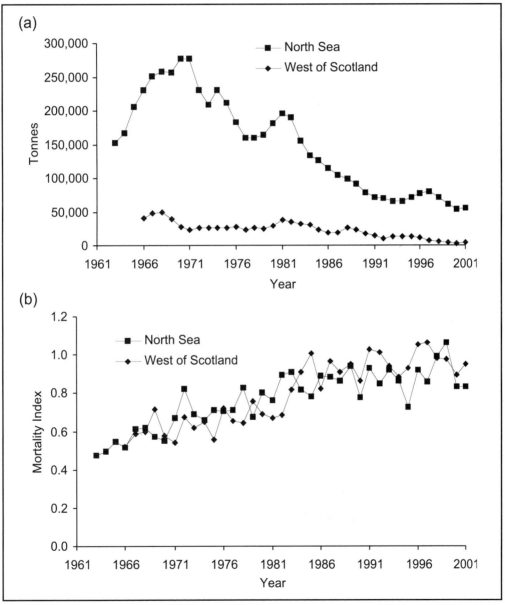

Figure 12.11. Trends in the status of North Sea and West of Scotland cod (*Gadus morhua*) stocks 1962 to 2001. (a) Spawning stock biomass. (b) Fishing mortality (source: ICES, 2001).

typically targeted as mid-water schools of high species uniformity and can be identified visually or by a characteristic acoustic signature. Avoidance of a particular species as a conservation measure is thus relatively easy and effective. Demersal trawling gears are far less selective and although controls on the landing of a particular species may be in place, incidental capture of both adults and juveniles cannot be avoided without the closure of entire grounds (Hutchings, 2000). At present, cod stocks from the North Sea, Irish Sea and West of Scotland are reported to be in danger of collapse (ICES, 2001) and recovery plans were initiated during 2000, incorporating limited area closures and modifications to gears, to increase selectivity. Doubts over the effectiveness of such measures have been widely expressed, with many pointing to disturbing parallels between the present state of the European cod stocks and the situation just prior to the catastrophic collapse of the Canadian cod fishery in the early 1990s (MacGarvin, 2001). Moreover, the Canadian experience has shown that a failure to introduce rapid and appropriate action, however severe, may leave stocks at a level from which recovery may not be possible in the foreseeable future.

The wider ecological impacts of fisheries continue to be the subject of much debate. Estimates for the North Sea suggest that around a quarter of the total biomass of exploitable fish species is presently removed by man every year (Figure 12.12). This is clearly a substantial quantity and is likely to constitute a significant modification of the North Sea ecosystem. By examining past records, Greenstreet *et al.* (1999b) demonstrated that selected areas off eastern and north-eastern Scotland, which had historically supported prolonged fishing pressure, had undergone changes in demersal fish community structure over a 72 year period. Where fishing was most intense, along the eastern Scottish seaboard, a consistent decrease in diversity coupled with the dominance of a few species was detected in non-target fish populations. Statistical analyses suggest that these changes may have occurred in the late 1970s or early 1980s, perhaps reflecting the increase in the use of demersal gears.

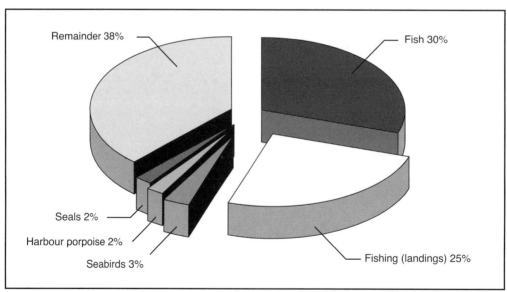

Figure 12.12. The fate of fish in the North Sea (compiled from the following sources: Fifth International Conference on the Protection of the North Sea, 1997; Anon., 1991; Camphuysen and Garthe, 2000; Hislop, 1992; Sea Mammal Research Unit, pers. comm.).

Similarly, Rogers and Ellis (2000) reported length-frequency distribution changes of both exploited and non-target species from the North Sea and Irish Sea over an 80 year period in favour of smaller individuals. There was also a coincident increase in the abundance of smaller, non-target species and it has been suggested that the continuous removal of larger predatory fish, such as cod, may be implicated in the observed increases in stocks of juveniles and smaller fish.

Brander (1981) and Walker (1996) noted the decline in catches of the common skate (*Raja batis*) in both the Irish Sea and North Sea, where it was previously considered to be a common and commercially important component of the retained bycatch. Moreover, an examination of the catch rates of selected ray (*Raja*) species from North Sea fishery survey data from 1929 to 1939 and 1991 to 1995 revealed a shift toward fewer species and smaller individuals (Walker, 1996). Major changes in the relative abundance of the eight ray species found in UK waters have also been demonstrated and it is likely that this can largely be attributed to their size at maturity and thus vulnerability to the fishery. The common skate, by these criteria, is the most vulnerable and is now considered to be commercially extinct in most areas.

The impact of fishing gear, particularly trawls and dredges, on seabed habitats and species is yet another area of concern. Jennings and Reynolds (2000) outlined the likely ways in which fishing may influence species diversity, by killing target and non-target species of fish or invertebrates, by modifying the ecological relationship between species, and by changing habitat structure. Examples of the first and, to some extent, the second point in relation to fish populations have been discussed, but direct evidence of lasting effects on the benthos has been difficult to demonstrate. This is primarily due to the lack of opportunities for study on areas entirely free of present and past fishing and the inability to disentangle the influence of other factors such as climate change and eutrophication (Jennings and Reynolds, 2000). Rumohr and Kujawski (2000) examined one of the few benthic data sets that allow comparisons between past (1902 to 1912) and contemporary (1986) North Sea communities. They concluded that there had been a decline in bivalve mollusc abundance, but scavenging or predatory crustaceans, gastropods and starfish had increased in abundance in response to the availability of fishery discards and animals killed or injured by the passage of fishing gear. These conclusions remain controversial and although Frid *et al.* (2000), in a similar study, found some evidence for benthic community changes in three of five selected areas of the North Sea, they were unable to detect a decrease in bivalve abundance.

This aside, there remains a consensus of scientific opinion that fishing activity has, and continues to have, an impact on the entire north-eastern Atlantic region and may even be the main ecological structuring force on the benthos in areas of intense exploitation (Lindboom and de Groot, 1998).

12.5 Marine mammals

There are 23 regularly occurring marine mammal species in the seas around Scotland. Of these, whales, dolphins and porpoises account for 21 species, many of them seasonal or migratory visitors.

The population status of most Cetacea occurring in Scottish waters, and indeed those around the whole of the UK, is largely unknown, with reliable scientific data restricted to observations on distribution rather than numerical abundance. In the past, commercial whaling activities reduced populations of target species throughout the north-east Atlantic and northern North Sea. Although quantitative estimates of the scale of such reductions are not possible, anecdotal evidence combined with catch records suggest that sperm (*Physeter macrocephalus*) and sei (*Balaenoptera borealis*) whale sustained at least moderate population reductions while blue whale (*Balaenoptera musculus*), fin whale (*Balaenoptera physalus*), humpback whale (*Megaptera novaengliae*) and northern right whale (*Eubalaena glacialis*) populations were greatly reduced (Brown, 1976; Evans, 1992; Thompson, 1928). Scottish-based whaling operations ceased around 1951 and cetaceans are currently protected throughout British waters under the Wildlife and Countryside Act (1981, reviewed 1986) and the Whaling Industry (Regulation) Act (1934, as amended 1981).

The OSPAR Commission (2000b) reported that, following the moratorium on commercial whaling, most species of large whale are showing signs of recovery in European waters. It is suggested that an increase in reported strandings, particularly of sperm whale in the North Sea, is a reflection of an overall increase in population sizes. At present, however, there is very little direct evidence on which to base unequivocal statements of any population recovery. Formal recording of strandings around Scotland began in 1992 and in the period up to 2000 stranding events of both large and small Cetacea have shown no clear pattern.

Smaller whales, dolphins and porpoises have remained largely unaffected by direct commercial exploitation, but have nevertheless been faced with a range of threats from other sources, the greatest of which is entanglement in fishing gear. The harbour porpoise (*Phocoena phocoena*) is the most abundant of Scottish Cetacea with the highest reported concentrations around the western and north-eastern coasts (Evans, 1992, 1997). A survey of North Sea harbour porpoise in 1994 estimated a population size of around 300,000 (Hammond *et al.*, 1995). Of these, some 7,000 per year are thought to have perished as a result of incidental capture in the Danish gillnet fishery alone (Lowry and Teilmann, 1994; Vinther, 1994). Overall, fishery-related mortality of harbour porpoise is believed annually to exceed 2 per cent of the total North Sea population, a rate considered to be unsustainable by the International Whaling Commission. As a first step towards a marine mammal conservation strategy, the Agreement on Small Cetaceans of the Baltic and North Seas has recently pressed the European Commission to restrict incidental capture to less than 1.7 per cent per year. Additional data on the rate of incidental capture specifically relating to Scottish fisheries are currently being gathered on a number of co-operating fishing vessels.

The Moray Firth is host to the world's most northerly population of bottlenose dolphin (*Tursiops truncatus*) and the only known resident population of this species in the North Sea. Statistical studies have implied that this is an isolated, barely viable population, which may be in decline (Sanders-Reed *et al.*, 1999). It remains to be seen whether the protection afforded within a Special Area of Conservation will be enough to ensure the long-term survival of this population.

Internationally important numbers of grey seal (*Halichoerus grypus*) and harbour (or common) seal (*Phoca vitulina*) are present in Scottish coastal waters. Unlike cetaceans, seal numbers can be regularly assessed when they come ashore to pup or moult. Periodic counts are made on behalf of the Natural Environment Research Council to advise the UK Government on the size and status of British seal populations under the Conservation of Seals Act 1970.

Of the total world population of harbour seal, UK coastal waters support about 5 per cent, of which around 90 per cent are found around Scotland. In 1988 a viral epidemic swept through the North Sea and some Scottish west coast populations. The disease, caused by the previously unknown phocine distemper virus, reduced overall North Sea numbers by over 40 per cent and was most severe along the continental coasts (OSPAR Commission, 2000a). In England, 50 per cent of seals resident in The Wash were reported to have died, but Scottish populations were less affected. Mortality estimates for the Moray Firth populations vary between 10 and 20 per cent, with some west coast populations sustaining slightly greater losses. It is widely believed that this outbreak was a natural event, as similar epidemics are known to have occurred in the past. Throughout Europe and the UK, harbour seal numbers have rapidly returned to, or exceeded, pre-epidemic levels. In Scotland, a minimum of 32,075 was recorded between 1996 and 2000 (SCOS, 2001) and comparisons of periodic estimates taken from the late 1980s to the present suggest that populations have largely remained stable.

In 2000 the British grey seal population was estimated at 124,300 animals aged one year or older (SCOS, 2001). About 40 per cent of the world's grey seals breed at well-established sites around Britain. Of these, over 90 per cent are associated with Scottish coastal sites. Overall, British grey seal populations increased steadily between 1984 and 1997 with an average rise of about 6 per cent per year. Since the 1970s, pup production has increased greatly in the Orkney Isles and the Outer Hebrides, with a lesser expansion in the Inner Hebrides and North Sea (Figure 12.13). The reasons for the sustained growth in population are not known, but the disproportionate rise in areas such as the Outer Hebrides suggests that the availability of sites free of human disturbance may constitute an important factor in breeding success.

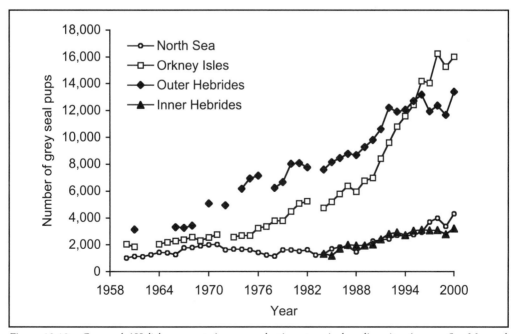

Figure 12.13. Grey seal (*Halichoerus grypus*) pup production at main breeding sites (source: Sea Mammal Research Unit).

12.6 Conservation and protection

12.6.1 Sites of Special Scientific Interest

The conservation of Scotland's coasts and seas for future generations is considered by many to be of the highest priority and a wide range of campaigns, management initiatives and conservation designations is currently being employed to this end. A pivotal point in the creation of a framework for statutory nature conservation in Britain was reached with the establishment of the first Sites of Special Scientific Interest (SSSI) under the National Parks and Access to the Countryside Act 1949. The application of this Act has facilitated the development of a network of scientifically evaluated sites notable for the quality, extent and/or rarity of the species, habitats or geological formations found within them.

SSSIs are identified under the Wildlife and Countryside Act 1981, which created a requirement for the owner or occupiers to be involved directly in the notification process. In Scotland, it is incumbent on SNH to identify activities that may damage or destroy the feature of interest. Owners and occupiers must then consult SNH prior to carrying out these activities, termed Potentially Damaging Operations. Thus, with additional (and currently controversial) compensatory awards in cases of financial loss, a reasonably durable conservation management structure has been achieved.

From the outset, the significance of Scotland's maritime natural heritage was reflected in the early selection of a number of coastal sites. Since 1949 the number of Scottish SSSIs with a coastal element has increased steadily, reaching 426 in 2001 (Figure 12.14a). The area covered by these sites has increased rather less steadily and it seems that there were periods up until the early 1970s where scientific enthusiasm, political climate and public support were particularly conducive to SSSI designation (Figure 12.14b). What is correspondingly clear is a tendency, after around 1975, towards the confinement of coastal SSSI boundaries to smaller areas. At present, Scottish SSSIs with a coastal element cover some 317,202 ha of coastal land, although some sites include only a small length of shoreline.

The benefits of the use of SSSIs and other types of designations as conservation management tools are becoming evident. Ritchie (1999) observed that over the last 30 years there has been a cultural change towards conserving and enhancing the environment, and commented that with direct conservation management applied to large areas of the eastern Scottish coastline '... the coastline is cleaner, more scenic, better managed and aesthetically conserved.'

SSSIs, though, carry a single major constraint that limits their effectiveness within the maritime zone. Since their inception they have explicitly excluded the area below the Mean Low Water Spring (MLWS) tides (The Scottish Office, 1998), thus excluding a key component of Scotland's maritime natural heritage from conservation management legislation. In 2001, an initial proposal to extend SSSI status beyond MLWS was subsequently modified in favour of a format specifically designed for marine conservation and presented to the UK Parliament as the Marine Wildlife Conservation Bill or the 'Randall Bill'. The legislative changes presently under debate are only relevant to England and Wales, and the implications of these for Scotland remain unresolved.

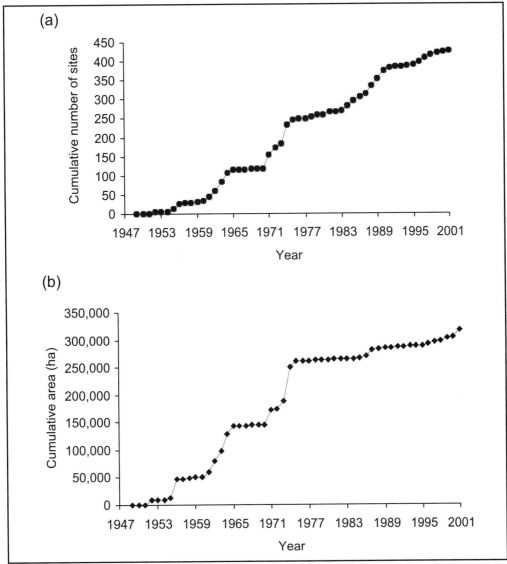

Figure 12.14. Scotland's Sites of Special Scientific Interest with a coastal interest (plants, animals and/or earth science features). (a) Cumulative number of SSSIs. (b) Cumulative SSSI area.

12.6.2 Special Areas of Conservation

In 1992 the European Union formally adopted the Habitats Directive with the aim of establishing a Europe-wide network of high quality conservation sites termed Special Areas of Conservation (SAC). SACs complement Special Protection Areas (SPAs) created under the Birds Directive. With the introduction of SACs came a clear priority to include a coherent mechanism for extending protection beyond the intertidal zone. Although provision for the establishment of statutory Marine Nature Reserves was included in the Wildlife and Countryside Act 1981, only a small number - all outside Scotland - have been established so far. With the introduction of SACs, statutory site-based conservation extending across both the littoral and sublittoral now applies for the first time in Scotland.

The Habitats Directive requires sites to be designated as SACs where they support typical, rare or vulnerable natural habitats and species of plants or animals as set out in Annex I and Annex II of the Directive. Scotland's territorial waters support seven of the nine marine and all but three of the coastal Annex I habitats (Table 12.4), together with ten of the eleven marine Annex II species (Table 12.5). The identification of possible SACs with subsequent public consultation has been a formidable undertaking, but considerable progress has been made. By September 2001, 30 marine SACs had been proposed to the European Commission (candidate SACs) and a further four were under consideration (proposed SACs). In total, this represents over 296,000 ha of shore, seabed and water column (Figure 12.15), a significant area, but still comparatively small, comprising only some 3.3 per cent of Scotland's territorial seas.

Table 12.4. Habitats Directive Annex I marine and coastal habitat types.

Habitats	*Present in Scotland*
Marine	
Estuaries	✓
Large shallow inlets and bays	✓
Lagoons	✓
Mudflats and sandflats not covered by seawater at low tide	✓
Reefs	✓
Sand banks which are slightly covered by seawater at all times	✓
Posidonia beds	no
Submerged or partly submerged sea caves	✓
Marine 'columns' in shallow water made by leaking gases	no
Coastal	
Atlantic salt meadows (*Glauco–Puccinellietalia*)	✓
Decalcified fixed dunes with *Empetrum nigrum*	✓
Coastal dunes with *Juniperus* spp.	✓
Dunes with *Salix repens* ssp. *argentea* (*Salicion arenariae*)	✓
Embryonic shifting dunes	✓
Atlantic decalcified fixed dunes (*Calluno-Uliceteal*)	✓
Dunes with *Hippophae rhamnoides*	no
Fixed dunes with herbaceous vegetation (grey dunes)	✓
Humid dune slacks	✓
Machair	✓
Annual vegetation of drift lines	✓
Perennial vegetation of stony banks	✓
Salicornia and other annuals colonising mud and sand	✓
Spartina swards (*Spartinion maritimae*)	no
Shifting dunes along the shoreline with *Ammophila arenaria* (white dunes)	✓
Vegetated sea cliffs of the Atlantic and Baltic coasts	✓
Mediterranean and thermo-Atlantic halophilous scrubs (*Sarcocornetea fruticosi*)	no

Table 12.5. Habitats Directive Annex II marine, estuarine and coastal species.

Species	Present in Scotland
Fishes	
Sea lamprey (*Petromyzon marinus*)	✓
River lamprey (*Lampetra fluviatilis*)	✓
Allis shad (*Alosa alosa*)	✓
Twaite shad (*Alosa fallax*)	✓
Mammals	
Bottlenose dolphin (*Tursiops truncatus*)	✓
Harbour porpoise (*Phocoena phocoena*)	✓
Otter (*Lutra lutra*)	✓
Grey seal (*Halichoerus grypus*)	✓
Common seal (*Phoca vitulina*)	✓
Plants	
Shore dock (*Rumex rupestris*)	no

12.6.3 The UK Biodiversity Action Plan

In 1994, as a direct response to the 1992 United Nations Convention on Biological Diversity, the UK Government convened a Biodiversity Steering Group and published *Biodiversity: The UK Action Plan*. Subsequently, specific action plans were prepared for a range of UK species and habitats that are considered to be representative, rare or at risk. The marine environment is well represented, with around 25 per cent of the identified priority habitats (Mackey *et al.*, 2001). Overall, there are 81 marine, estuarine or brackish-water species incorporated within action plans and about 74 of these species are found around Scottish coasts (U.K. Biodiversity Group, 1999).

12.7 The deep seas

In November 1999, as a result of a case initiated by the environmental pressure group Greenpeace, the UK High Court ruled that Council Directive 92/43/EEC (the Habitats Directive) applied to 'the UK continental shelf and superadjacent waters up to a limit of 200 nautical miles'. Prior to this, designations under the Habitats Directive were limited to sites within the 12-mile limit of UK territorial waters. This action was stimulated by concern over the latest in a series of rounds in which the UK Government was considering granting licences allowing seismic surveying and exploratory drilling for the presence of oil and gas deposits. The area under greatest scrutiny lies to the north and west of the Hebrides, Shetland and Orkney. This is considered to be a region of major importance for large cetaceans, a group particularly vulnerable to seismic survey techniques, but not included in Annex II of the Habitats Directive. The deep waters off the continental shelf break, although not well studied, are known to support a wide range of habitats ranging from mud plains and undulating sandbanks to reefs dominated by cold-water corals. It is the latter rocky reef habitats that are regarded as qualifying features under Annex I of the Habitats Directive.

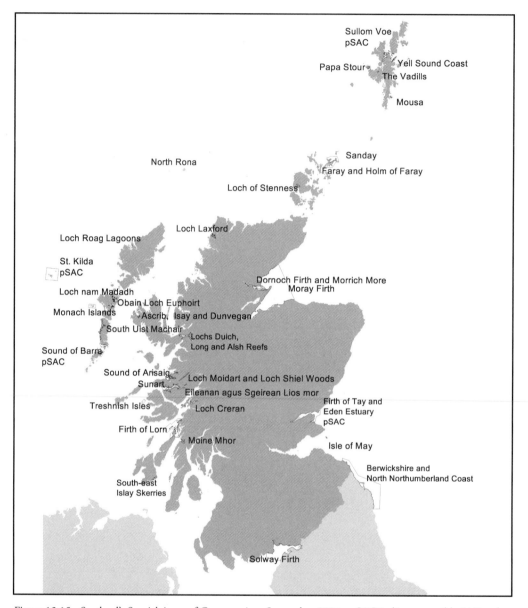

Figure 12.15. Scotland's Special Areas of Conservation, September 2001. pSAC indicates possible SAC, other sites are candidate SACs. Produced by Scottish Natural Heritage Geographic Information Group based on the Ordnance Survey 1:25000 map. © Scottish Natural Heritage. Licence Number GD315 G0005. © Crown Copyright.

The perceived threat posed by deep-sea oil and gas exploration is small when compared to a more immediate and tangible problem and one that currently lies outside the jurisdiction of the United Kingdom's application of the Habitats Directive. As the traditional fisheries of the European continental shelf have declined, catch unreliability and the introduction of fishing quotas have stimulated a growing interest in species that are considered largely outside the range of conventional fishing gears. Some deep-water fisheries are historically well established, notably around oceanic islands with steep inshore slopes such as Madeira and the Azores, but the fishery to the north-west and west of Scotland is a relatively recent development.

Commercial exploitation dates back to eastern European activity in the 1960s, but in the late 1970s French trawlers, traditionally operating along the outer shelf, began moving into deeper water. A market was initially established for blue ling (*Molva dyptergia*), but by the late 1980s demand for other deep-water species formerly landed as bycatch began to grow. By 1992, larger French vessels had extended their fishing activities still deeper in pursuit of the valuable orange roughy (*Hoplostethus atlanticus*) stocks (Gordon, 2001).

Although the French fleet continues to be the most active along the continental slope, markets have developed in Spain and the United States and increasing numbers of Norwegian, Icelandic and Faeroes vessels have begun trawling and longlining in the deep water. Both Ireland and the UK have commenced limited exploitation (Brennan and Gormley, 1999), but landings by Scottish vessels are largely of deep-water monkfish (*Lophius piscatorius*), with other species retained as bycatch. Irish fishing started around 1988 but a rapid decline in one of the target species, the greater argentine (*Argentina silus*), coupled with damage sustained to expensive gear, forced the fishery to close in 1990.

Deep-water fish largely conform to the life history adaptations of much of the deep-water biota, with slow growth rates, long natural life spans and maturation at a late age. These characteristics render them particularly vulnerable to overexploitation and landings of most species have declined rapidly soon after commencement of exploitation (Figure 12.16). At

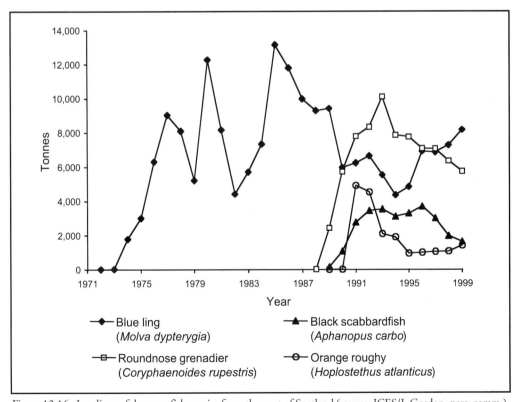

Figure 12.16. Landings of deep-sea fish species from the west of Scotland (source: ICES/J. Gordon, pers. comm.).

present, deep-water fisheries are entirely unregulated although most species are believed to be harvested outside safe biological limits. Recent advice to the European Commission recommends an immediate reduction in these fisheries unless they can be shown to be sustainable (ICES, 2001).

Deep-water fishing, although not of the intensity of the shallower fisheries, may still constitute a major destructive influence on established habitats and species. Trawl marks between depths of 200 to 1,400 m have been observed all along the north-east Atlantic shelf break and may form continuous furrows for up to 4 km (Fosså *et al.*, 2000; Hall-Spencer *et al.*, 2002; Roberts *et al.*, 2000; Rogers, 1999). The impacts of such disturbance on sedimentary habitats are unknown, but the physical effects on harder substrates, particularly deep-water coral reefs, are perhaps easier to assess. Reef structures dominated largely by *Lophelia pertusa*, but incorporating a number of other coral species, are present throughout the North Atlantic with large aggregations in Norwegian waters and smaller, scattered colonies widely distributed to the west of Shetland. These structures support a rich associated fauna with over 850 species living on or within the reefs of the north-eastern Atlantic (Rogers, 1999) and a single reef habitat may be host to some 200 to 300 species.

The complex topography of *Lophelia* reefs provides a particularly favoured habitat for non-target and target fish species, simultaneously supplying a refuge from predators and access to a high concentration of prey items. Consequently, fishing vessels in pursuit of the highest densities of exploitable species often recover large sections of reef after hauling in their trawling gear (Hall-Spencer *et al.*, 2002).

Clearly, the prospects for deep-water habitats and the species that inhabit them are bleak unless internationally enforced conservation measures are put in place. Designation of SACs under the Habitats Directive is being considered for deep-water coral reefs, but such protection will only apply to features within precisely defined areas. In addition, whereas designation as an SAC under the Habitats Directive will require incorporation into UK legislation, fisheries are controlled at the European level. Protection of both corals and deep-water fish will require the European Commission to exercise control over fishing in these designated sites through amendments to the CFP, perhaps incorporating the use of satellite tracking technology to evaluate accurately the distribution and extent of fishing effort in deep-sea areas.

12.8 Conclusion and prospects

Scotland is undeniably well endowed in the extent and variety of its natural marine heritage. The coastline is one of the longest of all European countries, but is also one of the least densely populated. In consequence, much of the inshore and coastal zone, particularly to the north and west, has received little or no human disturbance and remains largely pristine.

Land-based industrial development and subsequent urbanisation has, in general, been restricted to the areas surrounding the major inlets or firths of the Central Belt. Of a total Scottish population of 5.2 million, about 1.8 million live around the Clyde Estuary catchment and a further 1 million around the Firths of Tay and Forth. The cumulative effects of prolonged domestic and industrial discharges from these areas into the nearby estuaries have been severe and persistent. Statutory controls on discharges have, however, promoted a steady recovery since the 1970s and an increasing number of species are returning and re-establishing at locations where past contamination levels excluded all but a few highly tolerant taxa.

The long-held belief that the high seas constitute an inexhaustible repository for waste has been vigorously and successfully challenged in recent times and the practice of dumping at sea has been addressed at international level. Resultant UK legislation has put an end to the marine disposal of most types of waste. Disposal of radioactive waste at sea stopped at the end of 1982, burning of waste at sea has not been permitted since 1990, dumping of industrial waste stopped at the end of 1992, and dumping of sewage sludge stopped at the end of 1998.

Substantial pressure for environmental improvement will in the future be maintained through the provisions of the Water Framework Directive. The Directive aims to restore all water, except designated heavily modified waters needed for essential human activity, to a condition that deviates only slightly from those normally associated with undisturbed conditions. Even the heavily modified waters will be expected to realise their maximum ecological potential, given their existing physical modifications.

Scotland's eastern and north-eastern shores define the north-western boundary of the North Sea, one of the most biologically productive areas in the world and probably among the most exploited. Offshore areas have undergone intensive extraction of oil and gas, an industry that has dominated the economy of the North Sea basin for almost three decades. Initial warnings of the likely broad-scale physical, ecological and visual impacts caused by the extraction of natural energy resources have, however, proved largely groundless. Today, the offshore industry is contracting as reserves are gradually exhausted. Although advances in technology may allow access to new fields, or extend the life of existing production platforms, it is anticipated that the, already small, coastal effects will continue to diminish (Ritchie, 1999).

In general, the overall level of coastal development is low and in many areas has declined steadily over a period of perhaps 30 years. A comparison of North Sea coastal development in 1988 with that of 1999 revealed little change, apart from an increase in the relative importance of leisure and recreational uses (Ritchie, 1999; Ritchie and McLean, 1988). Expectations of population growth and an associated increase in industrial development have not been realised. Indeed, current predictions are of a future decline in population and this, combined with a widespread desire for improved scientific knowledge and effective, integrated management, presents an encouraging prospect for Scotland's coastal zone.

The ruggedness and relatively unspoilt nature of the Scottish coastline has long been a major tourist attraction that contributes significantly both to national and local economies. Excursions to view wildlife in their natural surroundings are increasingly popular and marine wildlife tourism in Scotland generated revenues of some £57 million and provided around 2,670 full-time jobs in 1996 (Masters, 1998). In some areas whale-watching may provide up to 12 per cent of the local tourism revenue (Hebridean Whale and Dolphin Trust, 2001). Wildlife tourism also provides major opportunities for education and the raising of public awareness, but it remains underdeveloped. A future programme of co-ordinated and sustainable tourism development, with due regard to the delicate balance between access and conservation, is likely to provide important socio-economic benefits for communities that possess few other means of generating income. This might, for example, be achieved by integrating a strategy for the development of marine wildlife tourism with the management of SACs and SPAs.

Fish farming has raised various issues. The Scottish aquaculture industry is one of the most heavily regulated in the world, with adequate control mechanisms on the release of therapeutic chemicals and on the extent of organic deposition. Growth of the industry has prompted concern about the effects of nutrients over wider areas and, although there is little relevant hard evidence, this will receive more attention in the future. A future strategy for Scottish aquaculture will take account of these matters as well as the associated conflicts between the aquaculture industry and the salmon fishery dependent on wild stocks.

There is less optimism for the status of the Scottish, European and world fisheries. Till now, exploited species or stocks were managed in isolation and are often harvested to a level where there is only a theoretical prediction of sustainability. The reality has proved more complex and the treatment of a natural resource as an economic commodity has brought stocks of some species close to collapse. A review of the CFP is currently underway and a revised policy will be introduced in January 2003. Among the proposals being considered are a reduction in fleet sizes, decentralised zonal management with access based on historic fishing rights, and a broader, ecosystem approach to fisheries management. From a natural heritage perspective, the latter is of considerable importance and there is increasing urgency to adopt an integrated policy that recognises the significance of ecological community structure. There is now very good evidence, for example, that areas protected from fishing activity, often referred to as 'no-take zones', provide not just a refuge for exploited and other vulnerable species, but an environment in which target species grow larger and produce more offspring. This increase in production has been shown to enhance populations outside the protected areas by means of a 'spill-over effect' and could play a future role in restocking fishing grounds (Roberts *et al.*, 2001; Roberts and Hawkins, 2000).

Overall, the current data suggest that Scotland's seas are reasonably healthy adjacent to the sparsely inhabited areas and are improving where anthropogenic discharges previously displaced natural, marine or estuarine communities. Conversely, the state of commercially exploited fish populations, and the ecological effects of the gear used to catch them, are of serious concern and will probably remain so for some time.

Nevertheless, there is no room for complacency. Over 80 per cent of the world's commodities are transported by shipping. Sea-borne freight traffic around Europe and the UK has continued to increase. In 2000, the Forth and Sullom Voe ports accounted for cargoes of 41.1 and 38.2 million t respectively, making them the fourth and fifth largest ports in the UK (DTLR, 2001). Two-thirds of Scotland's coastal traffic is liquid bulks, primarily crude petroleum from North Sea terminals, and accidental spillage is an ever present threat to marine habitats. In addition, the uncontrolled proliferation of non-native species introduced from ballast water discharges has occurred in some parts of the world and may yet present problems in Scotland.

The inevitable exhaustion of fossil fuel reserves will require the development of technology to harness renewable energy supplies. The UK, especially Scotland, is geographically well placed for the coastal and offshore exploitation of wind, wave and tidal currents. The design and construction of energy generating installations will present both new technological challenges and issues of aesthetic and environmental sensitivity.

Worldwide debate now rages over the extent and implications of changes in sea temperature. Scotland lies at the northern and southern extreme for many marine species and only minor changes in sea temperature may bring new species and expel others

(Hiscock *et al.*, 2001). Scotland's seas remain a difficult and demanding environment and new research and survey techniques will inevitably be required to detect change if, or when, it occurs.

Acknowledgements

We thank Drs Myles O'Reilly, Richard Park, Brian Miller, Tom Leatherland, John Baxter, Rupert Ormond and David Donnan for their important contributions. We are additionally grateful to Dr John Baxter, Professor Michael B. Usher and an anonymous referee for their helpful comments on the draft manuscript. The essential effort of the captains and crew of the SEPA survey vessels 'Forth Ranger' and 'Endrick' are cordially acknowledged.

References

Anonymous (2000). Scottish fish farming: past and present. *Aquaculture Magazine*, **26**, 48-54.

Balls, P.W., Brockie, N., Dobson, J. and Johnston, W. (1996). Dissolved oxygen and nitrification in the upper Forth Estuary during summer (1982-1992): patterns and trends. *Estuarine Coastal and Shelf Science*, **42**, 117-134.

Balls, P.W., MacDonald, A.M., Pugh, K.B. and Edwards, A.E. (1995). Long-term nutrient enrichment of an estuarine system, Ythan, Scotland (1958-1993). *Environmental Pollution*, **90**, 311-321.

Balls, P.W., Owens, R.E. and Muller, F.L.L. (1997). Dissolved trace metals in the Clyde, Forth and Tay estuaries - a synopsis and comparison with other UK estuaries . *Coastal Zone Topics*, **3,** 46-56.

Brander, K. (1981). Disappearance of the common skate, *Raja batis*, from the Irish Sea. *Nature*, **290**, 48-50.

Brennan, M.H. and Gormley, R.T. (1999). *The Quality of Under-utilised Deep-water Fish Species*. Irish Agriculture and Food Development Authority, Dublin.

Brown, S.G. (1976). Modern whaling in Britain and the north-east Atlantic Ocean. *Mammal Review*, **6**, 25-36.

Camphuysen, C.J. and Garthe, S. (2000). Seabirds and commercial fisheries: population trends of piscivorous seabirds explained? In *Effects of Fishing on Non-target Species and Habitats*, ed. by M.J. Kaiser and S.J. de Groot. Blackwell Science, Oxford. pp. 163-184.

Centre for Research into Environment and Health (1999). Faecal indicator organism sources and budgets for the Irvine & Girvan catchments, Ayrshire. Report to WOSWA, SEPA and South Ayrshire Council – Volumes 1 & 2.

Collett, W.F. (1961). *A Preliminary Investigation of the Pollution of the Upper Forth Estuary*. The Institute of Sewage Purification, Glasgow.

Collett, W.F. and Leatherland, T.M. (1985). The management of water pollution control in the Forth Estuary. *Water Pollution Control*, **84**, 233-24.

Coull, J.R. (1996). *The Sea Fisheries of Scotland. A Historical Geography*. John Donald Publishers, Edinburgh.

Cushing, D.H. (1988). *The Provident Sea*. Cambridge University Press, Cambridge.

Davies, I.M. (2001). Waste production by farmed Atlantic salmon (*Salmo salar*) in Scotland. *International Council for the Exploration of the Sea*, CM 2000/O:01 Sustainable Aquaculture Development.

Davison, I.M. and Baxter, J.M. (1997). The number of marine species that occur in Scottish coastal waters. In *Biodiversity in Scotland: Status, Trends and Initiatives*, ed. by L.V. Fleming, A.C. Newton, J.A. Vickery and M.B. Usher. The Stationery Office, Edinburgh. pp. 57-62.

Davison, D.M. (1996). An estimation of the total number of marine species that occur in Scottish coastal waters. Scottish Natural Heritage Review No. 63.

Department for Transport, Local Government and the Regions (2001). *Maritime Statistics: United Kingdom: 2000*. The Stationery Office, London.

Dobson, J. (1997). The role of suspended solids in the dissolved oxygen budget of the Forth estuary. *Coastal Zone Topics*, **3**, 38-45.

Dobson, J. (2000). Long-term trends in trace metals in biota in the Forth Estuary, Scotland, 1981-1999. *Marine Pollution Bulletin*, **40**, 1214-1220.

Dobson, J., Edwards, A., Hill, A. and Park, R. (in press). Burning issues of North Sea ecology. In *Proceedings of the 14th international Senckenberg Conference North Sea 2000, Senckenbergiana maritima 31 (2)*, ed. by I. Kröncke, M. Türkay and J. Sündermann.

Dobson, J and Park, R. (in press). The South Esk estuary: ecological and water quality status. *Coastal Zone Topics*.

Doody, J.P. (1999). The Scottish coast in a European perspective. In *Scotland's Living Coastline*, ed. by J.M. Baxter, K. Duncan, S. Atkins and G. Lees. The Stationery Office, London. pp. 15-29.

Evans, P.G.H. (1992). Status review of cetaceans in British and Irish waters. Unpublished report.

Evans, P.G.H. (1997). *Ecological Studies of the Harbour Porpoise in Shetland, North Scotland*. Worldwide Fund for Nature - UK, Godalming.

Fifth International Conference on the Protection of the North Sea (1997). Assessment report on fisheries and fisheries related species and habitats issues, ed. by M. Svelle, H. Aarefjord, H. Toretleir and S. Øverland. *Report from the Committee of North Sea Senior Officials to the Intermediate Ministerial Meeting on the Integration of Fisheries and Environmental Issues*, Bergen.

Fisheries Research Services (2001). *Scottish Fish Farms. Annual Production Survey, 2000*. Scottish Executive Environment and Rural Affairs Department, Edinburgh.

Fosså, J.H., Mortensen, P.B. and Furevik, D.M. (2000). Lophelia-korallrev langs norskekysten forekomst og tilstand. *Fisken og Havet*, **2**, 1-94.

Frid, C.L.J., Harwood, K.G., Hall, S.J. and Hall, J.A. (2000). Long-term changes in the benthic communities on North Sea fishing grounds. *ICES Journal of Marine Science*, **57**, 1303-1309.

Gillibrand, P.A. and Turrell, W.R. (1997). The use of simple models in the regulation of the impact of fish farms on water quality in Scottish sea lochs. *Aquaculture*, **159**, 33-46.

Gordon, J.D.M. (2001). Deep-water fish and fisheries: introduction. *Fisheries Research*, **51**, 105-111.

Greenstreet, S.P.R., Spence, F.B., Shanks, A.M. and McMillan, J.A. (1999a). Fishing effects in northeast Atlantic shelf seas: patterns in fishing effort, diversity and community structure. II. Trends in fishing effort in the North Sea by UK registered vessels landing in Scotland. *Fisheries Research*, **40**, 107-124.

Greenstreet, S.P.R., Spence, F.B. and McMillan, J.A. (1999b). Fishing effects in northeast Atlantic shelf seas: patterns in fishing effort, diversity and community structure. V. Changes in structure of the North Sea groundfish species assemblage between 1925 and 1996. *Fisheries Research*, **40**, 153-183.

Griffiths, A.H. (1987). Water quality of the estuary and Firth of Forth, Scotland. *Proceedings of the Royal Society of Edinburgh*, **93B**, 303-314.

Hall-Spencer, J., Allain, V. and Fosså, J.H. (2002). Trawling damage to Northeast Atlantic ancient coral reefs. *Proceedings of the Royal Society of London, Series B*, **269**, 507-511.

Hammond, P.S., Benke, H., Berggren, P., Borchers, D.L., Buckland, S.T., Collet, A., Heide-Jørgensen, M.P., Heimlich-Boran, S., Hiby, A.R., Leopold, M.F. and Øien, N. (1995). Distribution and abundance of the harbour porpoise and other small cetaceans in the North Sea and adjacent waters. Final Report, October 1995. *Life Project*, LIFE 92-2/UK/027.

Hebridean Whale and Dolphin Trust (2001). *Whale-watching in West Scotland*. Department for Environment, Food and Rural Affairs, London.

Hiscock, K., Southward, A., Tittley, I., Adam, J. and Hawkins, S. (2001). The impact of climate change on subtidal and intertidal benthic species in Scotland. Scottish Natural Heritage, Research Survey and Monitoring Report No. 182.

Hislop, J. (1992). The North Sea fishery: a case study. In *European Research in Cetaceans* 6, ed. by P.G.H. Evans. San Remo, European Cetacean Society. pp. 11-17.

Hutchings, J.A. (2000). Collapse and recovery of marine fishes. *Nature*, **406**, 882-885.

International Council for the Exploration of the Sea (1991). Report of the Multispecies Assessment Working Group. ICES, CM 1991/Assess:7.

International Council for the Exploration of the Sea (2001). Report of the Advisory Committee on Fishery Management. ICES Co-operative Research Report No. 223.

Jennings, S., Alvsvåg, J., Cotter, A.J., Ehrich, S., Greenstreet, S.P.R., Jarre-Teichmann, A., Mergardt, N., Rijnsdorp, A.D. and Smedstadt, O. (1999). Fishing effects in northeast Atlantic shelf seas: patterns in fishing effort, diversity and community structure. III. International fishing effort in the North Sea: an analysis of temporal and spatial trends. *Fisheries Research*, **40**, 125-134.

Jennings, S. and Reynolds, J.D. (2000). Impacts of fishing on diversity: from pattern to process. In *The Effects of Fishing on Non-target Species and Habitats. Biological, Conservation and Socio-economic Issues*, ed. by M.J. Kaiser and S.J. de Groot. Blackwell Science, London. pp. 235-250.

Jennings, S., Warr, K.J., Greensreet, S.P.R. and Cotter, A.J.R. (2000). Spatial and temporal patterns in North Sea fishing effort. In *The Effects of Fishing on Non-target Species and Habitats. Biological, Conservation and Socio-economic Issues*, ed. by M.J. Kaiser and S.J. de Groot. Blackwell Science, London. pp. 3-14.

Kelly, A.G. and Balls, P.W. (1995). Persistent organochlorine compounds in the Firth of Clyde. In *Coastal Zone Topics: Process Ecology and Management. 3. The Estuaries of Central Scotland*, ed. by D.S. McLusky. Joint Nature Conservation Committee. Peterborough. pp. 88-97.

Lindboom, H.J. and de Groot, S.J., (eds.) (1998). *Impact II. The Effects of Different Types of Fisheries on the North Sea and Irish Sea Benthic Ecosystems.* Netherlands Institute for Sea Research (NIOZ), Texel.

Lowry, N. and Teilmann, J. (1994). Bycatch and bycatch reduction of the harbour porpoise (*Phocoena phocoena*) in Danish waters. *Report of the International Whaling Commission*, **Special Issue 15**, 203-209.

Macaulay Land Use Research Institute (1993). *The Land Cover of Scotland 1988. Final Report.* Macaulay Land Use Research Institute, Aberdeen.

MacDonald, A.M., Edwards, A.C., Pugh, K.B. and Balls, P.W. (1995). Soluble nitrogen and phosphorus in the River Ythan system, U.K.: annual and seasonal trends. *Water Research*, **29**, 837-846.

MacGarvin, M. (2001). *Now or Never. The Cost of Canada's Cod Collapse and Disturbing Parallels with the UK.* WWF-UK, Godalming.

Mackey, E.C., Shaw, P., Holbrook, J., Shewry, M.C., Saunders, G., Hall, J. and Ellis, N. (2001). *Natural Heritage Trends: Scotland 2001.* Scottish Natural Heritage, Perth.

Masters, D. (1998). Marine wildlife tourism: developing a quality approach in the Highlands and Islands. Unpublished report.

Mathieson, S. and Atkins, S.M. (1995). A review of nutrient enrichment in the estuaries of Scotland: implications for the natural heritage. *Netherlands Journal of Aquatic Ecology*, **29**, 437-448.

McLusky, D.S. and Martins, T. (1998). Long-term study of an estuarine mudflat subjected to petro-chemical discharges. *Marine Pollution Bulletin*, **36**, 791-798.

Miller, B.S. (1999). Mussels as biomonitors of point and diffuse sources of trace metals contamination of the Clyde Sea area, Scotland. *Water Science and Technology*, **39**, 233-240.

OSPAR Commission (2000a). *Quality Status Report 2000, Region II - Greater North Sea.* OSPAR Commission, London.

OSPAR Commission (2000b). *Quality Status Report 2000.* OSPAR Commission, London.

Pearson, T.H. and Black, K.D. (2001). The environmental impacts of marine fish cage culture. In *Environmental Impacts of Aquaculture*, ed. by K.D. Black. Sheffield Academic Press, Sheffield. pp. 1-31.

Pugh, K.B. (1993). The nutrient status of the Ythan Catchment and Estuary. North East River Purification Board, Technical Report 93/1.

Raffaelli, D., Balls, P., Way, S., Patterson, I.J., Hohmann, S. and Corp, N. (1999). Major long-term changes in the ecology of the Ythan Estuary, Aberdeenshire, Scotland: how important are physical factors? *Aquatic Conservation: Marine and Freshwater Ecosystems,* **9**, 219-236.

Ritchie, W. (1999). The environmental impact of changing uses on the North Sea littoral of Scotland. In *Denmark and Scotland: the Cultural and Environmental Resources of Small Nations,* ed. by G. Fellows-Jensen. The Royal Danish Academy of Science and Letters, Copenhagen. pp. 103-122.

Ritchie, W. and McLean, L. (1988). UK - Scotland. In *Artificial Structures and Shorelines,* ed. by H. J. Walker, Kluwer, Dordrecht. pp. 127-135.

Roberts, C.M., Bohnsack, J.A., Gell, F., Hawkins, J.P. and Goodridge, R. (2001). Effects of marine reserves on adjacent waters. *Science,* **294**, 1920-1923.

Roberts, C.M. and Hawkins, J.P. (2000). *Fully-protected Marine Reserves: a Guide.* WWF and University of York, Washington DC and York.

Roberts, J.M., Harvey, S.M., Lamont, P.A., Gage, J.D. and Humphery, J.D. (2000). Seabed photography, environmental assessment and evidence for deep-water trawling on the continental margin west of the Hebrides. *Hydrobiologia,* **441**, 173-183.

Rogers, A.D. (1999). The biology of *Lophelia pertusa* (Linnaeus 1758) and other deep-water reef-forming corals and impacts from human activities. *Internationale Revue der gesamten Hydrobiologie,* **84**, 315-406.

Rogers, S.I. and Ellis, J.R. (2000). Changes in the demersal fish assemblages of British coastal waters during the 20th century. *ICES Journal of Marine Science,* **57**, 866-881.

Rumohr, H. and Kujawski, T. (2000). The impact of trawl fishery on the epifauna of the southern North Sea. *ICES Journal of Marine Science,* **57**, 1389-1394.

Sanders-Reed, C.A., Hammond, P.S., Grellier, K. and Thompson, P.M. (1999). Development of a population model for bottlenose dolphins. Scottish Natural Heritage, Research Survey and Monitoring Report No. 156.

Special Committee on Seals (2001). Scientific advice on matters related to the management of seal populations: 2001. Unpublished report.

Scottish Executive (2001). *Scottish Sea Fisheries Statistics 2000.* Scottish Executive, Edinburgh.

Scottish Office (1998). *National Heritage Designations in Scotland.* The Scottish Office, Edinburgh.

Thompson, D.A. (1928). On whales landed at the Scottish whaling stations during the years 1908-1914 and 1920-1927. *Scientific Investigations Fishery Board of Scotland,* **3**, 1-40.

UK Biodiversity Group (1999). *Tranche 2 Action Plans. Volume V - Maritime Species and Habitats.* English Nature, Peterborough.

Vinther, M. (1994). Incidental catch of the harbour porpoise (*Phocoena phocoena*) in the Danish North Sea gill-net fisheries: preliminary results. In *Proceedings of the Scientific Symposium on the North Sea Quality Status,* ed. by J. Andersen, H. Karup and U.B. Nielsen. Danish Environmental Protection Agency, Copenhagen. pp. 210-213.

Walker, P. (1996). Sensitive skates or resilient rays? Spatial and temporal shifts in ray species composition in the central and northwestern North Sea. *ICES,* CM 1996/Mini:4.

13 LONG TERM TRENDS IN MERCURY IN THE FORTH ESTUARY

J.E. Dobson

Summary

1. Inputs of mercury to the Forth Estuary have reduced substantially since 1985.

2. The concentration of dissolved mercury in the water column was always relatively low and fell rapidly as the input from a dominant point source discharge decreased. The concentration of mercury in biota has decreased slowly and there has been no detectable change in the amount found in the sediments.

3. Much of the mercury discharged has been retained on the sediments and is slowly released from the estuary.

13.1 Force for change

At the second Intergovernmental Conference in 1987 the UK Government agreed to reduce inputs of certain substances to the North Sea by 50 per cent between 1985 and 1995. Mercury was one of the substances identified because of its toxicity and bioaccumulation properties. The total load of mercury from riverine, industrial and sewage discharges to the Forth Estuary decreased from approximately 1,000 kg per year in the 1980s to 40 kg per year in the 1990s. Industrial inputs decreased from 2 kg per day to 1 kg per year and diffuse riverine inputs are now the dominant source of mercury.

13.2 Inputs

Inputs of mercury to the Forth Estuary were dominated by an industrial discharge at Grangemouth (Figure 13.1). The discharge from the factory declined from a peak in the 1980s to the current low level input (Figure 13.2). This reduction has been achieved through regulation of the process and the introduction of effluent treatment.

13.3 Environment

Trace metals interact with particulate matter in the environment and may be adsorbed onto that particulate matter. Because the Forth is a turbid estuary (Webb and Metcalfe, 1987), a relatively high percentage of the metals is found in the particulate phase (Balls *et al.*, 1997).

It has been estimated that over 90 per cent of the mercury discharged has been retained on the sediments of the estuary (Elliott and Griffiths, 1986). Routine monitoring of the mercury content of the sublittoral sediments has not shown any reduction consistent with the reduction in the discharge (Figure 13.3).

Mercury contamination is measured in fish and shellfish in the Forth Estuary (Figure 13.4). Both taxa will obtain mercury from the sediments via ingestion as well as from the water. Mercury in the flesh of flounder (*Pleuronectes flesus*) caught in the estuary

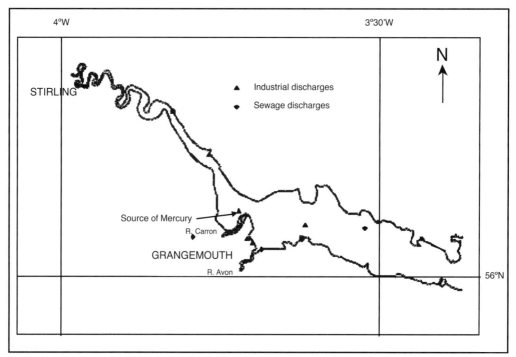

Figure 13.1. Location of discharges to the Forth Estuary.

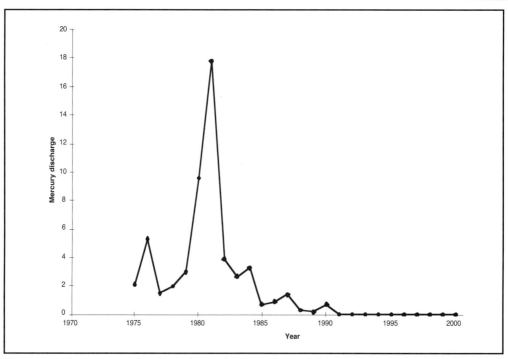

Figure 13.2. Long-term trend in the discharge of mercury (kg per day) to the Forth Estuary at Grangemouth.

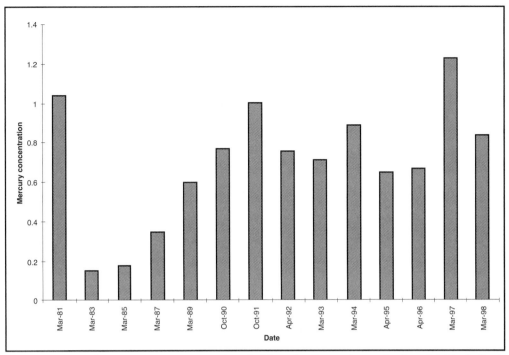

Figure 13.3. Annual average mercury concentration of sublittoral sediments (mg per kg dry weight) in the Forth Estuary.

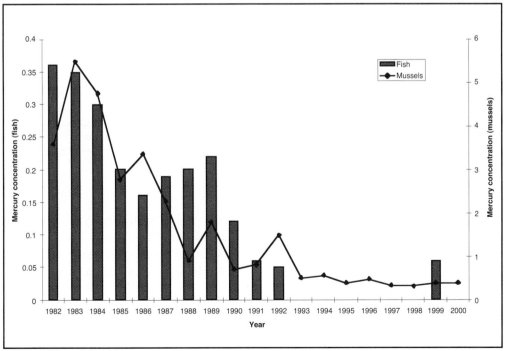

Figure 13.4. Long-term trends in mercury in flounder (μg per kg wet weight) and mussels (mg per kg dry weight) in the Forth Estuary.

has declined over the years. Monitoring stopped in 1993 due to the low concentrations being measured. Results in 1999 show that there has been no further decrease in mercury in flounder caught in the Forth.

Mercury in the mussel *Mytilus edulis* is measured at several locations in the Forth Estuary. Data collected from mussels at Grangemouth show a decline in body burdens consistent with the reduction of the discharge (Figure 13.4). Monitoring of mercury in the water column at a location close to the discharge began in 1986. Concentrations were always substantially below the Environmental Quality Standard of 300 ng per litre (dissolved, annual average) and dropped below the limit of detection of 3 ng per litre throughout most of the 1990s (Figure 13.5).

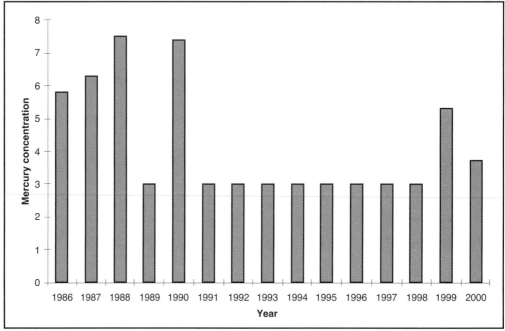

Figure 13.5. Annual average concentration of dissolved mercury (ng per litre) in the Forth. The limit of detection is 3 ng per litre, and hence in years such as 1989 and 1991 to 1998 the concentration may have been below this limit.

13.4 Discussion

The concentration of dissolved mercury in the water of the Forth Estuary remained low despite the substantial point source discharge because over 90 per cent of the total was present in the particulate phase. As the amount discharged has reduced, concentrations in the water column and biota have fallen but there has been no detectable reduction in the sediments. It can therefore be concluded that a large percentage of the mercury discharged to the Forth Estuary has been retained on the sediments. Sediment transport patterns in the estuary are complex, depending on variations in tidal range and river flow. In the Forth there is a strong near bed landward flux of sediments and a weaker seaward flux higher in the water column (Lindsay *et al.*, 1996). The weaker seaward flux provides a mechanism for contaminants to escape, but it is a slow process. Loss of mercury from the sediments of the Forth via this mechanism is expected to take decades (Davies *et al.*, 1986). Dredging activities constantly recycle the sediments and may encourage the seaward flux of fine particulate matter although there is no evidence that it releases mercury into the water column. The sediments of the Forth support a typical macrofaunal community determined by sediment structure and salinity, indicating that the mercury present is not acutely toxic, but there may be chronic effects which have not been detected (Anon., 1996).

References

Anonymous (1996). The biological quality of subtidal sediments off Grangemouth: changes since 1979. *Forth River Purification Board, Tidal Waters Report* No. 2/96.

Balls, P.W., Owens, R.E and Muller, F.L.L. (1997). Dissolved trace metals in the Clyde, Forth and Tay estuaries. *Coastal Zone Topics*, **3**, 46-56.

Davies, I.M., Griffiths, A.H., Leatherland, T.M. and Metcalfe, A.P. (1986). Particulate mercury fluxes in the Forth estuary, Scotland. *Rapports et Proces-Verbaux des Reunions du Conseil International pour l'Exploration de la Mer*, **186**, 301-305.

Elliott, M. and Griffiths, A.H. (1986). Mercury contamination in components of an estuarine ecosystem. *Water Science and Technology*, **18**, 161-170.

Lindsay, P., Balls, P.W. and West, J.R. (1996). Influence of tidal range and river discharge on suspended particulate matter fluxes in the Forth estuary (Scotland). *Estuarine and Coastal Shelf Science*, **42**, 63-82.

Webb, A.J. and Metcalfe, A.P. (1987). Physical aspects, water movements and modelling studies of the Forth estuary, Scotland. *Proceedings of the Royal Society of Edinburgh*, **93B**, 259-272.

14 TEMPORAL AND SPATIAL TRENDS OF ORGANOCHLORINE AND MERCURY CONTAMINATION IN GANNET EGGS

H.M. Malcolm, D. Osborn, T.H. Sparks, C. Wienburg, L.C. Dale, I. Newton and R.F. Shore

Summary

1.   Gannet eggs collected from Ailsa Craig and Bass Rock between 1971 and 2000 were analysed for organochlorine pesticides, polychlorinated biphenyls and mercury in order to establish temporal or spatial trends in residue concentrations.

2.   At both sites, organochlorine pesticide concentrations have declined exponentially, by at least three fold, since the 1970s. The declines in PCB and mercury concentrations are less well defined, with statistically significant decreases only reported at Ailsa Craig.

3.   The concentrations of all contaminants measured are believed to be below the levels at which breeding success is impaired.

14.1 Introduction

The use of organochlorine compounds including the pesticides DDT (1,1'-(2,2,2-trichloroethylidene)-bis[4-chlorobenzene]), aldrin, dieldrin, and industrial chemicals such as polychlorinated biphenyls (PCBs) have been increasingly restricted since the late 1970s due to their effects on health and the environment, particularly birds (see Pugh, Chapter 19). Due to their persistence in the environment, these chemicals are still present in wildlife, more than 20 years later. This raises important questions. Have residues of these contaminants in wildlife declined since their uses were restricted, and, if so, when are they likely to 'disappear' from the Scottish environment? Does the amount of contamination vary across the Scotland, and if not, does this provide information about sources and sinks of chemicals consistent with theoretical considerations?

Gannet (*Morus bassanus*) eggs were collected from various gannet colonies, including Ailsa Craig in the Firth of Clyde and Bass Rock in the Firth of Forth, on at least a bi-annual basis since 1971. These eggs have been analysed for DDE (1,1'-(2,2-dichloroethenylidene)-bis[4-chlorbenzene], a metabolite of DDT), HEOD (1,2,3,4,10,10-hexachloro-6,7-epoxy-1,4,4a,5,6,7,8,8a-octahydro-*endo*-1,4-*exo*-5,8-dimethanonaphthalene, a metabolite of the insecticides aldrin and dieldrin), PCBs and mercury (Hg). Such a dataset allows temporal and spatial trends of these chemicals to be established. As 40 per cent of the worldwide gannet population is found around Scotland, it is important to be certain that there are no biological effects of contamination by chemicals.

Eggs, in general, are useful bioindicators of pollution because they are highly consistent in composition, especially with regard to lipid content, and are produced by the same sector of the population each year (breeding females) (Newton *et al.*, 1990). There are four reasons why gannet eggs are particularly good bioindicators. First, seabirds usually accumulate higher contaminant levels than birds feeding from terrestrial habitats. Second, gannets live in discrete colonies that are easy to define spatially. Third, females lay eggs during the same few days each year, thus limiting seasonal fluctuations. Finally, the ecology of the gannet is well documented, allowing results to be understood in relation to location and feeding behaviour (Tasker *et al.*, 1985).

14.2 Materials and methods

Gannet eggs were collected from Ailsa Craig (55°15'N, 05°07'W) and Bass Rock (56°06'N, 2°36'W). This was done by trained naturalists, every 1 to 2 years between 1971 and 2000 (Newton *et al.*, 1990). On each occasion, the colony was visited during the laying or early incubation period and approximately ten eggs were taken. The intact eggs were transported to the laboratory where they were weighed and measured. The egg contents were homogenised and stored in glass jars at –20°C prior to organochlorine analysis by gas chromatography with an electron capture detector. Mercury was analysed using atomic absorption spectrophotometry after digestion in nitric acid. Details of the more recent analytical methods are reported in Pain *et al.* (1999). Developments in analytical methods over the years are not so great as to mask general trends or between-colony comparisons. In most years when eggs were received, at least seven eggs were analysed; fewer samples were analysed on only two occasions. The total number of eggs from Ailsa Craig and Bass Rock that have been analysed are 153 and 187, respectively. Only eggs which arrived at the laboratory with their shells intact were included for analysis, as eggs with cracked or broken shells may have potentially lost moisture, subsequently giving an uncharacteristically high residue concentration.

14.3 Results and discussion

For simplicity, data are discussed in terms of annual means. The mean concentrations of HEOD, DDE and total PCBs, expressed as mg per kg wet weight by year at each site, are shown in Figure 14.1. DDE and HEOD have both declined exponentially, and by at least three fold since the early 1970s. This is evident at both Ailsa Craig and Bass Rock. The decline in residue concentrations in eggs collected from Ailsa Craig and Bass Rock between 1971 and 1987 have previously been reported as a decline from the 1970s values followed by a slight rise during the mid-1980s (Parslow and Jefferies, 1975; Newton *et al.*, 1990). Updating the trends with the more recent data demonstrates that the increase in concentrations reported in the mid-1980s was either transient or within an overall downward trend.

The trend in the decline in total PCBs is less well defined, and the relationship between residues and time is best described by a linear regression model for Ailsa Craig. However, it is possible that the data can also be appropriately described by a two phase model that consists of a rapid decrease during the 1970s, with a slower rate of decline, or no decline at all, during the 1980s and 1990s. Changes over time in PCB concentration in eggs from Bass Rock were not statistically significant.

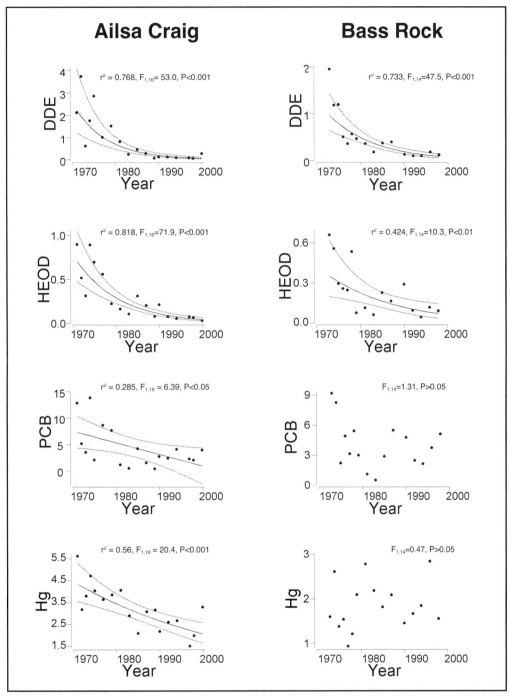

Figure 14.1. Annual mean concentrations of DDE (1,1'-(2,2-dichloroethenylidene)-bis[4-chlorbenzene]), HEOD (1,2,3,4,10,10-hexachloro-6,7-epoxy-1,4,4a,5,6,7,8,8a-octahydro-*endo*-1,4-*exo*-5,8-dimethanonaphthalene), total PCBs (polychlorinated biphenyls) and mercury (Hg) are plotted against time for gannet eggs from Ailsa Craig and Bass Rock. Concentrations are expressed as mg per kg wet weight, with the exception of mercury, which is expressed as mg per kg dry weight. Regression lines (±95 per cent confidence intervals, based upon a linear regression model) are shown where the change in contaminant concentration over time is statistically significant.

In this brief chapter, only the simplest spatial trends in Scotland, and inter-colony variation and in contaminant levels, can be described. Inter-colony differences for metals in puffins (*Fratercula arctica*) were described many years ago, where it was found that puffins on St. Kilda were more contaminated with cadmium than birds from the Isle of May (Osborn, 1979). More recently, Sparks *et al.* (2000) showed temporal and spatial differences amongst PCBs in peregrine (*Falco peregrinus*) eggs from different parts of Scotland (levels in eggs from coastal areas were higher, with a peak in the 1980s). In the gannet eggs, mercury levels at Ailsa Craig are now similar to those at Bass Rock, whereas in the 1970s, they were higher. This may reflect the reduced outputs from industrialised estuaries such as the Clyde. The lack of evidence of any decline in PCBs at Bass Rock is of some interest, as it provides clues about the global dynamics of PCBs. Mercury concentrations have declined steadily on Ailsa Craig, whereas at Bass Rock, there is no sign of an overall trend.

Although both the temporal and spatial trends established can be used as an environmental index, it is important to bear in mind that the residue levels are influenced by changes in both the contamination of the marine environment and the diet and feeding areas of the birds. The gannet diet consists of various species of pelagic shoaling fish, including mackerel, herring, sandeel and sprat, with birds foraging at a distance of up to 232 km away from the colony during the breeding season (Hamer *et al.*, 2000).

The levels of organochlorine contaminants reported in all eggs included in this study are below those thought to impair reproductive output (Newton *et al.*, 1990). Impaired breeding success was reported at Canadian gannet colonies where DDE concentrations in sampled eggs were greater than 5 mg per kg wet weight (Chapdelaine *et al.*, 1987). Even when the organochlorine concentrations were at their highest, the breeding success of gannets on Ailsa Craig and Bass Rock were reported to be within normal limits (Nelson, 1964; Wanless, 1979), suggesting that the breeding success of gannets in Scotland is unlikely to have been affected by organochlorines (Newton *et al.*, 1990). Some egg-shell thinning was, however, noted on Ailsa Craig in the past, so impacts on individuals may have occurred.

Overall, these data tell a good news story for gannets in Scotland. Levels of these contaminants in gannet eggs are, for the most part, in decline and biological effects at these levels of contamination might be expected to be small, unless there are unknown effects due to interactions between different contaminants that have not been monitored.

Acknowledgements

This work was supported by Joint Nature Conservation Committee and the Natural Environment Research Council's Centre for Ecology and Hydrology (Monks Wood) as part of the Predatory Bird Monitoring Scheme.

References

Chapdelaine, G., Laporte, P. and Nettleship, D.N. (1987). Population productivity and DDT contamination trends of northern gannets at Bonaventure Island, Quebec, 1967-1987. *Canadian Journal of Zoology*, **65**, 2922-2926.

Hamer, K.C., Phillips, R.A., Wanless, S., Harris, M.P. and Wood, A.G. (2000). Foraging ranges, diets and feeding locations of gannets, *Morus bassanus*, in the North Sea: evidence from satellite telemetry. *Marine Ecology Progress Series*, **200**, 257-264.

Nelson, J.B. (1964). Factors influencing clutch size and chick growth in the North Atlantic gannet *Sula bassana*. *Ibis*, **106**, 63-77.

Newton, I., Haas, M.B. and Freestone, P. (1990). Trends in organochlorine and mercury levels in gannet eggs. *Environmental Pollution*, **63**, 1-12.

Osborn, D. (1979). The significance of metal residues in wild animals. In *Management and Control of Heavy Metals in the Environment*, ed. by R. Perry. CEP Consultants, Edinburgh. pp. 187-192.

Pain, D.J., Burneleau, G., Bavoux, C. and Wyatt, C. (1999). Levels of polychlorinated biphenyls, organochlorine pesticides, mercury and lead in relation to shell thickness in marsh harrier (*Circus aeruginosus*) eggs from Charente-Maritime, France. *Environmental Pollution*, **104**, 61-68.

Parslow, J.L.F. and Jefferies, D.J. (1975). Geographical variation in guillemot eggs. In *Annual Report of the Institute of Terrestrial Ecology – 1974*. HMSO, London. pp. 28-31.

Sparks, T., Newton, I., Dale, L. and Osborn, D. (2000). Organochlorines in bird of prey eggs: a terrestrial case study. In *Statistics in Ecotoxicology*, ed. by T. Sparks. John Wiley, Chichester. pp. 211-245.

Tasker, M.L., Jones, P.H., Blake, B.F. and Dixon, T.J. (1985). The marine distribution of the gannet in the North Sea. *Bird Study*, **32**, 82-90.

Wanless, S. (1979). Aspects of population dynamics and breeding ecology in the gannet (*Sula bassana* (L.)) of Ailsa Craig. PhD Thesis, University of Aberdeen.

15 THE ATLANTIC SALMON: A CASE STUDY OF SCOTLAND'S ENVIRONMENT AND NATURAL HERITAGE

John Baxter and Peter Hutchinson

Summary

1.   Located in the middle of the latitudinal range of the species, Scotland is a major state of origin of wild Atlantic salmon, *Salmo salar*. Salmon occur in almost 400 rivers in Scotland, migrating considerable distances inland and reaching an altitude of almost 600 m.

2.   As smolts and returning adults, Scottish salmon pass through estuaries and coastal waters and their wide-ranging migrations can include the Norwegian Sea and even, for some, the waters off West Greenland. With this dependency on freshwater, estuarine and marine environments, the anadromous salmon is a potentially useful indicator of the state of these environments in Scotland and of the marine environment of the North Atlantic.

3.   There is currently grave conservation concern about salmon throughout its range. In Scotland, the declared all-methods catch of salmon has declined by about 70 per cent from a ten-year average of almost 1,700 t in the 1960s to an average of less than 500 t in the 1990s. During this period of declining catches there have been major reductions in netting effort and restrictions on rod fisheries, but nevertheless the abundance of many wild stocks has continued to decline due to a combination of pressures. The marine mortality of some monitored stocks has doubled in recent years compared with the 1970s.

4.   The chapter reviews the status of salmon stocks in Scotland and compares it with the situation throughout the North Atlantic in an attempt to identify what factors are driving abundance and whether they simply reflect the state of Scotland's environment or larger-scale influences. The measures being taken nationally and internationally to conserve and restore this flagship species are reviewed.

15.1 Introduction

Atlantic salmon, *Salmo salar*, and Scotland, a major state of origin for the species, are synonymous (NASCO, 2001a). This highly prized and economically valuable species occurs in almost 400 river systems in Scotland, migrating considerable distances inland, commonly reaching an altitude of 300-450 m and up to 600 m in some systems (Gardiner and Egglishaw, 1986). The largest rivers are on the east coast and salmon may enter some of these rivers in every month of the year (NASCO, 2001a).

The anadromous life-cycle of the salmon (Plate 27) involves a variable period of residence in fresh water, usually 2-3 years in Scotland (Youngson and Hay, 1996), after which the fish migrate through estuarine, coastal and offshore waters to northern marine ecosystems where they grow rapidly on the abundant food resources (Friedland, 1994) before returning to their natal river to spawn. The salmon is a potentially useful indicator both of the state of aquatic environments in Scotland and of the wider marine environment of the North Atlantic, frequented during extensive migrations which take some Scottish salmon as far as the waters off West Greenland. This chapter reviews the status of salmon stocks in Scotland and compares it with the situation throughout the North Atlantic in an attempt to identify what factors are driving abundance and whether they simply reflect the state of Scotland's environment or larger-scale influences. The measures being taken nationally and internationally to conserve and restore this flagship species are discussed.

15.2 Status of salmon stocks

The Atlantic salmon is more abundant now than at any time, although approximately 98 per cent of this biomass comprises farmed fish (Parrish *et al.*, 1998); many wild salmon stocks and fisheries in Scotland, as in other parts of the species' range, are in decline (Youngson *et al.*, in press).

Assessment of the status of wild salmon and identification of the factors influencing them is complicated, not least because salmon exist as a large number of discrete, self-sustaining populations (Youngson *et al.*, in press). They are widely dispersed at sea, and different populations and sea-age classes within populations may go to different areas at sea and be subject to different environmental conditions (Potter, 1994).

Catch statistics have been collected on a systematic basis in Scotland since 1952 (Youngson, 1996) and are available for the North Atlantic area from 1960 (ICES, 2001). These statistics, following adjustments for assumed exploitation rates and unreported catches, allow time series of pre-fishery abundance (i.e. recruits) and numbers of spawners to be generated for each country using run reconstruction models (see Potter and Dunkley, 1993), although there is a need for caution in interpreting trends in abundance generated from models based on catch data.

Fishery-independent information on stock status is available for about 40 monitored rivers in the north-east Atlantic area but many of these rivers are small, contribute only a small proportion of the total production in this area (ICES, 2001) and may not be representative of the situation in other rivers. However, the information from these monitored rivers is valuable since it may allow partitioning of the recruitment variability between the freshwater and marine phases of the life-cycle (Reddin *et al.*, 2000), facilitating the development of appropriate stock conservation and restoration measures (Potter and Crozier, 2000). In Scotland, information on smolt counts and adult returns is available for the River North Esk (37 years of data) and two tributaries of the Aberdeenshire Dee (the Girnock Burn (35 years of data) and the Baddoch Burn (13 years of data, although this system has been manipulated (J.C. MacLean, pers. comm.) and is not considered further in this review)).

The all-methods catch of salmon in Scotland has declined from an average of almost 1,700 t in the 1960s to an average of less than 500 t in the 1990s. The catch of 199 t in 1999 was the lowest recorded (Figure 15.1). The trend in catches in Scotland closely follows that of the total catch for the North Atlantic area. However, over this period there have been significant reductions in fishing effort around the North Atlantic and these must be taken into account in deriving trends in abundance. In Scotland, netting effort declined by 83 per cent between 1975 and 1999 (NASCO, 2000a), but this accounts for only part of the decline and constancy in rod catches, despite greatly reduced netting effort, suggests

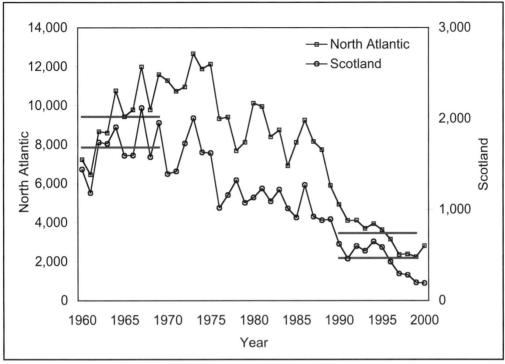

Figure 15.1. Total declared catch of salmon (in tonnes) for the North Atlantic area and for Scotland. Horizontal lines show the mean catch for the decades 1960-1969 and 1990-1999.

a major decline in abundance (NASCO, 2001a) or non-linearity between rod catch and stock abundance.

Modelled estimates of the pre-fishery abundance of Scottish salmon (Figure 15.2) indicate a decline from about 2.25 million fish in the early 1970s to around 700,000 fish in the late 1990s, i.e. a reduction of about 70 per cent. The estimated number of spawners remained relatively stable during the 1970s and 1980s, but declined in the 1990s by about 40 per cent. Figure 15.2 also indicates that salmon abundance has declined on a European basis, although there is greatest concern about the status of southern European stocks (Ireland, UK, France, Spain).

Counts of smolts emigrating from the North Esk indicate that there has been no statistically significant trend in smolt production since the mid-1960s when monitoring began, but that marine survival in the 1990s has been only about half the level in the 1960s (Dunkley, 1995; Shelton *et al.*, 2000). Counter data from the North Esk indicate that spawning escapement has remained relatively stable (ICES, 2001), suggesting that reductions in fishing mortality have, to date, compensated for reduced abundance. The Girnock Burn has also produced annual smolt runs of near-uniform strength, suggesting that the decline in the Dee spring fishery is due to increased marine mortality (Youngson, 1996). The situation appears to be particularly severe in a number of small rivers in the West Highlands. Of nine rivers surveyed, the salmon populations were considered to be extinct in two and endangered in another five. These small populations are considered to be particularly vulnerable during periods of high marine mortality (WRFT, 2000).

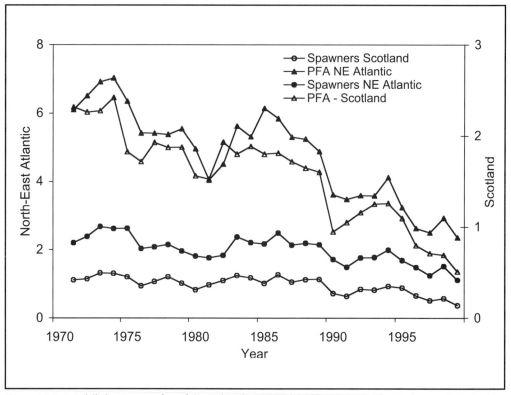

Figure 15.2. Modelled estimates of pre-fishery abundance (PFA) and spawners (millions of salmon), derived by run-reconstruction modelling, for Scotland and for the North-East Atlantic region (Source: ICES,2001).

Data from nine monitored European rivers indicate that marine survival was generally lower in the 1990s than in the 1980s (Potter and Crozier, 2000). A marked decline in abundance associated with low marine survival is also evident for North American stocks (ICES, 2001), leading to the conclusion that common events are influencing the production of salmon from widely different geographical areas (Reddin *et al.*, 2000). However, for the River Bush in Northern Ireland, average survival from egg to smolt has been about one-thirtieth of that from smolt to adult (Potter and Crozier, 2000). Most likely stocks have been affected by a range of factors across both freshwater and marine environments. Interpretation of the data is further complicated by the fact that factors operating in fresh water may subsequently affect survival at sea (Hutchinson and Mills, 2000).

15.3 Factors affecting salmon abundance

Throughout their life-cycle Atlantic salmon inhabit a variety of habitats and will face many factors affecting their survival. These range from population-specific, local factors such as discrete impacts on particular spawning redds, to large-scale influences such as climate change. Some impacts will be transient, although the repercussions may persist, while other impacts may be longer lasting. This brief review cannot examine all these factors in detail but serves to highlight both the national and international dimensions of the challenges faced when trying to conserve and restore the salmon.

15.3.1 Fisheries

Permitted salmon fishing gear in Scotland is restricted to rod and line, net and coble and, outside estuary limits (except for in the Solway Firth), fixed engines (Williamson, 1986; NASCO, 2001c). Table 15.1 shows the average catch by rod and line (excluding fish subsequently released), net and coble and fixed engine for the four decades 1960-1969 to 1990-1999. Net and coble and fixed engine catches have declined significantly over this

Table 15.1. Ten-year average catches of Atlantic salmon and grilse in Scotland for the period 1960–1999 and the catch for 2000. (Source: Scottish Executive Environment and Rural Affairs Department)

Period	Rod and line (excluding fish caught and released)	Net and coble	Fixed engine	Total catch
1960-69	68,435	204,355	196,641	469,431
1970-79	63,828	166,226	176,436	406,490
1980-89	73,018	103,807	129,619	306,444
1990-99	65,382	27,051	44,342	136,775
2000	44,653	12,521	22,988	80,162
Per cent reduction from 1960-69 to 1990-99	4.5%	86.8%	77.4%	70.9%

time, associated with a major effort reduction (NASCO, 2000a). Rod and line catches for Scotland as a whole have, in contrast, remained relatively stable (Figure 15.3) and as a result the proportion of the catch taken by rod and line has increased from approximately 15 per cent in the 1960s to almost 50 per cent in the 1990s. The economic value of the resource in Scotland is now dominated by angling exploitation (Youngson *et al.*, in press). However, there have been marked declines in the rod and line catch in some regions, particularly the West, North-West and North-East regions. This decline is illustrated in Figure 15.3 for the West Region. Catch and release angling is being increasingly practised in Scotland. Details of the number of salmon caught and released by anglers have been collected by the Scottish Executive since 1994. These indicate that the proportion of fish caught and subsequently released has increased from 7.9 per cent in 1994 (about 6,600 fish) to 32 per cent in 2000 (about 21,000 fish). It is important that these statistics are taken into account in assessing any trend in rod and line catches.

Scotland is a significant contributor to distant water fisheries but as a result of various international agreements, the catch of salmon in these fisheries has declined from a peak of more than 3,000 t in the early 1970s to only 29 t in 2000 (Hutchinson and Windsor, 2001). Fishing for salmon in international waters in the late 1980s and early 1990s threatened to undermine the effectiveness of these international agreements but diplomatic initiatives co-ordinated by NASCO appear to have successfully addressed this problem.

Closer to home, around 80 per cent of the salmon caught in the English North East Coast Salmon Fishery are of Scottish origin (Anon., 1996). However, there was a 49 per

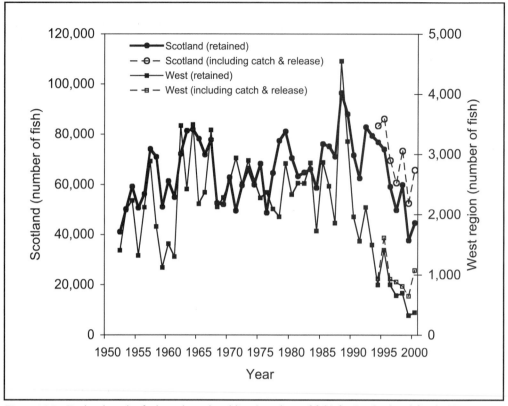

Figure 15.3. Declared catch of salmon by rod and line (numbers of fish) for Scotland and for the West region of Scotland. Statistics for the number of salmon caught and subsequently released are shown from 1994.

cent reduction in licences issued for this fishery between 1992 and 1999 (NASCO, 2000a) and compensation arrangements are presently being discussed with a view to closure of the fishery. Scottish-origin salmon are also known to be harvested in the Irish drift net fishery.

Despite major reductions in fisheries exploiting Scottish-origin salmon over the last 40 years, abundance has not increased. The problems facing these stocks do not, therefore, appear to be related to the directed fisheries (Dunkley, 1995; Youngson, 1996; Jacobsen and Hansen, 2000) and a range of biological and environmental factors likely to affect marine survival is now being investigated (Jacobsen and Hansen, 2000). There is, however, concern about possible by-catch of salmon in pelagic fisheries, in the Norwegian Sea, which overlap spatially and temporally with post-smolt migration routes (Anon., 2001; ICES, 2001).

15.3.2 Climate

Dickson and Turrell (2000) described large-scale changes in climate and circulation patterns of the North Atlantic associated with changes in the North Atlantic Oscillation (NAO), the dominant recurrent mode of atmospheric behaviour in the region. The NAO alternates between 'high index' years, associated with warming in the south but cooling in the Labrador and Nordic Seas, while 'low index' years generally show the reverse (Turrell and Holliday, 2001). The NAO index was generally low in the 1960s and 1970s when salmon catches were high, and high in the 1980s and early 1990s when salmon catches were low.

A number of recent studies has demonstrated correlations between marine survival of salmon and thermal habitat indices, based on sea surface water temperature (Friedland and Reddin, 1993; Friedland, 1998; Friedland *et al.*, 1998, 2000). For example, the pattern and timing of encroachment of warm water into the North Sea in spring is correlated with marine survival of salmon (Friedland *et al.*, 2000). As the NAO strengthens, the area of the salmon's preferred thermal habitat shrinks and there are changes in production of zooplankton and other biological effects (Dickson and Turrell, 2000). Reduced growth rates in years when temperatures are unfavourable result in an extended period of vulnerability to predation of both smolts and post-smolts leading to lower marine survival and suggesting that climatic influences on growth-mediated predation are the dominant causes of recruitment variability (Friedland *et al.*, 2000). The detection of a significant increase in the incidence of growth checks on the scales of Scottish salmon in recent years may assist in understanding trends in salmon abundance (MacLean *et al.*, 2000; ICES, 2001). It should be noted, however, that recent increases in the extent of thermal habitat in the North-West Atlantic have not yet led to improved marine survival of North American salmon stocks (Potter and Crozier, 2000).

Changes in weather in the catchment areas of salmon rivers, and thus the conditions experienced by salmon during their freshwater phase, are also associated with the different phases of the NAO Index. However, these will be more regionally variable than the larger-scale changes affecting the oceanic environment (Dickson and Turrell, 2000). Studies on the Girnock Burn have shown that winter, and especially spring, water temperatures have tended to increase since the mid-1960s (Langan *et al.*, 2001). The median date of smolt migration has also advanced over the same period, but it has not proved possible to link changes in migration timing directly with temperature changes, suggesting that complex processes are involved (A. Youngson, pers. comm.).

15.3.3 Freshwater habitat

There has been considerable damage and loss of salmon habitat over the last 150 years as a result of a variety of human activities and this must have been a major contributing factor in the decline of wild salmon stocks. For example, in Canada there has been a net loss of productive capacity of salmon of 16 per cent since 1870 (NASCO, 2000b). Only very few, if any, Scottish salmon rivers have completely escaped habitat damage (NASCO, 2001b).

Various obstructions such as dams and weirs have been constructed on Scottish rivers to provide power to drive mills. Hydroelectricity generating facilities exist in a number of river systems including the Shin, Conon, Beauly, Spey, Tay and Awe, and dams have also been created for water supply purposes. Dams and weirs can create a barrier to salmon reaching spawning and nursery habitat, delay upstream migration, flood spawning and nursery areas and result in injury to migrating smolts (Mills, 1980; NASCO, 2001b). Altered flow regimes and inappropriate compensation flows and freshet releases can affect migration.

Forestry, agriculture and general estate management operations can result in increased siltation, erosion, eutrophication due to fertiliser run-off, acidification and diffuse pollution by pesticides and other poisonous chemicals. Other factors include reduced dissolved oxygen concentrations, elevated temperatures and habitat destruction through gravel extraction and other civil engineering works (SAC, 1991; Elliott *et al.*, 1998). These may affect the productivity of the individual river systems.

Water quality in Scotland's rivers and large lochs is mainly excellent, with the major causes of deterioration being sewage effluent, agricultural pollution and acidification (Doughty *et al.*, this volume). Point-source pollution of rivers is being reduced through improvements in effluent treatment, as a result of changes in the structure of Scottish industry and other factors (NASCO, 2001b), and some waters are showing signs of recovery from acidification (Doughty *et al.*, this volume).

15.3.4 Predators

Salmon face a wide range of predators throughout their life-cycle (SAC, 1996). These have been thoroughly reviewed by Anthony (2000) who identified 50 predators of salmon in the Atlantic area. Various piscivorous birds prey on salmon. On a number of Scottish rivers juvenile salmon made up a significant proportion of the diet of both red-breasted mergansers (*Mergus serrator)* (30 to 56 per cent by mass in winter and spring) and goosanders (*Mergus merganser*) (9 to 41 per cent). On rivers where predation is high it could have a significant impact on the salmon stock (Marquiss *et al.*, 1998).

Mortality during smolt migration can be high in some rivers in some years (Anthony, 2000). The impact of predation at sea is poorly understood but post-smolts are the target of a range of fish, including various commercial species such as cod (*Gadus morhua*), saithe (*Pollachius virens*) and pollack (*Pollachius pollachius*), and predation is thought to be heaviest in the months immediately after smolts enter the sea (Hansen and Quinn, 1998). Larger adult salmon are preyed on by various sharks and rays, and also by a wide range of cetaceans and phocids (SAC, 1996).

The diet of seals has received considerable attention in Scotland (e.g. Rae, 1968, 1973; Pierce *et al.*, 1991a,b; Thompson *et al.*, 1991; Hammond and Fedak, 1994; Hammond *et al.*,1994a,b; Carter *et al.*, 2001). However, the results of these studies need to be interpreted with caution, since the methods used have in-built bias which affects their utility in assessing overall levels of seal predation on salmon (SAC, 1996). In most cases salmon comprised only a small part of the diet of seals except when the seals examined were close to salmon nets (Rae, 1968). There have been few studies of the diet of seals at the mouths of salmon rivers (Carter *et al.*, 2001) although there are frequent reports of salmon, caught by anglers, showing evidence of damage thought to have been caused by seals especially, in winter and spring. Similarly, data collected at net fisheries near Montrose and in the River North Esk during 1970-1997 show a four-fold increase during this period in the percentage of seal-damaged salmon in the catch taken before 1 June (Shearer, 2000). Carter *et al.* (2001) showed that, as a cause of mortality, seal predation on large salmonids in the estuaries of the Rivers Dee and the Don was ten times less important than mortality caused by angling. Whereas the mortality rate inflicted by man on salmon has been reduced, the view has been expressed that no management action is being taken to address the mortality caused by birds and marine mammals, partly because of the high social value placed on them (Anthony, 2000).

15.3.5 Salmon aquaculture

Salmon farming has developed rapidly throughout the North Atlantic region over the last 20 years. In Scotland, annual production of farmed salmon is now more than six hundred times the harvest from salmon fisheries. Escapes from salmon farms can occur at all stages of the production cycle, in fresh water and at sea, and the abundance of escapees in nature is large (Jonsson, 1997). In 1991, 5.1 per cent of fry sampled in rivers in western and northern Scotland were shown to be progeny of escaped farmed salmon and this was known to be an underestimate because of the methods used (Webb *et al.*, 1993). Furthermore, monitoring at one west coast netting station has shown that while the proportion in catches fluctuates widely, in 1999 47 per cent of the catch was escaped farmed salmon (WRFT, 2000).

There is evidence that escapes from salmon farms have spawned in Scottish rivers (Webb *et al.*, 1991, 1993), and elsewhere in the North Atlantic region (e.g. Crozier, 1993; Carr *et al.*, 1997), giving rise to concerns about adverse genetic and ecological interactions. McGinnity *et al.* (1997) showed that, in the wild, the progeny of farmed salmon grew fast and competitively displaced the smaller native fish downstream. However, while the competitive ability of farmed salmon may be higher than wild fish, their survival is probably lower (Jonsson, 1997). It has recently been hypothesized that escapes from Scotland (and Ireland) are transported with ocean currents close to the Norwegian coast and that they enter rivers there to spawn (ICES, 2001). This hypothesis remains to be tested but it raises an interesting international dimension.

There is also concern about high infestation rates of wild salmon post-smolts with salmon lice, *Lepeophtheirus salmonis*, in areas with salmon farms (WRFT, 2000; ICES, 2001). Serious epizootics in wild salmon have been associated with movements of live salmon for farming and restocking. Examples are the spread of the disease furunculosis from Scotland to Norway (Hastein and Lindstad, 1991) and of the parasite *Gyrodactylus salaris* from Sweden to Norway (Johnsen and Jensen, 1991).

Genetic, ecological, disease and parasite impacts on wild salmon can also result from other forms of aquaculture, including ranching and stocking, and from inadvertent transport. In this regard, the possible introduction of *G. salaris* is a serious risk to Scottish salmon populations which are highly susceptible to the parasite (Bakke and MacKenzie, 1993). Transfers of salmonids among locations have been common on both local and extensive scales in the past although much of the information is anecdotal (Youngson *et al.*, in press). Many organizations involved in stocking salmon rivers in Britain used stock from rivers other than the rivers being stocked (Harris, 1978). In response to declining salmon abundance more than 6.5 million eggs and juvenile salmon have been stocked annually in Scottish rivers in recent years using broodstock native to the river (NASCO, 2001b). It is important that future stocking operations continue to respect the genetic characteristics of the recipient population.

15.4 Recent management initiatives

Prior to the early 1960s the exploitation and management of Atlantic salmon originating in Scottish rivers were largely under national control (Mills, 1983). However, rational salmon management can be achieved only through actions at international, national and local levels, and a brief review of recent initiatives follows.

15.4.1 North Atlantic Salmon Conservation Organization

The inter-governmental North Atlantic Salmon Conservation Organization (NASCO) was established in 1984, with the objective of conserving, restoring, enhancing and rationally managing Atlantic salmon. Scottish salmon interests are represented in this forum through the European Union, which is a Contracting Party. The achievements of NASCO during the period 1984-1994 have been summarised by Windsor and Hutchinson (1994).

Recently, in response to continuing concerns about salmon abundance, NASCO and its Contracting Parties have agreed to adopt and apply a precautionary approach, and to date consideration has been given to the application of this approach both to the management of salmon fisheries and to habitat protection and restoration. In accordance with a decision structure for management of salmon fisheries, presently being implemented on a trial basis, conservation limits or other measures of abundance are being established at an appropriate management scale, in most cases for each salmon river, to ensure that only the harvestable surplus is exploited. With regard to habitat protection and restoration, NASCO's Contracting Parties and their relevant jurisdictions will develop plans containing a general strategy for protection of habitat for all salmon rivers and identifying and prioritizing the requirements for habitat restoration. Detailed inventories of salmon rivers will also be established. Categorising river systems and quantifying the scale of different impact factors are important steps in rationalizing salmon management (Armstrong *et al.*, 1998). A key element of both these initiatives under a precautionary approach is the need for effective monitoring and application of the findings in future management. Such an adaptive management approach is considered to be essential to salmon conservation (Parrish *et al.*, 1998).

There are two other recent initiatives within NASCO. First, it has established an International Board to identify priorities and funding opportunities for research into the factors responsible for the increased marine mortality of salmon. Second, it has fostered the development internationally, in cooperation with the salmon farming industry, of Guidelines on Containment of Farm Salmon. Under these guidelines national or regional action plans will be established so as to provide a systematic basis for minimising escapes.

15.4.2 *European Union*

The salmon is listed in Annex II of the EU's Habitats Directive as a species of Community interest whose conservation requires the designation of Special Areas of Conservation (SACs) in fresh water. Thirteen Scottish rivers have been proposed as candidate SACs, with a further three rivers still under consideration. Designated rivers will be subject to greater protection through the implementation of management schemes developed in partnership with all stakeholders. The EU's Water Framework Directive also offers a range of potential benefits to salmon conservation, such as the compilation of a register of protected areas, the introduction of a system for water abstraction control and catchment management.

15.4.3 *National and local initiatives*

The Salmon Conservation (Scotland) Act 2001 makes provision for fishery managers and Scottish Ministers to make regulations for the conservation of salmon (NASCO, 2001c). Recently, the Scottish Executive has published a Green Paper containing a number of proposals for better conservation and management of freshwater fish, including salmon (SEERAD, 2001). Seven of the proposals are the consolidation of existing salmon and freshwater fisheries legislation; a ban on the introduction, keeping or release of exotic, non-indigenous species; a ban on the use of live fish as bait; control of transfers of fish between catchments; funding of research on seal predation; a ban on the sale of rod-caught salmon; and updating of guidance on stocking practices.

Recent changes in the fisheries include the introduction of regulations prohibiting the use of certain baits and lures in 17 rivers, increasing use of catch and release angling for salmon, and a voluntary six-week deferment of the netting season by the Salmon Net Fishing Association of Scotland to protect 'spring' salmon (NASCO, 2001a).

A programme of surveys of juvenile salmon covering about 2,000 sites in Scotland has been developed by the Scottish Fisheries Co-ordination Centre, the results from which should enhance the scientific basis on which management decisions are taken (WWF, 2001). The data will be collected by Fishery Trusts and Foundations which now cover most areas of Scotland and which are also undertaking valuable habitat improvement work. For example, on the River Tweed approximately 100 km of river has been fenced off so as to improve spawning and nursery habitats, and access has been improved to over 400 km of the system by removal or modification of man-made obstructions (D. Glen, pers. comm.).

The Tripartite Working Group, comprising wild and farmed salmon interests and regulators, is continuing to develop Area Management Agreements designed to reduce the impacts of salmon farming on wild stocks. Also, many of the Local Biodiversity Action Plans in Scotland recognise the importance of salmon and its habitats.

15.5 Conclusions

The abundance of wild Atlantic salmon in Scotland and elsewhere in the North Atlantic has declined markedly in the last decade, to such a degree that there are now serious concerns about the threat of local extinctions, and the need for careful consideration of the causal factors and the identification of realistic solutions. This decline has occurred in spite of restrictive fishery management measures and other important initiatives introduced both nationally and internationally. It is the consequence of various factors operating at different spatial and temporal scales in a complex hierarchical inter-relationship in which factors on a given tier override those on lower tiers (Armstrong *et al.*, 1998). As such, caution must be applied when using overall salmon abundance figures as an indicator of the general state of Scotland's environment.

For example, changes in climate, operating over large geographic scales, appear to be having an effect on salmon abundance throughout the North Atlantic, although the causal mechanisms are not yet fully understood. It is important to recognise the influence of such factors and the need to increase understanding of them, but it is equally important to acknowledge that they may be beyond human control. It is in this context that remedial measures should be developed and the consequent recovery of stocks assessed.

Carter (2000) stressed that there is a need to focus on rectifying the situations where human actions have caused declines in abundance and that focusing on single issue solutions would simply not be good enough. Furthermore, he suggested that maximising juvenile production should be the key objective, although this will be effective only if human-induced mortality beyond the natal rivers, such as that associated with by-catch, fishing in international waters, impacts of salmon farming and coastal and marine pollution, are effectively controlled.

Potter and Crozier (2000) drew attention to the serious lack of data on long-term trends in the survival and productivity of salmon in fresh water and cautioned that, without this information, stock status cannot be properly interpreted, and management advice might, therefore, be flawed. Similarly, Doughty *et al.* (Chapter 9) refer to the difficulty in establishing trends in freshwater natural heritage features as a result of the limited available data, and problems of interpretation of existing data. However, in this regard the recent development of a suite of juvenile salmon monitoring sites by the Scottish Fisheries Co-ordination Centre, and initiatives arising from NASCO's decision structure on fisheries management and the inventories envisaged under the habitat protection and restoration plans, should enhance our ability to use the salmon as an indicator of the health of the Scottish freshwater environment so critical to the species' survival.

The future conservation of salmon will require a truly holistic approach to research and management, and replacement of the culture of blame with one of enhanced cooperation between all interested groups (Windsor, 2000). In this regard the Water Framework Directive, with its requirement for the development of catchment management plans and closer working between interest groups, and the designation of a number of rivers as Special Areas of Conservation for salmon, should further complement the existing management initiatives. There are some initial encouraging signs that abundance is increasing, particularly for European stocks, but not to the extent that consideration can yet be given to relaxing the restrictive measures that have been introduced to conserve and restore this flagship species.

15.6 Acknowledgements

We are grateful to Julian MacLean (SEERAD) for providing the catch data in Table 15.1 and Figure 15.3, and to the General Secretary of ICES for permission to use the data in preparing Figure 15.2 and to cite from the Report of the Advisory Committee on Fishery Management. Julian MacLean, Dick Shelton, Derek Mills and two anonymous referees kindly provided helpful comments on earlier drafts of this review.

References

Anonymous (1996). Report of the Technical Working Group on the English North East Coast Salmon Fishery. Unpublished report prepared by MAFF, SOAEFD and EA scientists following a meeting held in London on 17 December 1996.

Anonymous (2001). *Biennial Review 1999-2001. Fisheries Research Services, Freshwater Laboratory, Pitlochry, Scotland.* Scottish Executive Environment and Rural Affairs Department, Edinburgh.

Anthony, V.C. (2000). Predator-prey dynamics of Atlantic salmon. In *Managing Wild Atlantic Salmon: New Challenges - New Techniques*, ed. by F.G. Whoriskey and K.B. Whelan. Atlantic Salmon Federation, St Andrews, Canada. pp. 50-73.

Armstrong, J.D., Grant, J.W.A., Forsgren, H.L., Fausch, K.D., DeGraff, R.M., Fleming, I.A., Prowse, T.D. and Schlosser, I.J. (1998). The application of science to the management of Atlantic salmon (*Salmo salar*): integration across scales. *Canadian Journal of Fisheries and Aquatic Sciences,* **55** (Suppl. 1), 303-311.

Bakke, T.A. and MacKenzie, K. (1993). Comparative susceptibility of native Scottish and Norwegian stocks of Atlantic salmon, *Salmo salar* L., to *Gyrodactylus salaris* Malmberg: laboratory experiments. *Fisheries Research,* **17**, 69-85.

Carr, J.W., Anderson, J.M., Whoriskey, F.G. and Dilworth, T. (1997). The occurrence and spawning of cultured Atlantic salmon (*Salmo salar*) in a Canadian river. *ICES Journal of Marine Science,* **54**, 1064-1073.

Carter, T.J., Pierce, G.J., Hislop, J.R.G., Houseman, J.A. and Boyle, P.R. (2001). Predation by seals on salmonids in two Scottish estuaries. *Fisheries Management and Ecology,* **8**, 207-225.

Carter, W.M. (2000). A gathering of people. In *Managing Wild Atlantic Salmon. New Challenges - New Techniques,* ed. by F.G. Whoriskey and K.B. Whelan. Atlantic Salmon Federation, St Andrews, Canada. pp. 5-11.

Crozier, W.W. (1993). Evidence of genetic interactions between escaped farmed salmon and wild Atlantic salmon (*Salmo salar* L.) in a Northern Irish river. *Aquaculture,* **113**, 19-29.

Dickson, R.R. and Turrell, W.R. (2000). The NAO: the dominant atmospheric process affecting oceanic variability in home, middle and distant waters of European Atlantic salmon. In *The Ocean Life of Atlantic Salmon - Environmental and Biological Factors Influencing Survival,* ed. by D.H. Mills. Fishing News Books, Oxford. pp. 92-115.

Dunkley, D.A. (1995). Investigations into Atlantic salmon smolt production on the North Esk. *The Salmon Net,* **36**, 35-39.

Elliott, S.R., Coe, T.A., Helfield, J.M. and Naiman, R.J. (1998). Spatial variation in environmental characteristics of Atlantic salmon (*Salmo salar*) rivers. *Canadian Journal of Fisheries and Aquatic Sciences,* **55** (Suppl. 1), 267-280.

Friedland, K.D. (1994). History of salmon fisheries and management in the North Atlantic. In *Atlantic Salmon: a Dialogue.* International Council for the Exploration of the Sea, Copenhagen. pp. 6-22.

Friedland, K.D. (1998). Ocean climate influences on critical Atlantic salmon (*Salmo salar*) life history events. *Canadian Journal of Fisheries and Aquatic Sciences,* **55** (Suppl. 1), 119-130.

Friedland, K.D. and Reddin, D.G. (1993). Marine survival of Atlantic salmon from indices of post-smolt growth and sea temperature. In *Salmon in the Sea and New Enhancement Strategies,* ed. by D.H. Mills. Fishing News Books, Oxford. pp. 119-138.

Friedland, K.D., Hansen, L.P. and Dunkley, D.A. (1998). Marine temperatures experienced by post-smolts and the survival of Atlantic salmon, *Salmo salar* L., in the North Sea area. *Fisheries Oceanography,* **7**, 22-34.

Friedland, K.D., Hansen, L.P., Dunkley, D.A. and MacLean, J.C. (2000). Linkage between ocean climate, post-smolt growth, and survival of Atlantic salmon (*Salmo salar* L.) in the North Sea area. *ICES Journal of Marine Science,* **57**, 419-429.

Gardiner, R. and Egglishaw, H. (1986). *A Map of the Distribution in Scottish Rivers of the Atlantic Salmon,* Salmo salar *L.* Department of Agriculture and Fisheries for Scotland, Edinburgh.

Hammond, P.S. and Fedak, M.A. (Eds.) (1994). Grey seals in the North Sea and their interactions with fisheries. Unpublished report to the Ministry of Agriculture, Fisheries and Food, London.

Hammond, P.S., Hall, A.J. and Prime, J.H. (1994a). The diet of grey seals around Orkney and other islands and mainland sites in north-eastern Scotland. *Journal of Applied Ecology,* **31**, 340-350.

Hammond, P.S., Hall, A.J. and Prime, J.H. (1994b). The diet of grey seals in the Inner and Outer Hebrides. *Journal of Applied Ecology,* **31**, 737-746.

Hansen, L.P. and Quinn, T.P. (1998). The marine phase of the Atlantic salmon (*Salmo salar*) life cycle, with comparison to Pacific salmon. *Canadian Journal of Fisheries and Aquatic Sciences,* **55** (Suppl. 1), 104-118.

Harris, G.S. (Ed.) (1978). Salmon propagation in England and Wales. Unpublished report by the Association of River Authorities and National Water Council Working Party, London.

Hastein, T. and Lindstad, T. (1991). Diseases in wild and cultured salmon: possible interactions. *Aquaculture,* **98**, 277-288.

Hutchinson, P. and Mills, D.H. (2000). Executive Summary. In *The Ocean Life of Atlantic Salmon – Environmental and Biological Factors Influencing Survival,* ed. by D.H. Mills. Fishing News Books, Oxford. pp. 7-18.

Hutchinson, P. and Windsor, M.L. (2001). Salmon fisheries in the North Atlantic. In *Encyclopaedia of Ocean Sciences*, ed. by J.H. Steele, S.A. Thorpe and K.K. Turekian. Academic Press, London. pp. 2451-2461.

ICES (2001). Report of the ICES Advisory Committee on Fishery Management. International Council for the Exploration of the Sea, Copenhagen. pp. 170-192.

Jacobsen, J.A. and Hansen, L.P. (2000). Feeding habits of Atlantic salmon at different life stages at sea. In *The Ocean Life of Atlantic Salmon - Environmental and Biological Factors Influencing Survival*, ed. by D.H. Mills. Fishing News Books, Oxford. pp. 170-192.

Johnsen, B.O. and Jensen, A.J. (1991). The Gyrodactylus story in Norway. *Aquaculture*, **98**, 289-302.

Jonsson, B. (1997). A review of ecological and behavioural interactions between cultured and wild Atlantic salmon. *ICES Journal of Marine Science*, **54**, 1031-1039.

Langan, S.J., Johnston, L., Donaghy, M.J., Youngson, A.F., Hay, D.W. and Soulsby, C. (2001). Variation in river water temperature in an upland stream over a 30-year period. *The Science of the Total Environment*, **265**, 199-211.

MacLean, J.C., Smith, G.W. and Whyte, B.M. (2000). Description of marine growth checks observed on the scales of salmon returning to Scottish homewaters in 1997. In *The Ocean Life of Atlantic Salmon - Environmental and Biological Factors Influencing Survival*, ed. by D.H. Mills. Fishing News Books, Oxford. pp. 37-48.

McGinnity, P., Stone, C., Taggart, J.B., Cooke, D., Cotter, D., Hynes, R., McCauley, C., Cross, T. and Ferguson, A. (1997). Genetic impact of escaped farmed Atlantic salmon (*Salmo salar* L.) on native populations: use of DNA profiling to assess freshwater performance of wild, farmed and hybrid progeny in a natural river environment. *ICES Journal of Marine Science*, **54**, 998-1008.

Marquiss, M., Carss, D.N., Armstrong, J.D. and Gardiner, R. (1998). *Fish-eating Birds and Salmonids in Scotland. Report on Fish-eating Birds Research (1990-97)*. Stationery Office, Edinburgh.

Mills, D.H. (1980). Scottish salmon rivers and their future management. In *Atlantic Salmon: Its Future*, ed. by A.E.J. Went. Blackwell Scientific, Cambridge, Mass. pp. 71-81.

Mills, D.H. (1983). *Problems and Solutions in the Management of Open Seas Fisheries for Atlantic salmon*. Atlantic Salmon Trust, Pitlochry.

NASCO (2000a). Exploitation of salmon in the United Kingdom and Ireland. North-East Atlantic Commission document NEA(00)6. North Atlantic Salmon Conservation Organization, Edinburgh.

NASCO (2000b). Report of the Special Session on Habitat Issues held in 1999. Council document CNL(00)28. North Atlantic Salmon Conservation Organization, Edinburgh.

NASCO (2001a). Implementation of the Oslo Resolution on measures to minimise impacts of aquaculture on the wild stocks - the position in Scotland. Council document CNL(01)25. North Atlantic Salmon Conservation Organization, Edinburgh.

NASCO (2001b). Report of the Standing Committee on the Precautionary Approach - application of a precautionary approach to habitat protection and restoration. Council document CNL(01)17. North Atlantic Salmon Conservation Organization, Edinburgh.

NASCO (2001c). Background note on European Union measures taken to protect salmon. North-East Atlantic Commission document NEA(01)11. North Atlantic Salmon Conservation Organization, Edinburgh.

Parrish, D.L., Behnke, R.J., Gephard, S.R., McCormick, S.D. and Reeves, G.H. (1998). Why aren't there more Atlantic salmon (*Salmo salar*)? *Canadian Journal of Fisheries and Aquatic Sciences*, **55** (Suppl. 1), 281-287.

Pierce, G.J., Boyle, P.R. and Diack, J.S.W. (1991a). Digestive tract contents of seals in Scottish waters: comparison of samples from salmon nets and elsewhere. *Journal of Zoology*, **225**, 670-676.

Pierce, G.J., Thompson, P.M., Miller, A., Diack, J.S.W., Miller, D. and Boyle, P.R. (1991b). Seasonal variation in the diet of common seals (*Phoca vitulina*) in the Moray Firth area of Scotland. *Journal of Zoology*, **22**, 641-652.

Potter, E.C.E. (1994). Is scientifically-based management of salmon possible in the Atlantic area? In *Atlantic Salmon: a Dialogue*. International Council for the Exploration of the Sea, Copenhagen. pp. 63-70.

Potter, E.C.E. and Crozier, W.W. (2000). A perspective on the marine survival of Atlantic salmon. In *The Ocean Life of Atlantic Salmon - Environmental and Biological Factors Influencing Survival*, ed. by D.H. Mills. Fishing News Books, Oxford. pp. 19-36.

Potter, E.C.E. and Dunkley, D.A. (1993). Evaluation of marine exploitation of salmon in Europe. In *Salmon in the Sea and New Enhancement Strategies*, ed. by D.H. Mills. Fishing News Books, Oxford. pp. 203-219.

Rae, B.B. (1968). The food of seals in Scottish waters. *Marine Research*, **1968(2)**, 1-23.

Rae, B.B. (1973). Further observations on the food of seals. *Journal of Zoology*, **169**, 287-297.

Reddin, D.G., Helbig, J., Thomas, A., Whitehouse, B.G. and Friedland, K.D. (2000). Survival of Atlantic salmon (*Salmo salar* L.) related to marine climate. In *The Ocean Life of Atlantic Salmon - Environmental and Biological Factors Influencing Survival*, ed. by D.H. Mills. Fishing News Books, Oxford. pp. 88-91.

Salmon Advisory Committee (1991). *Factors Affecting Natural Smolt Production*. MAFF Publications, London.

Salmon Advisory Committee (1996). *The Effects of Predation on Salmon Fisheries*. MAFF Publications, London.

SEERAD (2001). *Scotland's Freshwater Fish and Fisheries: Securing their Future*. Scottish Executive Environment and Rural Affairs Department, Edinburgh.

Shearer, W.M. (2000). Can the impact of seals on salmon and salmon fisheries be reduced? *The Salmon Net*, **31**, 39-44.

Shelton, R.G.J., Holst, J.L., Turrell, W.R., MacLean, J.C. and McLaren, I.S. (2000). Young salmon at sea. In *Managing Wild Atlantic Salmon. New Challenges - New Techniques*, ed. by F.G. Whoriskey and K.B. Whelan. Atlantic Salmon Federation, St Andrews, Canada. pp. 12-23.

Thompson, P.M., Pierce, G.J., Hislop, J.R.G., Miller, D. and Diack, J.S.W. (1991). Winter foraging by common seals (*Phoca vitulina*) in relation to food availability in the Inner Moray Firth, NE Scotland. *Journal of Applied Ecology*, **60**, 283-294.

Turrell, B. and Holliday N.P. (2001). *The 2000/2001 Annual ICES Ocean Climate Status Summary 2000/2001*. International Council for the Exploration of the Sea, Copenhagen.

Webb, J.H., Hay, D.W., Cunningham, P.D. and Youngson, A.F. (1991). The spawning behaviour of escaped farmed and wild Atlantic salmon (*Salmo salar*) in a northern Scottish river. *Aquaculture*, **98**, 97-110.

Webb, J.H., Youngson, A.F., Thomson, C.E., Hay, D.W., Donaghy, M.J. and McLaren, I.S. (1993). Spawning of escaped farmed Atlantic Salmon, *Salmo salar* L., in western and northern Scottish rivers: egg deposition by females. *Aquaculture and Fisheries Management*, **24**, 663-670.

Williamson, R.B. (1986). Status of exploitation of Atlantic salmon in Scotland. In *Atlantic Salmon: Planning for the Future*, ed. by D.H. Mills and D. Piggins. Croom Helm, London. pp. 91-116.

Windsor, M.L. (2000). International Cooperation. In *Managing Wild Atlantic Salmon. New Challenges - New Techniques*, ed. by F.G. Whoriskey and K.B. Whelan. Atlantic Salmon Federation, St Andrews, Canada. pp. 164-171.

Windsor, M.L. and Hutchinson, P. (1994). International management of Atlantic salmon, *Salmo salar* L., by the North Atlantic Salmon Conservation Organization, 1984-1994. *Fisheries Management and Ecology*, **1**, 31-44.

WRFT (2000). *Wester Ross Fisheries Trust Annual Review 1999-2000*. Wester Ross Fisheries Trust, Fochabers.

WWF (2001). *The Status of Wild Atlantic Salmon: A River-by-River Assessment.* WWF-US, Washington, DC.

Youngson, A.F. (1996). The decline of spring salmon. In *Enhancement of Spring Salmon*, ed. by D.H. Mills. Atlantic Salmon Trust, Pitlochry, Scotland. pp. 3-12.

Youngson, A.F. and Hay, D. (1996). *The Lives of Salmon. An Illustrated Account of the Life-history of Atlantic Salmon.* Swan Hill Press, Shrewsbury.

Youngson, A.F., Jordan, W.C., Verspoor, E., Cross, T. and Ferguson, A. (in press). Management of salmonid fisheries in the British Isles: towards a practical approach based on population genetics. *Fisheries Research.*

PART THREE

ISSUES INFLUENCING SUSTAINABILITY

PART THREE

ISSUES INFLUENCING SUSTAINABILITY

The Earth Summit held in Rio de Janeiro in 1992 brought the concept of sustainable development into everyday thinking. However, it is not a trivial step to move from thinking to practice. This was emphasised by the speech of Scotland's First Minister, Jack McConnell MSP, on 18 February 2002 when he said "Today's generation of decision makers and politicians, business owners and local leaders in communities right across Scotland are uniquely placed in time. We know we must deal with the legacy of historically unsustainable development. There are wrongs still to be righted." Sustainable development is still most commonly defined in the words of the Brundtland Commission as "development that meets the needs of the present without compromising the ability of future generations to meet their own needs" (World Commission on Environment and Development, 1987). This places a strong emphasis on the importance of inter-generational equity. It implies that a modern society should therefore seek simultaneous growth in economic, social and environmental capital and also ensure that no irreversible environmental damage is passed on to future generations.

It is not surprising that climate change is often cited as a prime example of failures in the past to understand and adopt the principles of sustainable development. The EU's Sustainable Development Strategy (Dunion *et al.*, Chapter 20) and the Sixth Environmental Action Programme (Currie, Chapter 2) both recognise the urgency for remedial action.

The global community must face up to living with some of the impacts of climate change for several centuries to come, whatever actions we take now. Many of the underdeveloped parts of the world will face disproportionately serious consequences without adequate resources to adapt.

Amongst the four chapters in this part of the book, Kerr and Ellis (Chapter 16) summarise the likely future climate scenarios in Scotland and the actions that should be taken to promote adaptation. It is important that land use management provides the flexibility for habitats and species, as far as possible, to migrate and retain viability in a rapidly changing future. Langan *et al.* (Chapter 17) provide a vivid example showing that climate change is already having a measurable impact on Scotland's freshwater habitats. Kerr and Ellis (Chapter 16) also argue that Scotland must make its own equitable contribution to mitigating future problems by reducing emissions of greenhouse gases. They show that appropriate actions, taken within a sustainability framework, can generate multiple benefits.

Another long-term legacy, due to past practices, is the leakage into the environment, and the subsequent accumulation, of a huge range of man-made chemicals. Pugh (Chapter 19) argues that previous practices have been inadequate in preventing potentially damaging chemicals being released and that retrospective risk assessments are progressing only very slowly. Many of these materials underpin our modern lifestyle but a more integrated approach, requiring life cycle analysis of man-made products, will promote an improved holistic quality of life.

It is often argued that biodiversity is the touchstone of sustainable development. Its stabilisation and recovery would be a key test of our commitment to change our social and economic modes. Usher (Chapter 18) looks at the methods by which we should evaluate Scotland's biodiversity and the current mechanisms by which its recovery is promoted. His conclusions are optimistic in that the task has at least started, but there are many future obstacles to be overcome.

These four chapters reveal the apparently Herculean task that faces society in correcting past mistakes. There is no River Alpheus into which we can wash the accumulated pollution in the stable but, as the authors indicate, there are sensible and practical steps which will gradually reverse the damage.

Reference

World Commission on Environment and Development (1987). *Our Common Inheritance*. Oxford University Press, Oxford.

16 MANAGING THE IMPACTS OF CLIMATE CHANGE ON THE NATURAL ENVIRONMENT

Andy Kerr and Noranne Ellis

Summary

1.   Scotland is likely to become warmer, at a faster rate than has been historically observed in Scotland since the last Ice Age, and wetter, particularly in autumn and winter.

2.   Scotland's natural environment will be one of the most difficult sectors to manage with respect to climate impacts. For example, designated sites for nature conservation will be compromised as optimal climatic conditions for habitats and species move north and/or uphill at a rate faster than the capacity of species to migrate.

3.   Managing the adverse effects of climate change ideally requires a strategic approach to rural land use. Policies covering agriculture, forestry and nature conservation should be designed to improve the capacity of land uses to adapt to the impacts of climate change. In particular, habitats and species of nature conservation value need space to move across the landscape.

4.   Whereas adaptation to a changing climate will be necessary, the rate of climate change can be much reduced by measures to reduce human-induced greenhouse gas emissions. Examples of such measures will include the increased use of biomass for heat and electricity generation and enhanced opportunities for sequestering carbon in biomass or soils.

16.1 Introduction

The Scottish landscape reflects the history of glacier inundation in past millennia, producing the familiar topography of mountains and glens, and also the parent material for Scotland's soils. More recently, human influences have interacted with climate, topography, soils, fauna and flora to produce the environment and ecosystems that many seek to protect today.

The last 20 years have seen an internationally concerted attempt through the Intergovernmental Panel on Climate Change to develop the knowledge necessary to tackle the impacts of climate change (Houghton *et al.*, 2001). More recently, work by the UK Climate Impacts Programme (UKCIP) and related work by the Scottish Executive has provided the tools to examine the implications of, and possible responses to, UK climate change (McKenzie Hedger *et al.*, 2000; Kerr *et al.*, 1999; Kerr and McLeod, 2001). This chapter draws heavily on these works.

Concurrently, work through the United Nations Framework Convention on Climate Change (UNFCCC) and, at a national level, the UK Climate Change Programme has focused attention on mechanisms to reduce greenhouse gas emissions. Scotland's rural sector emits a similar quantity of greenhouse gas emissions to the transport sector, so the policy implications for reducing emissions are profound (Scottish Executive, 2000).

This chapter is structured to illustrate briefly the trends in Scottish climate, the sensitivity of the natural environment to these trends, and the prospect for managing climate change in the light of these sensitivities.

16.2 Trends in Scottish climate

16.2.1 Present Scottish climate

Scotland has a cool maritime climate (Tables 16.1 and 16.2), with a pronounced gradient of precipitation across the country from west to east. Stormy weather is not uncommon. In general, water is plentiful, though changes in precipitation across Scotland are now becoming apparent. Although precipitation across the Northern Hemisphere increased by about 1 per cent over the twentieth century (Nicholls *et al.*, 1996), within Scotland it appears to have been greater. For example, by 1993 the two wettest decades on record ended in 1990 and 1992, both of which had about 14 per cent more than the average decadal value (Smith and Werritty, 1994). Both long-term and short-term records show precipitation increasing in the north and west of Scotland, and decreasing in the east and south. Similarly, significant increases have been observed in the spring, autumn and winter in the north and west, while there have been decreases in the east in summer (Mayes, 1996) (Plate 28).

Table 16.1. Historic average summer and winter temperatures for the areas covered by the UKCIP98 Climate Scenarios grid-cells (°C). The summer is taken as the three months June, July and August; the winter as the three months December, January and February.

Region	Summer			Winter		
	1901-1930	1931-1960	1961-90	1901-1930	1931-60	1961-1990
Scotland	12.1	12.4	11.9	2.9	2.6	2.2
Scottish Borders	13.3	13.6	13.3	3.8	3.3	3.0

Table 16.2. Historic average summer and winter precipitation for the areas covered by the UKCIP98 Climate Scenarios grid-cells (mm). The terms 'summer' and 'winter' are defined in Table 16.1.

Region	Summer			Winter		
	1901-1930	1931-1960	1961-90	1901-1930	1931-60	1961-1990
Scotland	284	302	289	434	431	427
Scottish Borders	323	320	307	432	418	413

16.2.2 UK climate scenarios

In 1998 the UKCIP produced a set of national climate change scenarios, termed the UKCIP98 scenarios (Hulme and Jenkins, 1998). These are currently being updated (Hulme *et al.*, 2001). Predicting future climate is difficult because of the complexity and natural variation in climate over a range of time-scales and space-scales, and the ongoing human-induced alteration of the global atmosphere. Since no single climate change scenario can adequately capture the range of possible climate futures, the work described four possible climate futures for the UK from a baseline of the 1961-90 climate averages. These encompass a reasonable range of possible future climates. At present, probabilities cannot be attached to the likelihood of any one of the scenarios. This range of climate futures reflects different assumptions about the direction of future socio-economic change and hence the amount of global greenhouse gas emissions, and about the sensitivity of the global climate to a change in greenhouse gas concentrations.

The climate scenarios are based on a coarse model grid, which does not resolve the characteristically complex landscape or the variations of climate within Scotland. Hence it ignores such existing trends for wetter weather in the west and drier areas in the east.

16.2.3 Future Scottish climate

The UKCIP climate scenarios suggest that Scotland will become warmer over the next century. Average temperatures are likely to rise by between 0.9° and 2.6°C, with relatively more warming in winter than summer (Table 16.3). Annual precipitation is likely to increase by between 3 and 17 per cent by the end of the next century, with autumn and winter seeing the greatest increases. In contrast, spring amounts are expected to be lower with little change in summer (Table 16.4). The intensity of rainfall events is likely to increase, leading to an increased risk of flooding. The scenarios suggest there may be an increase in the frequency of very severe gales but a decrease in the number of gales overall. The water balance is likely to remain favourable, while direct short-wave solar radiation is likely to reduce over the next century because of increased cloud cover. Natural variability of the climate system is likely to modify the magnitude and patterns of these human-induced changes, which makes it difficult to attach high levels of significance to some of these suggested changes.

Table 16.3. The temperature rise from the 1961-90 average in the 'Scotland' grid cell under different climate scenarios (°C). Source: Hulme and Jenkins (1998)

Scenario	2010-2039	2040-2069	2070-2099
Low	+0.4	+0.7	+0.9
Medium-low	+0.8	+1.2	+1.5
Medium-high	+1.1	+1.6	+2.3
High	+1.2	+1.9	+2.6

Table 16.4. The precipitation rise from the 1961-90 average in the 'Scotland' grid cell under different climate scenarios (as a percentage). Source: Hulme and Jenkins (1998)

Scenario	2010-2039	2040-2069	2070-2099
Low	+3	+3	+3
Medium-low	+4	+5	+6
Medium-high	+6	+5	+16
High	+7	+6	+17

16.3 Impacts of climate change

The elements of Scotland's natural environment will be sensitive to the changing climate. Direct effects include flood events, erosion and different responses by species in their distribution, abundance and phenology. Indirect effects occur because of measures taken to protect the existing environment, such as flood defences along coasts and in river floodplains, and secondary effects on species, for instance changes in the nutritional quality of their plant food sources.

16.3.1 Water

The increase in total annual precipitation in Scotland has been associated with an increase in the number of heavy rain events, as well as a greater number of days with rain (Smith and Werritty, 1994). Consequences are rapid stream discharges producing erosion of banks and riverbeds. For example, it is surmised that excessive stream discharges are dislodging spawning grounds of young fish and freshwater pearl mussel (*Margaritifera margaritifera*) beds, particularly in north-west Scotland (e.g. Hastie *et al.*, 2001).

Whilst extremes in stream flow may be considered detrimental in many cases, higher levels of precipitation in some areas can dilute concentrations of pollutants in water courses, such as was observed in the Clyde at the end of the twentieth century (Curran, 1998). However, dissolved organic carbon (DOC) in upland freshwaters across the UK increased by 65 per cent between 1989 and 2001; this has been associated with an increase of temperature of $0.6^{\circ}C$ (Freeman *et al.*, 2001).

16.3.2 Soils

Altered seasonal precipitation patterns are now believed to be affecting the structure of upland peatlands across central and northern Scotland. Overgrazing was once a factor causing erosion through denudation of vegetation, but has been reduced. In areas where few sheep have been grazed, however, gullying and erosion have markedly increased by the end of the twentieth century. It is believed that drier summers followed by heavy rain events are the cause (Plate 28). This loss of habitat for associated plant, invertebrate and bird species is concurrent with increasing concentrations of DOC in upland streams, as described by Freeman *et al.* (2001).

Peatlands cover about 17 per cent of Scotland's area (M. Shewry, pers. comm., using data from MLURI, 1993) and are a characteristic feature of the Scottish landscape. These peat accumulations store significant quantities of carbon, so its loss as DOC and oxidation to carbon dioxide is of concern. Remediation, however, is not likely to be easy.

16.3.3 Biodiversity

Changes in temperature and precipitation patterns markedly affect species. Temperature usually determines the limits of a species' distribution by governing whether a physiological process can occur (such as pollen tube growth) or determining water availability (freezing temperatures can also cause drought stress). Temperature also plays a part in regulating lifecycle processes such as dormancy, leafburst, hibernation or egg-laying. Precipitation has a major influence on vegetation, high rainfall encouraging peatland or forest habitats, according to the temperature, whilst areas of low water availability are associated with species adapted to water stress. The volume and intensity of seasonal precipitation can also affect the physical structure (e.g. erosion) and chemical quality (e.g. pollution content) of freshwater and terrestrial habitats.

Species have a limited ability to adapt to multiple changes in their environment. Their response to change is mainly through alterations in distribution determined by physiological requirements rather than adaptation of long-established genetic characteristics. For example, mobile species like southern species of butterflies (see Usher, Chapter 18) and birds are now being seen in southern Scotland (e.g. brimstone butterfly (*Gonepteryx rhamni*) and nuthatch (*Sitta europaea*)), yet work to determine the potential for native trees of birch to alter the timing of their budburst in spring indicated that their response was slower than the rate of temperature rise (Billingham and Pelham, 1991).

Changes associated with climate change are manifold. There are not only alterations in both precipitation and temperature patterns and extreme weather events, but increases in atmospheric levels of carbon dioxide which encourage vegetative productivity, and increases in deposition and atmospheric concentrations of other pollutants such as nitrogen compounds and ozone, the effects of which are outlined in Fowler *et al.* (Chapter 7). Predicting the responses to climatic changes by ecosystems and/or species is therefore difficult, particularly so because of the individualistic responses by species. For example, northern species may retreat poleward whilst southern species expand northwards, but each species will shift its range limits at different rates.

Research has, thus far, therefore concentrated on determining the changes in distribution of different species under varying future climatic scenarios, e.g. Hill *et al.* (1999), Hossell *et al.* (2000) and Harrison *et al.* (2001). However, a number of species are observed to be entering spring-time events earlier in the year, thereby affecting inter-species relationships (such as predator-prey, flower and pollinator) which cannot be ignored (Table 16.5). Differential rates of response to shifts in climate and to earlier spring-time cues may cause the decline of species that are reliant on a prey food source being available at the time of the production of their young; for example, capercaillie (*Tetrao urogallus*) chicks hatching after peak emergence of their invertebrate food supply.

The difference in rates of dispersal, death and displacement suggest that new assemblies of species will be created. The complexity of relationships between species therefore makes it difficult to predict some of the changes in biodiversity that will result from climate

Table 16.5. Examples of earlier springtime events in Britain related to an increase of 1°C in temperature.

Springtime event	Days earlier/1 °C	Source
Trees in leaf	5-7	Sparks and Carey (1995)
Robins (*Erithacus rubecula*) and chaffinches (*Fringilla coelebs*) laying eggs	3 and 2 respectively	Crick (1999)
Swallows (*Hirundo rustica*) arriving in Britain	2-3	Sparks and Loxton (1999)
Springtime arrival of newts (*Triturus* spp.) to ponds	9-10	Beebee (1995)
First flights of the butterflies: painted lady (*Vanessa cardui*), small copper (*Lycaena phlaeas*) and orange tip (*Anthocharis cardamines*)	10, 9 and 6 respectively	Sparks and Yates (1997)

change. Within Scotland, biodiversity may increase as species enter from the south. However, a number of 'characteristically Scottish' species (e.g. Scottish primrose (*Primula scotica*), capercaillie and twinflower (*Linnaea borealis*)) are at the southern edges of their ranges and might be lost from Scotland (Harrison *et al.*, 2001).

16.3.4 Managed resources

Predicting the impacts of climate change on fisheries is complex. Fish are sensitive to many attributes of the physical and biological environment that may be influenced by the changing climate. The sensitivity to these attributes depends on the fish species and on the particular stage of their life cycle (Kerr *et al.*, 1999). At a local fisheries level, Parry (2000) reports that short-term changes in the climate are likely to result in both local changes in species composition and biodiversity, and local changes in population levels and in fisheries production. Changes in migration patterns and species movements are easier to achieve in the marine environment than in small lakes and rivers, so freshwater fisheries are, in general, more vulnerable than marine fisheries to the changing climate. Future impacts of climate on fisheries are uncertain because of the interdependence of factors such as over-fishing and other environmental pressures, including the introduction of many non-native species and the impacts of pollution.

In theory, warmer temperatures and higher atmospheric carbon dioxide concentrations will be beneficial to agriculture in northern Europe, though in Scotland increasing rainfall and less solar radiation may limit or negate any benefits. The former UK Ministry of Agriculture, Fisheries and Food reviewed the impact of climate change on UK agriculture and suggested (Muriel *et al.*, 2000) that

- the range of crops will move northward;
- high quality horticultural crops are more susceptible to changing conditions than arable crops, particularly if water availability becomes a problem;
- the relative suitability of different types of livestock is unlikely to change significantly;

- the potential for soils to support agriculture will be strongly influenced by changes in soil water balance;
- there will be increasing problems of vehicular access in waterlogged soils; and
- pests and diseases will change.

Kerr *et al.* (1999) argued that the key sensitivity of the agricultural system is to an increase in the variability of Scotland's climate, in addition to indirect factors such as the difficulty of access to waterlogged fields. The wet autumn of 2000 provided evidence of how climate impacts could affect business profitability.

Parry (2000) noted that most common tree species have a sufficiently large genetic variability to acclimatise to the forecast average changes in temperature and precipitation, but that changes in frequency of extreme events may cause problems. Forestry Commission (2000) provided advice on the implications of climate impacts for forestry. For forests, it is anticipated that

- rising atmospheric carbon dioxide concentrations are likely to lead to increasing tree growth rates;
- warmer temperatures mean buds are likely to break earlier in the year for most species, although for some budburst may be delayed after milder winters (Murray *et al.*, 1989);
- the continuing presence of late frosts may increase frost damage;
- warmer winters are likely to allow the survival of southern pests and pathogens;
- the expected increase in occurrence of storms may make woodlands more vulnerable to wind damage; and
- wood quality could be affected by both the changing climate and the rising carbon dioxide concentrations, with some changes being detrimental, and some beneficial.

16.4 Prospects for managing climate change in Scotland

16.4.1 Managing climate risk

Most natural systems are sensitive to the changing climate. The extent to which these systems are vulnerable depends on the magnitude of the change and their capacity to adapt, which is determined largely by the framework for managing Scotland's rural environment. The four key themes for managing climate risk are (McCarthy *et al.*, 2001) vulnerability to change being determined by the frequency and magnitude of extreme events; adapting to current climate risk being generally consistent with adapting to future changes; the capacity to adapt varying by region and through time; and enhancing the capacity to adapt being necessary to reduce vulnerability.

Policies for adapting to climate change must be integrated into an existing, often complex, policy framework with multiple drivers and demands on resources. The four core objectives for adapting to climate change, identified by Klein and Tol (1997), included increasing the flexibility of vulnerable managed systems; enhancing the adaptability of vulnerable natural systems, such as reducing non-climatic stresses; reversing existing bad practice; and improving societal awareness and preparedness. The extent to which such options can be undertaken in Scotland will reflect the existing legislative and management frameworks. They illuminate the importance of ensuring that management frameworks are predicated on enhancing the capacity to adapt to change.

The process of managing climate change must operate within the limits of scientific certainty about future climate and socio-economic change. Organisations will never have 'enough' information to take a decision without uncertainty - increasing precision of climate forecasting will not solve this problem. In this sense, climate adaptation strategies are simply a form of risk management.

16.4.2 Managing forestry

In the context of climate change, forestry provides two key roles. The first is providing low carbon sources of energy and both consumer and business products, such as construction materials. The second is sequestering carbon. By their nature, forest rotations are managed over long time-scales so an awareness of the likely climate impacts is important. These impacts are being built into the existing management systems. Perhaps most importantly, integrating forestry policy into a more sustainable land use policy is crucial for allowing the different ecosystems the flexibility to adapt to the changing climate. Changes in the subsidy structure for agricultural produce are likely to affect the management of the forest estate markedly over the next generation. A potential adaptation strategy needs to build in the changing framework in which forestry is undertaken in Scotland.

The development of an implicit cost of carbon dioxide emissions arising from Government policies to mitigate greenhouse gas emissions provides a driver for developing substantially more bio-energy from wood products, primarily for heating purposes, and harvested wood products, such as construction materials. The UK Climate Change Programme also makes clear the important role of forestry in protecting and enhancing carbon sinks, both through the Government's commitment to expand the forest estate in Scotland and through private initiatives and carbon offset schemes (DETR, 2000). The UK Government calculates that afforestation since 1990 will contribute a reduction of over 2.2 million t of CO_2 towards its Kyoto target between 2008 and 2012.

16.4.3 Managing agriculture

The changing climate is but one of many drivers of change in the agricultural sector. The adaptation priority is to ensure that the ongoing transformation in the industry builds in the flexibility necessary to cope with the changing climate and to take advantage of economic opportunities associated with mitigating emissions.

Policies for adapting to climate change must provide the flexibility for farmers to adapt their land use and farming systems whilst working with the practical implications of a changing climate. At present in Scotland, waterlogged fields appear to provide one of the biggest business risks from climate change. The inherent variability of Scotland's climate means that events such as the timing of planting and harvesting are likely to change incrementally year by year. Opportunities for Scottish agriculture inevitably depend on farm type and locality. With the increasing divergence in climate between Scotland and south-east England, it is clear that use of crop research from southern England will have less utility in future. One consequence of the drive for more flexibility in the agricultural sector, coupled to tighter environmental obligations, will be the blurring, and perhaps in the longer-term the removal, of the historic distinction between forestry, agricultural and nature conservation policy.

The Climate Change Programme is likely to be a driver of land use change in the UK, and Scotland has particular opportunities for enhancing its carbon sequestration. With a renewable energy target of 17 to 18 per cent by 2010, Scotland would appear to be an ideal location for the development of energy crops, though the development of associated biomass infrastructure is by no means certain and maximum benefit is only obtained in local markets.

16.4.4 Managing fisheries

Climate change is one of many drivers of change in Scotland's fisheries. Change will require a move away from single species resource assessment towards a proper ecosystem approach to sustainable fisheries management, both offshore and in fresh waters. A range of legislative mechanisms is in place at both European and Scottish levels to conserve marine and freshwater fish stocks and the habitats on which they depend. Declines in Atlantic salmon (*Salmo salar*) and brown trout (*Salmo trutta*) catches in Scotland in recent years, and of marine species around Scotland such as haddock (*Melanogrammus aeglefinus*) and cod (*Gadus morhua*), highlight the difficulties in formulating policies that provide adequate protection for these species. A cod recovery operation is now in place. The Salmon Conservation (Scotland) Act was brought into force in April 2001 in an attempt to reduce exploitation of wild stocks of salmon following record low catches in 1999. The measures that are envisaged under the new Act will help to reduce local exploitation of stocks and encourage sustainable management of fisheries.

Climate change is likely to worsen an already dire situation, because of the lack of flexibility both within the marine policy framework and by the users and consumers of the resources. Parry (2000) argued that adaptive management plans are required at several levels, including local, regional, national and EU, in order to address resource allocations and reduce the likely conflict between users of the resource. In the short-term, Parry (2000) suggested moving away from single-species stock assessment and allocations towards species groups or assemblages in order to increase flexibility. The Water Framework Directive provides one opportunity to integrate the work undertaken by many different agencies and private owners. It also provides the strategic context in which to reduce the non-climatic stresses on Scotland's freshwater fisheries.

16.4.5 Managing biodiversity

There are a number of possible management responses to climate-induced changes in biodiversity, although each will be difficult to implement. Habitats can be managed in an attempt to maintain them in their current condition despite their natural response to climate change or natural responses can be allowed to occur. For species, attempts can be made to control competitors, translocate threatened species to more suitable areas, or create new habitats. Much more research will be needed to allow prioritisation of these management responses, and assess their feasibility and effectiveness.

The historical approach to nature conservation within the UK has been to protect and designate sites, such as Sites of Special Scientific Interest (SSSIs), harbouring specific habitats and/or species of conservation interest. Since the mid-1980s, a series of agri-environmental schemes has sought to integrate land used to produce commercial goods with that used for nature conservation purposes. Although direct conservation objectives are not explicit within agri-environmental schemes, they aim to encourage greater biodiversity through more sensitive management (the Rural Stewardship Scheme in

Scotland explicitly makes this link). In principle, the EC Habitats Directive has married conservation on sites with that in the wider countryside by directing that its listed habitats and species be maintained at 'favourable conservation status' across the EU.

At the individual site level, the obligation to avoid deterioration of qualifying habitats and species may be difficult to achieve with warming temperatures encouraging northward shifts of species' ranges, potentially causing redundancies of some sites designated for their protection. Overall, the objective of favourable conservation status may still be possible if such changes in distribution and range are accepted.

There is also a need to reconsider conservation objectives of designated sites and the Biodiversity Action Plans produced in response to the UK signing the Convention on Biological Diversity. This would need to be done using assessments of potential adjustments in the rate of change in distributional limits and species' sensitivity under potential future climate scenarios. It may be necessary to reconsider the definition of habitat types as defined within the Habitats Directive and the Biodiversity Action Plans to ensure that transitional states of habitat are recognised. Modelling potential changes in the status of Europe-wide habitats and species is clearly important to enable the appropriate decisions to be made.

Monitoring at strategic locations is important to validate models, both of predictions of meteorological conditions and ecosystem responses. Strategic locations include sensitive and vulnerable habitats or species, and/or where climate change is most readily detected. The UK Environmental Change Network (Sykes and Lane, 1996) provides a suitable template for the development of such monitoring schemes.

The current rate of climate change exceeds the rate of historical distributional migration and dispersal capabilities. To keep pace with current movements of isotherms, species would need to move north by 240 to 400 km, or uphill by 200 to 275 m for each rise of 1°C. Historic rates of movement north for tree species have been in the order 20 to 80 km per century, which equates to a rise of temperature of only 0.1° to 0.4°C per century. This compares to the forecast rate of 1.5° to 5.8°C for this century. There will therefore be a need to aid the dispersal of some species such as through the provision of a strategic network of sites like the Natura 2000 network. However, there would need to be a large number of sites to be effective even if strategically allocated land is left available for the species, although this is being done for areas of coastal realignment (or managed retreat) around Scotland. However, habitats and species that depend on a specific geology which is not widespread (e.g. limestone) will lose out. Assisted dispersal through translocation may therefore be necessary.

16.5 Conclusions

There are already, and will continue to be, disruptions in the biological, physical and chemical structures of ecosystems. This will lead to the loss of some species and changes in key habitats. The current rate of climate change is large in comparison to historical records and unfolds against the background of changing air chemistry.

One consequence of the drive for more flexibility in the rural sector as a means of adapting to climate change, coupled to tighter environmental obligations, will be the blurring and perhaps in the longer-term the removal of the historic distinction between forestry, agricultural and nature conservation policy. Changes in land use policies are inevitable because of climate mitigation policies. The existing framework already creates incentives to encourage the use of renewable resources, such as biomass for energy production and, in future, for consumer end-use products. There are also incentives for a reduction in land use emissions, by reducing fertiliser use or by protecting the characteristically carbon-rich Scottish soils (i.e. peat). There is the potential for the sequestering of carbon through sustainable forestry. However, use of land for renewable energy sources, such as wind power, is likely to increase, especially over the next decade or two.

References

Beebee, T. (1995). Amphibian breeding and climate. *Nature,* **374**, 210-220.

Billingham, H.L. and Pelham, J. (1991). Genetic variation in the date of budburst in Scottish birch populations: implications for climate change. *Functional Ecology,* **5**, 403-409.

Crick, H.Q.P. (1999). Egg laying dates of birds. In *Indicators of Climate Change in the UK,* ed. by M.G.R. Cannell, J.P. Palutikof and T.H. Sparks. Department of the Environment, Transport and the Regions, Wetherby. pp. 64-65.

Curran, J. (1998). Climate change: the perspective of the Scottish Environment Protection Agency. In *Climate Change Impacts in Scotland: Workshop report.* Organised by The Scottish Office and the UK Climate Impacts, Edinburgh, September 1998. pp. 4-5.

DETR (2000). *UK Climate Change Programme.* Department of the Environment, Transport and the Regions, London.

Forestry Commission (2000). *Information Note 31. Climate Change: Implications for Forestry in Britain.* Forestry Commission, Edinburgh.

Freeman, C., Evans, C.D., Monteith, D.T., Reynolds, B. and Fenner, N. (2001). Export of organic carbon from peat soils. *Nature,* **412**, 785.

Harrison, P.A., Berry, R.M. and Dawson, T.E. (2001). *Climate Change and Nature Conservation in Britain and Ireland: Modelling Natural Resource Responses to Climate Change (the MONARCH Project).* United Kingdom Climate Impacts Programme, Oxford.

Hastie, L.C., Boon, P.J., Young, M.R. and Way, S. (2001). The effects of a major flood on an endangered freshwater mussel population. *Biological Conservation,* **98**, 107-115.

Hill, M.O., Downing, T.E., Berry, P.M., Coppins. B.J., Hammond, P.S., Marquiss, M., Roy, D.B., Telfer, M.G. and Welch, D. (1999). Climate changes and Scotland's natural heritage: an environmental audit. *Scottish Natural Heritage Research, Survey and Monitoring Report* No. 132.

Hossell, J.E., Briggs, B. and Hepburn, I. (2000). *Climate Change and UK Nature Conservation: A Review of the Impact of Climate Change on UK Species and Habitat Conservation Policy.* Department of the Environment, Transport and the Regions, London.

Houghton, J.T., Ding, Y., Griggs, D.J., Noguer, M., van der Linden, P.J., Dai, X., Maskell, K. and Johnson, C.A. (eds.) (2001). *Climate Change 2001: The Scientific Basis. Contribution of Working Group I to the Third Assessment Report of the Intergovernmental Panel on Climate Change.* Cambridge University Press, Cambridge.

Hulme, M. and Jenkins G.J. (1998). *Climate change scenarios for the UK: scientific report, UKCIP Technical Report No. 1.* Climatic Research Unit, Norwich.

Hulme, M., Crossley, J. and Xianfu, L. (2001). *An exploration of regional climate change scenarios for Scotland.* Scottish Executive Central Research Unit, Edinburgh.

Kerr, A. and McLeod, A. (2001). *Potential Adaptation Strategies for Climate Change in Scotland.* Scottish Executive Central Research Unit, Edinburgh.

Kerr, A., Shackley, S., Milne, R. and Allen, S. (1999). *Climate Change: Scottish Implications Scoping Study.* Scottish Office Central Research Unit, Edinburgh.

Klein, R.J.T. and Tol, R.S.J. (1997). *Adaptation to Climate Change: Options and Technologies. An Overview Paper.* Institute for Environmental Studies Publication, Vrije Universiteit, Amsterdam.

Macaulay Land Use Research Institute (1993). *The Land Cover of Scotland 1988: Main Report.* MLURI, Aberdeen.

Mayes, J. (1996). Spatial and temporal fluctuations of monthly rainfall in the British Isles and variations in the mid-latitude westerly circulation. *International Journal of Climatology,* **16**, 585-596.

McCarthy, J.J., Canziani, O.F., Leary, N.A., Dokken, D.J. and White, K.S. (eds) (2001). *Climate Change 2001: Impacts, Adaptation, and Vulnerability. Contribution of Working Group II to the Third Assessment Report of the Intergovernmental Panel on Climate Change.* Cambridge University Press, Cambridge.

McKenzie Hedger, M., Gawith, M., Brown I., Connell, R. and Downing, T.E. (eds.) (2000). *Climate change: Assessing the impacts – identifying the responses. The first three years of the UK Climate Impacts Programme..* UK Climate Impacts Programme and Department of the Environment, Transport and the Regions, Oxford.

Muriel, P., Downing, T., Hulme, M., Harrington, R., Lawlor, D., Wurr, D., Atkinson, C.J., Cookshull, K.E., Taylor, D.R., Richards, A.T., Parsons, D.J., Hillerton, J.E., Parry, M.L., Jarvis, S.C., Weatherhead, K. and Jenkins, G. (2000). *Climate Change and Agriculture in the UK.* Ministry of Agriculture, Fisheries and Food, London.

Murray, M.B., Cannell, M.G.R. and Smith, R.I. (1989). Date of budburst of fifteen tree species in Britain following climatic change. *Journal of Applied Ecology,* **26**, 693-700.

Nicholls, N., Gruza, G.V., Jousel, J., Karl, T.R., Ogallo, L.A. and Parker, D.E. (1996). Observed climate variability and change. In *Climate Change 1995. The Science of Climate Change,* ed. by J.T. Houghton, L.G. Meiro Filho, B.A. Callander, N. Harris, A. Kattenberg and K. Maskell. Cambridge University Press, Cambridge. pp. 137-181.

Parry, M.L. (ed.) (2000). *Assessment of Potential Effects and Adaptations for Climate Change in Europe: The Europe Acacia Project.* Jackson Environment Institute, University of East Anglia, Norwich.

Scottish Executive (2000). *Scottish Climate Change Programme.* Scottish Executive, Edinburgh.

Smith, K. and Werritty, A. (1994). Hydroclimatic and water management functions of Scottish hydro-electric plc. Unpublished report.

Sparks, T.H. and Carey, P.D. (1995). The responses of species to climate over two centuries: an analysis of the Marsham phenological record, 1736-1947. *Journal of Ecology,* **83**, 321-329.

Sparks, T.H. and Loxton, R.G. (1999). Arrival date of the swallow. In *Indicators of Climate Change in the UK,* ed. by M.G.R. Cannell, J.P. Palutikof and T.H. Sparks. Department of the Environment, Transport and the Regions, Wetherby. pp. 58-59.

Sparks, T.H. and Yates, T. (1997). The effect of spring temperature on the appearance dates of British butterflies, 1883-1993. *Ecography,* **20**, 368-374.

Sykes, J.M. and Lane, A.M.J. (1996). *The United Kingdom Environmental Change Network: protocols for standard measurements at terrestrial sites.* The Stationery Office, London.

17 THE POTENTIAL IMPACT OF CLIMATE CHANGE ON THE HYDROTHERMAL REGIME OF SELECTED RIVERS DRAINING THE CAIRNGORMS

S.J. Langan, L. Johnston, M. Donaghy and A. Youngson

Summary

1.   Both flow and temperature variation for rivers draining the Cairngorm massif reflect the seasonal pattern in precipitation and radiation budget inputs.
2.   In general terms the rivers selected for the study vary in a synchronous manner.
3.   In the Girnock, a tributary of the River Dee, there is a suggestion that winter and spring maximum and spring mean temperatures have increased over the 32 years of record.
4.   The most plausible explanation for this is the greater variability in the seasonal snowpack, brought about by changes in the prevailing climate.

17.1 Introduction

The timing and form of precipitation provides the driving variable determining the temporal differences in hydrological response of rivers. In mountainous areas, such as the Cairngorms, both seasonal and short term snow accumulation and ablation provide a key role in determining the nature of the hydrological regime of the rivers draining the region (Langan *et al.*, 1997). Further differences in the hydrological response of rivers occur as a result of flow routing through catchment soils and underlying geology. These differences in turn may have important consequences for the ecology that the rivers can support. Similarly the variation in a stream's thermal regime may have important consequences for changes in water quality, both chemical and ecological, of the stream and also for water resources further downstream. The causes of such variation can be both spatial and temporal. In general terms these can be related to the energy budget and thermal capacity of a water body.

This chapter aims to introduce the available flow and temperature records for a number of rivers draining the Cairngorms. It is only by establishing the nature of recent changes and variations in both flow and temperature that we will be able to model and predict future implications of climate change for the ecology and geochemistry of such systems.

17.2 The study area

Nine catchments that drain the Cairngorm massif in north-east Scotland and encompass a range of environmental attributes, such as aspect and altitude, have been established as sites for the present study. The characteristics of each catchment are given in Table 17.1. The Girnock catchment has been instrumented since 1968. All of the other sites were established for flow measurement in the late 1980s and temperature measurement in the last two years. All of the sites form part of SEPA's secondary flow gauging network. Flows at

Table 17.1. Summary catchment characteristics and flow and temperature records for the year from August 2000 to July 2001.

	Catchment Area (km²)	Dominant land cover	Altitude (m) Min	Max	Mean	Flow (Cumecs) Min	Max	Mean	Temperature (°C) Min	Max	Mean
Gairn	146	Heather moorland/rough grassland	229	1160	557	0.3	42.0	4.8	-0.6	18.4	7.2
Shee	143	Heather moorland/montane	326	1060	637	1.6	105.5	14.8	-0.4	17.5	7.1
Girnock	30	Heather moorland	250	860	505	0.1	8.3	0.8	-0.6	18.1	7.0
Tilt	166	Heather moorland/peatland	234	1120	674	1.0	41.6	8.5	-1.2	18.9	7.0
Don	101	Heather moorland	405	829	582	1.0	58.5	3.8	0.4	17.1	6.9
Feshie	230	Heather moorland/peatland	234	1347	617	1.5	55.9	7.8	-0.2	15.9	6.3
Nethy	38	Heather moorland	230	1228	489	0.7	4.6	1.1	0.0	14.1	6.1
Dee	293	Heather moorland	326	1442	683	2.3	72.6	12.9	-0.4	15.9	5.6
Avon	543	Heather moorland/peatland	303	1292	681	4.5	260.4	17.0	-1.5	15.7	5.3

the sites are computed from the continuous measurement of stage height on a natural rated reach of the stream. Temperature measurements are made on an hourly basis using Tiny Talk data loggers that are periodically downloaded to a computer for analysis and data archiving.

17.3 Results

Figure 17.1 shows a typical annual flow record for the study catchments. In common with other stream hydrographs, the data demonstrate three response modes. First, there is a rapid response to precipitation events which generate peak discharges. Typically these occur over three to seven days in the catchments studied. As the peak discharges recede, on the recession limb, there is the second response type that is typically a slower more damped response. This can last up to several weeks or longer. Finally, at a seasonal level there is a baseflow component derived from groundwater. During the early part of the summer this is augmented by the melting snowpack. Flows tend to be at their lowest during the summer months, which are associated with lower rainfall and higher rates of evapotranspiration caused by higher radiation. Maximum peak flows are commonly associated with the onset of autumn rains and later in the winter and spring, when they are associated with rain falling and melting snow already lying on the catchment.

Table 17.1 shows the highest mean flows are generated at the Avon, Shee and Dee sites, reflecting a combination of catchment size and higher altitude. In other respects such as

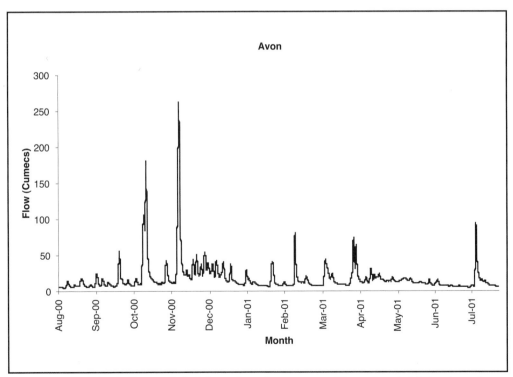

Figure 17.1. Variation in flows typical of the study catchments over a 12 month period (River Avon, August 2000 to July 2001). The unit of measurement for flow is expressed as a volume leaving the catchment in the river per unit time, cumecs (m³ per second).

timing and flow duration there is little systematic variation between the catchments. Over the relatively short duration of the records there is no evidence of a change in the flow regimes. Modelling of flows by Dunn *et al.* (2001) on the Dee suggested that inter-annual variations on a seasonal basis could be explained by the variation in the annual snow-pack characteristics. This suggests that if winter precipitation in the region changes (such as a higher incidence of rain and less snow) there will be a change in the hydrological regimes of these rivers.

Temperature variations at the site are dominated by the solar energy inputs. Table 17.1 suggests that on the basis of data collected over the last two years the rivers show the mean annual temperature to vary between 5.3°C (the Avon) and 7.2°C (the Gairn). The minimum temperatures all show that the monitoring sites where temperature is measured become iced up for periods during the winter. The River Nethy has the lowest maximum and range of temperature and also shows the highest proportion (24 per cent) of the mean flow to maximum flow. This suggests that the River Nethy may have a larger component of groundwater that maintains a more even temperature distribution through time compared to surface waters. The longest record for the sites monitored is that of the Girnock Burn, a westerly tributary of the River Dee in Aberdeenshire. An updated analysis of the data collected since 1968, previously reported by Langan *et al.* (2001), suggested that over the last 32 years there has been a change in the temperature regimes, towards higher temperatures associated with winter and spring, as described by mean and maximum seasonal temperatures. This is shown in Figure 17.2. Over the same period of record there was no change in either annual temperatures or the annual flow or seasonal flow distributions.

17.4 Discussion and conclusion

Rivers draining the Cairngorms are the headwater catchments for some of Scotland's and the UK's largest rivers, with the range and type of ecology within the rivers also being of international importance. Further, any change to the hydrothermal regime of these rivers is likely to have an influence far beyond the Cairngorms biota. For example, one species likely to be affected is the Atlantic salmon, *Salmo salar*. Amongst the populations of salmon in rivers draining the Cairngorms there is a unique component referred to as spring salmon. In recent years, this component has exhibited a decline in the numbers of returning adults. The Girnock study shows that the major changes in the temperature regime have occurred in winter and spring. Some important events in a salmon's life cycle occur in these periods and these stages are likely to be affected by the changes in the hydrothermal regime. For example, the hatch and emergence of alevins from redds occur in spring. Also the subsequent growth and survival, and the timing of the smolt migration, will all be strongly influenced by a river's hydrothermal regime.

The original monitoring network has been broadened as described in this paper. This is to examine if there is a regional change in the hydrothermal regime of the Cairngorm rivers and, if there is, whether it occurs in a synchronous manner across all catchments. Further analysis of the data generated, coupled with information on salmon growth and smolting, is currently in progress. This analysis, together with continued monitoring of the range of sites, should allow a more in-depth analysis and modelling of the spatial and temporal changes in both temperature and flow regimes in response to changes in climate.

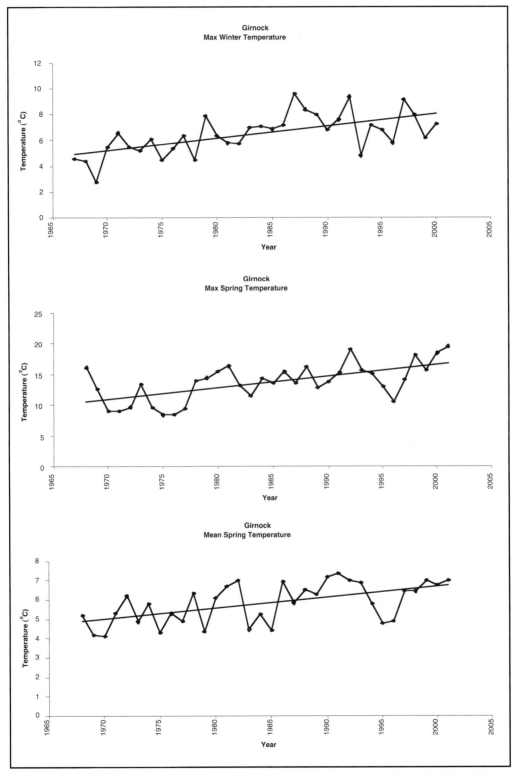

Figure 17.2 Variation in river water temperature indices at the Girnock, north-east Scotland, 1968 to 2000.

Acknowledgement

The authors are indebted to Derek Fraser and David Faichney of SEPA for their help in providing the flow records for the sites.

References

Dunn, S.M., Langan, S.J. and Colohan, R. (2001). The impact of variable snowpack accumulation on a major Scottish water resource. *Science of the Total Environment*, **265**, 181-194.

Langan, S.J., Wade, A.J., Smart, R., Edwards, A.C., Soulsby, C., Billett, M.F., Jarvie, H.P., Cresser, M.S., Owen, R. and Ferrier, R.C. (1997). The prediction and management of water quality in a relatively unpolluted catchment: current issues and experimental approaches. *Science of the Total Environment*, **194/195**, 419-435.

Langan, S.J., Johnston, L., Youngson, A.F., Soulsby, C., Donoghy M and Hay, D. (2001). Variation in an upland stream water temperatures over thirty years. *Science of the Total Environment*, **265**, 195-207.

18 Scotland's Biodiversity: Trends, Changing Perceptions and Planning for Action

Michael B. Usher

Summary

1.   Counting the number of species in Scotland, about 90,000, is not a sensitive measure of biodiversity trends.

2.   Two case studies explore trends in abundance and distribution of butterfly and bird species. Butterfly data are predominantly focused on geographical distribution, whereas bird data are more strongly focused on population size.

3.   Non-native species should not be included in estimates of biodiversity. The 10:10 rule, whereby 10 per cent of introduced species become established and 10 per cent of these become pests, is supported by plant data but not by animal data.

4.   Good progress has been made on the establishment of infrastructures associated with the Habitat, Species and Local Biodiversity Action Plans. However, it is not so clear that equivalent progress has been made on implementing the actions and achieving the targets.

5.   Habitats continue to be fragmented and species isolated into metapopulations. The climate appears to be becoming warmer and wetter. The implications of these changes for Scotland's biodiversity are discussed.

18.1 Introduction

The review of Scotland's biodiversity by Fleming *et al.* (1997) provided an insight into the species and communities that existed towards the end of the twentieth century. It did not, however, attempt to provide any kind of 'baseline' against which changes could be measured. It concentrated primarily on the diversity of species, with relatively little attention to genetic variation within species, an element of biodiversity that is very difficult to assess. It did, however, take a wider view of biodiversity, setting it into the context of the sustainable management of all of Scotland's resources.

The aim of this chapter is not to update the Fleming *et al.* (1997) review, but to assess some of the developments of the last decade. In spring 1996 the Scottish Biodiversity Group (SBG) was established to take forward the work of the UK's Biodiversity Action Plan (Anon., 1994) in Scotland. It is probably too early to ascertain if the SBG has had an impact, but at least some of the actions and activities under its aegis can be reviewed. It is also too early to detect trends in the last five years: a longer period of time is needed. However, questions can be asked about what has happened and whether the detection of trends will be easier in the future.

A difficult question to answer was 'how many species are there in Scotland?'. An attempt to answer it (Usher, 1997) estimated the total as approaching 90,000, with c. 50,400 on land and in freshwater environments and c. 39,200 in the seas around Scotland. Although there have been no subsequent refinements to these estimates, increased knowledge of the ubiquity of the protozoa (Finlay and Maberley, 2000) implies that perhaps these totals, particularly that for the marine environment, could be reduced, although new research in the deep sea may increase the marine proportion (Priede, 2001). There is also continued speculation about the global species richness of free-living bacteria, with a suggestion that the number of species might only be moderate (Finlay and Clarke, 1999).

Thus, until a better estimate can be derived, the total number of species in Scotland stands at about 90,000. Of this total, 49.2 per cent are viruses and single celled organisms, about which there is limited taxonomic understanding. About 21.3 per cent are fungi, algae and bryophytes and about 27.6 per cent are invertebrate animals; amongst these there are still many taxonomic uncertainties, and essentially only very limited monitoring (except for the butterflies). That leaves a mere 1.2 per cent which are the vascular plants and 0.7 per cent which are vertebrates; it is amongst these groups that the best data on geographical range, population size, extinction, and colonization exist.

There is, therefore, very unlikely to be any significant change in Scotland's species richness due to the arrival of new species or the extinction of existing species over the next century. Numerical changes are more likely to come about by increased research on the less well-known groups, by taxonomic advances, and by a greater understanding of what is meant by the concept of a species in the viruses, bacteria of all kinds and protozoa. Understanding change in Scotland's species richness will inevitably rest upon a knowledge of just a very few per cent of the species for which time-series data have been collected, and for which distribution maps at more than one time have been prepared.

However, the Biodiversity Action Plan process has attempted to explore some of the lesser known groups. Plans have been published for 226 species that occur, or have occurred, in Scotland (Usher, 2000a). An analysis of the plans shows that none has been prepared for the single celled organisms, most of which are poorly known. Comparison of the species richness of the taxonomic groups with the species for which Species Action Plans have been published (Table 18.1) demonstrates the preponderance of plans for both the vertebrate animals and the vascular plants.

Table 18.1. A comparison of the contribution of various taxonomic groups to the overall species richness of Scotland with the number of species included in Species Action Plans (SAPs). The data for the estimated number of species in Scotland are taken from Usher (1997), and the statistics for numbers of species occurring in Scotland with SAPs from Usher (2000a). The table excludes the estimated 44,100 species of viruses, bacteria and protozoa.

Taxonomic group	Estimated no. of species in Scotland	Percentage of total species richness	No. of species with SAPs	Percentage of plans
Fungi, algae and bryophytes	19,069	41.9	87	33.6
Vascular plants	1,080	2.4	41	15.8
Marine invertebrates	5,527	12.1	13	5.0
Terrestrial and freshwater invertebrates	19,184	42.1	61	23.6
Marine vertebrates	349	0.8	28	10.8
Terrestrial and freshwater vertebrates	310	0.7	29	11.2
Totals	45,519	100.0	259	100.0

The species richness of Scotland is just one aspect of Scotland's biodiversity. Trends will be reviewed in the next section, followed by an analysis of successes and failures in the implementation of the Action Plans. The chapter will be concluded with a section that looks to the future, identifying pressures on biodiversity and some of the possible responses.

18.2 Case studies

18.2.1 Scotland's changing butterflies

Scotland has 28 resident species of butterflies (Insecta: Lepidoptera), but it is likely that this number could be as large as 32 by the middle of this decade (Table 18.2). An intensive survey of butterflies was carried out between 1995 and 1999, and the results, compared with previous surveys, were published in Asher *et al.* (2001). Interpretations of the results are contained in Anon. (2001a) and Shaw (2001), though the data in Table 18.2 differ slightly from those previously published interpretations since they focus on Scotland rather than the whole of Britain and Ireland.

Table 18.2. A re-interpretation of the changing distributional ranges of butterflies in Scotland, based on the data in Asher *et al.* (2001).

Trend	Number of species	Species included
Range declining	6	dingy skipper, large heath, marsh fritillary, pearl-bordered fritillary, small blue and small white
Range more-or-less stable	15	chequered skipper, common blue, dark green fritillary, grayling, green hairstreak, green-veined white, large white, meadow brown, northern brown argus, Scotch argus, small copper, small heath, small pearl-bordered fritillary, small tortoiseshell and wall
Range expanding	7	large skipper, mountain ringlet, orange-tip, peacock, purple hairstreak, ringlet and speckled wood
Recent arrivals or expected soon	4	brimstone, comma, holly blue and small skipper

Four species have either recently arrived in Scotland, or might do so this decade. The brimstone (*Gonepteryx rhamni*) has a few recent records in Dumfriesshire, but its spread into Scotland will be restricted by the very local distribution of its larval foodplants. The holly blue (*Celastrina argiolus*) (Plate 29), however, with recent records in Dumfriesshire and Fife, is unlikely to be limited by foodplant availability. The comma (*Polygonia c-album*) has expanded northwards through England during the last two decades at c. 16 km per year, and there have been recent records in the Borders and Lothians. The small skipper (*Thymelicus sylvestris*) has been spreading north at over 6 km per year. Having moved well into Northumberland during the last 20 years, it is now poised to become established in Scotland.

Another seven species are expanding their ranges (Table 18.2). Most of these are spreading outwards from well established geographical areas but one, the large skipper (*Ochlodes venata*), is spreading northwards at about 4.5 km per year. If this trend is continued, it could reach Edinburgh between 2012 and 2015 and Glasgow between 2020 and 2025. The ringlet (*Aphantopus hyperantus*) has been spreading northwards through the Grampian Highlands and could reach Inverness about 2015.

Speculation about why five of the six species listed in Table 18.2 are declining is included in Anon. (2001a,b). The small white (*Pieris rapae*), which Asher *et al.* (2001) record as "range stable", has declined in northern Scotland. North of the Highland Fault, the number of records has dropped by nearly 40 per cent, and the species appears now to be absent from Caithness and only rarely encountered in Sutherland (and absent from Orkney since before 1970). It is difficult to think of a reason for this decline.

Ranges, as interpreted from biological recording and distribution maps, do not give a complete picture; population sizes are also needed. However, the studies of butterflies indicate that Scotland's fauna is changing, with the possibility of some new species becoming established, and with some of the more specialist species (i.e. those confined to single larval foodplants or to habitats of limited occurrence) continuing to decline in both distributional range and abundance.

18.2.2 *Trends in bird populations*

Data, collected annually on many bird species in the United Kingdom, demonstrate trends (e.g. Gregory *et al.*, 2000, 2001). For some species there is a definite long-term downward trend. With an index value of 100 in 1970, the skylark (*Alauda arvensis*), after a small initial rise in the 1970s, reached an index value of less than 50 (i.e. more than halving the population) by 1999. Other species, such as the grey partridge (*Perdix perdix*), tree sparrow (*Passer montanus*) and corn bunting (*Miliaria calandra*) decreased from an index value of 100 to less than 20 over the same period. Index values indicate the frequency with which species are encountered, and hence their population size, but they do not indicate the changes in geographical distribution.

It is easy to focus on the species that are in decline. However, a number of species are increasing. For example, the marsh harrier (*Circus aeruginosus*) increased from almost none in the early 1970s to about 150 breeding pairs in the mid-1990s. Osprey (*Pandion haliaetus*), a species that returned naturally in the 1950s, has increased from about 10 breeding pairs in 1970 to 110 pairs in the late 1990s. Similarly, the red kite (*Milvus milvus*), which has been re-introduced to several sites in Scotland and England, has increased from about 25 pairs in 1970 to over 400 pairs in the late 1990s.

How do all of these changes compare with each other? Change in the number of species is likely to be an insensitive measure of biodiversity; it is unlikely that many have been gained or lost during the 30 years over which the index has been measured. It is true that the number of breeding bird species in the UK has increased slightly from an average of 199 during the first five years of the 1970s to an average of 207 during the mid-1990s. However, it is when groups of ecologically similar species are examined that the pattern in the increases and decreases can be more clearly seen (Gregory *et al.*, 2001). The group of 20 common farmland birds has an index value that has declined between 1970 and 1999 from 100 to about 60. The group of 41 common woodland birds has declined only slightly, from an index value of 100 to about 90, over the same period. One hundred and thirty-nine species of common bird have remained reasonably stable, with an index value only just greater than 100 during the 1990s. In contrast, the 33 rare species, which have fewer than 500 pairs in the United Kingdom, have virtually doubled their index score.

In Scotland, P. Shaw (pers. comm.) analysed the 20 species for which Species Action Plans have been published. Only one, the common scoter (*Melanitta nigra*), appeared to have extended its geographical range (Figure 18.1). There were no data for two species, the red-backed shrike (*Lanius collurio*) and the Scottish crossbill (*Loxia scotica*), although the former is virtually extinct and it is unlikely that the latter will have declined in range. In terms of population changes, some have decreased; for example, the population size of the capercaillie (*Tetrao urogallus*) appears to have halved between 1992/94 and 1998/99. Others, such as the corncrake (*Crex crex*), have increased.

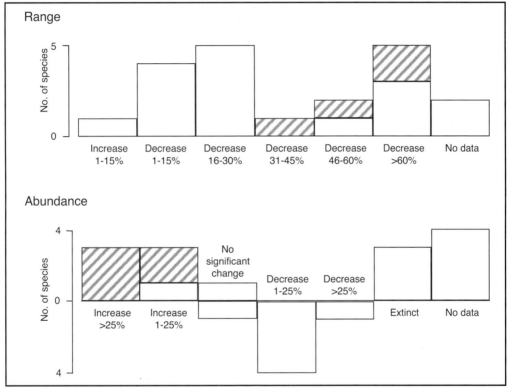

Figure 18.1. Trends in the 20 bird species in Scotland for which Species Action Plans have been prepared. The upper set of histograms shows the change in geographical range between 1968/72 and 1988/91. The lower set of histograms shows the change in population size, usually between 1994 or 1995 and 1999. Shaded portions of the histograms indicate either no statistical significance from the null hypothesis of 'no change' or that little confidence can be placed in the magnitude of the change.

The existence of annual monitoring schemes has allowed data to be collected which are sufficiently accurate to determine changes in both distribution and population size. It is, however, difficult to establish a clear picture of how the avian fauna of Scotland is changing. Some species appear to be becoming more abundant and a few to be increasing their range. Some species are apparently both decreasing their range and their population size. The overall picture is that the avian fauna is changing, not so much in species composition, but more in terms of relative species abundance. A decline in abundance is particularly evident in the set of common farmland birds, but the increasing abundance of a few 'charismatic' species, such as the red kite, may give a false sense of well-being in efforts to conserve Scotland's birds.

18.2.3 The problems of non-native species

Do non-native species contribute to an area's biodiversity? Virtually the whole of Scotland's terrestrial biodiversity has arisen during the last 12,000 or so years since the last glaciation, and hence all species are 'incomers' for a longer or shorter period. Those that have arrived 'naturally' (i.e. without human assistance) are considered to be 'native', whereas those that have been dependent directly or indirectly on human assistance are termed 'non-native' (Usher, 2000b). However, arrival 'naturally' on mainland Scotland does not imply that the species is 'native' throughout Scotland; for example, the hedgehog (*Erinaceus europaeus*) is 'native' in mainland Scotland but 'non-native' in the Outer Hebrides. Some 'non-native' species are 'long-established', having been introduced by the Romans about two thousand years ago. It is, therefore, difficult to divide species categorically into those that are native and those that are not.

In the audit of non-native species in Scotland's terrestrial environment, Welch *et al.* (2001) catalogued 988 species, including 824 species of vascular plants, 50 species of molluscs, 49 species of birds (of which only eight are breeding), 30 other vertebrate species (fish, mammals and an amphibian), 27 other species of invertebrates, six species of bryophytes and two species of fungi. Eno *et al.* (1997) recorded a much smaller number of non-native species in the marine environment. Although for most of these groups the numbers are small in comparison with the numbers of native species, this is not true for vascular plants. The native flora of Scotland contains 1,075 species (Usher, 1997); how should the 824 non-native species be viewed? If species richness is a measure of biodiversity, has Scotland's biodiversity been increased by some 77 per cent with the arrival of these non-native species?

Some would argue that the non-native species augment Scotland's biodiversity (e.g. Dickson *et al.*, 2000). Others would suggest that non-native species are potentially problematic. Williamson (1996) enunciated the 10:10 rule, whereby 10 per cent of non-native species become established, and 10 per cent of these become problematic. This rule can be tested with the audit data. Of the 832 species of all plants and fungi, 80 are considered to be naturalised, and seven either have, or have had, targeted control programmes. These figures are close to the 10:10 rule. Of the 77 species of invertebrates, 47 are considered naturalised and two have control programmes. Of the 79 species of vertebrates, 28 are considered naturalised and 11 have control programmes. These two groups of animals differ markedly from the 10:10 rule. Eight times as many non-native species have had to be controlled than would have been predicted by the 10:10 rule.

This result may be important, underlining the potential problems of non-native species. Alternatively, if the 10:10 rule is true, it could be surmised that the number of non-native animal species arriving in Scotland has been hugely underestimated. Either way, we know of 13 terrestrial and freshwater non-native species that either have or have had control programmes. This certainly implies that the 'precautionary principle' (Anon., undated) should be more widely invoked so that the risk of future problems is reduced. Controls on the importation of non-native species are important and are likely to become more important in the future. Attempting eradication of non-native species that have arrived is easier the earlier it begins; it is virtually impossible to eradicate unwanted species once they have become ecological or environmental problems. Non-native species clearly can present substantial problems and should not be viewed as increasing Scotland's biodiversity.

18.2.4 Gaining knowledge of change

These three examples have indicated that knowledge about biodiversity, at least about species, has been gained at four levels. These are

- casual observations by interested people and passed to local or national record centres (e.g. much of the data relating to non-native species);
- irregular audits, when information about the target subject can be amassed, retrieved and analysed (e.g. the audit of non-native species (Welch *et al.*, 2001));
- periodic surveys, as for the 2000 butterfly atlas (Asher *et al.*, 2001), where the main aim is to gain information on change in geographical range; and
- annual surveillance, when changes in the abundance of species can be estimated (usually by recording at a number of pre-determined geographical locations, as with the wildfowl and wader counts in the *Wetland Bird Survey* (Cranswick *et al.*, 1999), focused on about 1,500 sites surveyed during each winter month).

Amongst British wildlife, it is only really some of the bird species that are continuously under surveillance because of the large number of enthusiastic and dedicated birdwatchers, and hence good data exist. It is for this reason that bird data are being used for one of the 14 'headline' indicators for sustainable development published by the UK Government (Anon., 1999). The aim for this indicator is to "reverse the long-term decline in populations of farmland and woodland birds". Other indicators include trends in plant diversity; biodiversity action plans; landscape features such as hedges, stonewalls and ponds; extent and management of SSSIs; countryside quality; access to the countryside; and native species at risk (Anon., 1999). Some can be measured, but others, such as 'countryside quality', are difficult conceptually.

What we need to ask is whether we are collecting the right sort of data to measure biodiversity. Should annual surveillance be introduced for some other groups of species, perhaps expanding the butterfly monitoring scheme (Greatorex-Davies and Roy, 2000), monitoring other insects such as dragonflies and damselflies, or focusing on a set of plant species, such as the recent 'Cowslip Count' (Duckworth, 2001)? There are many other groups of organisms that could also be considered; what we still need to determine is which form the best indicators of biodiversity.

Are the periodic surveys accurate enough to determine with precision changes in species distributions? If $A_{i,t}$ is the abundance of species i, and $D_{i,t}$ is its geographical distribution, both at time t, and if we can define a function, f, then

$$I_{i,t} = f(A_{i,t}, D_{i,t})$$

where $I_{i,t}$ is an index value for the combined abundance and distribution of species i at time t. If we can do this, then the time series of $I_{i,t}, I_{i,t+1}, I_{i,t+2}, \ldots$ will tell us how species i is changing. For a whole suite of n species, say the grassland butterflies, a composite index I_t, which combines the separate species indices at time t, is

$$I_t = \sum_{i=1}^{n} w_i I_{i,t}$$

where w_i is a weighting for species i. The sequence of I_t, I_{t+1}, I_{t+2}, would be a time series demonstrating the changes in this group of species.

We have not yet defined which species should be investigated. Only then can we set up the surveillance or surveys needed to collect the data. The farmland and woodland bird indices are a start, but they are heavily slanted towards abundance rather than distribution. The National Bat Monitoring Programme has stimulated an interest in monitoring mammals. However, what is not clear is whether it is the widespread interest in birds and mammals that has stimulated these programmes, or whether birds and mammals are likely to be the best indicators of biodiversity. There is a lot of thinking that needs to be done; data collection, storage and analysis needs to be revised; and the indices developed. Only in this way will we gain a clearer and more objective picture of how biodiversity is changing, and be able to incorporate biodiversity fully into the thinking on sustainable development in Scotland.

18.3 Action planning: altering the trends

Following the publication of the UK's Biodiversity Action Plan (Anon., 1994), the first tranche of 14 Habitat and 116 Species Action Plans was published (Anon., 1995b). Further plans were produced such that over 40 Habitat and about 400 Species Action Plans have now been published. An analysis of those that relate to Scotland has been undertaken by Usher (2000a).

The work following publication of the UK's Biodiversity Action Plan also included guidance on preparing Local Biodiversity Action Plans (Anon., 1995a). It was seen to be essential to have a hierarchy of plans within the UK, and this is reflected in the structure of Biodiversity Groups – UK, Country and Local. Although perhaps somewhat bewildering to an outsider, this structure has endeavoured to involve a maximum number of contributors and interested groups in the biodiversity process. A broadly based review of plan implementation across the UK is given in Anon. (2001c). However, a further dimension is provided by Europe-wide plans for species that occur in the UK (e.g. the plan for the greater horseshoe bat (*Rhinolophus ferrumequinum*) (Anon., 2000)).

18.3.1 Habitat Action Plans in Scotland

Forty-one Habitat Action Plans relate to Scotland. Of these, there are two habitats (machair and native pine woodlands) where the total UK extent is in Scotland, and five where more than half (but less than 100 per cent) is in Scotland. With the plans being published between 1995 and 1999, it is hardly surprising that Steering Groups had only been set up for 21 of the habitats at the reporting round in autumn 1999. However, a survey in March 2001 indicated that there are Steering Groups for 39 (95 per cent) of the habitats and that workplans exist for 21 (51 per cent) of them. Progress is being made, albeit slowly, in getting started.

The important aspect, however, is whether the actions in the plans are being undertaken and the targets being met. The survey of plans relevant to Scotland in March 2001 provided indicators of progress (Table 18.3). The four habitats showing signs of recovery are the native pine woodlands, cereal field margins, reed beds and upland oakwoods.

In assessing success or failure, it should be noted that it generally takes a long time for recovery in a habitat. Some habitats, such as cereal field margins, have a shorter time-span, though to restore them to a condition with a set of arable field plants and the associated invertebrates will take many years. Restoration of woodlands, with slow growing trees, will take centuries, though incentive schemes have led to the planting of areas with pine of native provenance, to the planting of new oak woodlands in upland areas, and to the recognition of the importance of upland birch woodlands (for which a plan was agreed in 2001).

Table 18.3. The status of Habitat and Species Action Plans that relate to Scotland, assessed in March 2001. The numbers of plans in each category are shown; numbers in brackets relate to habitats or species that, within the UK, are restricted in their distribution to Scotland. These data relate to progress within Scotland and not necessarily to progress within the UK.

Plans	Total number of plans		Recovered or signs of recovery		No change		Signs of decline		Lost*	Insufficient information	
Habitats	41	(2)	4	(1)	19	(1)	5		0	13	
Vascular plants	38	(12)	5	(2)	10	(7)	8	(3)	7	8	
Other plants and fungi	54	(17)	1		38	(16)	4		3	8	(1)
Vertebrates	40	(7)	4	(1)	11	(2)	21	(3)	0	4	(1)
Invertebrates	52	(10)	1	(1)	22	(6)	14	(3)	6	9	
All species†	184	(46)	11	(4)	81	(31)	47	(9)	16	29	(2)

* All of these 16 species had disappeared from Scotland before the biodiversity process began, and hence they relate to historical data.

† The number of 184 relates to the number of plans because some of the plans relate to more than one species that occurs in Scotland.

18.3.2 Species Action Plans in Scotland

Of the Species Action Plans relevant to Scotland, there are 46 species which, within the UK, only occur in Scotland. A few of these are endemic, though the majority also occur elsewhere, often in Scandinavia. A further 37 species have more than half (but less than 100 per cent) of their UK populations in Scotland.

The March 2001 survey indicated that Steering Groups had been established for 113 (61 per cent) of the plans, and that workplans had been prepared for 53 (29 per cent). This may indicate rather more limited progress in establishing the infrastructure associated with starting action. Progress is again shown in Table 18.3. The largest category is that of 'no change', with 81 (44 per cent) of the plans indicating no change in the condition of the habitat or species. It is, however, disappointing that the number of species, where there are signs of decline, is four times as great as the number which are recovering, although the ratio is not so large for the species that are confined to Scotland within the UK. The species within the 'recovered or signs of recovery' group include Norwegian mugwort (*Artemisia norvegica*), Newman's lady fern (*Athyrium flexile*), pillwort (*Pilularia globulifera*), yellow marsh saxifrage (*Saxifraga hirculus*), Killarney fern (*Trichomanes speciosum*), river jelly lichen (*Collema dichotomum*), corncrake (*Crex crex*), otter (*Lutra lutra*), pipistrelle (*Pipistrellus pipistrellus*), vendace (*Coregonus albula*) and the New Forest burnet moth (*Zygaena viciae argyllensis*).

This analysis leaves no room for complacency. The greatest successes have been where there has been the greatest investment in both research and positive conservation action. Detailed research can determine the reasons for population decline, and can then test, often experimentally, hypotheses about restoring the populations. Research results, to be published in a special issue of the *Botanical Journal of Scotland* in 2002, will demonstrate a range of reasons for population decline, and the need for scientifically-based management if the targets of the Species Action Plans are to be realised. This is a long-term process - undertaking research, conducting appropriate hypothesis-based experiments, interpreting the results, and then transferring the results into practical advice for conservation managers. We need at least five years before we can expect results, but it is essential to ask now if appropriate research and experimentation has been initiated.

18.3.3 Local Biodiversity Action Plans in Scotland

The UK plans have an element of local implementation. Locally there may also be biodiversity priorities that are not recognised nationally. The Local Biodiversity Action Plans therefore contain a useful mixture of work on the national species and habitats as well as work on locally important species and habitats.

By 2001 Local Biodiversity Action Plans were being prepared for the whole of Scotland. In some instances, a plan relates to the geographical area of one local authority, but in a number of instances adjoining local authorities have worked together on a single plan (Table 18.4). By the end of 2001 nearly half of the plans will have been published (Abernethy and Scott, 2001).

Table 18.4. Progress with publishing the 25 Local Biodiversity Action Plans in Scotland. The table records the progress up to mid-September 2001.

Progress	*Number*	*Local Biodiversity Action Plans*
Plan published	11	Argyll & Bute, Borders, Dumfries & Galloway, Edinburgh, Falkirk, Fife, Glasgow, North Lanarkshire, North-east Scotland, Stirling, West Lothian
Plan far advanced or in draft	4	Ayrshire, Orkney, South Lanarkshire, Tayside
Plans for publication awaited	10	Cairngorms, Clackmannanshire, East Dunbartonshire, East Lothian, Highland, Midlothian, Renfrewshire, Shetland, West Dunbartonshire, Western Isles

Again progress is perhaps slower than one might have wished, but it is encouraging that there are Steering Groups for each of the 25 plans listed in Table 18.4, and for a majority of these the biodiversity audit has either been completed or is in progress (22 plans) and a project officer is in post (19 plans). The infrastructure associated with publishing and implementing the plans is well advanced, but questions need to be asked about the success of implementation and achievement of targets.

18.4 Biodiversity trends in the future

This review has focused on a number of trends, both in terms of species and habitats and in terms of the infrastructure that has been created to reverse trends that are undesirable. This indicates that the two main influences on biodiversity are environmental and social. The former relates to the response of the species or habitat to environmental pressures of all types, be they of anthropogenic or more natural origin, and the latter to the desire of the human population to do something that changes the trend. The sociology associated with biodiversity will not be discussed here, other than to note that the two most important aspects are educational (why biodiversity is important and what it means to every individual person) and political (the will to do something and the provision of resources with which to do it).

Various pressures on Scotland have reduced the estimated extent of semi-natural ecosystems and have also resulted in fragmentation (Mackey *et al.*, 1998). Between the 1940s and 1980s the extent of mire was reduced by 21 per cent, of heather moorland by 23 per cent and the length of hedgerows by 54 per cent. Fragmentation has resulted in smaller (and often more) individual areas of mire and heath, and smaller lengths of hedgerows, all of which are more isolated from one another. The habitat remains, but many species that inhabit it will only rarely be able to move from one patch to another, or even unable to move. Thus the process of fragmentation may have changed a population into a metapopulation (Hanski, 1999) whereby a large and coherent population has been divided into a series of subpopulations with at least some gene flow between each. As the process of fragmentation proceeds some (or all) of the subpopulations become totally isolated, gene flow stops, and they have once again become populations in their own right.

A number of ecological and demographic processes will be operating on each population, subpopulation or metapopulation. Some subpopulations will go extinct for purely stochastic reasons, other habitat fragments may be colonised as new subpopulations are formed, there may be local genetic problems due to inbreeding, and there may be unusual (and unpredictable) events such as disease outbreaks. The effects of the dynamics of metapopulations on biodiversity have still not been determined because the theory of metapopulation dynamics has only relatively recently been enunciated (reviewed by Hanski, 1999). The theory has been associated with static landscapes within which patches of habitat are neither created nor go extinct. As Keymer *et al.* (2000) said "… as for species living in ephemeral (patchy) habitats, landscapes are highly dynamic rather than static". This dynamism will be affected by climate, but also by implementation of the action plans themselves. For example, the native pine woodlands plan will influence both the spatial pattern of patches and the size of pine woodlands, which ultimately influences the dynamics of plants and animals associated with this habitat. There is a large amount of research, of both a theoretical and practical nature, that needs to be undertaken before these interactions can be incorporated into management practices.

However, perhaps a more important driver of change relates to the predicted global climate change. A brief review of the effects of climate change in Scotland, including the likely effects on the species and habitats for which action plans have been published, was given by Hill *et al.* (1999). However, Scotland has a very small-scale climatic pattern (steep gradients of temperature, precipitation, windiness, etc., across short distances), so that the local effects also need to be considered. This is one of the aims of the MONARCH project (Harrison *et al.*, 2001), which provided a more detailed bioclimatic classification of the UK and Ireland, reviewed the impacts of climate change on various habitat types, and modelled a variety of species characterising these habitat types.

Ecological succession will undoubtedly lead to changing communities of plants and animals. Conditions will change as the action plans are implemented, and there might be some unexpected effects due to the implementation of one plan on the species or habitat of another plan. The climate will change, both terrestrially (Hill *et al.*, 1999) and in the sea surrounding Scotland (Hiscock *et al.*, 2001). We have started to address the causes of climate change; we have hardly really started to address the consequences for biodiversity. We can either take a *laissez-faire* approach, and accept that changes will happen, with the loss of some species, the arrival of others, and alteration in the character of habitats. Alternatively, we may be more interventionist, and take proactive action to protect pine woodland from invasion by broadleaf species, or to move populations to more northern or higher localities. These are decisions that we need to make now, before it is too late to take action if we so wish. The future trends in biodiversity are, therefore, for us to determine now; that discussion must be started soon.

References

Abernethy, V. and Scott, M. (eds) (2001). *A Flying Start: Local Biodiversity Action Plans in Scotland.* The Scottish Executive, Edinburgh.

Anonymous (1994). *Biodiversity: the UK Biodiversity Action Plan.* HMSO, London.

Anonymous (1995a). *Biodiversity: the UK Steering Group Report. Volume 1: Meeting the Rio Challenge.* HMSO, London.

Anonymous (1995b). *Biodiversity: the UK Steering Group Report. Volume 2: Action Plans.* HMSO, London.

Anonymous (1999). *A Better Quality of Life: a Strategy for Sustainable Development in the United Kingdom.* Department of the Environment, Transport and the Regions, London.

Anonymous (2000). *Action Plan for the Conservation of the Greater Horseshoe Bat in Europe* (Rhinolophus ferrumequinum). Council of Europe, Strasbourg.

Anonymous (2001a). *The State of Britain's Butterflies.* Butterfly Conservation, Wareham; Centre for Ecology and Hydrology, Huntingdon; and Joint Nature Conservation Committee, Peterborough.

Anonymous (2001b). New butterfly atlas launched. *Butterfly Conservation in Scotland,* (Spring/Summer 2001), 2-3.

Anonymous (2001c). *Sustaining the Variety of Life: 5 years of the UK Biodiversity Action Plan.* Department of the Environment, Transport and the Regions, London.

Anonymous (undated). *Sustainable Development and the Natural Heritage: the SNH Approach.* Scottish Natural Heritage, Perth.

Asher, J., Warren, M., Fox, R., Harding, P., Jeffercoate, G. and Jeffercoate, S. (2001). *The Millennium Atlas of Butterflies in Britain and Ireland.* Oxford University Press, Oxford.

Cranswick, P., Pollitt, M., Musgrove, A. and Hughes, B. (1999). *The Wetland Bird Survey 1997-1998: Wildfowl and Wader Counts.* The Wildfowl and Wetlands Trust, Slimbridge.

Dickson, J.H., Macpherson, P. and Watson, K. (2000). *The Changing Flora of Glasgow.* Edinburgh University Press, Edinburgh.

Duckworth, J. (2001). *The Cowslip Count: Charting the Health of British Primulas.* Plantlife, London.

Eno, N.C., Clark, R.A. and Sanderson, E.G. (eds) (1997). *Non-native Marine Species in British Waters: a Review and Directory.* Joint Nature Conservation Committee, Peterborough.

Finlay, B.J. and Clarke, K.J. (1999). Ubiquitous dispersal of microbial species. *Nature,* **400,** 828.

Finlay, B.J. and Maberley, S.C. (2000). *Microbial Diversity in Priest Pot: a Productive Pond in the English Lake District.* Freshwater Biological Association, Ambleside.

Fleming, L.V., Newton, A.C., Vickery, J.A. and Usher, M.B. (eds) (1997). *Biodiversity in Scotland: Status, Trends and Initiatives.* The Stationery Office, Edinburgh.

Greatorex-Davies, J.N. and Roy, D.B. (2000). The butterfly monitoring scheme: progress report for 1999/2000. Centre for Ecology and Hydrology Report.

Gregory, R.D., Noble, D.G., Campbell, L.H. and Gibbons, D.W. (2000). *The State of the UK's Birds 1999.* Royal Society for the Protection of Birds, Sandy.

Gregory, R.D., Noble, D.G., Cranswick, P.A. Campbell, L.H., Rehfisch, M.M. and Baillie, S.R. (2001). *The State of the UK's Birds 2000.* Royal Society for the Protection of Birds, Sandy.

Hanski, I. (1999). *Metapopulation Ecology.* Oxford University Press, Oxford.

Harrison, P.A., Berry, R.M. and Dawson, T.E. (2001). *Climate Change and Nature Conservation in Britain and Ireland: Modelling Natural Resource Responses to Climate Change (the MONARCH Project).* United Kingdom Climate Impacts Programme, Oxford.

Hill, M.O., Downing, T.E., Berry, P.M., Coppins, B.J., Hammond, P.S., Marquiss, M., Roy, D.B., Telfer, M.G. and Welch, D. (1999). Climate change and Scotland's natural heritage: an environmental audit. Scottish Natural Heritage Research, Survey and Monitoring Report No. 132.

Hiscock, K., Southward, A., Tittley, I., Jory, A. and Hawkins, S. (2001). The impact of climate change on subtidal and intertidal benthic species in Scotland. Scottish Natural Heritage Research, Survey and Monitoring Report No. 182.

Keymer, J.E., Marquet, P.A., Velasco-Hernández, J.X. and Levin, S.A. (2000). Extinction thresholds and metapopulation persistence in dynamic landscapes. *The American Naturalist,* **156,** 478-494.

Mackey, E.C., Shewry, M.C. and Tudor, G.J. (1998). *Land Cover Change: Scotland from the 1940s to the 1980s.* The Stationery Office, Edinburgh.

Priede, M. (2001). The stuff of science fiction. *The University of Aberdeen Newsletter,* **12,** 7-8.

Shaw, P. (2001). Natural heritage trends: species diversity: butterfly species. Scottish Natural Heritage Information and Advisory Note No. 131.

Usher, M.B. (1997). Scotland's biodiversity: an overview. In *Biodiversity in Scotland: Status, Trends and Initiatives,* ed. by L.V. Fleming, A.C. Newton, J.A. Vickery and M.B. Usher. The Stationery Office, Edinburgh. pp. 5-20.

Usher, M.B. (ed) (2000a). *Action for Scotland's Biodiversity.* The Scottish Executive, Edinburgh.

Usher, M.B. (2000b). The nativeness and non-nativeness of species. *Watsonia,* **23,** 323-326.

Welch, D., Carss, D.N., Gornall, J., Manchester, S.J., Marquiss, M., Preston, C.D., Telfer, M.G., Arnold, H. and Holbrook, J. (2001). An audit of alien species in Scotland. Scottish Natural Heritage Review 139.

Williamson, M. (1996). *Biological Invasions.* Chapman and Hall, London.

19 HAZARDOUS SUBSTANCES: CHEMICAL, BIOLOGICAL AND RADIOACTIVE

Ken Pugh

Summary

1. Chemicals are the building blocks of life. It is difficult to imagine life in modern Western society without them; they have many benefits.

2. Tens of thousands of chemicals are manufactured and moved within Europe annually; 30,000 are marketed in quantities of over 1 tonne per annum (tpa); 10,000 in quantities of over 10 tpa; and 2,500 in quantities over 1,000 tpa.

3. Chemicals are used as intermediates in further chemicals and materials manufacture, directly in a range of industrial processes, and are incorporated in a number of consumer products. Through all pathways there is the potential for emission, discharge or loss.

4. Despite their widespread use only a very small percentage of the chemicals have been assessed in order to evaluate the risk they pose to human health and the environment. In many cases it is not known whether there is a threat, or, if there is, over what timescale. Very few chemicals are monitored regularly.

5. This chapter provides a brief overview of chemicals in the Scottish environment. Attention is drawn to the fragmentation of the controlling legislation; to the growing awareness (by industry and the regulator) of the need for an holistic and integrative life-cycle approach to the sustainable production, use and disposal of chemicals; to the emerging UK, European and International initiatives; and to the challenges and opportunities which these provide.

19.1 Introduction

In the widest possible sense, chemicals are the materials of life. Without them life in modern Western society would be difficult to imagine. For example, Gross (2001), corporate vice president and director of Research and Development at Dow Chemical, Michigan, has summarised the role and contribution of chemicals to society:

"If you have ever owned a refrigerator, listened to a compact disc, used a computer, taken medicine or owned an automobile you have benefited from the chemical manufacturing industry. People live longer today than at any time in history. Better and more plentiful food is affordable because of fertilisers, pesticides and herbicides. Energy efficient home insulation is brought to you by improved technology. The chemical industry helped develop controlled release medicine for better delivery of therapeutic ingredients to patients. Ion exchange resins are being used in drug discovery and antibiotic synthesis".

As knowledge and experience increases the benefits appear to be offset by some disbenefits. Current concerns about effects on health and the environment centre on brominated flame retardants, endocrine disrupting agents, dioxins, polychlorinated biphenyls, and fish farm chemicals, to name but a few. In response, pressure groups, specialist organisations and the general public pursue to varying degrees so called chemical free products and activities, e.g. organic farming, or alternative medicines and therapies.

Almost daily there are new alerts to the potential dangers of our dependence on modern chemicals. Who would wish to return to the days of scrubbing the residues of burned milk and sauces from pans? What a boon the advent of polytetrafluoroethylene (PTFE) and the teflon coating! But beware; recent research (ENDS, 2001) has shown that thermal decomposition of fluoropolymers such as PTFE generates trifluoroacetic acid, a chemical with no known mechanism of loss from the environment, perfluoroctonoic acid, chlorofluorocarbons (CFCs) and fluorocarbons (with their impact on stratospheric ozone depletion and global warming).

We have long known that in the physical world every force has an equal and opposite reactive force. Maybe in the chemical world every benefit has an equal and opposite dis-benefit, but not as conveniently focused to catch our attention. For example, society has been quick to maximise the use of the myriad chemicals which make up computers, mobile phones and other apparently essential electrical equipment, but slower to handle the mountain of discards, with its end of life plastics, battery and microchip cast-offs, cadmium, mercury, nickel, germanium, etc. When use and disposal are separated by space and time, use can turn to abuse without provisions like those of the proposed European Union Waste Electrical and Electronic Equipment Directive which considers reuse, recycling and appropriate disposal routes.

Chemicals are at the heart of the economic/social/environment sustainability triangle, with its debate and its challenge for action and innovation. Chemicals manufacture is a multi-billion pound industry - even in Scotland. Chemicals provide social and economic benefits through employment, both in their original manufacture and in their subsequent formulation into products. The products have far-reaching social impacts. And yet there are substantial environmental concerns associated with chemicals, for example the availability and depletion of raw materials, energy use (the chemical industry is one of the more demanding energy users), waste management (gaseous, liquid and solid), and hazard control (the impact of intrinsic properties on consumer protection, food safety, industrial health and safety, and the natural environment). The conflicting pressures and priorities within the sustainability triangle are subject to social amplification through attention from non-governmental organisations (NGOs), other pressure groups and the media attention, and changing lifestyles.

This chapter provides a brief overview of chemicals in the Scottish environment; chemicals being construed as commercial chemicals, materials used in and emanating from the manufacture and use of products, and including pesticides, biocides, pharmaceuticals and radioactive substances. Attention will be drawn to the past fragmentation of the controlling legislation, to the growing awareness (by industry and the regulator) of the need for an holistic and integrative life-cycle approach to the sustainable production and use of chemicals, and to the exciting emerging UK, European and International initiatives.

19.2 Production and use of hazardous substances

Whilst there may be millions of chemicals capable of synthesis, there are over 100,000 chemicals registered in the European Union (EU). Those substances manufactured in, or imported into, the EU between January 1971 and 18 September 1981 are referred to as Existing Substances, and are listed in EINECS (the European Inventory of Existing Commercial Chemical Substances). This list is now closed and no further substances will be added. Eighty-two thousand are well defined substances, 18,000 are of unknown or variable composition, complex reaction products and biological materials. About 200 new substances enter the market each year. Those manufactured in, or imported into, the EU since 18 September 1981, once notified (see below), are listed in ELINCS (the European List of Notified Chemical Substances).

About 90 per cent of the registered substances are estimated to be on the market currently. Around 30,000 are marketed in quantities of over 1 tonne per annum (tpa) (Figure 19.1); of these 10,000 are in quantities of over 10 tpa and 2,500 in quantities over 1,000 tpa - the latter are referred to as the High Production Volume (HPV) chemicals.

European chemical production accounted for 403 billion Euros in 1999; this was around 29 per cent of global production. Approximately 36,000 companies make up the European chemicals industry; 96 per cent are small to medium sized enterprises accounting for 28 per cent of sales. The remaining 4 per cent of larger companies generate 72 per cent of sales.

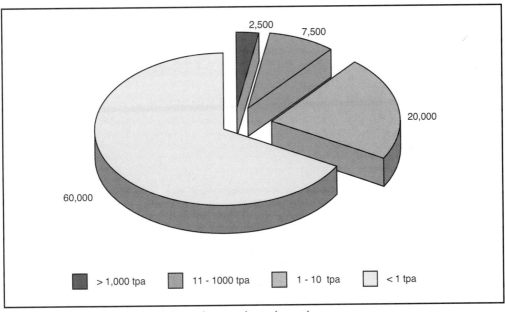

Figure 19.1. Estimated number of chemicals currently on the market.

There is growing concern about the sustainable production, use, release and disposal of chemicals and the effect that they have on human health and the environment (e.g. phthalates leaking from soft PVC toys; brominated flame retardants measured in human breast milk; bisphenol A leaching from the lining of tin cans; nonyl phenol in detergents, with most of these believed to have endocrine disrupting properties). Apart from 200 to 300 recently notified new substances and a similar number of chemicals receiving positive approval under specific (pesticide or pharmaceutical) schemes, none of this vast range of chemicals has been subject to risk assessment and little is known about their effects and fate in the environment or their impacts on human health.

Following a European lead (EC Regulation 793/93), UK regulations requiring risk assessment of new substances were made in 1993 (NONS, 1993) and for existing substances in 1994 (ESR, 1994). The Environment Agency is the competent authority for risk assessment in the UK; SEPA maintains an informal watching brief. Prior to October 2001 there were 110 substances on the first three priority lists awaiting risk assessment; currently only 47 (12 led by the UK) have agreed risk assessments. A fourth priority list containing another 20 or so chemicals was issued on 25 October 2000. Overall progress with implementation of the requirements at national, European or global levels has been slow; so far only 200 to 300 recent substances have gone through the notification process (NONS, 1993) and been entered on the ELINCS list, and less than 50 chemicals on the EINECS list of existing substances have been assessed fully.

Risk assessment is a complex, and somewhat subjective, process. It endeavours to cover all aspects of a chemical's use and impacts on human health and the environment, including its hazardous properties (structure and physical-chemical data), use and exposure information, environmental fate and pathways (including persistence, bioaccumulation), toxicity (carcinogenicity, mutagenicity, teratogenicity), and ecotoxicology (aquatic and terrestrial). European regulation specifies the type and presentational format of assessment in relation to the volume of chemical destined for the market. But often there are few data available, especially for new materials (where there is an urgency in the face of development and production needs), and the dialogue between experts is slow and hitherto has tended not to take account of public concern. Overall, the process is seen as being too slow and onerous, demanding excessive information and being complicated. In the meantime society and the chemical industry, in its widest sense, move on and the environment continues to absorb increasing numbers and amounts of chemicals. Change is needed; it is anticipated.

19.3 The Scottish dimension

19.3.1 Chemicals production and use

Although three of the world's major chemicals companies operate in Scotland and there are two nationally important oil and gas complexes operating continuously at Grangemouth and Mossmoran, chemicals production in Scotland has been described as the 'unknown industry'. However, there are more than 20 sites across Scotland employing directly about 8,000 people (6 per cent of those employed in the UK chemicals industry). They generate an output worth about £2bn (contributing to £26bn UK output), based on assets of £3bn (£30bn for the UK), with current year investments of £330m. Sixty per cent of the Scottish output is contributed to UK export; only a minute portion enters Scottish manufacture and downstream use directly, and much of the remainder (e.g. ethylene) feeds into national grid systems (Chemical Industries Association, pers. comm.).

The location and range of chemical manufacture in Scotland, as listed in Table 19.1, shows extremes. The majority of the industry is located diagonally across Scotland from the south-west, across the central belt, and along the east coast (Figure 19.2). At one end of the range there are the major companies in terms of volume - the combined Scottish capacity for ethylene production at Grangemouth and Mossmoran is 1.5m tonnes per annum - whereas at the other end there are those who manufacture specialities in quantities measured in kilogrammes or just a few tonnes per annum but where the products can be valued at up to £1 m per tonne. Scotland has one of the few plants in the world which manufacture

Table 19.1. The Scottish Chemical Manufacturing Industry (Chemical Industries Association, pers. comm.).

Company	Location	Mode (Note 1)	Chemical Manufacturing activity
Air Products	Baillieston	B	Speciality (medical) and welding gases
Avecia	Grangemouth	B	Pharmaceuticals, fine organics and intermediates
BOC	Glasgow	B	Speciality (medical) and welding gases
Boots Contract Manufacturing	Airdrie	B	Formulation and packaging, e.g. shampoos, soaps and cosmetics
Borden Chemicals	Stirling	B	Formaldehyde and formaldehyde resins
BP	Grangemouth	C	Oil refining – petrochemicals (ethylene)
Ciba Speciality Chemicals	Paisley	B	Pigments for printing inks, paints, etc
Diosynth	Methil	B	Pharmaceutical intermediates
Dupont - Teijin	Dumfries	B	High grade film for packaging and magnetic tape
Elementis	Livingston	B	Bentonite products – drilling muds; nail varnish colour carriers
Enichem	Grangemouth	B	Synthetic rubber
Exxon Mobil	Mossmorran	C	Ethylene
GE Plastics	Grangemouth	B	Plastics
GlaxoSmithKline	Irvine	B	Pharmaceutical intermediates and antibiotics
GlaxoSmithKline	Montrose	B	Pharmaceutical intermediates
ICI	Ardeer	B	Nitro-cellulose for paints, lacquers, propellants; chemical devices (detonators)
Inveresk Research	East Lothian	R&D	Toxicology testing laboratory
ISP Alginates	Girvan	B	Seaweed based products
Lanstar (Scotland) Ltd	Paisley	B	Environmental services
Macfarlane Smith	Edinburgh	B	Opiates and analgesics
Norit	Cambuslang	B	Activated carbon for water treatement; decolourant for food
Organon Laboratories	Newhouse	R&D	Pharmaceutical research, especially drugs for neurological disorders
Quest International	Menstrie	B	Food additives and fragrances (based on yeast chemistry)
R & J Garroway	Glasgow	B	Acids (e.g. sulphuric) for agricultural purposes
Rhodia ChiRex	Annan	B	Pharmaceuticals and pharmaceutical intermediates
Roche	Dalry	B	Vitamins
Rohm & Haas	Grangemouth	B	Acrylate resins
Royal Ordnance	Bishopton	B	Propellants
Scotia	Lewis, Western Isles	B	Fish oil products; evening primrose oil
Shanks & McEwan	Granton, Edinburgh	B	Environmental services - solvent recovery
Syngenta	Grangemouth	B	Agrochemicals (pesticides)

Note 1: B = batch process; C = continuous process; R&D = research and development

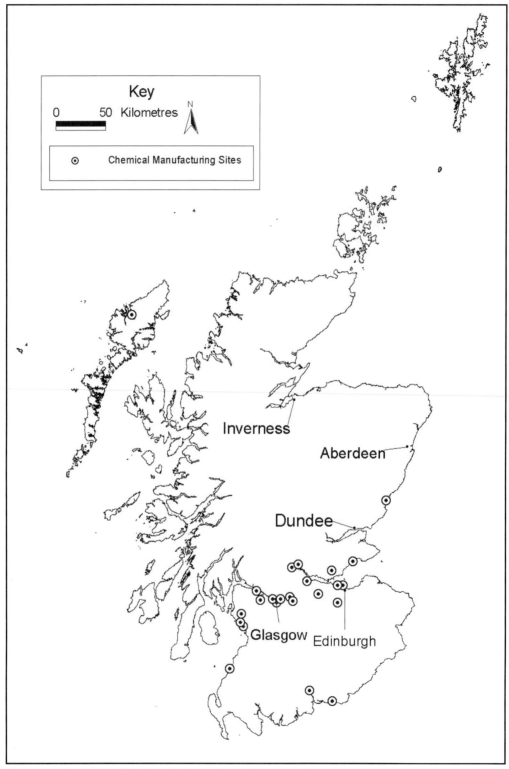

Figure 19.2. Locations of the Scottish chemical manufacturing industry.

some of the fermented antibiotics, and one of the biggest plants in the world for manufacturing one of the vitamins (Chemical Industries Association, pers. comm.).

Chemicals are used as intermediates in further chemicals and materials manufacture, directly in a wide range of industrial processes, and are incorporated in a number of consumer products. Market demands and supply chains are extremely complex, and because of limited internal supply and relatively high re-import in products it has not been possible to establish the number, volume or pattern of use of chemicals within the scope of this overview.

19.3.2 State of the environment

With the very extensive range of chemicals in existence there is the potential for their occurrence in the environment through releases, emissions and losses to air, water and land from point and diffuse sources during their manufacture and use and from products. Pathways once in the environment can be complex and are often not well understood. Analytical resources do not permit an all embracing surveillance of all of the chemicals in the environment. Indeed, the capability of the best resourced UK environmental analytical laboratories does not exceed 200 determinands, representing a very small fraction of the tens of thousands of chemicals in existence.

Effort is invariably focused on the relatively small number of hazardous substances entering the aquatic environment which have been included on 'lists' for several decades. The OSPAR (Oslo–Paris Convention for the Protection of the Marine Environment of the North-East Atlantic), Annex 1A, Red List, Dangerous Substances (I and II) lists contain all the 'usual suspects'. Newer initiatives may cause an increase in the range for consideration and a diminishing interest in those listed substances banned many years ago and whose concentrations in the environment are now below analytical detection limits. In the meanwhile data exist for only a relatively narrow range of metals, pesticides and solvents. Knowledge about hazardous substances in the aquatic environment far outstrips knowledge about their occurrence in air and soil; but overall it has been said of chemicals that "ignorance outweighs knowledge at every point" (RCEP, 2001). Details of the available data and trends are presented in the chapters on water, land and air (see Doughty *et al.*, Chapter 9; Saunders *et al.*, Chapter 12; Birnie *et al.*, Chapter 5; Fowler *et al.*, Chapter 7), and also in the various State of the Environment Reports produced by the Scottish Environment Protection Agency – general (SEPA, 1996), air (SEPA, 1999a), water (SEPA, 1999b) and soil (SEPA, 2001). Scottish data generated for the Harmonised Monitoring Scheme can be accessed via www.sepa.org.uk/data.

Biologically active substances in the environment - pesticides, biocides, veterinary products and pharmaceuticals - receive relatively scant pro-active, systematic monitoring attention despite the fact that they receive positive approval for use. Only six currently used pesticides, and a similar number of those whose use is now banned, are routinely monitored at end of river (Harmonised Monitoring) sites in Scotland, whereas there are approximately 400 pesticides currently authorised for use. Of those investigated, only one or two are reported above the analytical detection limits during routine river monitoring, and there are no cases of exceedence of the relevant environmental quality standard (EQS). The frequency of sampling in this programme may conceal the true picture where the combination of crop, location, season and climatic condition determines the actual pesticides chosen for use and their occurrence in the environment. Local, reactive, *ad hoc* monitoring occurs in response to poor ecological indications and action programmes involving more intense monitoring may then be developed to resolve the issues. Through this process there is some understanding of the use of timber treatment chemicals, sheep dips and fish farm chemicals, and of some local environmental concentrations, but there are insufficient data to report on concentrations and trends in the wider environment. Further details and a discussion of the data gaps for all environmental compartments have been presented in a report on Monitoring of Pesticides in the Environment (PEWG, 2000). Biocides will come under positive authorisation once the recently adopted Biocidal Products Directive (98/8/EC) has been translated into regulation; meanwhile little is known about their occurrence and effect in the environment. The use of veterinary products is the subject of a review which is just being finalised (Environment Agency, 2001) and attention is beginning to be focused on the environmental effects of medicinal products for human use (CSTEE, 2001).

Radioactivity has a somewhat higher profile; this occurs because of the perceived hazards associated with radioactive materials coupled with public reaction to events such as the Chernobyl disaster. In Scotland, the major nuclear installations for power generation are at Chapelcross (Dumfries and Galloway), Dounreay (Highland), Hunterston (Ayrshire) and Torness (East Lothian). There are nuclear defence establishments at Faslane and Coulport and Holy Loch (Argyll and Bute) and at Rosyth (Fife). SEPA undertakes measurements around these nuclear sites and other potential sources of elevated radioactivity (e.g. the Scottish Universities' Research Reactor Centre (South Lanarkshire), some major hospitals, and some landfills). A series of annual reports of monitoring in the UK - the latest for 1999 (FSA and SEPA, 2000) - show the overall diligence of the industry. In summary, at all monitored locations specific radioactivity results are very low; gamma dose rates are difficult to distinguish from natural background rates; and doses to the most exposed group of the population from external radiation and the consumption of fish and shellfish is always less than 2 per cent of the principal dose limit (1 millisievert) for members of the public. Full details are contained in FSA and SEPA (2000).

19.4 Existing control mechanisms

The regulations controlling hazardous substances are complex, diverse and dispersed with no one piece of legislation covering each aspect of the life cycle of a chemical or a chemical product - its manufacture, distribution, use, disposal and re-cycling. There are several compendia listing relevant legislation. One such regularly updated catalogue, Croner (2001), lists eight categories of statutory instruments, namely environmental hazard classification, chemical notification and risk assessment, warning, controls on marketing and use, regulation of biologically active products, sites storing or handling hazardous substances, pollution control, and environmental risk assessment. Each sub-section can be examined to reveal a multitude of regulations.

Even though some recent legislative regimes have taken a more integrated approach, e.g. Integrated Pollution Control (IPC) and latterly the Pollution Prevention and Control (PPC) and Control of Major Accident Hazards (COMAH) Regulations, generally the legislation remains fragmented, reactive and media specific, and tends to be implemented with little cross-referencing. However, it is encouraging that some rationalisation is beginning to occur through European influences. Perhaps the challenge for the future is to allow 'chemicals' to provide an over-arching framework and perspective under which an integrated and holistic view of environment (all media) and natural heritage can be held and balanced against other pressures (e.g. hydraulic regimes, habitat loss), so that priorities and policies need no longer be determined in a piecemeal or sectoral manner.

19.5 Current initiatives

As implied above, there was a perception that the control of hazardous substances was not working. For this reason, during the mid and late 1990s, a number of groups have been formulating initiatives, albeit separately, and are still refining them. The commonality in several of these programmes is emerging and is adding weight to their purpose, importance and urgency of delivery.

After two years of deliberation, in December 1999 the UK published its Chemicals Strategy (DETR, 1999). The Chemicals Strategy sets out Government policies to avoid harm to the environment or to human health through environmental exposure to chemicals. It covers chemicals entering the environment through commercial production and use (but not pesticides, biocides and human and veterinary medicines which are (or will be) regulated by existing positive approval schemes). The Strategy's overall goals are

- to make full information about the environmental risks of chemicals publicly available;
- to continue reduction of the risks presented by chemicals to the environment and human health while maintaining the competitiveness of industry; and
- to phase out early those chemicals identified as representing an unacceptable risk to the environment and human health.

It is anticipated that the Chemicals Strategy will help the UK to meet its international commitments - such as those under the OSPAR Convention (Convention for the Protection of the Marine Environment of the North-East Atlantic) to reduce continuously the discharges, emissions and losses of hazardous substances to the marine environment.

The Government believes that there is a basic duty of care on those who manufacture, supply, use or import chemicals. Manufacturers should provide enough information to allow the risks of chemicals to the environment and human health via environmental exposure to be assessed. This package of information should be passed down the manufacturing chain so that users of the chemical can make environmentally sound decisions about the products they buy and sell. The Government will continue to encourage development and dissemination of environmental best practice, for example through the Environmental Technology Best Practice Programme which has been extended until April 2005. This will help reduce exposure to hazardous chemicals, and increase their substitution by safer alternatives.

An international programme (see below) has been agreed to assess the hazards of chemicals which are produced in high volumes. By the end of 2004, the chemical industry (as opposed to the regulator) should complete hazard assessments for 1,000 high production volume chemicals - a very ambitious target. These assessments will provide the information needed to decide whether a chemical is likely to be of concern. The Government will press the international chemical industry to complete all hazard assessments on high production volume chemicals by 2015.

The international programme will be kept under review by the UK Government; progress will be evaluated by 2004 at the latest. If sufficient progress has not been made, the Government intends to press for legislation in Europe to make assessments mandatory and within an agreed time-scale. The legislation sought would provide that failure to comply with the assessment requirement would lead to the chemical being withdrawn from the market.

The UK Chemicals Strategy provided for the establishment of a Chemicals Stakeholder Forum (CSF) by Summer 2000. This new advisory body, which was set up on time, comprises representatives of the chemicals industry, chemical users, consumers, environmental interests and NGOs. Supported by the Advisory Committee on Hazardous Substances (ACHS), the CSF aims to promote a better understanding between stakeholders and provide advice to the Government so that concerns about chemicals in the environment inform Ministers' decisions and the development of policy. The Stakeholder Forum (DETR, 1999)

- acts as a barometer for the views and opinions of stakeholders;
- advises on the selection of criteria for identification of chemicals needing priority attention, and the risk management strategies required for them;
- will report on such chemicals, advising on precautionary controls, and restrictions and time-scales for action;
- will advise on the development of indicators of environmental exposure to hazardous chemicals, including targets for reducing overall exposure of the environment; and
- conducts its business in an open fashion, making its documents, minutes and advice public.

The work of the UK CSF is gaining momentum and dovetails with a number of other national and international initiatives. In 1990 the Organisation for Economic Co-operation and Development (OECD) agreed a programme to investigate chemicals. Whilst the programme provided a detailed screening and reporting protocol, progress with actual assessment of chemicals was slow. In 1998 the International Council of Chemical Associations (ICCA) announced a voluntary programme of accelerated testing and hazard assessment of around 1,000 HPV chemicals (selected from a list of 4,100) to be completed by the end of 2004. This programme is currently very active and there is an expectation that the targets will be realised (there are 1,293 chemicals in the programme, with commitments to 700 recorded so far in the years 1999 to 2003 – see www.iccahpv.com). Input to the ICCA initiative in Europe is managed by CEFIC (the European Chemical Industry Council), and in the UK by the Chemical Industries Association (CIA) with co-operation from the Environment Agency (EA) and the UK Department of the Environment, Food and Rural Affairs (DEFRA). The CIA is the UK chemical industry's leading trade and employer organisation and is committed to continual improvement in all aspects of health, safety and environmental performance, and to openness about its achievements through its 'Responsible Care' programme. It is also committed to chemical management and has developed a new initiative known as 'Confidence in Chemicals' which in essence is its response and contribution to the ICCA HPV programme.

A 'Strategy with regard to Hazardous Substances' was adopted at the ministerial meeting of OSPAR, in Sintra, on 23 July 1998. This OSPAR strategy requires the development of programmes and measures to identify, prioritise, monitor and control (i.e. prevent and/or reduce and/or eliminate) the emissions, discharges and losses of hazardous substances which reach, or could reach, the marine environment of the North-East Atlantic. The ultimate aim is to achieve concentrations in the marine environment near background values for naturally occurring substances and close to zero for man-made substances. The Sintra meeting 'committed to implement this strategy progressively by making every endeavour to move towards the target of the cessation of discharges, emissions and losses by the year 2020'.

The EU Water Framework Directive (2000/60/EU) was adopted in September 2000. Article 16 of the Directive defines the Community strategy for the establishment of harmonised quality standards and emission controls of certain substances posing a significant risk to, or via, the aquatic environment. Thirty-three chemicals or groups of chemicals have been identified as 'priority substances', 11 of which have been ascribed 'priority hazardous' status, with the intention that emission, discharge or loss of these priority hazardous substances should end or be phased out within 20 years.

The European Commission White Paper entitled 'Strategy for a Future Chemicals Policy' was agreed by ministers in June 2001 and work is now progressing towards the draft of a new Directive(s) by 2002. Under these proposals existing and new substances will be subject to the same procedure under a single system for gathering hazard information, assessing risks, classification, labelling and restricting the marketing and use of individual chemicals and mixtures ('REACH' - **R**egistration, **E**valuation, and **A**uthorisation of **CH**emicals). All chemicals produced or imported into the European Union in quantities above 1 tpa will be registered in a central database. Testing requirements will be tiered according to volume and use; higher tonnage chemicals will be tested for long term chronic effects. Chemicals deemed to be of most concern will need authorisation for a specific use. Responsibility will be placed on manufacturers, importers and users of industrial chemicals to assess hazard and exposure.

The United Nations Environment Programme (UNEP) uses the term Persistent Organic Pollutants (POPs) to describe chemical substances that persist in the environment, bioaccumulate through the food web, and pose a risk of causing adverse effects to human health and the environment. At the UNEP Stockholm Convention on 22-23 May 2001 more than 100 countries agreed control measures covering the production, import, export, use and disposal of POPs, and governments agreed to promote best available technologies and practices for replacing POPs and prevent the development of new ones. Twelve materials - aldrin, chlordane, DDT, dieldrin, endrin, heptachlor, mirex, toxaphene, PCBs, hexachlorobenzene, dioxans and furans - entered the initial list of POPs for action, most of them being subject to an immediate ban, and a review mechanism was put in place to ensure the treaty remains dynamic and responsive to new scientific findings and that the candidate POPs list is updated regularly. There is pressure to apply the Stockholm Convention globally.

Beyond these collaborative approaches various countries (e.g. Sweden and the Netherlands) have developed their own strategies for chemical manufacture, use and disposal, and the assessment and management of the risks to the environment and human health. Most of the strategies, including those listed above, envisage controls being in place within the foreseeable future, and set timescales such as 'within one generation', 20 years, etc.

There is much current activity as the public perception of chemicals grows and the industry itself becomes more conscious of its image. Agreement is still required on the precise criteria by which materials are prioritised onto lists for action. Persistence, Bioaccumulation and Toxicity (PBT) are the usual criteria, but entry thresholds are not always the same (UK CSF, 2000). The multiplicity of lists of chemicals grows; combining the lists from the Water Framework Directive, the EU Dangerous Substances Directives, the North Sea Conference, OSPAR (substances for priority action and candidates for 2002), and the UK CSF (candidates for priority action) generates a list of 107 chemicals or groups of chemicals proposed for priority action (Pugh, 2001).

There are fears that all of these new initiatives are 'more of the same' (RCEP, 2001). Undoubtedly there will be an accumulation of new data about specific chemicals. More is needed about environmental and health effects. Better knowledge is also required about the occurrence of chemicals in, and from, products, particularly in the Scottish context.

But an excursion through the current arena of chemicals can be likened to engaging with a tired 1,000 piece jigsaw puzzle, with its pieces faded, worn and loosely fitting, some of them scattered, 'lost' and requiring retrieval back to their battered container, when its solution is hampered by the lack of a lid and a clear picture of the completed puzzle. At this moment in time the chemical community - manufacturers, users, and regulators - have a challenging opportunity to redesign and repackage the multi-dimensional complexity of chemicals under a new, holistic, integrated, system so that the 'puzzle' can be solved and society can be assured of a safe and healthy environment.

References

Croner (2001). *Substances Hazardous to the Environment*. Croner Publications, Kingston upon Thames.

CSTEE (2001). Opinion on draft discussion paper on Environmental Risk Assessment of Medicinal Products for Human Use. Paper 12062001/D(01) expressed at the 24th plenary meeting of the Scientific Committee on Toxicity, Ecotoxicity and the Environment, Brussels, 12 June 2001.

DETR (1999). *Sustainable Production and Use of Chemicals – a Strategic Approach: The Government's Chemicals Strategy*. Department of the Environment, Transport and the Regions, London.

ENDS (2001). ENDS Environment Daily, 1034, 19 July 2001. Environmental Data Services, London.

Environment Agency (2001). *Review of Veterinary Medicines in the Environment (Draft)*. Environment Agency, Bristol.

ESR (1994). Notification of Existing Substances (Enforcement) Regulations 1994 (SI 3247). HMSO, London.

FSA and SEPA (2000). *Radioactivity in Food and the Environment, 1999 (RIFE-5)*. Centre for Environment, Fisheries and Aquaculture Science, Lowestoft.

Gross, R. (2001). Chemistry: essential to our progress. *Chemistry and Industry*, **13**, 402.

NONS (1993). Notification of New Substances Regulations 1993 (SI 3050). HMSO, London.

PEWG (2000). *Monitoring of Pesticides in the Environment - Report Prepared for the Pesticides in the Environment Working Group*. Environment Agency, Bristol.

Pugh, K.B. (2001). Chemicals and the Environment - a compendium. Unpublished report. Scottish Environment Protection Agency, Aberdeen.

RCEP (2001). *Fresh Approaches to Chemical Use and Control - Seminar Notes*. Royal Commission on Environmental Pollution, London.

SEPA (1996). *State of the Environment Report*. Scottish Environment Protection Agency, Stirling.

SEPA (1999a). *State of the Environment Report: Air Quality Report*. Scottish Environment Protection Agency, Stirling.

SEPA (1999b). *State of the Environment Report: Improving Scotland's Water.* Scottish Environment Protection Agency, Stirling.

SEPA (2001). *State of the Environment Report: Soil Quality Report.* Scottish Environment Protection Agency, Stirling.

UK CSF (2000). Criteria for concern. Paper CSF/00/7 prepared for the UK Chemical Stakeholder Forum, 2 October 2000.

PART FOUR

TOWARDS A SUSTAINABLE SCOTLAND

Part Four

Towards a Sustainable Scotland

Drawing on analyses by SNH (such as Mackey *et al*, 2001) and SEPA (such as SEPA, 2001), as well as other sources published and unpublished, the latest assessments of environmental and natural heritage trends have been documented in this book. In Part 1, it is noted that Scotland encounters and contributes to a range of environmental pressures, in common with other parts of the United Kingdom and Europe. The conference therefore addressed some fundamental questions, such as 'What effects are airborne pollutants having?', 'What are the implications of changing land use on landscapes and wildlife?', 'Are Scotland's fresh waters being managed properly?' and 'How has a long history of exploitation affected the seas?'. Underlying the whole conference was the question of sustainability, and whether Scotland was playing its part both in the protection of the environment and in the pursuit of sustainable development.

Dunion *et al.* (Chapter 20) tackle the question head on. In the absence of a unifying sustainable development strategy, and indicators with which to monitor progress, they could not declare whether Scotland is becoming more or less sustainable. Furthermore, they argue that alternative benchmarks may prove to be misleadingly skewed, with potentially damaging outcomes. A key message is that sustainable development is not 'out there' waiting to be discovered and mapped, but that sustainable development indicators can help to crystallise what the concept is, set priorities, monitor progress and shape future action and decisions.

O'Riordan (Chapter 21) calls for a more assertive attitude to sustainable development at the heart of government, within its agencies and throughout all walks of life. His thesis is that, in the major sustainability themes, what will happen depends on how society values certain choices, how it judges actions and how it is governed. Among his far-reaching proposals, he recommends that both SNH and SEPA establish a joint workshop to look at a more clearly defined sustainability strategy.

The Chief Executives of SNH and SEPA, Crofts and Henton (Chapter 22), conclude with five requirements for sustaining Scotland's environment. First is the collection of data that are accessible and reliable, and relevant to decision making. Second is the need for clarity in the interpretation and explanation of data, to inform policy and action. Third is a recognition of the importance of ecosystem functions and environmental services. Fourth is the need for sectoral policies to be founded on cross-sectoral principles of environmental stewardship. And, fifth is the need for a longer-term vision, with participation at local and national levels, to be delivered throughout the advisory, regulatory and fiscal instruments of government.

Unsurprisingly perhaps, a conference on the state of the environment and natural heritage has not been able to present a simple or straightforward answer to the question of sustainable development. Nevertheless, it accomplished what it set out to do, by presenting facts clearly and opening up debate. There appears to be a continuing need to understand the world around us, by monitoring trends and by seeking to understand the causes and consequences of change. The conference has exposed some of the problems and opportunities of bringing together the requisite information. That, in itself, is a step forward.

References

Mackey, E.C., Shaw, P., Holbrook, J., Shewry, M.C., Saunders, G., Hall, J. and Ellis, N.E. (2001). *Natural Heritage Trends: Scotland 2001*. Scottish Natural Heritage, Perth.

SEPA (2001). *State of the Environment: Soil Quality Report*. Scottish Environment Protection Agency, Stirling.

20 THE ROLE OF INDICATORS IN REPORTING ON THE STATE OF SCOTLAND AND ITS ENVIRONMENT

K. Dunion, J. Holbrook and B. Sargent

Summary

1. Despite the clear commitment to sustainable development made by the Scottish Parliament and Scottish Executive at their inception, we do not know whether Scotland has become more or less sustainable because no measures or indicators have been put in place with which to monitor progress.

2. This chapter looks at the approach taken in Scotland to establish indicators of sustainable development. It compares the environmental components of indicator sets produced by the United Nations, the European Commission, the Department of the Environment, Transport and the Regions with the Scottish set. The latter was produced for consideration by the Scottish Executive, and from it the Executive's proposed Waste, Energy and Travel (WET) indicator set was derived.

3. The indicator set comparison demonstrates the shortfalls of using solely the WET indicators to monitor progress towards achieving a sustainable Scotland, especially so far as environmental indicators are concerned. The chapter recommends that a high-level sustainability strategy for Scotland, coupled with a full sustainability indicator set incorporating a measure of Scotland's ecological footprint, needs to be progressed urgently.

20.1 Introduction

When the Scottish Parliament and its Executive came into being in 1999, the programme for government was set out with a commitment to deliver environmentally and socially sustainable development. This was clearly intended to be, and was received as, a significant undertaking. It could only be understood to mean a departure from conventional ways of gauging progress and clearly pointed to the areas - environmental and social - in which progress would be expected to be evident if the commitment was being delivered.

Nevertheless there was vagueness about what this signalled. There was, after all, no definition of sustainable development running alongside this commitment. There was no strategy paper setting out more fully what the Scottish Executive understood by the term and how it would then seek to shape its approach to policy, legislation and spending. Fundamentally, no measures or indicators had been put in place by which performance overall, by sector or by agency, could be evaluated.

Three years on if we were to ask "is Scotland more environmentally and socially sustainable?" then the answer has to be "we don't know". Clearly there has been some unease about having a political proclamation that is not testable by relevant, verifiable and commonly accepted reference points. The widespread development of sustainable development indicators (which in turn have grown out of environmental indicators) bears witness to the common need of international institutions, national governments, local communities and private companies to describe, test and monitor what is meant when they claim to be pursuing sustainable development.

Indeed it could be argued that the existence of indicator sets are themselves indicators of whether or not a commitment to sustainable development is being taken seriously and is intended to be more than a declamatory statement. The role of indicators is to summarise the characteristics of a system or highlight what is happening in a system. Indicators simplify complex phenomena.

The trouble is that we are facing a dual and conflicting problem. The more we consider and unpack the concept of environmentally and socially sustainable development, the more complex the undertaking becomes. However, in our anxiety to draw more people into the endeavour and to explain the concept, the more insistent becomes the requirement for simplicity in articulating the complexity to the public and to political decision takers.

There are other conflicting notions. We would like indicators to be capable of international (or, within countries, regional) comparison so that a high degree of commonality in indicator sets is seen as desirable. However, there is also a growing conviction that indicators have to reflect the priorities and diverse circumstances of the groupings that they are intended to influence.

What seems now to be well understood is that sustainable development is not 'out there' waiting to be discovered and mapped. Nevertheless, there is still a strongly held view that by adopting the right set of sustainable development indicators we can help to crystallise and define what the concept is, set priorities, monitor progress and shape future action and decisions. As a consequence, hundreds of indicator sets have now been formulated and adopted across the globe. Research projects have unpicked the methodology, and identified the strengths and weaknesses. One important attempt to synthesise principles of good practice drawing upon expertise from five continents gave rise to the so called ten Bellagio principles which set out tests which we would do well to consider whether we are meeting in Scotland (Hardi and Zdan, 1997).

These tests include recommendations that the assessment of progress towards sustainable development should be guided by a clear vision of sustainable development and the goals that define that vision. The assessment of progress should review the whole system as well as its parts. Essential elements of assessment should consider equity and disparity within the current population and present and future generations, dealing with concerns such as resource use, over-consumption and poverty, human rights and access to services, the ecological conditions on which life depends, and economic development and other non-market activities that contribute to human and social well-being.

Practically, this requires an explicit set of categories that links vision both to goals, and to assessment criteria, as well as a selecting a limited number of key issues for analysis and choosing a limited number of indicators to provide a clear signal for progress.

20.2 Environmental indicators and sustainable development

It is against these and other tests that we must consider whether the approach taken in Scotland is sufficient to the challenge. By early 2002, Scotland had no extant set of sustainable development indicators to underpin the commitments given in 1999. There have, of course, been attempts to encourage the development of such indicator sets. As far back as 1995 Scottish local authorities, such as the former Fife Region and the former Strathclyde Region, responded to the initiative fostered by the Local Government International Bureau by drawing up indicator sets for their regions (Fife Regional Council, 1995; Strathclyde Regional Council, 1995). These reflected the desire to use indicators that both resonated with local people and encompassed sustainable development, not simply state of the environment measures. Fife's set, for example, was grouped around four clusters comprising basic needs, community, quality of the environment and resources.

The Advisory Group on Sustainable Development (AGSD), which had been established prior to devolution to advise the Secretary of State for Scotland, concluded its final report in 1999 by calling for indicators for current resource, energy and land use, social inclusion and economic performance, holding the view that "the sustainable development indicators should become as regular a part of public monitoring information as the unemployment figures" (AGSD, 1999).

Sustainability indicators have often grown out of a process of compiling state of the environment indicators, which Scotland has also lacked at Governmental level. The requirement to monitor progress, and to do so by use of indicators, was recognised by Scottish Natural Heritage (SNH) and the Scottish Environment Protection Agency (SEPA) at early stages in their own development. In *Sustainable Development and the Natural Heritage - the SNH Approach* (SNH, 1993), SNH looked to the government to "provide for the monitoring of progress towards the achievement of national targets". SEPA in its first State of the Environment report in 1996 indicated its intention to pursue the development of environmental performance indicators in discussion and collaboration with other environmental organisations (SEPA, 1996).

SEPA and SNH were both instrumental in setting up a Scottish Environmental Indicators Group which, as well as drawing upon the expertise of the staff in the two agencies, also included representatives from the Scottish Executive, the Macaulay Land Use Research Institute, the Natural Environment Research Council, Friends of the Earth Scotland, Scottish Environment Link, the Department of the Environment and the Environment Agency. Although some conclusions of the group were published (Singleton *et al.*, 2000), its work was brought to a premature end by the Scottish Office indicating that it expected that the devolved administration would wish to draw up its own official set of indicators.

For a while, however, this anticipation seemed misplaced. Despite the enthusiasm for indicators from a variety of sources there seems to have been a deep-seated reservation from within the Scottish Executive that militated against quick resolution. The most obvious course of action would have been to adopt the set of 150 indicators which had been drawn up by the Department of the Environment, Transport and the Regions (DETR). The *Quality of Life Counts* sustainability indicators go well beyond a state of the environment list by encompassing social, economic and environmental measures (DETR, 1999). Hence, indicators such as educational attainment, level of crime and long-term unemployment are included. However, of the 150 listed, 94 could be classified as environmental, of which 15 deal with biodiversity. This preponderance of environmental indicators is not unusual. The post-Rio UN Commission for Sustainable Development (UNCSD) working list of 131 indicators of sustainable development includes 72 that are environmental, of which eight deal with biodiversity (UNCSD, 2001). Even a smaller international set, such as the set of

35 indicators drawn up by the Organisation for Economic Co-operation and Development, includes 24 that are environmental, of which five relate to biodiversity (OECD, 1998).

The reason for this should be well-known, yet still too often in Scotland we hear complaints that the sustainable development agenda is too environmental, and somehow should be rebalanced towards economic or social imperatives. First, it is inescapably the case that the development agenda has been dominated by economic growth, tempered to a greater or lesser degree by social concerns. The environment has never been predominant. Secondly, and more fundamentally, sustainable development has grown out of the environmental movement, which has alerted humankind to notions of depletion of natural capital, exceeding carrying capacity, and living outwith our environmental space. Environmental indicators predominate, not because the environment is more important than concerns over poverty but because such indicators measure whether we are pursuing social and economic ends in a way that can be continued indefinitely. Whilst acknowledging the right of current generations elsewhere on the globe (especially in poor nations) to expand their share of world resources, environmental indicators help gauge whether overall we are safeguarding the right of future generations to inherit a viable ecosystem.

20.3 The Scottish approach to indicators of sustainable development

Generally, the DETR set of indicators has been well received. The UK Round Table on Sustainable Development (2000) considered the set to be "a robust and useful way of keeping track of the progress of sustainable development in the UK".

There has been some criticism of the DETR set from south of the border - CAG Consultants (2001) have argued that there are "serious gaps and limitations in the quality of life counts indicators" arguing that "what they measured, the way they measured it and the things left out, projected a particular interpretation of sustainable development. Aspects of this, especially the identification of quality of life with economic activity and growth, were highly contentious" (CAG Consultants, 2001). This is unlikely to be the reason why it was decided that Scotland would not report on progress on sustainable development using the *Quality of Life Counts* set. This is a decision that has significant consequences as the indicators purport to be a UK set; furthermore regional reports using the headline indicators are now being produced, but excluding Scotland.

No official statement has been made as to why the set has not been adopted, and the best that can be proffered are impressions. Immediately after devolution there was a general assertion of the right not simply to adopt approaches from Westminster where these related to devolved matters. The impression has been given that the DETR set of indicators were felt to be inappropriate for Scotland. The antipathy may not have had much to do with the content of the set but rather the size and purpose of the set itself. Concerns have been aired that the set is too large and unwieldy to allow conclusions to be drawn. At the same time, the set was seen as not sufficiently precise to be useful in altering the practice of those whose actions would have an impact upon sustainable development. This attitude extended to doubting whether any indicator set, however restricted in scope, should be drawn up. However, the issue in principle was resolved in early 2000 when the Scottish Executive's Ministerial Group for a Sustainable Scotland was formed. A contract was let to ENTEC UK to consult and to draw up a suggested Scottish set. The conclusions were published in

June 2001 (ENTEC UK, 2001). The consultants demonstrated that they had considered indicators in use and had addressed their aim, scope, strength and weaknesses. These included international indicators such as those from the UNCSD (2001), OECD (1998), Statistical Office of the European Communities (2001) and the DETR *Quality of Life Counts* set. The report recommended the adoption of 42 indicators split into three categories: pressures (or drivers), policy responses and high-level status. Despite the expectation that this would at last equip Scotland with a suite of sustainability indicators, the final report made it clear that the indicators only encompassed the themes of waste, energy and travel (the WET themes), which had been adopted by the Ministerial Group as its priorities to be addressed when considering the challenge of sustainable development. The report suggested further that, so long as the methodology adopted in drawing up the report was accepted, it could be extended over a period of time to encompass other themes. The suggested indicators, although still dominated by environmental concerns, include only two biodiversity elements.

The scope was restricted even further when only 12 of the indicators were actually adopted in the consultation document 'Checking for Change' (Scottish Executive, 2001a). This document, as well as asking for views on a more limited suite of indicators, also raised the prospect of whether or not a single indicator might be adopted. It was suggested that CO_2 emissions per capita would provide a headline indicator of Scottish performance.

Responses to the consultation were generally critical of the restricted form of the list of 12 and were concerned about UK and international comparability (Scottish Executive, 2001b). SEPA responded that Scotland needs comprehensive indicators along the line of *Quality of Life Counts*, whereas SNH recommended the approach taken by the Welsh Assembly by which around half of the UK set was adopted unchanged, augmented by others which better suited the Welsh situation. Non-governmental organisations such as Friends of the Earth Scotland, RSPB Scotland, WWF Scotland and Scottish Wildlife Trust broadly agreed that the UK set adapted to Scottish circumstances would be appropriate. Local authorities were more mixed, with some like Aberdeen City, Glasgow and Comhairle nan Eilean Siar, advocating the more holistic UK approach, whilst others suggested a more limited expansion of the WET themes.

The picture was further complicated when, in 2002, the Cabinet Sub–committee on Sustainable Scotland, chaired by the First Minister, replaced the Ministerial Group. Thinking within the Scottish Executive seemed to have moved to a position that, whilst the indicators could be expanded beyond the WET themes so as to encompass social and economic indicators, targets should accompany these. This reflected a desire to be able to articulate a combined statement of aspirations, indicators and commitments to outcomes. However, the consequence of this approach is that coherent methodology is diluted. Indicators may be chosen because a target has been announced, e.g. reducing the amount of waste to landfill. Conversely, other indicators would be omitted in the absence of a previously agreed target. Thus the rate of recycling, which was in the original WET list, would be omitted as an indicator. The targets themselves may be ill-defined. For example, climate change emissions are a crucial element of every set of indicators, but the target in Scotland is simply to contribute an equitable share of the UK's reductions, neither defined nor quantified. Whilst we may eventually have a Scottish set, the process exhibits failings.

We have lacked what has been called 'the story'. We need an articulation of our understanding of sustainable development and its application to historical and current Scottish circumstances. Sustainable development is not out there to be discovered, but rather it is value based and values can vary between cultures and change over time. Only by describing our current situation and our understanding of context can we apply judgements as to what will be important and what changes in substance and process we want to see over time. The Ministerial Group recognised this and a paper on sustainable Scotland was prepared in 2002, which partly performed this function. It argued for the Scottish Executive to maintain its focus on a few key areas. However, it extended the scope of WET beyond resources, energy and travel and drew into the frame issues of natural resources such as fish stocks and biodiversity. Indicators would be expected to be linked to the issues highlighted in the statement.

Even allowing for this, it is evident that there are other pressing sustainable development issues which are not encompassed by this trio of priorities. For instance, if we compare the WET themes and their indicators to the environmental components of the proposed sustainable development indicators produced for the Statistical Office of the European Communities (2001), then a number of blind spots are apparent, e.g. eutrophication of coasts and marine waters, which has been identified by the United Nation Environment Programme and the European Commission as a priority concern for European nations, would fall outside the set of WET indicators. So too would quality of bathing water, protected area as a percentage of total area, or use of agricultural pesticides. Many of these European indicators were included in the report of the Scottish Environmental Indicators Group (Singleton *et al.*, 2000). Appendix Table 20.1 provides a comparison of environmental indicators incorporated in indicator sets put forward by the United Nations, the European Statistical Office (Eurostat), the Department of the Environment, Transport and the Regions and the Scottish Executive. There are 11 environmental indicators that are common to all four sets. For reporting on environmental sustainability, the WET indicators will only allow for a limited comparison or integration with trends at the UK or the international levels. The UNCSD and Eurostat sets contain 12 more environmental indicators, which are also found in the DETR set, but absent from the WET set. The DETR set has the broadest range of environmental indicators, extending well beyond the three main issues of the WET set and those of the Eurostat and UNCSD sets.

20.4 Developing a way forward

The consequence of not having a high level strategy and full sustainable indicator set is that other key players are creating their own benchmarks which are not only skewed but may lead to damaging outcomes. This is illustrated by the report of the Joint Performance Team set up to measure the effectiveness of both Scottish Enterprise and Highlands and Islands Enterprise. Its report *Measuring Progress Towards a Smart Successful Scotland* (Scottish Enterprise, pers. comm) proposed that 'balanced economic development' is achieved by equilibrium between standard of living, the employment rate and output per head. It suggested that a standard of living index should be drawn up to measure what sustainable economic development is ultimately trying to achieve - but until such an index is designed it is proposed that income per head should be used as a proxy.

On this model Scotland could be judged successful even if it severely damaged its natural heritage and profligately consumed the world's finite and renewable resources. It ignores not only what had been agreed at Rio de Janeiro in 1992 and fails properly to accommodate the commitment given by the Scottish Executive for environmentally and socially sustainable development. What Scotland is trying to achieve should be spelt out by articulating what is meant by this commitment and outlining what form measurements will take.

The preference would have been to establish first principle agreement to the process by which the indicators were going to be arrived at. The norm, which has been observed, is that international and national indicator sets tend to be top-down; that is that an expert group proposes indicators, which are adopted by the decision-making body. Conversely, it has been observed that sub-national, regional and local authorities tend to derive indicators from a bottom-up process of consultation. This may reflect the differing expectations of the indicator set, the international and national being expected to be either aggregated from the activities of many actors and thereby describing the efficacy of operational activities in delivering on international and national targets. At a lower level, it may be part of a public education programme designed to articulate the complex concept of sustainable development in a series of measurements, which resonate with local populations.

The approach adopted by the Scottish Executive has been top-down, but seeking to involve and consult nationally significant organisations. However, the views of those bodies tended to be at variance with the Scottish Executive and Scottish ministers as to the scope and extent of the indicators adopted. In the course of debating whether to have indicators, including wrangling over what should be included and political considerations as to what may be implied from the set, we have lost coherence in what makes for a good indicators set.

A commended approach was that taken by Seattle where the process was driven by a broad based grouping, which established from the outset shared values and vision, before a draft set of indicators was drawn up. Readily available data were used, but essential indicators were not discarded for statistical or policy expediency. The set is kept under review not only to measure progress but also to ensure appropriateness (Bossel, 1999).

In addition to clarity of process, we could also have had some articulation of methodology to provide a commonly agreed approach to deriving indicators so that they can be made capable of cross-referencing. A common approach at present appears to be to adopt the methodology of pressure (or driver), state and response. For example, if climate change was the issue being addressed, the pressure would be emissions of greenhouse gases, the state could be sea level change and the response would be the rate of renewable energy generation. By having too limited a set, this balance between identifying what is the problem, how it manifests itself and what is being done about it, will be lost.

Even here interpretation can be difficult. For instance the UK government's judgement is that it is making good progress on climate change as gauged by its immediate objective of meeting a target for a 12.5 per cent reduction of greenhouse gas emissions from 1990 levels by 2010. Consequently it awarded itself a 'green light' in its self-evaluation of *Quality of Life Counts*. By contrast, however, the UK Round Table on Sustainable Development (2000) cautioned that it should have produced a 'red light' as scientific analysis showed that much larger reductions would be necessary to reduce the impact of global warming. It concluded "in our view the government is misleading itself and the public in showing a green signal for climate change'".

Others have criticised the pressure-state-response model as being too linear in suggesting relationships between cause and effect. It has also been criticised for failing to take account of the systemic and dynamic nature of the processes involved in sustainability (Bossel, 1999). However, it is essential that, whatever indicator set is adopted, it is capable of allowing conclusions to be drawn as to the state of Scotland insofar as it is making progress either towards or away from sustainable development (however we have chosen to define that term).

Looking at the UK set of 150 indicators or the 138 indicators of the state of environment produced by the Scottish Environmental Indicators Group, it is not easy to come to such an overall conclusion. Whilst criticism of the truncated draft Scottish Executive sets may be justified, it should not be presumed that simply beefing up the number of measurements would solve deficiencies.

In seeking a unifying measure, many studies draw attention to the use of gross domestic product as a commonly accepted single proxy indicator of the economic progress and presumed well-being of a nation. This has persisted notwithstanding the myriad criticisms of it. There is a hankering therefore for something similar in sustainable development. The International Institute for Sustainable Development has expressed a colourful scepticism by saying that "searching for a single indicator of sustainable development is something like the quest for the unicorn" (www.iisd.org/measure/faqs.htm).

Nevertheless, the Welsh Assembly has decided that the ecological footprint of Wales shall be used when considering how it meets its constitutional requirement to pursue sustainable development. Ecological footprinting is a mass balance tool which measures the flow of materials and energy through a system. It quantifies the materials, energy and water used and the amount of waste produced to make a product or to sustain an activity, and then applies conversion factors to arrive at an estimate of the amount of land required to sustain these consumption and waste patterns. So, for example, electricity from coal has a larger footprint than electricity generated from renewable sources because the conversion factors not only address the amount of land required to produce fossil fuels but also include a figure for the amount of land that would need to be set aside to act as a sink for the carbon dioxide emitted.

Recently Anglian Water measured its footprint. This allowed it to conclude that the biggest improvement in its ecological impact would be to tackle its energy use. The company has now set itself a target to obtain 10 per cent of its energy from renewables by 2010; this includes powering two of its sites from biogas generated during sewage treatment, as well as building and operating a wind turbine at another of its sites (ENDS, 2001).

Even the ecological footprint fails to provide an entirely satisfactory single indicator. Leaving aside the problems in acquiring the data regarding the inputs, it has difficulty encompassing all of the pollution outputs from the process. The ecological footprint crucially also says nothing about people's quality of life. It would certainly be helpful to carry out the exercise of establishing Scotland's ecological footprint because it would allow for international comparisons and may help to influence operational priorities. It is, however, unlikely to provide a satisfactory single indicator, and certainly it will not provide one that allows us to dispense with a wider set.

We are not here proffering our own indicator set for Scotland. Our respective organisations have made submissions to the Scottish Executive and broadly agree by advocating the adoption of the UK set adapted to Scottish circumstances. The view being taken is that the realities of current circumstances should not be ignored. The benefits of UK comparability, the desirability of making a report to the World Summit on Sustainable Development in 2002, and the pressure to focus on delivering changes to key areas where unsustainable development is most pronounced, all outweigh the advantages of further prolonged debate about a bespoke Scottish set of indicators.

20.5 Conclusions

Given these problems, do we really need indicators? After all, they could be described as an attempt to measure the immeasurable. It could be argued that "we will never achieve a universal and unchanging set of sustainability indicators and the challenge is one of keeping pace with people's dreams and trying to make them real". We do not have to disagree with that sentiment whilst also holding to the more prosaic view that "evidence is the best safeguard against prejudice and fantasy, and numbers help make evidence rigorous". Sustainability indicators should provide us with

- the benchmark as to whether we are moving towards, or away from, sustainability, however that is defined;
- the capacity for international comparison to see if we are doing as well as, less well or better than comparable nations;
- the methodology that can shape and spawn sub-sets of sectoral indicators;
- the ability to prioritise issues that need particular attention in Scotland; and
- the information to refine policies and decision taking by identifying where progress in one area may have detrimental impacts on another area.

The UN called for Governments to report on progress towards sustainable development at the World Summit in Johannesburg in the second half of 2002 and it charged civil society to attest as to whether the official conclusions are widely shared. Sustainability indicators would allow us to make a credible response and to indicate where we intend to improve for the future.

Acknowledgement

We would like to thank Dan Barlow for his assistance and work on Appendix Table 20.1.

References

Advisory Group on Sustainable Development (1999). *Scotland the Sustainable?* The Scottish Office, Edinburgh.

Bossel, H. (1999). *Indicators for Sustainable Development.* International Institute for Sustainable Development, Winnipeg.

CAG Consultants (2001). *Report to the Sustainable Development Commission: State of Sustainable Development in the UK.* CAG Consultants, London.

Department of the Environment, Transport and the Regions (1999). *Quality of Life Counts.* The Stationery Office, London.

ENDS (2001). Anglian Water's search for sustainability indicators. *The ENDS Report*, March 2001, pp. 24-26.

ENTEC UK (2001). *Sustainability Indicators for Waste Energy and Travel for Scotland.* Scottish Executive Central Research Unit, Edinburgh.

Fife Regional Council (1995). *Sustainability Indicators for Fife.* Fife Regional Council, Glenrothes.

Hardi, P. and Zdan, T. (1997). *Assessing Sustainable Development – Principles in Practice.* International Institute for Sustainable Development, Winnipeg.

Organisation for Economic Co-operation and Development (1998). *Sustainability Indicators beyond the Environment.* OECD, Paris.

Scottish Environment Protection Agency (1996). *State of the Environment Report.* Scottish Environment Protection Agency, Stirling.

Scottish Executive (2001a). *Checking for Change – a Consultation Paper.* Scottish Executive, Edinburgh.

Scottish Executive (2001b). *Checking for Change – Report of the Consultation.* Scottish Executive, Edinburgh.

Scottish Natural Heritage (1993). *Sustainable Development and the Natural Heritage: the SNH Approach.* Scottish Natural Heritage, Perth.

Singleton,P., Holbrook, J., Sargent, B. and Mackey. E.C. (2000). Potential environmental indicators for Scotland. Scottish Natural Heritage Review No. 136.

Statistical Office of the European Communities (2001). Measuring progress towards a more sustainable Europe – proposed sustainable development indicators (draft). Eurostat/F3. April 2001.

Strathclyde Regional Council (1995). *Sustainability Indicators.* Strathclyde Regional Council, Glasgow.

UK Round Table on Sustainable Development (2000). *Indicators of Sustainable Development.* UK Round Table on Sustainable Development, London.

UN Commission for Sustainable Development (2001). *Indicators of Sustainable Development, Guidelines and Methodologies.* United Nations, New York.

Appendix Table 20.1. A comparison of environmental indicators incorporated in indicator sets proposed by the United Nations (UNCSD), the European Union (Eurostat), the Department of the Environment, Transport and the Regions (DETR), the consultants to the Scottish Executive (ENTEC) and the Scottish Executive (WET). The table is ordered by levels of commonality. The abbreviations UNCSD, Eurostat, DETR, ENTEC and WET are defined in the text with appropriate references.

UN sub–theme	Indicator	UNCSD	Eurostat	DETR	ENTEC	WET
Climate change	Greenhouse gas emissions	✓	✓	✓	✓	✓
Air quality	Air pollutants in urban areas	✓	✓	✓	✓	
Water quality	Rivers of good or fair quality	✓	✓	✓	✓	
Species	Native, rare (BAP) species trends	✓	✓	✓	✓	✓
Material consumption	Material consumption	✓	✓	✓	✓	✓
Energy use	Energy use per household	✓	✓	✓	✓	
Energy use	Share of consumption of renewable resources	✓	✓	✓	✓	✓
Energy use	Energy use eco-efficiency	✓	✓	✓	✓	
Waste generation and management	Waste arisings by sector	✓	✓	✓	✓	
Waste generation and management	Waste recycling and reuse	✓	✓	✓	✓	✓
Waste generation and management	Distance travelled per capita per mode of transport	✓	✓	✓	✓	
Ozone layer depletion	Ozone depletion	✓	✓	✓		
Agriculture	Area converted to organic production	✓	✓	✓		
Forests	Total forest area	✓	✓	✓		
Forests	Sustainable management of woodland	✓	✓	✓		
Urbanisation	Built up area/net loss of soils to development	✓	✓	✓		
Coastal zone	Estuarine water quality, marine inputs	✓	✓	✓		
Fisheries	Fish stocks around the UK fished within safe limits	✓	✓	✓		
Water quality	Water demand and availability	✓	✓	✓		
Water quality	Quality of bathing water	✓	✓	✓		
Ecosystem	Protected area as a percentage of total area	✓	✓	✓		
Ecosystem	Trends in natural habitats	✓		✓	✓	✓

UN sub–theme	Indicator	UNCSD	Eurostat	DETR	ENTEC	WET
Waste generation and management	Generation and disposal of hazardous waste	✓	✓	✓		
Waste generation and management	Generation and disposal of radioactive waste	✓	✓	✓		
Transportation	Passenger travel by mode		✓	✓	✓	✓
Transportation	Freight transport by mode		✓	✓	✓	
Climate change	Sea level change			✓	✓	
Air quality	Emissions of selected air pollutants			✓	✓	✓
Agriculture	Nitrogen balance	✓	✓			
Agriculture	Use of agricultural pesticides	✓	✓			
Urbanisation	New homes built on previously developed land			✓	✓	
Urbanisation	Development of vacant or derelict land compared to total			✓	✓	
Water quality	Dangerous substances in water	✓		✓		
Ecosystem	Biodiversity action plans			✓	✓	
Energy use	Energy efficiency measures in homes			✓	✓	
Energy use	Energy efficiency of road passenger travel/average fuel consumption of new cars			✓	✓	
Waste generation and management	Management of different waste streams			✓	✓	
Waste generation and management	Household waste and recycling			✓	✓	
Waste generation and management	Landfilling of biodegradable wastes			✓	✓	
Transportation	Traffic congestion			✓	✓	
Transportation	Road traffic			✓	✓	✓
Environmental protection	Environmental protection expenditure		✓	✓		
Environmental protection	Implementation of multilateral environmental agreements	✓		✓		
Environmental protection	Adoption of environmental management systems			✓	✓	
Information access	Use of environmental information services and consumer information			✓	✓	
Climate change	Carbon dioxide emissions by end user			✓		
Climate change	Rise in global temperature			✓		

UN sub–theme	Indicator	UNCSD	Eurostat	DETR	ENTEC	WET
Climate change	International emissions of carbon dioxide per head			✓		
Air quality	Concentrations of selected air pollutants			✓		
Air quality	Sulphur dioxide and nitrogen oxides emissions			✓		
Air quality	Acidification in the UK			✓		
Agriculture	Area under agreement within the Environmentally Sensitive Area and Countryside Stewardship agri-environment schemes		✓			
Agriculture	Concentrations of organic matter in agricultural topsoils			✓		
Forests	Area of ancient semi-natural woodland in GB			✓		
Forests	Number of countries with national forest programmes			✓		
Urbanisation	Loss of natural habitat for development (urban, agricultural, resource extraction, waste disposal)				✓	
Urbanisation	New retail floor space in town centres and out of town			✓		
Urbanisation	Buildings of Grade I and II at risk of decay			✓		
Urbanisation	Quality of surroundings			✓		
Urbanisation	Access to green space			✓		
Desertification	Land affected by desertification	✓				
Coastal zone	Percentage of total population living in coastal areas	✓				
Coastal zone	State of the world's fisheries			✓		
Water quantity	Water affordability			✓		
Water quantity	Water leakage			✓		
Water quantity	Abstractions by purpose			✓		
Water quantity	Sites affected by water abstraction (to be developed)			✓		
Water quantity	Energy and water consumption by sector; waste and hazardous emissions by sector			✓		
Water quantity demand	Household water use and peak			✓		

UN sub–theme	Indicator	UNCSD	Eurostat	DETR	ENTEC	WET
Water quality	Nutrients in water			✓		
Ecosystem	Landscape features – hedges, stone-walls and ponds			✓		
Ecosystem	Countryside quality			✓		
Species	Trends in plant diversity			✓		
Species	Populations of wild birds			✓		
Ecosystem	Biodiversity in marine and coastal area			✓		
Material consumption	Primary aggregates per unit of construction value			✓		
Material consumption	World and UK materials consumption levels per head			✓		
Material consumption	Amount of secondary or recycled aggregates used compared to virgin aggregates			✓		
Material consumption	Resource use eco-efficiency				✓	✓
Energy use	Depletion of fossil fuels			✓		
Energy use	Thermal efficiency of housing stock			✓		
Energy use	Energy and water consumption by sector/waste and hazardous emissions by sector			✓		
Energy use	Energy generation eco-efficiency				✓	
Energy use	Energy and water consumption by sector – waste and hazardous emissions by sector			✓		
Waste generation and management	Construction and demolition waste going to landfill			✓		
Waste generation and management	Generation of industrial waste	✓				
Waste generation and management	Discharge from the nuclear industry			✓		
Waste generation and management	Distance travelled by waste for disposal, by mode				✓	
Waste generation and management	Concentrations of persistent organic pollutants			✓		
Waste generation and management	Chemical releases to the environment			✓		
Transportation	Average journey length by purpose			✓		
Transportation	Heavy goods vehicle mileage intensity			✓		

UN sub–theme	Indicator	UNCSD	Eurostat	DETR	ENTEC	WET
Transportation	Leisure trips by mode of transport			✓		
Transportation	Overseas travel			✓		
Transportation	Sustainable tourism			✓		
Environmental protection	Expenditure on pollution abatement			✓		
Environmental protection	Greening government operations			✓		
Environmental protection	Enforcement of regulations			✓		
Environmental protection	Land covered by restoration and aftercare conditions			✓		
Environmental protection	UK companies implementing ethical trading codes of conduct			✓	✓	
Environmental protection	Corporate environmental engagement			✓		
Environmental protection	Environmental reporting			✓		
Science and technology	Expenditure on research and development		✓			
Natural disaster preparedness and response	Risks to human and natural capital		✓			
No theme	Number of local authorities with Local Agenda 21 strategies			✓		
No theme	Access to the countryside			✓		
No theme	Individual action for sustainable development			✓		
Total in source set		58	59	147	42	12
Total environmental indicators		31	30	96	32	9
Natural heritage coverage		8	7	21	4	2

21 GOVERNING FOR A SUSTAINABLE SCOTLAND

Tim O'Riordan

Summary

1.   Sustainable development is a process of reducing burdens on global life support functions, ensuring that every citizen enjoys health, security and reliable income and creating sufficient wealth for prosperity to be fully shared. This is an important ideal, but it is not yet being followed in Scotland, or elsewhere.

2.   For sustainable development to be pursued, changes in the manner of governing will be necessary. This may include a more coherent policy directorate in the heart of the Scottish Executive, supported by strong policy co-ordinating units in executive departments and non departmental public bodies.

3.   Sustainable development also requires public support and active engagement. This may mean the creation of a Scottish Sustainability Commission, a Sustainability Cabinet Committee in the Scottish Parliament, and a Scottish Citizens' Sustainability Network linking the local voice to national strategic decisions.

4.   For such a vision to be put into effect, the policy evaluation and auditing processes need to be based on sustainability appraisal. This is designed to ensure that all policy actions, including grant aid and legislation, must be tested against the criteria of sustainable development, and actually deliver as much in their implementation.

5.   All of these themes have huge implications for SNH and SEPA. The possible transformations to outlook and procedure in these two organisations are reviewed.

21.1 Defining sustainable development

By signing up even more to sustainable development, Scotland would be recognising its national commitment to the 'Rio Process'. This is more prosaically known as 'Agenda 21', the strategies towards sustainable development that all nations are expected follow in the wake of the UN Conference on Environment and Development, held in Rio de Janeiro in June 1992. The 'Rio Process' is the evolving aftermath of that event, the learning and understanding that accompanies the revelation of what sustainable development really means. Sustainability is an evolving vision, and a guiding aspiration: it can never fully be attained, but it should be striven for.

There are many definitions of sustainable development. The term is hugely amorphous. One of its qualities is the breadth of interpretation that ensures a general agreement that the concept is vital for progress. One set of definitions relates to eco-efficiency, namely the production of more wealth with fewer resources, reducing overall energy use and waste production. This was best promoted by Hawken *et al.* (1999). The task is to improve technological efficiency and market acceptance. Another set of principles circulates around social justice and environmental equity. One of the most coherent treatments of this approach was by Carley and Christie (2000). The aim here is to ensure that social spread of rights, well-being and opportunity is guaranteed across the most disadvantaged of citizens. Dobson (1999) also covered this theme from a theoretical point of view. A third strand applies to improved procedures of evaluation and governance. This relates to ways for calculating environmental and social burdens (Von Weizsäcker *et al.*, 1997), and improvements in cost benefit analysis and economic valuation (Turner *et al.*, 1994). There is also a theme on improved lines of policy integration and co-ordination of governmental structures, for which a good reference is Pezzoli (1997). The history of the concept of sustainability was well covered by Adams (1990).

For the purpose of this chapter, two recent books on the general topic are drawn in as background. One is by O'Riordan and Voisey (1998) and the other edited by O'Riordan (2001). These turn the basis of the discussion that follows. They also seek to capture the spirit of the broad debate summarised above. The main focus here is that of governance for sustainability, as this is the approach that forms the centrepiece of this chapter.

In Figure 21.1 the three governing 'hubs' lie in the south-west, north and south-east quadrants of the outer circle. These elaborate the four key features of governance for sustainability, listed below. The principal issue is that of multi-centred governance, for which the first two characteristics listed below are particularly pertinent. The remaining two points relate more to the changing role of science in an emerging participatory democracy, as well as to the linking of the global to the local in citizen awareness and behaviour.

The first observation is that governance is shared, multi-centred, operating on many scales from the planetary to the household, and involving business, voluntary organisations and citizens' groups across a suite of activities.

Second, governance differs from government in that it operates through networks, not hierarchies, and is adaptive, proactive and capable of rapid learning. It shares power through recognising a range of experiences, and is willing to act on intuition and instinct rather than just on rational analysis and established rules (see Held (1996) and Rhodes (1997) for a fuller analysis).

Third, participatory democracy is not just a consultative device. It involves deliberation and inclusion. Deliberation is the opportunity to probe deeply into aspects of decisions where science cannot find complete answers because the future is not analytically organised. Science provides a vital function of providing information and guidance as to prediction. But in the major sustainability themes, what will happen depends on how society values certain choices, how it judges actions and how it is governed. This is why there is a role for participatory science. The future of climate change, or biodiversity, or transport, or energy use, will be based on deliberative choices where public, private and civic all have many voices based on their particular experience, hopes and fears. For example, there may be no single global, or regional, climate in the future. Any climate will be a product of natural ocean-atmosphere-ice-biosphere interlinkages as modified and interfaced with human action. In essence, human behaviour and outlook form a fifth element of the climate system, and a third hand in biodiversity (ecosystems, climate, and human interpretation and valuation being the appropriate trio). So deliberative democracy provides a basis for genuine communication amongst those whose values, outlooks and starting positions may be hugely different, and initially incommensurable. Inclusionary procedures mean bringing

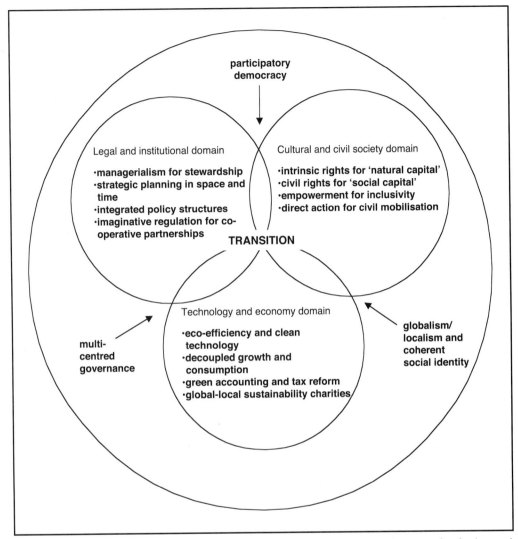

Figure 21.1. Sustainable development can mean almost anything, including the scope for fundamental contradiction. It is best to regard sustainable development as a constant process of transformation of a society and an economy towards acting as trustees that maintain and nurture life and habitability for future generations on this planet. The diagram emphasises three existing shifts in the pattern of governing. These are the scope for spanning space, time and active decision-makers into networks of adaptive and anticipatory policy making and strategic alliances. Such a move will lead to a more participatory democracy and a greater variety of partnerships in conducting the affairs of governing. These will embrace civil, public and private sectors in a variety of configurations. The circles in the middle represent the three inter-linked domains of sustainability, namely social fairness and natural social entitlements, eco-efficiency and price reform to reflect environmental footprints, and new forms of integrated policy making. Sustainability is a mix of economic, social, environmental and institutional factors: the intertwining whole is governance for sustainability.

in more and more interests as understanding evolves and as the ambit of relevant stakeholders enlarges. 'Inclusionary' means continuing to include until all representative interests are incorporated. In this way, participatory democracy includes both deliberation and participation (for a summary of the literature see Holmes and Scoones (2000).

Fourth, global to local is no longer a spatial phenomenon. Indeed, the psycho-space and self-esteem of the individual outlook play a crucial role in global-local identity. Arguably sustainability begins in the conscience, the persona, the social support matrix, and the intuition that guides us all in so many ways (see O'Riordan, 2000, p. 16) for further discussion). The point here is not to remove the analytical power of scientific evidence and discovery. It is to build on the scope for incorporating how people 'feel' and judge their moral positions. Sustainability carries many equity and ethical features, as indicated in Figure 21.1, so this combination of feelings and core beliefs, which themselves are shaped by patterns of trust and confidence, is an important addition for a wider science. It is a process of revealing how local and personal actions and responsibilities transcend the space of neighbourhood and turn the household to the nation and the planet (for a fuller analysis, see O'Riordan (2001, chapters 1 and 2)). There is no action, however 'micro' in scale, that does not have ultimate global consequences. And any global activity, or global pressure, will leave its mark on the local scene - possibly via the media, possibly through a new social norm or fad, or possibly via different consuming opportunities and habits. The sustainable citizen becomes the global-local citizen, who thinks and acts globally to locally via whatever spatial and social connections are necessary.

These four observations suggest that sustainable development is a process of building on existing patterns of changing governance in Britain. Scotland offers a distinctive home for this shared governance. It has, for the most part, its own Parliament, proportional representation, a joint governing party that arguably should better reflect a majority of electoral opinion, and a separate Executive with considerable room for manoeuvre. It also enjoys a strong area-based identity, and, again for the most part, its agencies of executive responsibility have established strong regional civic sounding boards. In principle, therefore, Scotland should be reasonably well prepared for sustainable governance. Sadly it is not, and I will discuss why below.

Turning to the rest of Figure 21.1, the viewer will see in the three 'domain circles' how the three strands of social justice, eco-efficiency, and strategic integration of policy programming and funding should ideally interact through the forms of shared governance summarised above. The key theme is the shift to a justice objective both through social rights and entitlement for natural processes. Rights to nature are steadily being increased via such measures as the EU Habitats Directive and the EU Water Framework Directive, both of which give considerable powers to SNH and SEPA to ensure that biodiversity and life support processes are managed so as to be robust. There are, of course, many devices by which these core responsibilities towards an 'entitlement of nature' will be accepted, or diluted. The key for sustainable development is to strengthen the existing arrangements, including sound scientific audits, built-in monitoring, the wider discretion of the precautionary principle and regular evaluation of success or failure. Many of these procedures are well developed by SNH and SEPA, and indeed many are summarised and analysed in these conference proceedings. But there is still plenty to do if the hard test of sustainability is fully to be met.

Social rights are beginning to become enshrined in the Human Rights Act 2000 which was passed in Scotland a year before passage in England and Wales. This Act does not guarantee the kind of deliberative and inclusionary democracy as outlined earlier. Nor does it require that all those who might be affected by a proposed course of action properly get identified. Above all, there is nothing in the legislation requiring executive agencies to ensure that those who should be included are actually involved, nor that the wishes of those who deliberate are actually taken account of. This important final point essentially means a process of community outreach, training and educational programmes, and of talking to people as they live out their own lives and hopes.

Through this chapter, I should like to make reference to the continuing fish farming controversy in Scotland. There are a number of pointers to the slowness of discernible shift to sustainable development. Some of these are highlighted in a recent report by Birley (2001), who looked at issues around biodiversity, waste, energy and transport for his message. The fish farming theme is illustrated here because it reflects many of the potentials for improving patterns of governance for sustainability in Scotland.

The fish farming dispute is summarised in a recent report by Friends of the Earth (Scotland) (2001). Essentially, the issues involve the continuation of the industry in areas that are essentially marginal, where many families are dependent on the survival of the industry, and where the distinctiveness and quality of salmon should determine its marketability. Yet the industry is plagued by disputes over toxic residues in feed, over toxic and nutrient rich residues below the cages from the fish faeces and various pesticides applied to the closely packed fish, and to the possibility of escape of farmed salmon into the wild. This in turn leads to claims that sea lice on farmed salmon may be transferred to wild salmon, and to claims that the two types of salmon are interbreeding. Furthermore, alleged toxicity of feed and aquichemicals is alarming food retailers and consumers, and hence affecting markets.

The controversy over fish farming in Scotland has not yet encouraged either SEPA or SNH actually to search for 'community correspondents'. These would be local people who feel the pulse of local feelings, and who can connect with all manner of people when they congregate and speak their own minds. The really effective outreach is that which taps people in their own social activities and linkages and which draws them into the sustainability issues of the locality through conversations and listening dialogue.

The principle of 'going to' the people, rather than expecting them to attend meetings or consult via formal representations is well established in the literature on participation. For a good review, the Community Development Foundation (2000) covered the main themes from a highly pragmatic vantage point. For a more theoretical interpretation, see Healey (1998) and Holmes and Scoones (2000).

For such an approach to be effective, however, SNH and SEPA have to be believed locally, understood locally and proven to be responsive locally. This is where the community correspondents could become part of wider networks of guidance forums that become the pulse of Sustainability Scotland. Just consulting, leaving some controversial disputes under-analysed or ignored (e.g. claims of toxification of fish feed, or of surrounding local environments from anti-viral or anti-bacterial agents, or incomplete answers to charges of cross-breeding of farmed stock to wild salmon stock), and retaining power in a narrow form of representative government, is not the way of sustainability.

The concept of community correspondents is much more located in existing 'grass roots' networks than in the current arrangement in the Scottish Civic Forum. The Civic Forum is an important initiative whose potential contribution to sustainability governance for Scotland still needs to be fully evaluated. Any national 'civic' body would be strengthened by such participatory networks.

The technology and economy domain in Figure 21.1 is certainly in the forefront of the economic ministries and businesses that are innovative in Scotland. Frankly, the 'ecological footprint' even for these new technologies is still too great. The notion of ecological footprint is covered by Dunion *et al.* (Chapter 20), and by Chambers *et al.* (2000) via case studies. Full life-cycle analyses, as well as these 'footprint audits' would show that even so-called Factor 10 technologies (i.e. those which reduce throughput of materials to value of output by a combination of 10-fold increases in efficiency) would be insufficient to the effective function of planetary life support. A good discussion was led by Hawken *et al.* (1999), with a controversial critique by Lomborg (2001).

The ecological footprint is a surrogate value of the total ecological and social damage, caused globally and over time, by any technological action right now. Such a calculation is still beyond any rational or verifiable analysis. But the kinds of governance approaches outlined in this chapter should help to create the conditions for sustainability appraisal that could be a decent surrogate for this 'footprint'. Indeed, the uptake of new regulatory and technological measures can anaesthetise the decision maker from recognising how partial is the movement to ecological integrity, social justice and reliable livelihoods for all Scots, when such technologies are considered. For example, the energy industry is still highly dependent on CO_2 emissions, but it has a high political influence so that by no means all of the local costs are incorporated in energy prices to the consumer. Similarly with the transportation industry and the housing industry, the costs of the service are greater than the prices paid. Moves towards more energy-lean economies, more waste recycling and more socially sensitive pricing strategies are fine. They genuinely represent a shift in direction for many business agents. But a full sustainability appraisal of the kind discussed below is vital if the shift in science and technology, and in social responsibility, are truly to meet the tests of sustainability.

21.2 Sustainability appraisal

Sustainability appraisal is an evaluative process that checks to see if a policy, or a programme of action, or a specific grant aid scheme, actually meets the tests of sustainability as broadly laid down in Figure 21.1. The National Assembly of Wales has a duty in its enabling legislation to further the cause of sustainable development. In so doing it now recognises that all of its policies and spending programmes should be tested against the yardsticks of sustainable development.

The appraisal process has long been problematic in the UK. The Government set up a number of policy appraisal procedures between 1992 and 2000. These resulted in papers prepared by the former Department of the Environment and the former Department of the Environment, Transport and the Regions, such as *Policy Appraisal and the Environment* (1991), *Environmental Appraisal of Development Plans* (1993), and *Policy Appraisal and the Environment: Policy Guidance* (1998). All of these are proving to be fairly controversial, basically variants of rational choice, cost benefit analysis, risk assessment and life cycle analysis. All of these schemes are technologically framed to be rational and ordered. None properly takes into account either the effects and consequences of cumulative outcomes (i.e. the consequences of many like measures), nor the surprise of chance combinations (e.g. climate change and air pollution effects, water abstraction and transfer in sensitive Highland environments). And none seriously considers, or incorporates, deliberative and inclusionary participatory approaches. In summary, current appraisal guidelines appear to suffer from the following four defects.

- They rely on particular forms of expertise, narrow frames of reference that primarily support functional technology and rational economic logic.
- They cannot readily cope with surprise, ignorance, multiple values and outlooks, and the broadening basis of the precautionary principle.
- They are designed primarily to be handed down by executive agencies rather than incorporated into local opinion and civic wisdom.
- They reinforce an economy that is primarily geared to the quantity of wealth rather than the quality of life, and cannot easily take into account social values of well-being, security and confidence-building, let alone alienation, anger and despair.

Sustainability appraisal begins with moves toward sustainability governance of the kind outlined above. It is a process of connecting and revealing rather than analysing and deciding. In the fish farming case, for example, it would take as one yardstick the quality and survival of wild salmon. It would use a wider range of experienced local knowledge to inform the science, and the scientists would listen to the judgements of local instinct and intuition as much as measures of temperature, salinity, toxicity, morphology and pathology when considering salmon monitoring evidence. It is no longer good practice to rely on 'sound science' alone in such matters. The incorporation of a more participatory and more 'civic' science is now widely accepted, if not yet translated into practice. O'Riordan *et al.* (2001) covered the issues surrounding this concept. If this meshing of evidence, analysis and community feelings and instinctive sensitivity is not carried out, then distrust is bred, and controversy is heightened. This is certainly the case in the fish farming dispute. Community networks might be activated to guide how farmed salmon could be managed to be less intensive, of higher nutritional quality, and more readily identifiable to the consumer as locally derived. Each salmon farm could conceivably generate a name and a brand and a cultural and local association that could be as beloved and as distinctive as the many labels of malt whisky are today.

In essence, sustainability appraisal covers the following four principles. First, it specifically rests on tests of ecological integrity or resilience and social wellbeing as its primary guide. If the tolerances of ecosystem functions are not known, then local opinion plus other intuitive opinion should be merged with scientific prognoses. The meshing of intuitive knowing with scientific analysis is an important combination for sustainability appraisal.

Second, it would activate a 'community correspondents network' to see just who is gaining and losing from all specific measures associated with any proposal, how their behaviour is being adapted to accord with the entitlements of nature, and what measures of liability compensation or cross-subsidisation, or corporate social responsibility, should be put into effect to ensure that the mix of interested stakeholders is at least better off as a result. This notion of community correspondents deserves more attention. These would be people who represent discernible strands of informal social networks in a locality. Such networks may be sports clubs, the Women's Institute, church groups or recreational associations (e.g. pigeon fanciers). The people selected would not be spies or troublemakers.

They would be trained to communicate, to listen, to report to their constituencies, and to offer opinion or advice or themes that require deliberation and wider debate. If the correspondents were linked by understanding and commitment to the two custodial agencies, they would trust and be trusted in turn. This is the issue of correspondence.

Third, it would analyse all subsidies, grants and other fiscal measures to see just how far these promote the cause of nature's entitlements or not, and how far they also advance social entitlements. Such measures cannot always be attained by an agency or even a network. But sustainability appraisal at least helps to point out the deficiencies of monetary biases and inappropriate fiscal measures so that the debate is introduced into a functioning participatory democracy.

Fourth, it would ensure that all relevant areas of government - at national and unitary (local) levels, plus regional groupings where appropriate - bring together their policies and practices to meet specific objectives that cross the economic, social and environmental realms. The appraisal would have to prove that all the relevant policy aims are entwined so as to meet the tests of natural and social entitlements. Again, various aspects of a fully deliberative democracy would be drawn in to support this appraisal, and to legitimise it once completed.

Sustainability appraisal is more than a process or a cluster of statutory duties. It is an unfolding examination of a new form of shared governing in which many players become responsible, where common outlooks are tested in discussion and revelation, and where all actors demonstrably shift their original positions in order to accommodate the whole. If needs be, then sustainability appraisal will have to evoke 'lateral policy analysis'. This means looking for creative approaches to finding solutions of both a local and an economic nature that transcend the normal rules of financing and auditing. Only a confident and co-operative form of governance will have the imagination, the strength of purpose, and the public support to explore such approaches.

An example of this might be to find EU regional development funds (Structure Funds) to finance the training for marketing of 'clean' farmed salmon by local people. This might include combining the marketing of the actual salmon with locally initiated cultural themes, such as clothing, weaving or music.

Sustainability appraisal should be the lifeblood of sustainability Scotland. It should be experimental within a spirit of joy, determination, exhilaration, learning and communitarianism. In this age of electronic connections, the good and the poor experiences can be shown and synthesised. The early examples will inevitably be fairly limited and rudimentary because the pattern of governance is still unhelpful and non-accommodating. Also the pioneers may be restricted in their vision by agency mindsets that are unfamiliar and unimpressed. If the following suggestions are put in place, then sustainability appraisal will become the pulse of change that Scotland can sense. It will be filled with growing excitement and pleasure in its special sustainability identity.

Figure 21.2 outlines a possible approach to managing a sustainability appraisal for salmon farming in Scotland. The diagram is designed to be illustrative, and to form the basis for a workshop on this topic. It is highly desirable that such a workshop be held by the custodial, development and social agencies in Scotland as a basis for moving this concept into practice.

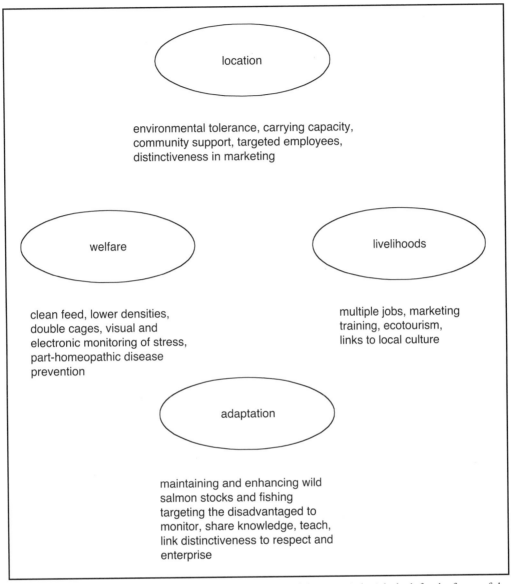

location

environmental tolerance, carrying capacity,
community support, targeted employees,
distinctiveness in marketing

welfare

livelihoods

clean feed, lower densities,
double cages, visual and
electronic monitoring of stress,
part-homeopathic disease
prevention

multiple jobs, marketing
training, ecotourism,
links to local culture

adaptation

maintaining and enhancing wild
salmon stocks and fishing
targeting the disadvantaged to
monitor, share knowledge, teach,
link distinctiveness to respect and
enterprise

Figure 21.2. This is a first attempt at suggesting how a sustainability appraisal might look for the future of the Scottish fish farming industry. The point of the appraisal is that patterns of coalescing governance, as outlined in Figure 21.3, should be in place. Then the appraisal is undertaken partly by the people themselves, including the industry and the regulators, and partly by the policy machinery of the Scottish Executive. The focus is on the economic, social and environmental chains of inter-linked responsibility along the lines outlined in Figure 21.1. The actual format and procedure of such an appraisal awaits a workshop and a series of participatory pilot studies.

21.3 Governing structures for sustainability Scotland

Figure 21.3 indicates one possible arrangement for linking together the suggestions from this analysis. The aim is to lay out a framework of governing arrangements that will enable sustainability Scotland to emerge. What follows is very much the basis for a discussion; it is not a blueprint. The essence of shared governance is that Scots themselves will create the appropriate mix. All I can do is provide the basis for the beginning of the discussion.

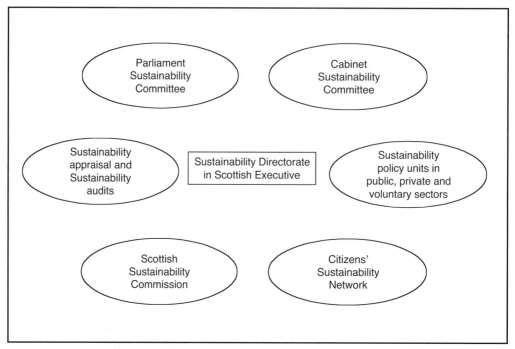

Figure 21.3. The idea here is to establish a central nervous system of sustainability thinking within the heart of Scottish government. This would centre the policy machinery in the Scottish Executive to ensure an equivalent policy focus for cabinet and for the Parliament, and reach out to resonant policy co-ordination in collective agencies. The application of sustainability appraisal and auditing by a Sustainability Commission and a citizens' network would ensure participatory democracy and a true sense of combined ownership for the future of sustainability governance in Scotland.

'Sustainability Scotland' is used as a term of art for a Scotland that is progressing beyond sustainable development as it is currently interpreted into the shared governance of sustainability indicated in the previous section.

This is the observation of an optimist. I am all too aware of the enormous impediments to transformation of governing structures. These obstacles cover structural, budgetary, administrative and individual personnel hopes, fears and customary ways of doing things. Birley (2001, p. 8) found scant evidence of ministerial commitment, agency interest, clarity of purpose, or personal mission around the notion of sustainable development. Dunion *et al.* (Chapter 20) point to the failings of sustainability appraisal techniques in the Scottish Executive and executive agencies. Birley (2001) also noted a 'persistent confusion' between environmental policy and sustainable development strategy throughout Scotland, with no vision or delivery function for the latter.

I have no illusions that any of the proposals that follow will be even considered seriously, let alone implemented. But there are straws in the wind. There is to be some sort of sustainable development commission for Scotland. There is a Scottish Civic Forum that could form the basis of a wider citizens' network, and there are sustainability policy units in the Scottish Executive and non-departmental executive agencies. So what follows is meant to provide a more coherent vision for sustainability governance for Scotland, building on these developments, and providing confidence for more progressive improvements.

21.3.1 *A sustainability nerve centre in the Scottish Executive*

At present (Autumn 2001), the heart of sustainable development thinking lies in a small unit within the Environment Group in the Scottish Executive. This group of people is too small in number for the kind of tasks envisioned in Figures 21.1 and 21.2, and too bureaucratically marginal in the scheme of Scottish government. Sustainability covers four domains - environmental, social, economic and institutional. So the sustainability nerve centre, the 'Sustainability Directorate', should be created in the First Minister's office, it should straddle the whole of the Executive, and it should report to the First Minister. Its operations should be accessible to interactive involvement with other organs of government (sustainability policy units in the various groupings in the Executive, and also the non-departmental agencies) and with a network of active citizens, through a Scottish Sustainability Commission and Citizens' Sustainability Network. Hence its centrality in Figure 21.3.

The Sustainability Directorate would encourage the inclusion of sustainability thinking across governance generally, including the private and voluntary sectors. It would initiate and guide sustainability appraisals at least in terms of codes of practice, timing in decision making, and reporting styles. It would also undertake sustainability audits of the actual programmes and spending schemes, in order to be sure that the appraisal mechanism meets its objectives.

The key to the Sustainability Directorate is that it should be small, adaptable and highly interactive. It should contain civil servants, business people, academics and a range of informed citizens, many of whom would be on secondment. It should be capable of commissioning research, yet of using the organs of governing outlined in Figure 21.3 for its own analysis and commentary. It should be both initiatory and responsive. Such a Directorate would be the strategic arm of the new governance for sustainability - open-minded, sharing, listening and far-seeing, guiding and being guided. It will only succeed as the patterns of interconnected governance evolve around it, and which it, in turn, helps to shape.

21.3.2 *Sustainability policy units in Scottish Executive groupings and agencies*

Each functional grouping within the Executive, plus the policy nerve centres of the various executive agencies, should also consider developing strategic sustainability policy units in their midst. Such units would act in a similar way to the Sustainability Directorate, but at the group or agency level. They would foresee, guide, initiate, respond and evaluate. They would set the framework for sustainability appraisals, and post-implementation audits, and would be the link-point between the executive arm and the policy arm of governance. These units would also be electronically connected to each other and to stakeholders so that they are genuinely accessible. There is every reason why all major businesses and sizeable voluntary organisations should also include directors and directorates for sustainability to create a 'sustainability family' in Scottish civic life.

21.3.3 *Parliamentary and Cabinet Committees*

If sustainability joins up natural and social wellbeing, economic gain and governance redesign, then there needs to be a Parliamentary and a Cabinet-level co-ordination of these four domains. This suggests a powerful, and highly focused, Parliamentary Committee for Sustainability Scotland, and a Sustainability Cabinet Committee. Their secretariat would be closely connected to the Directorate, to the sustainability policy units, and to the two outreach mechanisms for citizens as a whole. Such a cabinet committee will work best if the 'silo' mentality of functional and fiscal independence, which is already beginning to disappear, became largely extinct.

It is worthy of note that the Province of British Columbia has recently created a Ministry of Sustainable Resource Management. This reports to a group of ministers with a sustainability tag to their policy propositions covering land use, agriculture, aquaculture, fisheries, forestry and mining, along with parks and wildlife. If British Columbia can do this, it should be possible for Scotland, with a similar population and economic structure, to follow suit.

21.3.4 A Scottish Sustainability Commission

I call this body a Sustainability Commission to distinguish it from the UK counterpart, the Sustainable Development Commission. That particular body has a remit to inspire the notion of sustainable development in government, business and society throughout the UK. It is not matched by any noticeable change in governing structures, though, as in Scotland, there is a loosely defined and somewhat *ad hoc* grouping of ministers to whom it reports. But because there is no essential mechanism for delivering sustainable development in the UK, the UK Commission remains at present somewhat of an isolate. It is too small to overturn obstacles, too quiet to be heard above the existing sustainable development clamour, and too marginal to day to day activities for the wider body politic to take note.

I understand that some form of link between the UK Sustainable Development Commission and a Scottish counterpart is actively being created in Scotland. I welcome this. For such a Scottish commission to be effective, it has to enjoy a supportive institutional apparatus. This is why Figure 21.3 illustrates the interconnections of seven innovative institutional arrangements which ideally ought to evolve, if Sustainability Scotland is ever to become a reality.

The Scottish Sustainability Commission should be encouraged to network, to facilitate, to co-ordinate, to comment, and to enable training in sustainability awareness to cross the land and the culture. It should hold workshops, initiate seminars, support best practice, and offer prizes and recognition for those who try and who succeed, even those who fail but demonstrably learn. It should initiate training schemes for members of local authorities, for board members of all agencies, for senior Scottish Executive managers, and for parliamentarians. It should encourage schools to initiate and create sustainability projects and practices within their schools and in their neighbourhoods. Such projects could focus on food, energy and waste, and would involve co-operative and far-seeing behaviour. It should not shy away from spirituality or intuition in encouraging fresh ways of learning and sharing. Its job is always to encourage, demonstrate, proclaim and connect those who would not otherwise realise they have a common purpose.

21.3.5 A Scottish Citizens' Sustainability Network

This is a Scottish Civic Forum composed of representatives from voluntary organisations, community groups, trades unions and churches. This acts as a sounding board for civic opinion, and in its own way provides the basis of advice on sustainability issues. What I propose complements this Forum. There is also a strong case for a network of Scottish citizens and groups that work in their locality and in their daily socialising to promote the cause of Sustainability Scotland. This network would never meet, but it could link up electronically, regionally and locally. It will learn to understand its collective and disparate outlooks, which will help it guide appraisals and judge audits. It will assist many people, not currently part of any governance and for whom sustainability is an unfamiliar word, to see how their dreams and aspirations can become close to reality via the revelation of progressive sustainability. It will operate through existing social groupings, through schools and neighbourhood organisations and it will always strive to link livelihoods to security to quality of existence to new patterns of learning and consuming.

Such a network can be enormously assisted through regional and local variants in the executive and custodial agencies in Scotland. Indeed the national network might organically evolve through more localised arrangements. This is part of the task that the agencies could play to establish Sustainability Scotland.

21.4 Translating sustainability into SNH and SEPA

These proposals all have a bearing on the work of SEPA and SNH. I am aware that both organisations carry an interest in sustainability strategy, and have evolved many exciting initiatives. But there is still a lack of clarity and spirit of direction in both bodies for the sustainability ideal. As the larger structures are being created, here is a list of six actions for the two custodial agencies.

First, they should establish a sustainability induction programme for all board members and incoming employees, being trained together. This would ensure that the basic vision and principles of sustainable development are built into the very heart of management for both organisations. Above all, this should help to ensure an empathy for the evolving practice of sustainability, with all of its inherent contradictions and ambiguities.

Second, they need to create sustainability policy nerve centres in headquarters and the regions, and enable these to be visible, proactive, innovative, connecting and responsive to citizens' sustainability networks. The chapter indicates how such units should be staffed and designed to communicate through the organisations and out into the citizens' networks.

Third, they should establish the practice of sustainability appraisals and audits in all policies, programmes and budgetary measures, including grant aid schemes. This effort should be preceded by a series of workshops aimed at introducing and experimenting with sustainability appraisals and audits. By such means a dossier of how best to approach them would be part of agency intranets and websites.

Fourth, they should promote the cause of the co-decision principle with government and the voluntary sector for all key land use decisions and strategies. At present national and local elected governments distrust the notion of co-responsibility for decisions on the grounds that the agency, business and voluntary sectors are not democratically accountable. If democracy diffuses throughout the land, if elections become a small part of governing accountability, and if deliberative and inclusionary procedures become the custom, then co-decision making will slip into place as effortlessly as an osprey makes its catch! Such an arrangement is beginning to emerge from the proposed Cairngorm National Park planning machinery. This would involve the National Park Board and the local authority planning departments adopting complementary procedures. Similar administrative arrangements could evolve for water management associations, planning on coasts and floodplains (O'Riordan and Clayton, 2000), and for biodiversity enhancement, using planning betterment procedures to invest in comprehensive biodiversity provision based on amalgamating commitments by developers into a strategic framework for enhancing biodiversity.

Fifth, they should engage with schools, colleges and universities in developing common approaches to research, training and evaluation, and use local community networks as part of social and environmental monitoring. Schools could well become neighbourhood sustainability pivot points in the future. Targeting them now would give confidence to this prospect. Annual meetings should be participatory affairs that review commitment and experience. Ideally they should be a celebration of sustainability, and a hallmark of the contribution that SNH and SEPA actually have made, year on year, to making Sustainability Scotland a joyous reality.

Finally, they could widen a joint chairmen's group of the two custodial agencies to include the various development agencies and social betterment bodies. This may not meet often, but it would provide the basis for reflecting on best practice, co-ordinating outlooks and management strategies, and bonding through a common concern for sustainability. Needless to say, representatives of the Scottish Citizens' Sustainability Network should also attend.

21.5 Epilogue

I am hopeful that my proposals advanced here will have some effect on the Scottish scene. I would like to think that SNH and SEPA will establish a joint workshop to look at a more clearly defined sustainability strategy as part of their expanding statutory remit. And I do hope that they will embrace a series of pilot schemes and guidelines on sustainability appraisal techniques, and their subsequent evaluation. Also, the scope for establishing a community correspondents' network at the local level, feeding into the Civic Forum, is there for the designing. In the Scottish Executive and Parliament, I remain confident that the political reservoirs favouring a fresh appraisal to wellbeing for people, nature and prosperity will lead to a consensus move towards administrative and policy reform. I am a perennial optimist. That is why I believe in the mission of the UK Sustainable Development Commission, and in a viable vision for Sustainability Scotland.

References

Adams, W. (1990). *Green Development Paths*. Routledge, London.

Birley, T. (2001). *Reality Check: a Review of Scottish Executive Activity on Sustainable Development*. WWF Scotland, Aberfeldy.

Carley, M. and Christie, I. (2000). *Managing Sustainable Development*, 2nd edn. Earthscan, London.

Chambers, N., Simmons, C. and Wackernagel, M. (2000). *Sharing Nature's Interest*. Earthscan, London.

Community Development Foundation (2000). *The New Community Strategies: How to Involve Local People*. Community Development Foundation, London.

Dobson, A. (ed.) (1999). *Sustainability and Social Justice*. Routledge, London.

Friends of the Earth (Scotland) (2001). *The One that Got Away*. Friends of the Earth (Scotland), Edinburgh.

Hawken, P., Lovins, A. and Lovins, H. (1999). *Natural Capital*. Earthscan, London.

Healey, P. (1998). *A Theory of Communicative Planning*. Routledge, London.

Held, D. (1996). *Models of Democracy*. Polity Press, Cambridge.

Holmes, T. and Scoones, I. (2000). *Participatory Environmental Policy Processes: Experiences from North and South*. Institute of Development Studies, University of Sussex, Brighton.

Lomborg, B. (2001). *The Skeptical Environmentalist.* Cambridge University Press, Cambridge.

O'Riordan, T. (2000). Environmental science on the move. In *Environmental Science for Environmental Management,* ed. by T. O'Riordan. Prentice-Hall, Harlow. pp. 1-22.

O'Riordan, T. (ed.) (2001). *Globalism, Localism and Identity: Fresh Perspectives on the Sustainability Transition in Europe.* Earthscan, London.

O'Riordan, T. and Clayton, K. (2000). Coastal processes and management. In *Environmental Science for Environmental Management,* ed. by T. O'Riordan. Prentice-Hall, Harlow. pp. 243-247.

O'Riordan, T. and Voisey, H. (eds.) (1998). *The Transition to Sustainability: the Politics of Agenda 21 in Europe.* Earthscan, London.

O'Riordan, T., Cameron, J. and Jordan, A. (eds.) (2001). *Reinterpreting the Precautionary Principle.* Cameron May, London.

Pezzoli, K. (1997). Sustainable development: a transdisciplinary overview of the literature. *Journal of Environmental Planning and Management,* **40**, 507-575.

Rhodes, R. (1997). *Understanding Governance.* Open University Press, Milton Keynes.

Turner, R.K., Pearce, D.W. and Bateman, I.B. (1994). *Environmental Economics: an Elementary Introduction.* Harvest Wheatsheaf, Hemel Hempstead.

Von Weizsäcker, E., Lovins, A. and Lovins, H. (1997). *Factor Four: Doubling Wealth, and Halving Resource Use.* Earthscan, London.

22 Sustaining Scotland's Environment

Roger Crofts and Tricia Henton

Summary

1.   This chapter assesses five components for sustaining Scotland's environment: data, understanding, interpretation, policy development and new mechanisms.   A way forward is set out.

2.   Data availability has increased and it is now possible to detect longer term trends with positive and negative effects on the environment. It is essential that long runs of data are maintained, data gaps are filled, data requirements are reviewed rigorously and data are made more accessible.

3.   Understanding of the environment has increased.   However, it is often compartmentalised.   More work is required to improve understanding of how environmental systems work, and of the services which they provide.

4.   Interpreting environmental information is essential for improving policy and action.   Rigorous and objective analysis is required.   Composite indicators of environmental change should be developed.

5.   Policy needs to be developed in a more integrated way to achieve the greatest environmental benefit.   A number of achievements and failures in Scotland are identified.   Fundamental reform of the agriculture support mechanisms is the most necessary policy reform.

6.   A longer-term vision, supported by all relevant stakeholders, is essential. Ways of achieving this approach are set out.

22.1 Introduction

This chapter provides an overview and interpretation of the major issues for sustaining Scotland's environment. The earlier chapters focus particularly on the state of Scotland's environment, including its natural heritage, addressing trends in relation to air, land and water, as well as specific issues, such as biodiversity and the marine environment. Other chapters raise wider issues relating to the sustainable development agenda in Scotland from a number of significant perspectives: integration of policy, vision and strategic direction, measures of progress and new structures of governance. These two aspects of trend reporting and policy critiques are very closely related because improvements in policy and governance cannot be taken forward unless there are high quality data about trends in key environmental parameters, and there is an objective assessment of the trends using the most up-to-date scientific knowledge and methodologies. The interaction between scientific evidence and policy change has never been more important. It is essential that the development of policy and governance structures is informed by the outcomes of scientific investigation. This point is developed further in the concluding section of this chapter.

Scotland has two statutory environment bodies: Scottish Natural Heritage (SNH) and Scottish Environment Protection Agency (SEPA). These bodies work together effectively to secure Scotland's environmental assets of air, water, land and soil, landscape, landform and wildlife and to safeguard the processes and systems which support and sustain these assets. Both organisations have statutory sustainable development duties which give them wider roles to integrate the careful use and management of environmental assets with the social and economic needs and aspirations of society. As Chief Executives, we welcome the fact that the conference on which this book is based was jointly organised by SNH and SEPA, and that many of the key chapters represent joint effort by our colleagues. Such corporate working is critical in helping to address important environmental issues, defining strategies and putting in place appropriate actions. It is also recognised that there are many other stakeholders, in the public, private and voluntary sectors, who have important roles in working with SNH and SEPA to achieve their environmental objectives and the contribution which they make to a more sustainable and integrated Scotland.

This chapter considers the issues emerging from the preceding chapters under the headings of data, knowledge, interpretation, policy and mechanisms; and concludes with our views on the way forward.

22.2 Data

A great volume of data on the state of Scotland's environment and its natural heritage has been accumulated over the last decade. As a result, it is possible to detect trends in key parameters relating to air, land and water, and relating to species and habitats. The trends are very variable, with some implying environmental improvement, some indicating a more or less steady state, and some indicating a deteriorating situation. The chapters analyse the trends themselves and consider, with the data available, the amount of understanding we have about their causes.

Data collection is therefore critical to identify both positive and negative trends. However, there are often arguments that there are 'not enough data'. More information can always be used, but there are limits to what can be collected. Data must be used with caution and objective interpretation must be ensured. For example, do data show real anthropogenic effects or do they reflect long-term natural changes? The chapters on fisheries and marine waters demonstrate the uncertainties which surround interpretation. If a different approach is taken, such as a geologist's concept of time, then climate change takes on a different perspective. Overall the conclusion is that good data are essential if proper policy decisions are to be taken. There are three key points about data.

It is essential that long runs are maintained so that trends can be detected. Without this approach our knowledge could be overwhelmed by short-term variations which are insignificant in the longer term. Short runs of data, whilst of some assistance, are less valuable.

There is a need to ensure that gaps in data about the environment and the natural heritage are identified and efforts made to fill them. There is a number of significant data gaps, such as information on landscape change, the variety and classification of species at the genetic and unicellular levels, public attitudes towards the environment, the economic costs and benefits of environmental management, and the broader economic benefits of the environment to society. Plugging these gaps is essential so as to enable a more comprehensive overview of all of the three elements of sustainable development.

There is considerable variation in data availability. Rich data exist on some topics, such as the number, distribution and trends in some vertebrates and invertebrates. Is all of this material really needed, or can some be collapsed into meta-data sets to give a broader perspective of changes, for instance, in particular habitats? Are all of the bird monitoring data currently available required? It is suggested that the data need on this topic is rigorously reviewed. At a time when there are demands for more data sets, and the resources for data collection and analysis are not increasing, rigorous scrutiny of the purpose of continued collection of data is vitally important.

It is only relatively recently that many organisations have become aware of data availability. Efforts to ensure that these data are effectively catalogued and that quality is assessed has had to be undertaken. Too often in the past data were regarded as the property of those individuals in public bodies who were responsible for its commissioning or its collection. This can no longer be the case given the importance of the use of data to inform the broader policy process. In addition, excuses can no longer be made about the difficulty of release of data because of the statutory demands through Freedom of Access to Environmental Information Regulations and the availability of web-based systems. The major challenge, therefore, for all who are custodians of data is to ensure that the data's quality is properly assessed and the data are made accessible to all potential users, particularly through CD-ROM and web-based systems.

It is recognised that there can be risks in releasing data about the environment and natural heritage. Some of the material is sensitive because of the locations of scarce species and some of it is sensitive because it could lead to litigation by individuals who feel that they might be treated unfairly. These risks need to be assessed, but in the majority of circumstances the decision has to be to release data and make them accessible to all.

22.3 Understanding

The amount of investigation and accumulation of knowledge about the environment and natural heritage of Scotland are at an all time high. So what is the state of Scotland's environment and natural heritage? Sometimes it can be difficult to remain optimistic when looking at environmental issues. Many of the trends of the last 20 years, on whatever topic, wherever in the world, are negative. There is no doubt that on a global scale the pressures on the environment have grown exponentially. Even in Scotland, there are depressingly negative trends for species and habitats, often reflected in declining populations of birds, fish or flora. One of the questions is "do we understand the science well enough to make a difference: either to hold the line, or to make improvements?".

This book indicates that we do know quite a lot about the quality of land, air and water, and about habitats. The following are good examples of reversing negative impacts.

- International and local controls on emission of SO_x and NO_x are showing real reductions and therefore benefits for Scotland.
- Effective control of point source pollution into water is a success story, balanced by the bigger challenge of managing diffuse pollution. Data for Scotland's marine and fresh waters show this.
- Habitat improvements have stopped the decline in quality of some rivers and woodlands.

A lot is also known about ecosystem functions, as the integral of the interaction between species, and between species and their habitats, and the flows of energy, water and other substances. The level of understanding is improving about the importance of 'environmental services', i.e. the role which water, air and soil play in providing services to civil society in terms of productive media for food and fibre, and a wide range of species, and in terms of the supply of that essential nutrient of life: water. The complex concept of 'carrying capacity' is regarded by many as being one of the most critical limits of the environment to provide services to civil society and to natural systems. Despite all of the research which has been undertaken on these basic concepts, much more needs to be done to ensure that they are quantified in such a way that they can be brought into consideration alongside issues relating to society and business. Explaining how ecosystems function, and how the ecosystem approach proposed as the principal mechanism for implementing the Convention on Biological Diversity, can be applied in practice are vital tasks for the scientific community. Improving ways of measuring the contribution of the environment and also the limits to its capacity in providing services for society are equally vital. Alongside this scientific effort, there needs to be a much stronger effort to explain the concepts so that they are readily understood by civil society, and in particular, key decision-makers – the politicians themselves and those who advise them. Without this explanation there is a risk that policies will fail to safeguard the environment and will, ultimately, prove costly and damaging.

For instance, there is insufficient knowledge and acceptance of the services which ecosystems provide for society's benefit. It is essential to communicate better the ecosystem services of long-term natural capital for food and fibre; and the services of erosion control which allow the soil to be retained within the natural system and so enable society to benefit from reduced flood risk to farmland and settlements.

New concepts and new approaches are being developed and it is essential that these are taken forward in a Scottish context. An ecological and environmental footprint analysis (Dunion *et al.*, Chapter 20) of the activities of civil society is one which has not been addressed. Considering the environmental footprint of urban society on rural areas and rural society on urban areas is but one angle on this issue. Considering Scotland's ecological and wider environmental footprint on the rest of the UK, on Europe and, more especially, on the developing world are in urgent need of consideration. It is unlikely that decision-makers and the wider population really think about these matters, either when they are purchasing out-of-season fruit and vegetables which have been produced in developing countries such as Kenya, or when taking a foreign holiday in developing countries in Africa, Latin America or South-East Asia, for example. Put another way, the concept of environmental justice needs to be considered much more fully. This is an important element of the sustainable development equation because it means not only what is being done by civil society to nurture itself but also the equitable sharing of environmental resources (a key plank in the Convention of Biological Diversity) between civil societies.

Residents in industrialised areas readily understand the problems of environmental injustice in the management of major river systems, for example the Nile or Ganges, which cross international boundaries. However, they often fail to recognise the environmental injustice of the management of similar river systems in countries like Scotland. On the Tay, for instance, the UK's largest river in terms of its level of discharge, the residents of Perth consider that environmental justice is achieved if flood barriers are erected along the banks of the river through the City. Real environmental justice would be achieved if the flood banks upstream of Perth were removed and, at the same time, the fields on the floodplain were allowed to flood, and the methods of cultivation and seasonal exposure of soils and increases in drainage were moderated upstream. Farmers would be asked to play a role as floodplain managers. Equally, environmental justice means not putting the unpalatable developments next to deprived communities rather than next to upper and middle class communities. More particularly, it means giving all members of our society in Scotland an equal chance of access to environmental resources and the enjoyment of our natural heritage.

The challenge, therefore, is to develop the concepts of ecological footprint and environmental justice much more in a Scottish context, recognising our dependency on the wider world, and then applying the results to the decision-making process. That way, linkages between the environmental resources of the country and social well being and economic development should be more easily defined.

22.4 Interpretation

Interpretation of material on trends in the environment and natural heritage, within the context of existing and new scientific and allied concepts, is another vital part of the process of advising on the policy and practice of sustainable development from an environmental perspective. The 'state-pressure-response' model is now a well-accepted one and has formed the basis for environmental audit work by both SEPA and SNH. In recent years these organisations have covered the majority of their remits with SEPA publishing seminal statements on air, water and soil (SEPA, 1999a, 1999b, 2001) and SNH publishing on the state and trends in the natural heritage (Mackey, 1995; Mackey *et al.*, 2001). The amount of new knowledge and its more effective interpretation and presentation has increased understanding very significantly. It is interesting, for example, to contrast SNH's 1995 report *The Natural Heritage of Scotland: An Overview* with the recently published *Natural Heritage Trends: Scotland 2001*; the latter clearly demonstrates how data are more readily available, knowledge has increased and performance in interpreting it and making it more accessible has substantially improved.

The challenge, as always for public bodies, including SEPA, SNH and research institutes, is to maintain the highest level of objectivity possible. This is the way to ensure that debate about policy formulation and review is properly informed. It also helps to correct some of the misunderstandings which are deliberately put into the public domain by particular interest groups which look at things from a very narrow perspective and ignore much of the relevant information and its interpretation. Take, for example, the position of seals. There is substantive evidence that seals do prey upon Atlantic salmon (*Salmo salar*) but some commentators maintain that this is so significant that it fully justifies a cull of the seal populations. This fails to take into account both the protected status of both of the species of seals – common (*Phoca vitulina*) and grey (*Halichoerus grypus*) - under the European Union's Habitats Directive and the scientific appraisal of the many factors which have an impact on the salmon population: changes in water circulation patterns, salinity and temperature in the North Atlantic, intercepting fisheries offshore and near the coast, hybridisation with releases from salmon fish farms, and river engineering works which have an impact on the spawning beds being the major factors. In addition, it is often a concern of those involved in the research community that there is an insufficiency of data or that its quality is not of the highest level. Whilst these are valid concerns, perfection in data availability and data quality can never be reached. As a result, it is very important that the research community can indicate the levels of confidence which can be given to information which has been used in analyses.

It is a truism that the environment does not recognise political boundaries. Hence any indicators of environmental health, and of economic and social wellbeing, need to be framed in a context which allows comparisons between countries and regions. Consequently it is misguided to seek independent indicators of sustainable development, for example as proposed by the Scottish Executive (Scottish Executive, 2001b). The set of 147 UK indicators for sustainable development set out in the DETR's paper *A Better Quality of Life* should form the basis (DETR, 1999). The approach taken by the National Assembly of Wales in examining that larger data set, utilising those indicators which are relevant for Wales seen in the UK and wider contexts, and modifying slightly others to ensure that they are relevant to a Welsh context (National Assembly of Wales, 2001) is preferred by many commentators in Scotland to the proposals in the Scottish Executive's paper *Checking for Change* (Scottish Executive, 2001a). A thorough review of the UK set of indicators, so as to consider their relevance for Scotland and to ensure that Scotland can be placed within a European context, is important (see also Dunion *et al.*, Chapter 20)

There is also a challenge in developing composite indicators for the environment. Usher (Chapter 18) argues the case for using composite trends for bird species associated with particular habitats as one way forward. This is an appropriate approach. If it could be developed for other sets of species and other environmental factors then this would be beneficial. In addition, there is a challenge to the environmental community in developing composite indicators on similar lines to those which have been developed by economists, for instance the various measures of unemployment and gross domestic product. Whilst this is not easy, it is a better approach to that suggested in *Checking for Change* of taking carbon dioxide emission as the one single measure of environmental quality as this only reflects one part of the environment.

22.5 Moving policy forward

Now is a period of very fertile policy development, particularly since the establishment of the Scottish Parliament and the Scottish Executive. There are new policies for a variety of areas including agriculture, enterprise, tourism, social justice, culture and wildlife conservation. Whereas most of the individual aims are laudable, if they are inspected in detail to see how they match with the expectations emanating from the UNCED Summit in Rio de Janeiro and even from the Scottish Executive's own social and environmental sustainability ambitions, then many find these new policies wanting. In addition, these policies seem to have been drawn up in isolation, whereas the practice of sustainable development demands a much more integrated approach: in the words of the UK Government 'joined up Government'.

There seems to many still to be an insular approach, which is commonly called a 'silo' mentality, in relation to particular sectors, such as agriculture, and in relation to other areas of Government business, such as enterprise. If the integrated approach demanded by sustainable development is to be achieved then the barriers need to be broken down once and for all. This does not mean abandoning policies for supporting particular sectors, but it does mean ensuring that support for one sector does not have untoward effects on other aspects within the sustainability equation. Therefore, any new policy must be put to the test of its environmental, social and economic costs and benefits before it is finalised. In a sense, this is the equivalent of the 'triple bottom line' approach within the business community by checking out the environmental sustainability and social wellbeing components alongside business viability.

What can be done about trends that are environmentally damaging? How can society ensure that the right actions are taken? The key ultimately lies in government policies at national and international levels (see Currie, Chapter 2). He sets out very clearly the value of engagement with the European Union (EU) and the importance of providing information to the EU for use in the development of environmental protection policies and evolution of the EU's sustainable development strategy. He also stresses the importance of getting the timing right. The advice given by SNH and SEPA, as environmental advisors to the Scottish Executive, has an important role to play in this situation.

Policy changes that were adopted in the 1980s and 1990s have made a difference to environmental quality and habitats. There is a mildly encouraging picture in relation to acidification. Changes in forestry management practices and woodland planting have led to positive benefits. Protection and improvement of water quality is a success story across Scotland. The absolute necessity for further reform of the European Commission's Agriculture Policy is well recognised, as is the complexity and difficulty of carrying it out. This is possibly one of the greatest challenges to all parties interested in the environment. How do we get 'win/win' successes? The moves towards beneficial land use policies should hopefully be encouraged through the Water Framework Directive where a much more integrated approach will have to be adopted.

Part of the problem in the past, in Scotland and many other industrialised countries, is the issue of organisational cultures. Inevitably, within the public service risk aversion and caution, rather than pro-activity, tend to be the order of day. Seeking to move forward organisational cultures is a major issue: this cannot be resolved quickly but requires leadership within those organisations at all levels if it is to occur.

Looking at the situation in Scotland over the last 12 years with respect to the evolution of thinking, policy and action on sustainable development, gives a rather mixed picture, with both high and low points. Obvious high points were the fact that a Secretary of State was prepared to give a major speech on sustainable development in September 1989 to a predominantly business audience. This was followed a year later by the government, and supported by all parties in the House of Commons and House of Lords, giving the first statutory duty of sustainability on a public agency: SNH in the Natural Heritage (Scotland) Act 1991. Other high points were the publication of policy statements by SNH on its approach to sustainable development in 1994; the legislative provision for SEPA of a sustainability duty in the Environmental Protection Act 1995; the publication of the sustainable development report (Advisory Committee on Sustainable Development, 1999); the prominence given to sustainable development by the new administration elected in 1997 and in the *Programme for Government* document in 1999 (Scottish Executive, 1999); the decision by the Minister for Environment and Planning in 2000 to refuse permission for the Lingerabay superquarry application on sustainability grounds.

However, there have been some low points, including the fact that SNH was rebuked by Government for wishing to take into account sustainability considerations in its advice on the proposed second Firth of Forth Crossing. More fundamental is the fact that the emerging sustainable development strategy for Scotland related only to Waste, Energy and Transport (WET) and failed to take into account wider environmental matters or economic and social issues and policies and the fact that the proposed indicators for sustainable development remain wedded entirely to the narrower WET strategy. Indeed, the strategy fails to recognise the relevance of one of the major outcomes of the UNCED Summit in Rio de Janeiro - the Convention on Biological Diversity - despite the immense commitment at national and local level in Scotland for biodiversity conservation. In addition, there is the total failure to address the issues and practical steps set out so cogently in the Report of the Secretary of State's Advisory Committee (Advisory Committee on Sustainable Development, 1999).

In 1990, optimists felt that by the end of decade a great deal would have been achieved in relation to sustainable development policy and practice, but this has proved not to be the case. Rather there has been a series of setbacks. The case for a vision for sustainable development in Scotland, for the adjustment of the relevant policies and for new mechanisms to ensure its implementation, are still having to be made by former members of the Advisory Committee on Sustainable Development in Scotland, and members of the UK Sustainable Development Commission.

22.6 Mechanisms for delivering new policies for sustainable development

At present, the policy mechanisms available have not evolved sufficiently to allow the integrated approach demanded by sustainable development to be delivered effectively. Although there are many schemes which are positive and provide a challenge, there is still a great deal of subsidy and compensation within Government financial mechanisms. As has been argued in the case of nature conservation, these must now be regarded as outmoded. It is encouraging that new approaches that rely upon positive financial incentives are being put into place. Contracts on behalf of society between Government and its agencies and those delivering goods and services are an obvious way forward. As has been argued in the *Forward Strategy for Scottish Agriculture* (Scottish Executive, 2001c), the idea of Land Management Contracts is much more likely to deliver a range of goods and services provided by farmers and farmland to civil society than the current regimes which are based predominantly on price and production support. Whilst this will require fundamental reform of the EU's Common Agriculture Policy, and therefore agreement by Member States, there are opportunities within the subsidiarity arrangements already agreed by the European Commission for much greater progress to be made in Scotland. It is clear from talking to many farmers that they would be prepared to play a much wider role than food production, that they would be prepared to be stewards of biodiversity, of soil and water resources, of the cultural and landscape heritage of the countryside, of access to the countryside and, where appropriate, of managing floodplains and creating greater carbon stores. Multifaceted land management contracts with farmers to cover these issues have to be the way forward. However, the present sub-division of the agriculture budget in Scotland is not amenable to this. Of the total of around £550 million per annum only one-twentieth is devoted to direct environmental payments: does this mean that the environment represents only one twentieth part of the agriculture support regime? Many hope that this is not the case and would welcome a much greater and much faster increase in the programme of support for agriculture to deliver the wider range of environmental benefits.

Basically, the challenge is to move from a culture of compensation to a culture of paying for outcomes. More generally, economists have always argued that the taxation system is by far the most effective instrument for delivering outcomes of benefit to civic society. It is hoped that the government will explore these issues and implement changes: certainly the approaches to landfill have been very effective.

22.7 The way forward

There is no single recipe for taking matters forward.

Most fundamentally, many chapters indicate the need for a clear vision for Scotland: a vision for a sustainable Scotland. At present there is no such over-arching vision, other than that stated in the partnership for Government document of the Scottish Executive. Whilst this has positive elements, it needs to be teased out much further. A polluted, degraded, overexploited environment, where carrying capacity is exceeded, and where natural regenerative ecological and physical processes are abused, will lead ultimately to economic collapse and social upheaval. This is as applicable in Scotland as it is in the developing world. On the other hand, a healthy Scottish environment is an absolute necessity to the economic and social wellbeing of the country. This is not only to support our principal industries such as tourism, distilling, food production, petrochemicals and electronics but also for the intrinsic, aesthetic value of an attractive environment. This can be as variable as having a high quality river flowing through an area of urban deprivation or an area of highly diverse and attractive scenery in a rural setting. To start the debate on this issue, a possible vision for the future (Crofts, 2000) is that "sustaining Scotland means recognising that

- human society and its natural environment are accepted to be interdependent;
- people are an intrinsic part of the environment;
- the environment is recognised as a capital asset for society; and
- the environment can be used for human benefit provided that this is within its carrying capacity, that undue risks are not taken and that the functioning of natural systems are not significantly impaired".

To achieve a vision there needs to be a meaningful process to involve all relevant interests, both nationally and at the local level. The community planning process provides an important vehicle, provided that it fully embraces the Agenda 21 process. Leadership is required nationally and locally by politicians, by public servants, and by public bodies to ensure the culture change necessary within organisations to achieve the integrated approach to deliver sustainable development. Involvement of all parts of civil society is equally essential. A vision for the future, developed through proper participative measures, is required both at the national level and in the various component parts of Scotland. Allied to this, policy needs to be better integrated and needs to be tested against the environmental sustainability, social wellbeing and economic prosperity criteria of sustainable development. New instruments which seek to deliver positive outcomes for society and the environment are required, including potentially a reform of the taxation system and other incentives. More objectivity is also needed in getting over the messages arising from the measurement, monitoring and assessment of trends in the environment and the natural heritage so that the debate about vision, policy and its implementation are better informed than it is at present.

Public attitudes to the environment are also critical. Environmental awareness has risen rapidly since the late 1960s, not just in the public mind but also at corporate and political levels. This culminated in the tremendous awareness around the time of the UN Conference on Environment and Development at Rio de Janeiro in 1992, and the recognition of the need to integrate environmental, social and economic issues in policy making and decision taking.

The 1990s were a highly optimistic time, one when sustainable development was coming of age. Then suddenly momentum seemed to be lost. Public buy-in to environmental issues seems to have shifted. There is intense ambiguity in personal and societal behaviour relating to environmental issues. Environment is widely perceived as 'something negative which stops people doing what they want to do', and yet surveys show that the public does expect the environment to be considered by policy makers and government.

There is public detachment from the causes of environmental problems and their solutions. At its simplest, the majority of the population does not make the connection between the goods placed in the supermarket trolley every week, the packaging and other wastes that conveniently leave the premises through the wheelie bin, and the planning application for the new incinerator or landfill at the end of the road. Somewhere along the line the connections are neither being properly explained, nor are the links being made.

There is also a feeling of hopelessness that pervades the major environmental issues. What can individuals do about climate change? What difference can a person's small actions make, either positively or negatively? Against this rather depressing background, both SEPA and SNH have key roles as advisors, providers of information, commentators and, in SEPA's case, regulators.

Finally, it is essential that scientists and others in the research community play their part in explaining the concept and practice of sustainable development and the various aspects of the environment and natural heritage which are part of it. The Conference on which this book is based had a predominantly environmental audience. Whilst this is very valuable for the participants, in future it is our hope that there will be a much more diverse audience so that those in the environmental business, in both public and voluntary sectors, reach out into a wider world. In that way the validity of the environmental component of sustainable development will become increasingly recognised and the debate about a sustainable Scotland much better informed.

References

Advisory Committee on Sustainable Development (1999). *Scotland the Sustainable.* The Scottish Office, Edinburgh.

Crofts, R. (2000). *Sustainable Development and Environment: Delivering Benefits Globally, Nationally and Locally.* Scottish Natural Heritage Occasional Paper No. 8.

Department of Environment, Transport and the Regions (1999). *A Better Quality of Life.* HMSO, London.

Mackey, E.C. (ed.) (1995). *The Natural Heritage of Scotland: An Overview.* Scottish Natural Heritage, Perth.

Mackey, E.C., Shaw, P., Holbrook, J., Shewry, M.C., Saunders, G., Hall, J. and Ellis, N.E. (2001). *Natural Heritage Trends: Scotland 2001.* Scottish Natural Heritage, Perth.

National Assembly of Wales (2001). *A Sustainable Wales – Measuring the Difference: Indicators for Sustainable Development in Wales.* National Assembly of Wales, Cardiff.

Scottish Environment Protection Agency (1999a). *Improving Scotland's Water Environment: SEPA State of the Environment Report.* SEPA, Stirling.

Scottish Environment Protection Agency (1999b). *State of the Environment: Air Quality Report.* SEPA, Stirling.

Scottish Environment Protection Agency (2001). *State of the Environment: Soil Quality Report.* SEPA, Stirling.

Scottish Executive (1999). *Making it Work Together: a Programme for Government.* Scottish Executive, Edinburgh.

Scottish Executive (2001a). *Checking for Change.* Scottish Executive, Edinburgh.

Scottish Executive (2001b). *Sustainability Indicators for Waste, Energy and Travel for Scotland.* Scottish Executive Central Research Unit, Edinburgh.

Scottish Executive (2001c). *A Forward Strategy for Scottish Agriculture.* Scottish Executive, Edinburgh.

INDEX

Note: **bold** page numbers indicate chapters.
All references are to *Scotland*, unless otherwise indicated

Printed by The Stationery Office, 6/02 c7